A NOTE FROM THE AUTHOR

Congratulations on your decision to take the AP U.S. History exam! Whether or not you're completing a year-long AP U.S. History course, this book can help you prepare for the exam. No matter how deep your understanding of history is, it will take more than knowledge to earn a high score on this exam. Students who perform well on the AP exam possess a solid understanding of the chronology and events of history but also effectively apply and analyze the content knowledge through the various tasks on the exam itself.

In addition to offering a chronological content review of the most tested, up-to-date material on the AP exam, this review guide also features tips on how best to process the events, eras, and scope of U.S. history. You will learn how to dissect multiple-choice questions and quickly eliminate distractors to find the best answers. You will find different methods on how to process and outline information in your readings to write detailed and effective Document-Based Question and Free-Response Question essays. Finally, Kaplan has drafted a sample study schedule to keep you on track, whether you bought this guide in September—or two weeks before the exam!

Over 300 practice multiple-choice questions and over 20 sample essay questions give you the opportunity to see where your strengths and weaknesses lie and to practice the test-taking skills you learn in early chapters.

Good luck using this guide on your adventure in study and review!

Krista Dornbush

AP® U.S. HISTORY

2

RELATED TITLES

AP® U.S. HISTORY
2010 EDITION

Krista Dornbush

PUBLISHING

New York

© 2010 by Kaplan, Inc.
Published by Kaplan Publishing, a division of Kaplan, Inc.
1 Liberty Plaza, 24th Floor
New York, NY 10006

Printed in the United States of America

10 9 8 7 6 5 4 3 2 1

ISBN 13: 978-1-4195-5068-3

Kaplan Publishing books are available at special quantity discounts to use for sales promotions, employee premiums, or educational purposes. For more information or to purchase books, please call the Simon & Schuster special sales department at 866-506-1949.

TABLE OF CONTENTS

PART THREE: AP UNITED STATES HISTORY REVIEW

UNIT I: THE NEW WORLD TO THE AMERICAN REVOLUTION, 1492–1783

PART FOUR: PRACTICE TESTS

ABOUT THE AUTHOR

Krista Dornbush teaches AP U.S. History at Marina High School in Huntington Beach, California. Entering her 15th year of teaching and her 13th of teaching Advanced Placement, Ms. Dornbush serves as a College Board consultant and national leader for AP U.S. History and Pre-AP® workshops. She has also worked as a Faculty Consultant and Table Leader for the Educational Testing Service reading of the Advanced Placement U.S. History exam since 1998. In addition to authoring this book, Ms. Dornbush has penned a workshop for teachers offered by the College Board in regards to reading in the social studies.

KAPLAN PANEL OF AP EXPERTS

Congratulations—you have chosen Kaplan to help you get a top score on your AP exam.

Kaplan understands your goals and what you're up against—achieving college credit and conquering a tough test—while participating in everything else that high school has to offer.

You expect realistic practice, authoritative advice, and accurate, up-to-the-minute information on the test. And that's exactly what you'll find in this book, as well as every other in the AP series. To help you (and us!) reach these goals, we have sought out leaders in the AP community. Allow us to introduce our experts.

AP U.S. HISTORY EXPERTS

Gwen Cash is a Lead Consultant for the College Board and has served on the AP Advisory Council and the conference planning committee in the Southwest region. She also helped to write the AP Social Studies Vertical Teams guide. Ms. Cash holds a BA and an MD from The University of Texas at Austin, Texas, and she teaches on-level and AP U.S. History courses at Clear Creek High School in League City, Texas.

Anthony "Tony" Jones has taught AP courses for the past 10 years, including AP U.S. History, AP European History, and AP World History. He has taught at Houston County High in Warner Robins, Georgia, and Rutland High School in Macon, Georgia. He is a member of the World History Association and the National Council for Social Studies. He is a Table Leader and Reader for the AP World History exam. Additionally, he has been a presenter on integrating technology into the social studies and AP classroom at several conferences.

Steven Mercado has taught AP U.S. History and AP European History at Chaffey High School in Ontario, California, for the past 12 years. He has also served as a reader for the AP U.S. History exam and as a reader and table leader for the AP European History exam.

| **Part One** |

THE BASICS

CHAPTER 1: INSIDE THE AP U.S. HISTORY EXAM

INTRODUCTION

Congratulations on your decision to take the Advanced Placement exam in United States history! The test is a big one—its content measures your knowledge of United States history from roughly 1492 to the early 1990s. After taking a college-level class, you certainly will have a large base of historical knowledge heading into the exam. However, the AP exam asks you to take things one step further—to apply that knowledge in complex and analytical situations to show evidence of college-level learning.

This guide offers not only a full review of U.S. history but, more importantly, specific skills and strategies successful students use to score higher on the AP exam. In the following chapters, you will encounter reading strategies for your day-to-day assignments, writing strategies for the Document-Based and Free-Response questions (DBQs and FRQs), and analytical skills for both documents and multiple-choice questions. Rote memorization of facts, dates, and events alone does not ensure success. While a solid foundation of historical knowledge is critical to your learning, application of that knowledge earns top scores. Keep the skills and strategies you learn in chapter 2 of this guide in mind as you take the Diagnostic test in Part Two to assess where you stand before tackling the course review in Part Three.

Part Three is the meat of this guide. Its units and chapters are arranged chronologically to correlate with your classroom textbook and the College Board's course description guide for the AP exam. We have made sure to give you a solid review of the most-tested vocabulary, people, places, and concepts on the AP. Each chapter contains review questions and detailed explanations of test items to help you determine if you need further study of an era of history, or if you can move on to the next one.

Finally, Part Four offers two full-length practice tests that closely mirror the actual AP exam, with testlike DBQs, FRQs, and detailed answer explanations.

Are you ready for your adventure through the study and mastery of everything AP U.S. History? Good luck!

Introduction   Test Overview   Scoring   Registration & Fees   What to Bring

OVERVIEW OF THE TEST STRUCTURE

The AP U.S. History exam is designed yearly by the AP Test Development Committee as an opportunity for you to demonstrate mastery of skills typically found in introductory college U.S. history classes.

The exam, divided into two sections, is three hours and five minutes long. Section I is 55 minutes long and consists of 80 multiple-choice questions. These questions cover the entire course of study and increase in difficulty as the exam progresses. Section II is 130 minutes long and contains one Document-Based essay question and two Free-Response essay questions.

Section	Number of Questions	Time
I	80 multiple-choice questions	55 minutes
II	3 essay questions including	130 minutes
	one Document-Based essay question	(60 minutes recommended) and
	two Free-Response essay questions	(70 minutes recommended)
	Total 3 hours, 5 minutes	

PART I—MULTIPLE CHOICE

The 80 multiple-choice questions in Section I mostly cover the 19th and 20th centuries. Twenty percent of the questions will cover the period up to 1789, 45 percent will cover the period from 1790 to 1914, and 35 percent will cover the period from 1915 to the present (although very few questions will cover the period since 1985).

The multiple-choice questions are constructed with a standard question stem and five answer choices. It is important to note that the exam directions will ask you to choose the "best" right answer. This is because of the five answer choices, four will be "distractors"—tricky choices written to distract you from the better answer. Distractors can be written so well that you might be tempted to choose them if you have not read the rest of the answers thoroughly. We will discuss pacing yourself and other test-taking techniques later in this chapter.

PART II—FREE RESPONSE

Section II of the exam, the free-response portion, asks you to write three full-length essays in 130 minutes: a DBQ (Part A) and two standard FRQs (Parts B and C). A DBQ is different from a standard free-response essay, because it asks you to analyze and synthesize historical information. For your DBQ, you will be asked to relate documents, pictures, and other historical sources to a theme or era. It is important to remember to incorporate outside knowledge when writing your DBQ, which can be taken from any era of U.S. History. Part B essay questions generally ask for information prior to the end of the Civil War, and Part C questions generally ask for information from Reconstruction to roughly 1980.

Introduction   **Test Overview**   Scoring   Registration & Fees   What to Bring

On Test Day, you will be given a booklet containing the DBQ and four FRQs and a sealed booklet for your responses. Section II of the exam begins with a 15-minute mandatory planning period. You may not begin writing your answers in the sealed booklet until the proctor has signaled that 15 minutes have passed, but you can use this time to outline and plan your DBQ and to decide which two of the four essay questions you will answer. AP Exam graders will not see any work that occurs in the question booklet. Only answers in the sealed answer booklet will be read and scored.

After 15 minutes, you are given the remainder of the time to construct coherent essays that answer the questions in the booklet. Typically, students will spend 45 minutes on DBQ and then move on to Parts B and C. We suggest that you allow 35 minutes for these two essays—five minutes of planning time and 30 minutes of writing time per essay.

BREAKDOWN OF COVERED MATERIAL

Multiple-choice and essay questions focus on political, social, economic, cultural, and intellectual developments in the United States. In the multiple-choice section, political questions will account for approximately 35 percent of the total questions, and social change will account for 40 percent. Foreign policy (15 percent) and economics (10 percent) round out the areas covered. But remember, these categories are not black and white. That is, a question may cover more than one category (political and economic, for example).

The essay questions may ask you to explain change over time, to analyze cause and effect, to compare one time period to another, or to explain specific developments and changes in a category or categories. You must have a good understanding of historical analysis and the broader themes of U.S. history to answer the essay questions effectively. We will discuss the DBQ and FRQ essays in depth later on in this guide.

HOW THE EXAM IS SCORED

All AP exams are rated on a scale of 1 to 5, with 5 being the highest:

5 Extremely well qualified

4 Well qualified

3 Qualified

2 Possibly qualified

1 No recommendation

On the AP U.S. History exam, Section I and Section II each count for one half of your final score. You can receive a raw score of up to 80 points on Section I. This portion of the exam is "penalty" graded. That means incorrect responses are counted as 1.25 points off, as opposed to only 1 point off for an unanswered question. This way, you are not rewarded for merely guessing throughout

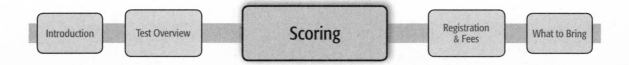

the exam. However, it will be to your advantage to answer a question if you can eliminate one or more of the answer choices.

You can receive a raw score of up to 27 points on Section II. But take note—in this section, the DBQ counts for half of your total points. That one essay holds twice as much weight as each of the FRQs.

These raw scores are entered into a formula that calculates your composite score of 1 to 5. This composite score is the one sent to students, schools, and universities. On page 353 of this guide, you will find the formula to convert your raw score into a composite score. After you complete the practice exams in the back of this guide, you can calculate your composite score to estimate how you would do on the actual exam.

Scoring Guides—DBQ and FRQ

Monitoring your own success on the exam's free-response section is straightforward. The scoring guides for the DBQ and the FRQ are very similar. Essays on the AP U.S. History exam are all scored on a nine-point scoring guide. Basic requirements hold true from year to year, with the content requirements changing for each question asked. A standard nine-point scoring guide would look something like this:

The 8–9 Essay

- Contains a clear, well-developed thesis that answers all parts of the prompt.
- Thesis is supported with substantial, relevant information.
- Provides evidence of thoughtful analysis.
- May contain minor errors.

The 5–7 Essay

- Contains a thesis that answers all parts of the prompt; may be unbalanced.
- Thesis is supported with some relevant information.
- Analysis is unbalanced and/or limited.
- May contain errors that do not seriously detract from the quality of the essay.

The 2–4 Essay

- Contains a confused or unfocused thesis or may simply restate the question.
- Contains minimal or irrelevant information or simply lists facts with no explanation.
- Contains little or no evidence of analysis and only a general treatment of information.
- May contain substantial errors.

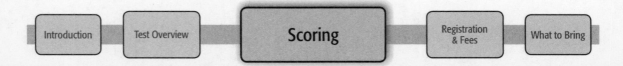

THE 0–1 ESSAY

- Lacks a thesis or rewrites the question.
- Incompetent or inappropriate response.
- Shows little or no understanding of the question.
- Contains major factual errors.

THE "–" ESSAY

- Is blank or off-topic.

Essays are scored holistically, with Faculty Consultants (Exam Readers) reviewing each essay from beginning to end. Scores are only given to answers within the sealed answer booklet. Only actual essays are scored, which means that even if you have a great outline of an essay, you will receive a score of "–" if you do not write the essay in full.

REGISTRATION AND FEES

You can register for the AP U.S. History exam by contacting your guidance counselor or AP Coordinator. If your school doesn't administer the exam, contact AP Services for a listing of schools in your area that do. The fee for each AP exam is $86. For students with financial need, a $22 reduction is available. To learn about other sources of financial aid, contact your AP Coordinator.

For more information on all things AP, visit **collegeboard.com** or contact AP Services:

AP Services
P.O. Box 6671
Princeton, NJ 08541-6671
Phone: (609) 771-7300 or (888) 225-5427 (toll-free in the United States and Canada)
Email: apexams@info.collegeboard.org

WHAT TO BRING

Testing conditions vary from site to site. However, there are several key items that all students should bring on Test Day.

- Several sharpened number 2 pencils with erasers. We suggest that you also bring along a separate eraser. White erasers work very well in erasing pencil from scan sheets.
- Several black or dark blue ballpoint ink pens. We suggest that you not use erasable ink or liquid ink pens. They can smear or run, affecting legibility.
- Your school code
- A watch that does not make noise. Some testing sites do not have clocks visible.

- Your Social Security number for identification purposes
- A photo ID
- A highlighter to use when preparing for the essay

Some items are prohibited or best left at home. These are items not to bring.

- Books, correcting fluid, dictionaries, highlighters, or notes
- Scratch paper
- Computers (unless you are a student with a disability and have been approved to bring the computer)
- Watches that beep or have an alarm
- Portable listening devices, such as MP3 players, CD players, radios, and tape players
- Cameras
- Beepers, cellular phones, or personal digital assistants (PDAs)
- Clothing with subject-related information

ADDITIONAL RESOURCES

The College Board website at **apcentral.collegeboard.com/apc/public/homepage/10460.html** is the best resource for additional information regarding AP courses, exams, and services. We suggest you visit often throughout the school year to access information regarding updates and test dates and to answer any questions you may have along the way.

CHAPTER 2: STRATEGIES FOR SUCCESS—IT'S NOT ALWAYS HOW MUCH YOU KNOW

READING STRATEGIES FOR THE AP U.S. HISTORY EXAM

Often students new to AP history courses struggle with the sheer amount of reading required to learn the material. Some instructors break up the reading into chunks of 10 to 15 pages a night, while others may assign the entire chapter in one sitting. Depending on your school schedule, the text you use, and the assignments your instructor gives, you must develop a system for completing your reading. Since this is an area of difficulty for many AP students, we will provide you with some active reading strategies that you can build into your daily schedule.

No matter if you have 10 pages to read every other day or an entire chapter to read in a week, it is critical that you are an active participant with your textbook. In AP U.S. History, it is no longer acceptable to read passively. By this, we mean that you must interact with your text by taking notes, asking questions, and summarizing. It is also not enough for most students to read the material once and only once. You must build time into your schedule for "rehearsal" of the material you have read—you must review your reading at a time well removed from your first read. This may be the next day, or in two days, or in a week, depending on your schedule. But remember, cramming material in the weeks before the exam will not improve your chances of scoring well. Only consistent and deliberate study of your material throughout the year will pay off.

Before we begin discussing specific strategies for daily reading, take a moment to reflect on how you read assigned material. *Where* do you read? Is it quiet? Noisy? Light? Dark? Comfortable? Do you have the necessary study aids close at hand (pencils, note paper, highlighters, dictionary)? If you read in the gym while waiting for basketball practice to start, chances are that your environment is noisy, dark, and uncomfortable and study aids will not be readily available. This is not the best place to complete your reading for your AP class. Similarly, if you read late at night in bed, you may find yourself falling asleep before you finish the assignment, only to find yourself rushing to read right before class. We suggest that you complete your reading assignment in a quiet, comfortable, well-lit place in which you have study aids readily available.

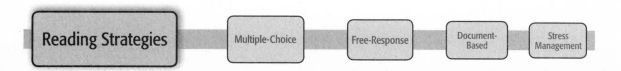

Reading Strategies   Multiple-Choice   Free-Response   Document-Based   Stress Management

CLEAR YOUR HEAD

Avoid interference from other subjects by making U.S. History the one you study right before you go to sleep.

When do you read? Immediately after school? After work/practice/rehearsals? Late at night in bed? You should try to complete your reading assignment as close to the end of your school day as possible. This way, the material you discussed in class will be fresh in your mind, and you can apply it to the material in your text.

How do you read? Do you take notes as you read? Do you simply recopy the text? If assigned questions to answer with the reading, do you simply search for the answers and avoid actually reading the chapter? These last questions are the most important to your comprehension and learning of the material you read for AP U.S. History. It is how you read that is the most critical. Let's take a look at some ways you can build active reading strategies into your daily homework routine.

UMBRELLA QUESTIONS

Have you ever wondered how your instructors or test developers come up with exam questions? We'll let you in on a secret. Predicting multiple-choice or essay questions is as easy as opening up your textbook. History texts are written in a very predictable formula. At the beginning of every chapter, you will find a short summary or introduction. Some authors like to "tease" you with an interesting fact or entertain you with flowery language. Other authors prefer to offer you chapter objectives or a glimpse of what will be covered in the pages that follow. In either case, the authors of your text provide you with clues to the important concepts that will be discussed within the text. Next comes the body of the chapter. Have you ever noticed that there are clever headings for each section of text? Again, the authors are providing you insight into the importance of the arguments that will follow. Finally, to wrap things into a neat package, the authors will provide you with either a chapter summary or a conclusion. Can you connect the summary or conclusion with the objectives, chapter introduction, and section headings?

If you answered yes to these questions, then you have already discovered the magic of the textbook formula. Let's look at a reading strategy that utilizes the textbook formula to assist you in comprehending your reading assignments.

THE HIGHLIGHT REEL

Highlight key phrases! Your life will be much easier when you need to go back and review text later. If you can't highlight in your textbook, try sticky notes.

Turn the objectives, headings, and conclusion into questions before you read the chapter. For example, if your textbook has a heading for a section called "The Impact of Dred Scott," your question initially might be "What was the impact of Dred Scott?" Write this question down in your notes before you read the text itself. Do the same for every other heading. Now, read each section that covers each question you have created. Is your question exactly answered by the text you have just read? For our example above, we may read the section and decide that "What was the impact of Dred Scott?" is not specific enough to cover the important discussion in the section. We may decide to change our question to "What impact did the Dred

Reading Strategies | Multiple-Choice | Free-Response | Document-Based | Stress Management

Scott decision have on sectional tension?" depending on the text of the section. This question can be answered with more depth and analysis than our previous question. Simply identifying what the impact is is not enough for the AP exam, however. By connecting the Dred Scott case to a greater historical theme, you will begin making the associations that score you points on the exam. While you can easily pick out the broader historical themes in your textbook by looking at chapter titles, it's the specific analysis that leads to mastery.

The next step is to answer the questions you have created for each section of text. If you have trouble answering your own questions, you may need to revise the questions or reread the section. Your last step is to predict a possible essay question that might come from each section. Then, write an overarching umbrella question that ties all your questions together to cover the entire chapter or era. Try to use academic terms to construct your question, much as in the AP U.S. History sample prompts you will find throughout this guide. Can you answer this question by using the evidence you have collected from the answers to all of your smaller umbrella questions? Now you have a study guide for your assigned reading that contains questions for each portion of the text, answers to those questions, and a broad, overarching question similar to an AP essay question.

PERSIA Chart

On almost every AP U.S. History exam, essay prompts will require you to understand various categories historians utilize to analyze events. It is beneficial for you to practice recognizing these categories as you read your text and primary source documents. Here is a method that you can use as you read to categorize the textual information presented in assigned reading.

PERSIA is an acronym that is easy to remember and use. **P** equals Political, **E** equals Economic, **R** equals Religion, **S** equals Social, **I** equals Intellectual, and **A** equals Arts. Historians may use categories like these to analyze or break down the components of an era of U. S. history. As you complete PERSIA charts covering significant time periods, you will have tools to assist you in identifying significant connections between categories and how a certain category may dominate a particular time period. Imagine the power these PERSIA charts will have when you are ready to review for your AP exam! You will have organized the significant aspects of each major era by the very categories you must know to construct an effective essay.

Let's look at a list of key words and questions that you can use to help you complete a PERSIA chart for any era or chapter in your text book.

P = Political

You may choose to include the following items: presidents/major leaders, judicial rulings, legislation, major movements, revolutions, rebellions, foreign policy, taxes, and tariffs.

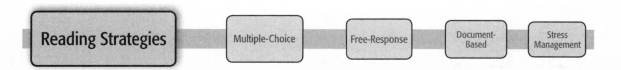

You should be able to answer the following types of questions after you have charted this section:

- How did the U.S. government react to events during this era?
- How did leadership change in the country during this era?
- Why did the government's foreign policy stance change?

E = ECONOMIC

Taxes, tariffs, recessions, depressions, panics, inflation, currency issues, scarcity, Gross National Product (GNP), and Gross Domestic Product (GDP) are a few possible terms that you can look for to determine economic issues in your reading.

Consider questions such as these:

- How did the government react to economic distress during the time period?
- Were the economic decisions of the ruling party helpful to the country's overall economic health?
- Did foreign policy play a role in the economic decisions of the country?

R = RELIGIOUS

As you search for examples for religion, keep in mind that you must consider the influence of religion on a given time period, event, or group of people.

Use questions such as these to guide your thinking:

- How did religion play a role in the development of government/society/culture during this era?
- How did religious divisions affect the arrival of a certain event?
- Can you list major religious leaders who influenced the United States during this time?

S = SOCIAL

Here you will want to look for instances of how an event has altered the way people in a culture interact with one another. You will want to keep your eyes open for race, gender, or ethnic relationships and how they have either changed or remained the same in the face of a historical event.

Consider these questions:

- How was the social structure altered during this era?
- Did your reading reveal any social or cultural norms?
- Can you list specific examples from your reading that reveal the social aspects of the culture/country at this time in history?

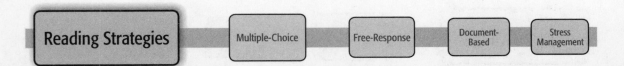

I = INTELLECTUAL

In this category, you are searching for achievements in many different areas. Literature, science, technology, academia, and schools of thought are just a few of the possible items you could look for. You may also consider ideologies during a time period, such as the philosophies of the Enlightenment, to fall under the category of "Intellectual."

These questions may be of assistance:

- How did advancements in technology change life for Americans during this time period?
- From what series of events did this school of thought emerge, and how did it impact American society?
- How does the literature of this time period reflect the events that surrounded its creation?

A = ARTS

The last section of the list can be one of the most challenging for AP U.S. History students. Most textbooks have very little discussion of art but rather use art to illustrate specific points throughout. Often, the AP exam will ask questions regarding the impact of an artistic movement on a given period.

Questions to consider are these:

- How did this artist portray events, people, or feelings of this era?
- Why did artists feel the need to produce pieces such as the ones in this section?
- How was the art received outside of the art community?
- Was there patronage of the art? In other words, was the art commissioned by a benefactor?

As you read a chapter or section of a chapter, fill in the areas of the PERSIA list as you read. Write down information you believe is significant or important to the era you are studying. Ask yourself, *Has the author or my instructor repeated this information in the text or in class?* If so, then chances are that the repeated information is important enough for you to write down.

CHAIN OUTLINES

Many students learn to take notes in a traditional outline format. We need to take this standard outline format and pump some historical skills into it! Try to think like a historian. How would a historian approach the material in your text? A historian would be looking for patterns, linkages, and causation. Therefore, your

---

BE C-R-E-A-T-I-V-E

Throughout the year, create acronyms or other mnemonic devices to jog your memory. For example, SADTWITS can help you remember the American Revolution:

S = Sugar Act
A = Admiralty Courts
D = Declaratory Act
T = Townshend Acts
W = Writs of Assistance
I = Intolerable Acts
T = Tea Act
S = Stamp Act

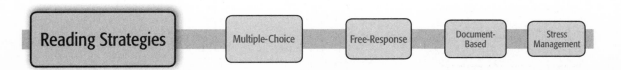

Reading Strategies   Multiple-Choice   Free-Response   Document-Based   Stress Management

outline should reflect these patterns, linkages, and causes. We will call this new outline our "Chain Outline." Think of the material you read in your text as a big metal chain with smaller chains attached. Sometimes the smaller chains connect, creating links between larger links within the chain. Let's use the example of the early years of the Civil Rights Movement in the 1950s as our topic for the following Chain Outline.

As you can see from our chain, we have been able to see patterns, links, and causes that show us much more than if we had simply placed theses items in a traditional outline. You can take this a step further and add specific details about these events in the margins of your paper. You may even be able to predict possible exam questions by looking at the major themes that run through a section or chapter. There are only so many ways exams can ask about major historical themes!

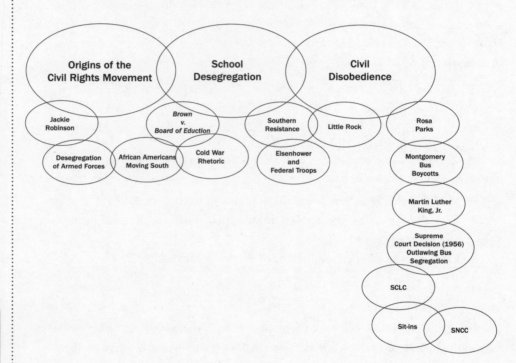

CHANGE IS GOOD

Don't be afraid to change your answer to a multiple-choice question. If you don't feel confident about your answer, trust your instincts and go back to it if time allows.

HOW TO APPROACH THE MULTIPLE-CHOICE QUESTIONS

Students often complain that they feel tired or that their brain seems like it doesn't work as well toward the end of the AP exam. This "test fatigue" can strike even the most seasoned test taker. Here are some strategies to help you avoid "test fatigue" and other common problems encountered during the long multiple-choice section of the AP exam.

PROCESS OF ELIMINATION

The multiple-choice questions on the AP U.S. History exam are complex, with answer choice distractors designed to keep you on your toes. It is important for you to develop a system to eliminate distractors so you can quickly arrive at the correct answer and move on. Remember, the directions of Section I of the exam direct you to choose the best right answer, not solely the right one. This means that there may be more than one correct answer but only one is the best one.

Make yourself comfortable with the style of questions that will be presented on the AP exam by practicing with examples from this guide. Practice eliminating at least three of the five answer choices for any multiple-choice question. Two of the five distractors will be so obtuse that you should, as you broaden your history knowledge, be able to eliminate them right away. The third will be somewhat close—it may just cover the same era as the question stem. That leaves you with two enticing possibilities to decide between. Remember, you need the best right answer, so look carefully for any clues in the two remaining answer choices. Does either contain words such as *all*, *most*, or *none*? If the answer is yes, then chances are that this answer is not correct. The AP exam does not like to make grand, overarching statements. Check the time period of the question and match it up with the remaining answer choices. Can you eliminate one of your answers because it is outside the time frame of the question? At this point, even if you have no means of elimination, it is in your best interest to guess—you've narrowed your chance of getting the right answer down to 50 percent.

TIME MANAGEMENT

With any timed exam, it is in your best interest to practice taking the test under the same time restrictions. You have 55 minutes to complete all 80 questions in Section I. And remember, you may not go back to complete Section I once these 55 minutes are over, even if you have time left over in Section II. Thus, it is critical that you practice to develop the ability to work effectively under time constraints.

As a basic rule, you should allot an average of 40 seconds per test item on Section I. Remember, however, the multiple-choice questions become more difficult as the exam progresses. Keeping this in mind, try to take about 30 seconds per item on the first third of the exam, 40 seconds per item in the second third, and 45 seconds or more per item during the last third. Use the sample test items in Part Four of this book to practice taking the exam under time constraints. Keep a watch with a second hand or a silent timer next to you as you answer test questions. The first time through, log in approximately how much time it took you to complete the entire test. Then figure out how much time elapsed per test item. Take careful note

> ### PICK YOUR BATTLES
>
> If a question deals with a map or graph and you *know* that is one of your weak spots, don't waste valuable time reviewing the question more than twice.

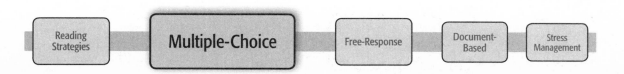

Reading Strategies | **Multiple-Choice** | Free-Response | Document-Based | Stress Management

of the types of questions that took you more time and when during the test you felt the need to slow down. Careful analysis of your test-taking methods at an early point allows you to determine where in the actual AP exam you will encounter difficulty. You can use this information to focus your study.

PENALTY SCORING

You may recall from chapter 1 that Section I of the exam is penalty scored. Incorrect responses are counted as a 1.25 point deduction from your score, so you will not benefit from random guessing. However, as a rule of thumb, you should aim to leave no more than 4 or 5 percent of the Section I questions blank. Leaving more than this percentage blank can have a greater negative impact on your overall score than if you had attempted to answer the questions.

So practice this simple method to help alleviate the need for guessing. When you work on a timed practice exam or as you sit for the actual AP exam, work straight through the 80 questions and answer those questions that you can with no hesitation. Skip the difficult questions that bog you down or leave you confused. Then, on the next pass, answer those questions that you can narrow down to two answer choices. Now you are only left with the questions you need time to think over. Spend the remainder of your testing period answering these questions. If you absolutely cannot come up with an answer, leave the item blank but only after you have spent a sufficient amount of time trying to eliminate distractors.

One final point to keep in mind: On most multiple-choice exams, students are encouraged to "go with their gut" when answering questions. On the AP U.S. History exam, this can be dangerous! Remember that distractors are designed to catch you off guard and make you think you have chosen the correct answer. Read all questions and answer choices completely and carefully! Many questions stems will have the words "all of the following EXCEPT." Questions like these give test takers the most trouble, because many do not take the time to read the question completely. The distractors for these questions are particularly tricky if you haven't read the question thoroughly.

If you have prepared thoroughly, then have confidence! If you can make an educated guess on a test item, using your knowledge of U.S. history, chances are that you will make the correct choice.

HOW TO APPROACH THE FREE-RESPONSE QUESTIONS

The essay questions on the AP U.S. History exam are designed to test your ability to apply knowledge of history in a complex, analytical manner. In other words, you are expected to treat history and historical questions as a historian would. This process is called historiography— the skills and strategies historians use to analyze and interpret historical evidence to reach a conclusion. Thus, when writing an effective essay, you must be able to write a strong and clearly developed thesis and supply a substantial amount of relevant evidence to support your thesis.

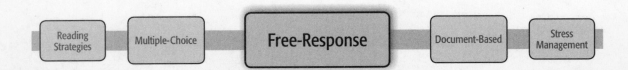

Reading Strategies | Multiple-Choice | **Free-Response** | Document-Based | Stress Management

Quite often, there are no "right" answers for the essay questions presented in Sections II and III. However, there are expectations for the depth and analysis of you responses.

Recall from chapter 1 that the essays you compose in Sections II and III of the exam are scored on a 9-point scale. For AP Readers, the critical "breaking point" for essay scoring is between a 4 and a 5. Oftentimes, it is also the "breaking point" for students. By this, we mean that scoring a 5 on your essay could mean the difference between a composite or overall exam score of 3 as opposed to a 2. What does it take to jump over the gap between a 4 and a 5? Or better yet, how can you earn a top score of 8 or 9? We will review some strategies here that can help you develop a plan of attack for the free-response section of the AP exam.

Success on the free-response section of the exam starts with breaking down the task of essay writing into specific steps. As part of your year-long preparation for taking the AP U.S. History exam, you should be writing at least two essays (one DBQ and one FRQ) each month. You can score your essays by using the scoring guide provided in chapter 1 of this guide. Aim high! If you can score above a 6 on your practice essays, you are well on the way to earning a top composite score on your exam.

STEP 1: DISSECT THE QUESTION

Always keep in mind that the AP U.S. History exam is written to be challenging and rigorous. Thus, the questions will have specific and important information that you must identify prior to constructing a response. When given an essay prompt, first take some of your 15-minute reading period to slow down and understand exactly what the question is asking you to do. The key here is to understand how to answer all parts of the question. Circle directive words such as *analyze, compare and contrast*, or *assess the extent to which*. Commonly, prompts will ask you to validate or refute a statement or to explain the impact of one event on another or the degree of impact. List these directives as pieces of the puzzle that you will attempt to put together with your history knowledge. Here is a sample AP U.S. History FRQ:

> Assess the extent to which advances in technology altered the social, cultural, and economic landscape of the United States in the years 1920–1930.

To start, circle the words *Assess the extent to which*. This question is asking you to show how much of an impact technology had on the United States. Next, you should realize that the question is asking you to discuss the impact of technology on *social, cultural, and economic* aspects of the United States. Remember, you must address all three areas to earn a top score. Finally, circle the years *1920–1930*. Each year at the AP reading, students are given scores of 0 for essays that do not address the proper time period. Your answer must attempt to cover the entire period given

STICK TO THE SUBJECT

In your essay, giving historical information before or after the time period in the essay topic will not get you any extra points.

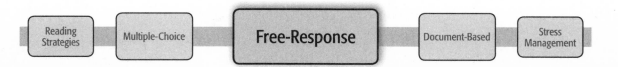

THERE'S NO *U* IN HISTORY

Don't include personal opinions in the essay. The reader is looking for your grasp of the history itself and your ability to write about it.

BE A DBQ REBEL

For DBQ questions, you don't have to write a thesis that agrees with their thesis. You can also take a "middle ground" approach.

by the question. Remember, too, your job is to be a historian, which means that you must take a stand. You must explain how much advances in technology changed the political, cultural, and economic areas of the United States during this decade.

STEP 2: FORMULATE A THESIS

A major area of concern each year for the Chief Readers of the AP exams is that students do not take the time to understand all parts of the question and plan their responses. We have already dissected the question; now it is time to plan a thesis. The thesis is your way of telling the reader why he should care about reading your essay. If you have a weak thesis, the reader will not be convinced that you understand the question. He will not trust that you have the depth of knowledge necessary to answer the question! Therefore, you must have a thesis that takes a stand, answers the entire question, and shows the reader that path you will take in your essay answer. It is not enough to merely restate the question as your thesis. One of the most important things to do is to take a position. Don't be afraid of taking a strong stand for or against a prompt, as long as you can provide the proper and relevant evidence to support your assertions.

Think of your thesis as the "road map" to your essay. It will provide the reader with the stops along the way to the final destination—the conclusion. For example, for the sample essay above, your thesis may be:

> Technological advances, such as radio, automobiles, and motion pictures, in the period 1920–1930 had a major impact on how Americans viewed themselves as a country. These advances connected people from all walks of life and helped spur a booming consumer culture that solidified what it meant to be an "American."

This thesis does not explicitly restate the prompt but rather alludes to it by discussing specific technological advances and how historians believe they impacted American culture. This thesis provides the reader with a "road map" by developing a structure for the rest of the essay. The body of the essay will discuss specific technological advances in the first paragraph, explain the impact of those advances on society and culture in the second paragraph, and will explain the growth of the consumer culture (economy) in the third paragraph. Finally, a good essay conclusion will argue that the "American identity" as mass consumer developed in this period and could not have occurred without these technological advances. Notice that none of the information in the thesis is provided by the prompt itself. Only through a thorough study of U.S. history can you construct a strong thesis.

STEP 3: PLAN YOUR EVIDENCE

Now that you have a "road map," you need to brainstorm all of the relevant evidence you can recall that relates to the question. There are several ways to do this. Some students prefer to use a cluster strategy, where they place the main thoughts in bubbles and then scatter supporting evidence around the main bubbles. Other students prefer to list facts and evidence in a bulleted list. Some like to create an outline of relevant information. Whatever you prefer, this is a step you cannot skip! Students who do not take the time to plan their evidence often find themselves scratching out irrelevant information during the exam, thus wasting valuable time. Also, you must learn to do this efficiently—you only should use about five minutes to complete the first three steps of essay writing. Use abbreviations, pictures, or other cues that are special but efficient to you. A sample list for the essay question above may look like this:

- **Social**—radio and movies connected Americans from all walks of life, all parts of the country, provided escape from life, established the "perfect" American, helped commercialization

- **Cultural**—movies and radio exposed people to different groups, ethnicities, literature, arts, created the first "idols" such as Valentino, Pickford, Babe Ruth, Joe Louis, popularized professional sports, cars connected people, freed them to travel to new areas

- **Economic**—bought consumer goods in large numbers, refrigerators, autos, helped spur growth in other industries, mass-produced goods became in vogue

Once you have a list, you can move to the next (and most important) step—writing!

STEP 4: WRITE YOUR ESSAY

As you practice writing essays using the strategies in the chapter, you will have the luxury of taking time to write topic sentences, list evidence, and construct "mini conclusions" for each prompt. However, on the AP exam, time is of the essence! You have about 30 minutes to construct a coherent essay response for each of the two FRQs and about 45 minutes for the DBQ. If you practice the prewriting strategies from steps 1 through 3 above, you will find it easy to write a developed paper in a short time.

There is no "standard" number of paragraphs you must have. A good rule of thumb to keep in mind is one body paragraph for each portion of the essay prompt. Some AP U.S. History exam questions will be structured to fit a five-paragraph essay, while others may need more and others less. You will not be penalized for writing a strong four-paragraph response. Likewise, you will not be rewarded for constructing a weak six-paragraph response. AP readers look for quality, not quantity.

THINK AHEAD

During the 15-minute reading session, make a short outline of all the outside information you're planning to use in your essay. That way, you have the info handy while you're writing.

WRITING TIP

When composing your essay, start with your most important information. That way, if you run out of time while you're writing, your key points are already in the essay.

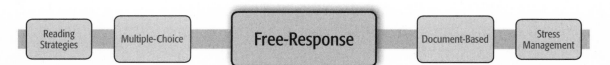

Reading Strategies | Multiple-Choice | **Free-Response** | Document-Based | Stress Management

Your first paragraph should always introduce your essay. Your thesis from step 2 is only part of your introduction. The first paragraph of your essay should include your thesis and any other organizational cues you can give your reader. Ask yourself, "Could a complete stranger understand where my essay is going from just my first paragraph?" If your answer is no, then you must rework the introduction. Do not spend time creating a "hook" or flashy statement for your first sentence. Do not use rhetorical questions. AP Faculty Consultants are reading for the items that are listed on the scoring guide. You will notice that creativity in language and structure is not a listed item. However, a well-written and developed argument is a desired item.

Your body paragraphs should follow the "road map" you set in your introduction and thesis. Don't stray from your plan, or you will find yourself straying from the question. You have taken the time to plan, so use the plan! Do not merely list facts and events in a "laundry list" fashion. You must have some element of analysis between each set of evidence you provide. In the example above, it would not be enough simply to mention that automobiles became affordable through the work of Henry Ford. You must explain why this fact is relevant to the question asked. Why were affordable cars important to changes in America between 1920 and 1930? How did cars impact the social, cultural, and economic makeup of the country? Using transition words such as *however*, *therefore*, and *thus* to show a shift in thought can make creating analytical sentences quick and easy. You should practice stringing facts and thoughts together using these "qualifying transitions" in your sentences.

Beware of telling a story rather than answering the question. Readers are looking for analysis, not a revised version of your textbook. Do not attempt to shower the reader with extra factoids and showy language. Say what you need to say cleanly and simply. Readers will be impressed with your ability to write clearly and concisely in a way that showcases your historical knowledge, rather than your ability to write creatively. Because this is a formal essay, you should avoid using personal pronouns such as *you*, *I*, or *we*. Avoid the use of terms that could be "loaded" unless you intend on explaining them to the reader. For instance, you would not want to use the term *liberal* to describe Thomas Jefferson unless you were prepared to explain your use of the word *liberal* in the historical context. Do not use slang in any part of your essay. Also, because your essay is about history, and thus is about the past, write your essay in the past tense. Do not write about Franklin D. Roosevelt as if he is still alive today.

You should end each body paragraph with a "mini conclusion" that ties the paragraph back to the thesis. It can serve as a transition sentence into the next paragraph or stand alone. In either case, the reader should be able to tell easily that you are shifting gears into another part of the essay.

KNOW THE LINGO

Whenever possible, use historical terms or phrases instead of general ones. For example, instead of saying that the South established laws against an owner freeing slaves, say that the South established laws against *manumission*. This shows the reader that you really know your stuff.

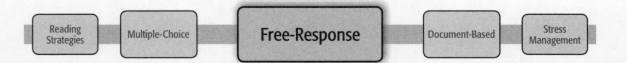

Reading Strategies | Multiple-Choice | **Free-Response** | Document-Based | Stress Management

Lastly, write your conclusion. Many students have learned that they should simply restate their thesis in the conclusion; these students may recopy what they wrote in the introduction word for word. This is incorrect. Yes, you should restate your thesis, but in a new way. Instead of rewriting it word for word, explain why your thesis is significant to the question. Do not introduce new evidence in your conclusion. The conclusion should tie all "mini conclusion" sentences together and leave the reader with a sense of completion. If for some reason you are running out of time when you reach the conclusion, you may leave it off without incurring a specific penalty on the scoring guide. However, if you practice writing timed essays, you will learn the proper timing it takes to write a complete essay, conclusion included.

HOW TO APPROACH THE DOCUMENT-BASED QUESTION

You can follow the guidelines above for the DBQ with some important additions. The DBQ requires the use of a "substantial number" of documents and "substantial and relevant" outside information. There is no prescribed number to make up "substantial," but we recommend using half of the documents plus one. So if there are eight documents for a DBQ, use five documents minimum in your response. It is better to use all of the documents than to use the minimum. Likewise, there is no magic formula for "substantial" outside information. A good goal to keep in mind is to use at least three pieces of outside information per body paragraph. Therefore, in a standard five-paragraph response, an essay would have nine pieces of outside information.

The DBQ requires you to analyze the documents in addition to the outside information you bring to the question. This is a difficult task, and you have only 15 minutes to plan before you begin writing. Don't panic! Use the same strategies for FRQs above for document analysis. Yes, we realize it is a big task for you to complete the strategies for each and every document on the AP exam as we have them outlined in this guide. However, the more you practice using these strategies, the better you will become at quickly finding significance in the documents.

DOCUMENT ANALYSIS

Many students new to AP may struggle with the reading and analysis of primary source documents. Since the DBQ response on the AP U.S. History exam makes up almost 23 percent of your overall score, it is important to practice this skill throughout the year. Primary sources are documents that are contemporary to the time period in which they were written. In other words, a letter written by Abigail Adams to her husband John Adams would be considered contemporary to the late-eighteenth century and, thus, a primary source document from this time period.

> ### PRACTICE MAKES PERFECT
>
> Mastering how to format the DBQ is half the battle. The more you practice writing DBQs, the more prepared you'll be to write one under pressure on Test Day.

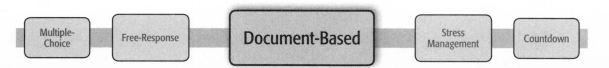

Multiple-Choice | Free-Response | **Document-Based** | Stress Management | Countdown

An example of a secondary source would be a textbook offering its interpretation of the same letter from Abigail Adams to John Adams. On the AP exam, you will be required to read, dissect, and analyze primary sources quickly and efficiently. Let's look at a method to practice document analysis that you can learn to adapt for the AP U.S. History exam.

Here is an example of a possible primary source document that could appear on the AP U.S. History exam:

> "A house divided against itself cannot stand....I do not expect the Union to be dissolved; I do not expect the house to fall; but I do expect it will cease to be divided. It will become all one thing, or all the other…" Abraham Lincoln, 1858

First we must consider what a historian would do when asked to analyze a primary source document. Are key features evident on the document, right there on the page? Our first step will be to scan the document for clues. Look at dates, authors, and possible indications of where this document came from. In this document, we can see that it was produced in 1858 and was written by Abraham Lincoln.

Our next step will be to catalog all of the possible outside information we may have about the dates, author, and place of the document. For this document we know that Abraham Lincoln was vying for the Republican nomination to run for president in 1858. Thus, we can show that this document is probably important because it illustrates that Lincoln was gravely concerned about the preservation of the Union well before secession and also concerned winning the presidency.

Next we will write down any inferences we may have regarding the document. These may be specific ideas we have that would further explain why this document would be important to a historian studying this period. For our sample document, we can infer that this speech would be important in the study of the coming of the Civil War. Lincoln was almost acting as a "fortune teller" by eerily predicting the troubles that lay ahead for the nation. A historian would be interested in discovering exactly how Lincoln was able to have that kind of foresight and how it prepared him to be president in such a turbulent time.

Last we will tie it all together. Create a thesis statement for this document by using your inferences, outside information, and important facts you have already listed. A thesis statement for our sample document may look something like this:

> By 1858, the Republican Party had been formed due to the divisions caused by the passage of the Kansas-Nebraska Act. Senator Abraham Lincoln delivered his prophetic "House Divided" speech to warn his fellow Republicans of the dangers that lay ahead for the strength of the Union.

USE YOUR OWN WORDS

When using documents, avoid quoting directly from the document. Your job is to paraphrase the information in the document and—most importantly—to use the source to support your own ideas.

CITATION TIP

When citing a document, you don't have to cite it as "Lincoln's speech of 1858." Save yourself some time and refer to it as "Document B."

A simple way to remember this strategy is to call it SCIT (pronounce the *c* as a *k* like in kitten.) S equals scan, C equals catalog, I equals infer, and T equals tie it together. You can practice and complete this strategy for all of the documents on your AP exam in the 15 minutes of mandatory reading time before you begin constructing your DBQ response.

STRESS MANAGEMENT

You can beat anxiety the same way you can beat the AP U.S. History exam—by knowing what to expect beforehand and developing strategies to deal with it.

SOURCES OF STRESS

In the space provided, write down your sources of test-related stress. The idea is to pin down any sources of anxiety so you can deal with them one by one. We have provided common examples—feel free to use them and any others you think of.

- I always freeze up on tests.
- I'm nervous about the DBQ.
- I need a good/great score to get into my first-choice college.
- My older brother/sister/best friend/girlfriend/boyfriend did really well. I must match their scores or do better.
- My parents, who are paying for school, will be quite disappointed if I don't do well.
- I'm afraid of losing my focus and concentration.
- I'm afraid I'm not spending enough time preparing.
- I study like crazy, but nothing seems to stick in my mind.
- I always run out of time and get panicky.
- The simple act of thinking, for me, is like wading through refrigerated honey.
- I have too many AP exams in one week.

MY SOURCES OF STRESS

_____

_____

_____

_____

_____

_____

Read through the list. Cross out things or add things. Now rewrite the list in order of most disturbing to least disturbing.

MY SOURCES OF STRESS, IN ORDER

_____

_____

_____

_____

_____

_____

Chances are, the top of the list is a fairly accurate description of exactly how you react to test anxiety, both physically and mentally. The later items usually describe your fears (disappointing mom and dad, looking bad, etc.). Taking care of the major items from the top of the list should go a long way toward relieving overall test anxiety. That's what we'll do next.

STRENGTHS AND WEAKNESSES

Take 60 seconds to list the areas of U.S. history that you are good at. They can be general, such as "colonialism," or specific, like "foreign policy in the 1930s." Put down as many as you can think of and, if possible, time yourself. Write for the entire time; don't stop writing until you've reached the one-minute stopping point. Go!

STRONG TEST SUBJECTS

_____

_____

_____

_____

_____

Now take one minute to list areas of the test you struggle with or simply do not understand. Again, keep it to one minute and continue writing until you reach the cutoff. Go!

TROUBLESOME TEST SUBJECTS

_____

_____

_____

_____

_____

_____

Taking stock of your assets and liabilities lets you know the areas you don't have to worry about and the ones that will demand extra attention and effort. It helps a lot to find out where you need to spend extra effort. We mostly fear what we don't know and are probably afraid to face. You can't help feeling more confident when you know you're actively strengthening your chances of earning a higher overall score.

Now, go back to the "good" list and expand on it for two minutes. Take the general items on that first list and make them more specific; take the specific items and expand them into more general conclusions. Naturally, if anything new comes to mind, jot it down. Focus all of your attention and effort on your strengths. Don't underestimate yourself or your abilities. Give yourself full credit. At the same time, don't list strengths you don't really have; you'll only be fooling yourself.

Expanding from general to specific might go as follows. If you listed "politics" as a broad topic you feel strong in, you would then narrow your focus to include areas of this subject about which you are particularly knowledgeable. Your areas of strength might include specific presidencies, legislative acts, Supreme Court decisions, etc. Whatever you know well goes on your "good" list. OK. Check your starting time. Go!

STRONG TEST SUBJECTS: AN EXPANDED LIST

_____

_____

_____

_____

_____

_____

RELAAAAAAAX

Another way to relieve stress is through progressive relaxation. For example, when you're sitting at your desk, clench your fists tightly for about five seconds, then unclench them slowly and feel the tension disappear.

After you've stopped, check your time. Did you find yourself going beyond the two minutes allotted? Did you write down more things than you thought you knew? Is it possible you know more than you've given yourself credit for? Could that mean you've found a number of areas in which you feel strong?

You just took an active step towards helping yourself. Enjoy your increased feelings of confidence and use them when you take the AP U.S. History exam.

HOW TO DEAL WITH STRESS

VISUALIZE

This next little group of activities is a follow-up to the strong and troublesome test item lists you completed above. Sit in a comfortable chair in a quiet setting. If you wear glasses, take them off. Close your eyes and breathe in a deep, satisfying breath of air. Really fill your lungs until your rib cage is fully expanded and you can't take in any more. Then, exhale the air completely. Imagine you're blowing out a candle with your last little puff of air. Do this two or three more times, filling your lungs to their maximum and emptying them totally. Keep your eyes closed, comfortably but not tightly. Let your body sink deeper into the chair as you become even more comfortable.

With your eyes shut, you can notice something very interesting. You're no longer dealing with the worrisome stuff going on in the world outside of you. Now you can concentrate on what happens inside you. The more you recognize your own physical reactions to stress and anxiety, the more you can do about them. You may not realize it, but you've begun to regain a sense of being in control.

Let images begin to form on TV screens on the back of your eyelids. Allow the images to come easily and naturally; don't force them. Visualize a relaxing situation. It might be in a special place you've visited before or one you've read about. It can be a fictional location that you create in your imagination, but a real-life memory of a place or situation you know is usually better. Make it as detailed as possible and notice as much as you can.

Stay focused on the images as you sink farther into your chair. Breathe easily and naturally. You might have the sensations of any stress or tension draining from your muscles and flowing downward, out your feet and away from you.

Take a moment to check how you're feeling. Notice how comfortable you've become. Imagine how much easier it would be if you could take the test feeling this relaxed and in this state of ease. You've coupled the images of your special place with sensations of comfort and relaxation. You've also found a way to become relaxed simply by visualizing your own safe, special place.

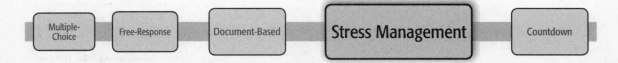

Multiple-Choice   Free-Response   Document-Based   **Stress Management**   Countdown

Close your eyes and start remembering a real-life situation in which you did well on a test. If you can't come up with one, remember a situation in which you did something that you were really proud of—a genuine accomplishment. Make the memory as detailed as possible. Think about the sights, the sounds, the smells, even the tastes associated with this remembered experience. Remember how confident you felt as you accomplished your goal. Now start thinking about the AP U.S. History exam. Keep your thoughts and feelings in line with that prior, successful experience. Don't make comparisons between them. Just imagine taking the upcoming test with the same feelings of confidence and relaxed control.

This exercise is a great way to bring the test down to earth. You should practice this exercise often, especially when you feel burned out on test preparation. The more you practice it, the more effective the exercise will be for you.

COUNTDOWN TO THE TEST

Studying for the AP U.S. History exam can seem daunting because of the sheer volume of material covered in a year-long course. Whether you have taken the course over a semester or over two years, the exam measures your knowledge and skills in exactly the same way. As we have said, it is only through the thorough study over the course of the year that you will earn a high score on the AP exam. This guide is an excellent addition to the class notes, reading notes, and practice essays you have accumulated throughout the year. This guide is not intended to replace your assigned readings, a textbook, or your instructor. You can, however, use this guide to assist you in studying throughout the year or closer to your exam.

Some students prefer to review what they learned last in class and work their way back to the beginning of the course as they study. This is perfectly acceptable. However, other students prefer to begin their studies with the material that is most distant—material learned at the beginning of the course. Again, this is a perfectly logical way to attack the material. Other students choose to skip around and study only those sections of the course with which they had difficulty. Whatever approach you decide to take, make sure it best suits your needs and helps you feel prepared and secure in your abilities in AP U.S. History.

There is one method we advise against. We do not recommend cramming material into your brain in the weeks before the AP exam. Students who score well on the exam are students who have carefully studied U.S. history and have both a breadth and depth of understanding of the material and how to think historically. Take your time. Allow yourself the opportunity to practice your material often by starting your review early.

> **JOG YOUR MEMORY**
>
> When you study, put extra emphasis on first-semester material. History from the second semester is usually easier to remember, because you learned it more recently.

Multiple-Choice — Free-Response — Document-Based — Stress Management — **Countdown**

Regardless of where you will take your AP U.S. History test, everyone preparing for the AP exam has a Friday morning in early May earmarked as "Test Day." For some, the purchase of this guide occurred in September. For others, mid-April. Yet in some cases it may already be May! Whatever your situation, we have provided study calendars below that you can use to help you set some goals.

MONTHLY STUDY CALENDAR

August/ September	Wow, you're ahead of the game and have already thought about AP study—you're off to a great start! Go through your reading calendar provided by your instructor and connect each chapter of this guide to the material you will be learning about in class. By the end of September, you should have completed your study and review of all chapters in this guide up to the **Revolutionary War**.
October	By the end of this month, you should have completed the chapters in this guide that discuss the **Revolutionary War** up through **Jacksonian Democracy**.
November	Funny how fast time flies! Be sure to make special arrangements for family holidays and gatherings that may change your study time. By the end of this month, you should be through **Jackson** and well into the growing **Sectional Crisis of the 1850s**.
December	The 20th century turns during this month, as you move from **Sectional Tension** through the **Rise of Industry, 1865–1900**.
January	During this month, you should devise a plan to review all of the material you have covered during this semester. Don't let final exams get you down. Use this time as an opportunity to revisit the content you covered in September! Additionally, you should be through the **Progressive Era**.
February	Don't let time slip away! This month takes you from the **Progressive Era** through the **Great Depression** and **New Deal**.
March	You are now in the home stretch! In March, you should cover the **Second World War** to the end of the **1950s**. You should also go back through the material you covered during the first part of this semester to get a head start on your review.
April	Can you believe that the exam is only a month away? Complete the guide in the first two weeks of April and concentrate on reviewing the entire guide during the last two weeks, concentrating on your weaknesses.
May	The exam is in a few days. Relax, but don't let up. Keep going over your trouble spots and practice writing free-response essays. Good luck!

The Quarter Study Calender

Quarter One	By Thanksgiving, you should have covered all chapters up to the **Sectional Tensions of the 1850s**.
Quarter Two	By your semester final exams, you need to have studied from the **1850s** through the **Progressive Era**.
Quarter Three	This can be a stressful period—the bulk of your review and study needs to occur here. You should have covered all material up to the end of the **1950s** by the end of this quarter.
Quarter Four	You do not have much time in this quarter before the exam. Here you need to finish the guide and start reviewing all materials from the beginning. Remember to concentrate on the areas where you have trouble.

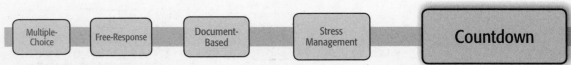

THE "I HAVE A MONTH" STUDY CALENDAR

We will presume that you purchased this guide sometime between the end of March and the beginning of April. With only a month or so before the exam, you don't have time to lose!

We recommend that you make a goal of covering eight chapters of this guide every week, with one day dedicated to reviewing those chapters before moving on. Be sure to concentrate on the material and chapters where you experienced difficulties over the course of the school year.

THREE DAYS BEFORE THE TEST

It's almost over. Eat an energy bar, drink some soda—do whatever it takes to keep going (but don't overdose on sugar and caffeine). Here are Kaplan's strategies for the three days leading up to the test.

Take a full-length practice test under timed conditions. Use the techniques and strategies you've learned in this book. Approach the test strategically, actively, and confidently.

WARNING: Do *not* take a full-length practice test if you have fewer than 48 hours left before the test. Doing so will probably exhaust you and hurt your score on the actual test. You wouldn't run a marathon the day before the real thing.

TWO DAYS BEFORE THE TEST

Go over the results of your practice test. Don't worry too much about your score or about whether you got a specific question right or wrong. The practice test doesn't count. But do examine your performance on specific questions with an eye to how you might get through each one faster and better on the test to come.

THE NIGHT BEFORE THE TEST

DO NOT STUDY. Get together the supplies you will bring to the test center.

Know exactly where you're going, exactly how you're getting there, and exactly how long it takes to get there. It's probably a good idea to visit your test center sometime before the day of the test so that you know what to expect—what the rooms are like, how the desks are set up, and so on.

Relax the night before the test. Do the relaxation and visualization techniques. Read a good book, take a long hot shower, watch some bad television. Get a good night's sleep. Go to bed early and leave yourself extra time in the morning.

LOOK TOWARD THE FUTURE

When reviewing your notes and books for your regular tests during the school year, highlight those areas in your notes that you think you have forgotten (or never fully understood). That way, when the AP exam rolls around, you'll be able to revisit those notes and fix up your weak spots.

THE MORNING OF THE TEST

First, wake up. After that…

- Eat breakfast. Make it something substantial but not anything too heavy or greasy.
- Don't drink a lot of coffee if you're not used to it. Bathroom breaks cut into your time, and too much caffeine is a bad idea.
- Dress in layers so that you can adjust to the temperature of the test room.
- Read something. Warm up your brain with a newspaper or a magazine. You shouldn't let the exam be the first thing you read that day.
- Be sure to get there early. Allow yourself extra time for traffic, mass transit delays, and/or detours.

DURING THE TEST

Don't be shaken. If you find your confidence slipping, remind yourself how well you've prepared. You know the structure of the test; you know the instructions; you've had practice with—and have learned strategies for—every question type.

If something goes really wrong, don't panic. If the test booklet is defective—two pages are stuck together or the ink has run—raise your hand and tell the proctor you need a new book. If you accidentally misgrid your answer page or put the answers in the wrong section, raise your hand and tell the proctor. He or she might be able to arrange for you to regrid your test after it's over, when it won't cost you any time.

AFTER THE TEST

You might walk out of the AP exam thinking that you blew it. This is a normal reaction. Lots of people—even the highest scorers—feel that way. You tend to remember the questions that stumped you, not the ones that you knew.

We're positive that you will have performed well and scored your best on the exam because you followed the Kaplan Strategies outlined in this section. Be confident in your preparation and celebrate the fact that the AP test is soon to be a distant memory.

Now, continue on to Part Two of this guide, where you can take a Diagnostic Test to determine where you stand right now. This short test will give you an idea of the format of the actual exam, and it will demonstrate the scope of topics covered. After the Diagnostic Test, you'll find answers with detailed explanations. Be sure to read these explanations carefully, even when you got the question right, as you can pick up bits of knowledge from them. Use your score to learn which topics you need to review more carefully. Of course, all the strategies in the world can't save you if you haven't built up a solid knowledge base of U.S. history. The chapters following the Diagnostic Test will help you review the primary concepts and facts that you can expect to encounter on the AP exam.

TIME TIP

Pay close attention to how much time you have for each section. Move quickly at the beginning and keep checking your progress periodically.

Multiple-Choice · Free-Response · Document-Based · Stress Management · **Countdown**

DIAGNOSTIC TEST

AP U.S. HISTORY DIAGNOSTIC TEST

To best use this guide, you must understand where your strengths and weaknesses in U.S. history lie. If you are looking at this guide at the beginning of your school year, the questions in the Diagnostic Test may seem difficult. If you are taking this Diagnostic Test at the end of your school year, your results on this test may assist you in developing a study plan before the AP U.S. History exam. In either case, it is important that you pay very close attention to areas of this test on which you score poorly. These results may indicate that you must study a particular section of this guide a bit more closely than areas in which you scored well. We will provide you with more information regarding how you can use your score on this Diagnostic Test at the end of this section.

Let's go ahead and begin your Diagnostic Test! Find a quiet room with no distractions, get a number 2 pencil and a silent timepiece, and take the entire test from start to finish. Explanations of all test items are provided at the end of this test. Try not to look at them now. Take this test without any other materials to obtain a true measure of your abilities.

Good luck!

DIAGNOSTIC TEST ANSWER GRID

To compute your score for the Diagnostic Test, calculate the number of questions you got wrong, then deduct $\frac{1}{4}$ of that number from the number of right answers. So if you got 5 questions wrong out of 20, subtract $\frac{1}{4}$ of that (1.25) from the number of questions you got right (15). The final score would be 13.75. To set this equal to a score out of 100, set up a proportion:

$$\frac{13.75}{20} = \frac{n}{100}$$

$$20n = 1,375$$

$$n = 68.75 = 69$$

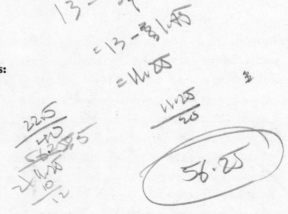

The approximate score range is as follows:

5 = 90–100 (extremely well qualified)

4 = 80–89 (well qualified)

3 = 70–79 (qualified)

2 = 60–69 (possibly qualified)

1 = 0–59 (no recommendation)

A score of 69 is approximately a 2, so, in this case, you could definitely do better. If your score is low, keep on studying to improve your chances of getting credit for the AP U.S. History exam.

1. Ⓐ Ⓑ Ⓒ Ⓓ Ⓔ

2. Ⓐ Ⓑ Ⓒ Ⓓ Ⓔ

3. Ⓐ Ⓑ Ⓒ Ⓓ Ⓔ

4. Ⓐ Ⓑ Ⓒ Ⓓ Ⓔ

5. Ⓐ Ⓑ Ⓒ Ⓓ Ⓔ

6. Ⓐ Ⓑ Ⓒ Ⓓ Ⓔ

7. Ⓐ Ⓑ Ⓒ Ⓓ Ⓔ

8. Ⓐ Ⓑ Ⓒ Ⓓ Ⓔ

9. Ⓐ Ⓑ Ⓒ Ⓓ Ⓔ

10. Ⓐ Ⓑ Ⓒ Ⓓ Ⓔ

11. Ⓐ Ⓑ Ⓒ Ⓓ Ⓔ

12. Ⓐ Ⓑ Ⓒ Ⓓ Ⓔ

13. Ⓐ Ⓑ Ⓒ Ⓓ Ⓔ

14. Ⓐ Ⓑ Ⓒ Ⓓ Ⓔ

15. Ⓐ Ⓑ Ⓒ Ⓓ Ⓔ

16. Ⓐ Ⓑ Ⓒ Ⓓ Ⓔ

17. Ⓐ Ⓑ Ⓒ Ⓓ Ⓔ

18. Ⓐ Ⓑ Ⓒ Ⓓ Ⓔ

19. Ⓐ Ⓑ Ⓒ Ⓓ Ⓔ

20. Ⓐ Ⓑ Ⓒ Ⓓ Ⓔ

DIAGNOSTIC TEST

1. Henry Clay's "American System" sought to

   (A) open trade relationships between the United States and Europe.

   (B) strengthen the U.S. economy.

   (C) divide the Republican party.

   (D) lower protective tariffs to encourage foreign investment.

   (E) establish a two-term limit for presidents.

2. President Harry Truman publicly justified his use of the atomic bomb on Hiroshima and Nagasaki by

   (A) assessing the risk of Soviet domination of Asia if the bomb had not been used.

   (B) calculating the loss of American life in a conventional military invasion of Japan.

   (C) using the fear of fascism as justification for the destruction.

   (D) seeking revenge on Japan for the surprise attack on Pearl Harbor.

   (E) releasing the contents of NSC-68.

3. According to the doctrine of "popular sovereignty," the slavery question would be decided by

   (A) Congress.

   (B) the popular vote in each territory.

   (C) a Supreme Court ruling.

   (D) an Executive Order.

   (E) a national popular vote.

4. Colonial opposition to the Stamp Act took all of the following forms EXCEPT

   (A) tarring and feathering tax collectors.

   (B) a boycott against British goods.

   (C) a meeting of a special congress to ask for a repeal of the tax.

   (D) wearing "homespun" clothing.

   (E) the dumping of British tea into the Boston Harbor.

5. The Grangers sought to combat the

   (A) loss of African-American civil rights in the South.

   (B) removal of the Plains Indians.

   (C) closing of the Western frontier.

   (D) high prices farmers were paying to railroads and middlemen.

   (E) Chinese Exclusion Act of 1882.

6. W. E. B. Du Bois differed from Booker T. Washington in that he

   (A) championed the direct election of senators.

   (B) advocated a return to the days of the Black Codes.

   (C) was inspired by social Darwinism.

   (D) wished to end prostitution.

   (E) stressed civil rights issues rather than economics.

GO ON TO THE NEXT PAGE

7. The 104th Congress ushered in an era of "divided government" in which

   (A) half of Americans voted Republican and half of Americans voted Democratic.

   (B) the Democratic President Clinton had to work hard to pass legislation in a Republican-led Congress.

   (C) the United States became more aggressive with regard to foreign policy.

   (D) the judicial and legislative branches joined forces to combat the president.

   (E) states' rights groups battled the federal government for power.

8. Conservative critics of President Franklin D. Roosevelt's "New Deal"

   (A) felt he was too slow to react to the crisis of the Depression.

   (B) urged him to allow the economy to repair itself.

   (C) were angered over the failure to get legislation passed.

   (D) feared the growth of the federal government and national debt.

   (E) argued that commercial banks should be dissolved.

9. The growth of large corporations was aided by the Supreme Court's interpretation of

   (A) the Fourteenth Amendment.

   (B) the Sherman Antitrust Act.

   (C) Interstate Commerce Act of 1887.

   (D) the Pendleton Act of 1883.

   (E) the Sixteenth Amendment.

10. The Articles of Confederation did not have provisions for Congress to

    (A) plan for the development of western lands.

    (B) wage war.

    (C) establish a post office.

    (D) enforce tax collection.

    (E) borrow money.

11. Ronald Reagan won the election of 1980 by garnering the vote of

    (A) women.

    (B) blue-collar voters.

    (C) liberal Democrats.

    (D) Keynesian economists.

    (E) African Americans.

12. The belief in the strength of the individual was best expressed by

    (A) the transcendentalists.

    (B) the Mormons.

    (C) the Presbyterians.

    (D) the temperance movement.

    (E) the Hudson River School.

13. "A woman is handicapped by her sex, and handicaps society, either by slavishly copying the pattern of man's advance in the professions, or by refusing to compete with man at all."—Betty Freidan

    The quote above can be attributed to which of the following books?

    (A) *Their Eyes Were Watching God*

    (B) *Silent Spring*

    (C) *The Feminine Mystique*

    (D) *A Century of Dishonor*

    (E) *Baby and Child Care*

GO ON TO THE NEXT PAGE →

14. The growth of the American suburbs in the 1950s can be attributed to

(A) a decrease in the overall birth rate in the United States.

(B) the discovery of the oolio vaccine.

(C) a rise in the income of racial minorities.

(D) the GI Bill and the Interstate Highway Act.

(E) movement of American business centers to the upper Midwest.

15. The issuance of the Emancipation Proclamation in January 1863 had the effect of

(A) immediately freeing all slaves in the United States.

(B) making slavery unconstitutional.

(C) weakening the Confiscation Acts.

(D) garnering much needed British support for the North.

(E) shifting the purpose of the war to a moral rather than a political cause.

16. Fear of radicalism and immigration in the 1920s is best illustrated by

(A) the Volstead Act.

(B) passage of the Nineteenth Amendment.

(C) the trial of Sacco and Vanzetti.

(D) the Scopes Monkey Trial.

(E) the banning of the Ku Klux Klan.

17. The presidential election of 1896 had as its major issue

(A) farmers' and laborers' rights.

(B) laissez-faire economic policies.

(C) free and unlimited coinage of silver.

(D) fundamentalist Christian values.

(E) the prohibition of alcohol.

18. New England colonies differed from Chesapeake colonies in that

(A) New England settlers were not members of the Church of England.

(B) New England colonies were settled purely for religious reasons.

(C) Chesapeake colonists were less tolerant of religious differences.

(D) there were fewer women in Chesapeake colonies.

(E) no Africans were brought to New England as slaves.

19. In his refusal to turn over taped conversations to Congress during the Watergate investigation, President Richard Nixon claimed that

(A) the tapes were his private property.

(B) national security was at stake.

(C) he had executive privilege.

(D) they were inadmissible as evidence.

(E) those taped did not know they were being recorded.

20. Thomas Jefferson contradicted his philosophy of "strict constructionism" with regard to the Constitution by

(A) owning slaves of his own.

(B) seeking to impeach Supreme Court justice Samuel Chase.

(C) purchasing the Louisiana territory from France.

(D) repealing the Embargo Act.

(E) participating in the "Revolution of 1800."

STOP

ANSWERS AND EXPLANATIONS

1. B

Henry Clay, a representative of Kentucky, sought to make the United States economically self-sufficient by protecting American manufacturing with protective tariffs, re-establishing the Bank of the United States, and providing for federal funding of internal improvements. This comprehensive plan to improve the economic status and health of the United States was called the "American System." Trade between Europe and the United States (A) remained difficult, as the country continued high tariffs on imported goods, and refused to ally with either Britain or France. The two-term presidential limit (E) was not imposed until the passage of the Twenty-second Amendment in 1951. Even though the Republican party was experiencing challenges, the "American System" was not devised to split the party (C).

2. B

Some military experts had estimated that as many as 1 million U.S. soldiers would be lost in a conventional invasion of Japan at the end of World War II. Faced with an impossible decision in the summer of 1945 to use the most powerful and destructive weapon on earth, Harry Truman chose to protect the lives of those Americans by dropping atomic bombs on Hiroshima and Nagasaki on August 6 and August 9, respectively. On August 11, Japan surrendered and later signed an unconditional surrender aboard the USS *Missouri* on September 2, thus ending World War II.

3. B

Lewis Cass, a senator from Michigan, devised a plan in which the determination of whether a new state or territory would be slave or free would be left up to the citizens of that state or territory. The plan was called "popular sovereignty." This idea became convenient for national politicians, especially Democrats, who could now sidestep the slavery issue by claiming the power to institute slavery rested with the territories and new states, not the federal government.

4. E

Colonials reacted swiftly to the British imposition of the Stamp Act by forming the Stamp Act Congress (C), amassing support for a boycott of British goods (B), and making the wearing of "homespun" clothing rather fashionable (D). The Sons and Daughters of Liberty were known to have intimidated tax collectors by tarring and feathering and many other such tactics (A). The dumping of British tea into Boston Harbor did not occur until the passage of the Tea Act in 1773.

5. D

A cooperative of western farmers who originally organized as a social fraternity for isolated farmers, the National Grange of Patrons of Husbandry (more commonly known as "the Grange") soon turned to politics as costs of farming rose and prices for farm goods plunged. The Grange established cooperatives for the purchase of machinery and the storage of grain that attempted to insulate farmers from the trusts. The Grangers later succeeded in enacting laws at the state and local level in Illinois, Wisconsin, Iowa, and Minnesota to protect farmers from unfair pricing practices of the railroads. However, the Granger Laws were dealt a fatal blow by the Supreme Court in *Wabash v. Illinois* (1886), which forbade states from regulating railroads that were involved in interstate commerce.

6. E

W. E. B. Du Bois disagreed with his popular counterpart in the struggle for African-American recognition on many counts. The most important difference was Du Bois's distaste for Washington's alleged complacency with regard to the lack of civil rights for African Americans. Washington emphasized economic independence rather than racial equality, a point that the sometimes militant Du Bois disputed publicly.

7. B

The 1994 midterm elections and the swearing in of the 104th Congress placed majority control of the legislative branch in the hands of the Republicans. *Divided government* is defined as a time in which the president is of one party and Congress is controlled by the other. President Clinton had to work very hard to convince members of Congress to follow his lead in reducing the federal deficit and reforming the welfare system.

8. D

There were many critics of the "New Deal." However, most of those critics feared the massive growth of the federal government and the rapid increase in government spending that would lead to higher national debt. More than any president before, Franklin Roosevelt was able to pass pieces of legislation in his "First Hundred Days" in office (C). Most economists had abandoned the classical model of market self-repair and were urging FDR to take swift action. He immediately closed all banks in the United States for a four-day "Bank Holiday" (A). However, never did he or any of his critics argue for the dissolution of the commercial banking system, only a reform of it (E).

9. A

The Fourteenth Amendment, passed in 1867 during Reconstruction, was intended to protect the legal rights of African Americans. However, large business owners in the late 19th and early 20th centuries argued that their corporations were being denied "due process" by not having the ability to sue the federal government in court. The Supreme Court agreed with the monopolists by ruling in their favor throughout the Gilded Age.

10. D

While the Articles of Confederation provided a solid foundation for an infant nation, it lacked a critical provision to ensure its success. That missing provision was the ability of the Confederation Congress to enforce the collection of taxes. After fighting the Revolutionary War, the Confederation had high war debts that had to be paid. Under the Articles, Congress could only ask for member states to donate to the cause. The deflated state and national currency only added to the Confederation's woes. The Articles did provide Congress a method of developing western lands (A), the ability to wage war (B), borrowing power (E), and the establishment of a post office (C).

11. B

The "Reagan revolution" ushered a wave of new conservatism in the United States. Capitalizing on his status as a "Washington outsider," Reagan was successful in pulling blue-collar workers and Southern Democrats into his voting block, taking 51 percent of the popular vote and almost 90 percent of the electoral vote. At first, Reagan was not popular with women (A), although they warmed up to him by the 1984 election. Liberals (C), Keynesians (D), and African Americans (E) never really supported Reagan in large numbers.

12. A

Ralph Waldo Emerson and Henry David Thoreau were the most prolific and best-known transcendentalists of their day. Their works stressed individualism, civil disobedience, and a return to nature to discover the mysteries of God and self. The Mormons (B), under the leadership of Joseph Smith, believed in communal and familial strength as their spiritual calling. Presbyterians (C), led by minister Charles Finney, amassed followers by preaching about the damnation of those who would not declare a renewed faith to God. The temperance movement (D) argued that blind individualism led to the dangers of alcoholism and sought to make the manufacture and sale of potent beverages illegal. The Hudson River School (E) was an American artistic movement that glorified the natural wonders of the American landscape.

13. C

In 1963, Betty Freidan shocked the American public by publishing her scathing commentary about the station of American housewives titled *The Feminine Mystique*. Her book served as a lightning rod for middle-class women across the country to join the feminist movement, which gained strength throughout the 1960s.

14. D

The two greatest factors in the housing boom that occurred in the 1950s in America's suburbs were the GI Bill and the Interstate Highway Act. The GI Bill provided government funding for war veterans to earn college degrees and purchase homes. The Interstate Highway Act made it possible to link outlying suburban areas with urban centers quickly and efficiently. Now, middle-class Americans could work in the city by day and return home to the suburbs after work. Unfortunately, lower-income and minority groups were not allowed or could not afford to purchase homes in these new suburban communities.

15. E

Abraham Lincoln waited until after the Battle of Antietam (September 17, 1862) to issue the Emancipation Proclamation, largely based on the advice of his cabinet that to offer such a proclamation without any decisive Union victories would render it meaningless from a political standpoint. The Emancipation Proclamation did not immediately free any slaves (A), because it applied only to those living in Rebel states. It did, however, strengthen the moral cause for thousands of Union soldiers fighting the war and those back home supporting them. Many European leaders were thrilled that the North and South were fighting a civil war, as this would presumably make Southern cotton cheaper while dealing a mortal blow to America's "democratic experiment." The Confiscation Acts of 1862 (that had established Confederate slaves as contraband and thus subject to confiscation and, in effect, freedom) were strengthened by the Proclamation in that Union soldiers no longer had to return liberated slaves as "property" to Southern slave owners (C).

16. C

Sacco and Vanzetti were Italian anarchists who were arrested in 1921 for the alleged robbery and murder of a paymaster in South Braintree, Massachusetts.

They were brought to trial amidst the heart of the "Red Scare," a time when Americans were terrified of radicals such as communists and anarchists. Despite contradictory and inconclusive evidence on behalf of the prosecution, the two were convicted and sentenced to death in 1923.

17. C

William Jennings Bryan became an overnight sensation after delivering his "Cross of Gold" speech, which demanded the free and unlimited coinage of silver. Favoring the old Populist platform of "free silver," the Bryan campaign traveled across the United States to garner support from farmers by convincing them that silver was their ticket to escape poverty. While farmers' issues were critical in this election, labor's were not (A). Laissez-faire economic policies (B) were not a problem until the late 19th century. Bryan was known for his fundamentalist ideals but not until the 1920s (D).

18. D

Settlers in the Chesapeake colonies tended to be young men in search of economic opportunity. Very few women made the voyage to settle in the South. English Puritans tended to immigrate in family units to New England in search of religious freedom and economic gain. These settlers believed themselves to be "nonseparatists" in that they intended to remain associated with the Church of England to "purify" it from within. Despite the Maryland Act of Toleration in 1649, Chesapeake settlers were just as intolerant of religious diversity as their New England neighbors.

19. C

President Richard Nixon claimed that he was protected by a special form of confidentiality called "executive privilege" and thus did not have to turn over the many hours of taped conversations to Congress. It actually took a Supreme Court ruling in the case *United States v. Richard Nixon* (1974) to force him finally to turn over the tapes. Consequently, the House Judiciary Committee voted for three articles of impeachment. However, before the full House of Representatives formally voted for impeachment and before he would have subsequently faced a trial and certain conviction in front of the Senate, Richard Nixon resigned on August 9, 1974.

20. C

Thomas Jefferson's actions often contradicted his own philosophy towards a literal application of the Constitution or "strict constructionism." One of the best examples is his purchase of the Louisiana Territory from France in 1803. The Constitution does not provide for a presidential purchase of land from a foreign power. However, for the good of his young nation, Jefferson set aside his interpretation, thus doubling the size of the United States. Jefferson did own slaves, but slavery was legal under the Constitution (A). The impeachment of judges is allowable in the Constitution (B). Jefferson did not repeal the Embargo Act but rather persuaded Congress to pass it in 1807 (D). The "Revolution of 1800" was simply the election of Jefferson, a Democratic-Republican rather than a Federalist, as president in that year (E).

HOW TO MAKE THIS BOOK WORK FOR YOU
BASED ON THE RESULTS OF YOUR DIAGNOSTIC TEST

First, you should know that only one-half of the composite score for the AP U.S. History exam will be multiple-choice. The essays are equally important and potentially easier to master with preparation. No matter what your results on the Diagnostic Test, you should review the essay exam format and expectations carefully.

How you interpret your diagnostic score depends on your situation. How soon is the exam? If you took the Diagnostic Test in the fall or winter, you are likely to score lower than if you took the test in early May. Analyze the types of questions that you missed. The Diagnostic has questions that span from the American Revolution, to World War I, to the Cold War, and many eras in between. Take note of the time periods that you found difficult to recall when taking the test.

This book reviews all eras of AP U.S. History that the AP exam will cover. Part Three is broken down into five chronological units, each spanning an era of U.S. history. Look over the chapters that comprise these units, paying special attention to your weaknesses. Each chapter in Part Three is followed by more practice multiple-choice questions to sharpen your understanding.

Part Four of this book provides more testing practice: two complete exams with 80 multiple-choice questions and three essays. You will be ready to take these full exams after the bulk of your review. Set a time and a place for taking these full practice exams under testlike conditions without interruptions or distractions.

Focus on:
Late 19th century (1880-1900)

Part Three

AP UNITED STATES HISTORY REVIEW

HOW TO USE THE REVIEW SECTION

As we enter the review portion of this guide, it is important for you to recall your success on the Diagnostic Test in Part Two. Before you begin your review, go back and determine the questions on the Diagnostic Test you had difficulty with and link them with the appropriate chapter(s) in this section. Keep track of your understanding of the material in these chapters by answering the review questions after each chapter. Throughout the chapters, words that appear in bold face are key terms you should know in full by the time you finish the chapter. Italicized words are vocabulary you might be unfamiliar with. All italicized words are defined in the Glossary on page 441. Once you have completed a thorough review with Part Three, go ahead and take one of the full-length AP U.S. History exams in Part Four to assess your understanding of the material.

HOW THIS REVIEW IS STRUCTURED

There are five major unit headings that serve as the "umbrella" themes for the chronological eras of United States history. Under each of these five themes are several chapters of historical content that cover specific time periods as they occur along the development of the United States.

UNIT I: THE NEW WORLD TO THE AMERICAN REVOLUTION, 1492–1783

UNIT II: THE NEW NATION TO THE CIVIL WAR, 1787–1877

This unit hasn't been covered in class yet. Perfect; read this unit in parallel to what's being read and taught for and in class

Might want to focus mostly on
{ Unit II
{ Unit III
In other words, the following time periods
_{ 1787–1877_
_{ 1863–1919_

UNIT I: THE NEW WORLD TO THE AMERICAN REVOLUTION, 1492–1783

CHAPTER 3: DISCOVERING AND SETTLING THE NEW WORLD, 1492–1700

IF YOU ONLY LEARN EIGHT THINGS IN THIS UNIT . . .

1. Political and religious reasons behind exploration of the New World by European countries
2. The effect of settlement on existing Native American tribes and the resulting tensions
3. Major differences among the New England, Middle, Chesapeake, and Southern colonies
4. Causes and effects of the Great Awakening
5. Specific events (laws, acts, skirmishes) that eventually led to the Revolutionary War
6. The results of the First and Second Continental Congress
7. The mission behind the Articles of Confederation
8. The events and results of the American Revolution

NATIVE AMERICAN CULTURES AND SOCIETIES

Prior to the arrival of the first Europeans to North America, millions of Native Americans lived in scattered settlements across the continent. These settlements were not large enough to be considered citylike. Some settlements could be easily moved to follow food sources or weather patterns, while others were more permanent. The more permanent villages had a division of labor in which male members of the community would spend time away hunting game or engaging in warfare while female members maintained the workings of the village. Females were responsible for rearing children, tending crops, and administering the laws and rules of the tribe. Many Native American tribes were **matrilineal** in that tribal rights and responsibilities and social station were determined by the bloodline of the mother as opposed to the father. In the Southwest (current-

Native Americans | Changes in Europe | Exploration | Protestantism | Key Terms

day New Mexico), the Pueblo-Hohokam peoples developed large, permanent communities with storied apartment housing and intricate irrigation systems for their crops. In the upper Northeast, the Adena-Hopewell peoples left behind evidence of complicated living arrangements similar to those of the Pueblos of the Southwest. The Ohio Valley was the home of the Cahokia peoples, whose massive burial mounds survive today.

And yet the Natives didn't seem to have those problems.

Despite the technological and social developments of Native American tribes before the arrival of Europeans, they had difficulty amassing any sort of full-scale defense to repel the newcomers. The geographical distance between tribes, frequent internal wars, and distinct cultural and linguistic differences made it difficult to unite to fight off European settlers.

CHANGES IN EUROPE LEADING TO EXPLORATION

Great discoveries in transportation, navigation, and communication of the Scientific Revolution during and after the European Renaissance (late 1400s–early 1500s) led to a thirst for adventure and exploration. Stronger and faster ships, more accurate maps, and the spread of the written word by way of the printing press helped to nurture a generation of young men seeking gold and glory. European heads of state sought to expand their empires by way of wealth, land, and religious conversion. Often, kings and queens would send explorers under the guise of a religious mission to evangelize native peoples when, in fact, the quest for gold and territory was the real goal.

Religion experienced massive change during this period, as well. The expulsion of the Moors from Spain and the reunification of the country under the leadership of the Catholic rulers Isabella and Ferdinand ushered in an age of Spanish exploration and expansion. The Roman Catholic Church experienced challenges to its power after the German monk, **Martin Luther**, posted his protests against the Church and its abuses. This powerful movement away from the Catholic Church was known as the **Protestant Reformation**. Roman Catholic countries strove to secure their power in the world by converting non-Christians in distant lands.

95 Theses

SPANISH, ENGLISH, AND FRENCH EXPLORATION

The Treaty of Tordesillas, signed between Spain and Portugal in 1494, decided how Christopher Columbus's discoveries of the New World would be divided. Because the treaty ensured Spain's claims in the Americas, Isabella and Ferdinand were quick to fund and send explorers to gain riches and civilize native populations. Men such as Vasco Nunez de Balboa, Juan Ponce de León, Ferdinand Magellan, and Hernán Cortés expanded the treasures of Spain with land, gold, and silver. Spanish *conquistadores* enslaved Native American populations using the *encomienda*, in which Spaniards were given land by the Crown and were obligated to care for their native slaves.

Spanish

A philosophy that is, in essence, similar to the landowners' self-idolatry/paternalism. some of

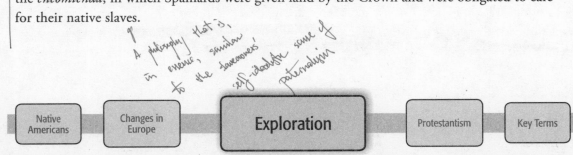

THE SPANISH IN THE AMERICAS

The Spanish influence stretched from what is now California to current-day Florida to the southern tip of Argentina. Their influence can still be seen in the languages spoken, the names of states and countries, and the heritage of many people who live in these regions.

Seeking an escape from overcrowding, unemployment, and oppression, many British citizens jumped at the chance to make the voyage to North America. The English monarchy wanted to keep up with Spanish, French, and Portuguese exploration by sending explorers of their own. The first English settlement of **Roanoke**, established by **Sir Walter Raleigh** in 1585, mysteriously vanished without a trace. The next attempt of colonization did not occur until the establishment of the Virginia Company in 1607. **Captain John Smith** was given charge to organize a colony at Jamestown in order to find gold, Christianize the natives, and secure a passage to India. More importantly, the **Virginia Company** gave the settlers a charter that guaranteed them the same rights as their brothers overseas, thus setting the foundations for the American Revolution. Captain John Smith was the savior of the Jamestown colony through his strong leadership in its early years.

The French arrived in North America around 1524, focusing mostly in what is today Canada and the upper northeastern United States. French explorers such as Jacques Cartier and Samuel de Champlain cultivated a friendly business relationship with Native Americans, dealing mostly in beaver pelts. These vast trade networks spanned the upper Northeast down the Mississippi River to current-day New Orleans. Unfortunately, the French also brought diseases, guns, and alcohol to the native populations. Warfare between tribes worsened as the French traded among warring groups and gave guns as presents.

THE PROTESTANT REFORMATION AND CALVINISM

After Martin Luther's 95 Theses were published in 1517, waves of Northern Europeans broke away from the Catholic Church, thus beginning the Protestant Reformation. Luther argued that faith alone was necessary to gain salvation through God's grace. "Good works" and following the Catholic Church's sacraments, in Luther's view, were not necessary. As Luther's protests circulated quickly throughout Europe, with a speed made possible with the advent of the printing press, Catholics began to fear this new threat to their power and prestige. An era of religious wars between the Protestants and Catholics greatly affected much of Northern and Western Europe from 1521 to 1648.

Changes in Europe | Exploration | Protestantism | Key Terms | Review Questions

John Calvin, a middle-class French-born intellectual, elaborated on and differed with the teachings of Luther, amassing an enormous international following of his own. Calvinists believed in the supreme power of God and that humans were by nature wicked and needed strict leadership to keep them from sin. The cornerstone of Calvin's theology was the concept of predestination, the idea that God knew before a person was born whether or not he or she was "chosen" to enter the gates of Heaven or condemned to eternal damnation. Calvinists believed that one could not get into Heaven by faith or good works alone but must be one of the "**elect**," or God's chosen people. A person would know if he or she was chosen for salvation through a conversion experience that revealed God's will. These followers of Calvin, the Puritans, made up the immigrants who settled New England colonies of Massachusetts, Connecticut, Rhode Island, and New Hampshire in the first half of the 17th century.

KEY TERMS	
Names	John Calvin
	Martin Luther
	John Smith
Events	Protestant Reformation
Documents and Laws	Treaty of Tordesillas
Places	Roanoke
	Virginia Company
Vocabulary	elect
	encomienda

REVIEW QUESTIONS

1. The greatest factor that enabled Europeans to conquer natives in the New World was the

   (A) submissiveness of the tribes that were encountered.
   (B) uncivilized and disorganized social structure of Native Americans.
   (C) lack of healthy tribal populations prior to the arrival of Europeans.
   (D) differences of population and cultural patterns among tribes.
   (E) the willingness of the natives to convert to Christianity.

2. Conquistadores were in the Americas searching for all of the following EXCEPT

   (A) gold.
   (B) glory.
   (C) conversion of natives to Christianity.
   (D) a shorter route to Asia.
   (E) horses.

3. European exploration was spurred by the Renaissance and

   (A) the Reformation.
   (B) the Scientific Revolution.
   (C) the Great Schism.
   (D) cheap and easy voyages made possible by clipper ships.
   (E) the Edict of Nantes.

4. John Smith is known for saving the English colony of

   (A) Jamestown.
   (B) Roanoke Island.
   (C) Boston.
   (D) Plymouth.
   (E) Charleston.

5. Puritans differed from Pilgrims in that they

   (A) were not Protestant.
   (B) remained members of the Church of England.
   (C) believed in antinomianism.
   (D) were not persecuted in England.
   (E) spoke in tongues when in church.

ANSWERS AND EXPLANATIONS

1. D

Native Americans were widely dispersed across the Americas with sometimes hundreds of miles between settlements. Tribes oftentimes did not share a common culture or language, which also contributed to their inability to join together to repel the European invaders.

2. E

It was the Spanish that first introduced the horse to the Native Americans. By claiming that their conquests were all in the name of "God, gold, and glory," the conquistadores were able to justify their actions and bring wealth and power to their countries.

3. B

The Renaissance opened the minds of Europeans to the possibilities of science. Because of that awakening, many inventors made travel and navigation easier than before. The Scientific Revolution brought about advances in cartography and nautical instruments to aid in navigation and the *caravel*, a ship that was lighter and quicker than the ships of the Middle Ages.

4. A

Hoping to avoid the same presumed fate as the lost colony of Roanoke, Captain John Smith was integral to the survival of the Jamestown colony. Through his leadership during the "starving time" of the early years and John Rolfe's knowledge of tobacco cultivation, the colony was able to weather a difficult start and survive.

5. B

The Pilgrims were known as separatists; they believed that they had to leave the Church of England to escape a life they did not believe in. The Puritans, on the other hand, believed that they needed to remain in the Church to stand as examples and purify it from within. However, once the Puritans left England for North America, they no longer remained active in the Church of England.

CHAPTER 4: THE ATLANTIC WORLD, 1600–1750

[handwritten annotation: Puritans — Non-Separatists, Separatists (Pilgrims); ie. Pilgrims were sub-branch of collective Puritan body]

THE NEW ENGLAND COLONIES

The driving force for English colonists to settle along the Atlantic coast of North America in New England was religion. **The Church of England** (Anglican Church) was founded in 1534 by King Henry VIII. The King sought to divorce his first wife Catherine of Aragon. However, Pope Clement VII refused to dissolve the marriage. Enraged, the king (who had named himself "Defender of the Faith") broke away from the Roman Catholic Church and created the Church of England. The Anglican Church remained similar to the Catholic Church in most ways. The **Puritans** in England protested against these similarities. Encouraged by the teachings of John Calvin, these Puritans sought to "purify" the Anglican Church by ridding it of the ceremony and regalia of the Catholic Church. King James I believed these people to be a threat to his power and vigorously attempted to expel them from England.

THE PILGRIMS AND THE MAYFLOWER COMPACT

The first group of Puritan immigrants was comprised of **separatists**, Puritans who felt that they needed to abandon the Church of England altogether and set up a new church independent of the monarchy. This group of Puritans, more commonly known as **Pilgrims**, set out in 1620 aboard the *Mayflower* bound for Virginia. Having agreed to work for seven years for the Virginia Company in exchange for a share of the profits, the Pilgrims set sail. The ship may have blown off course; it landed instead in Plymouth Bay, where a site was chosen for the settlement. While on the high seas, the Pilgrims drafted an agreement to set up a *secular* body to administer the leadership of the colony, known as the **Mayflower Compact**. This document set the stage for the concept of the separation of church and state and the rule of the majority. Despite this division between governance and church, religion remained the most important aspect of the Plymouth colonists' lives.

[handwritten annotation: Plymouth ≈ Pilgrims]

THE GREAT MIGRATION AND JOHN WINTHROP

The next wave of Puritans arrived in New England in 1629 due to oppression and persecution by the English crown. These colonists were **nonseparatists**; while in England, they believed they had to

| New England | Middle Colonies | Chesapeake & Southern Colonies | Resistance | Key Terms |

remain within the Church of England to reform it. The Puritan settlers led the "**Great Migration**" of the 1630s to the Massachusetts Bay Colony. Large numbers of Puritan families ventured across the Atlantic seeking religious freedom and a fresh start. The Governor of the Massachusetts Bay Colony was the outspoken Puritan minister **John Winthrop**. Proclaiming in his *Model of Christian Charity* (1630) that Boston would be a "city upon a hill" for the Christian world to see and emulate, Winthrop became one of the most influential of the leaders of the New England colonies.

LIFE IN THE MASSACHUSETTS BAY COLONY

Hallmarks of the Massachusetts Bay Colony were its success in fishing, timber, and shipbuilding; the development of a citizen democracy as witnessed in town hall meetings; and consistent leadership. The purpose of government in the colony was to ensure the adherence to God's will by all citizens, elect or nonelect. Governor Winthrop did not run his colony as a democracy, however. Only those Puritans who were members of the Congregational Church participated in the public airing of sins and transgressions called the *conversion experience*, and only males were allowed to vote.

NON-PURITANS AND DISSENTERS

The colony was also not known for its tolerance of non-Puritans, or those who were deemed *dissenters*. Dissenters were punished and often banished from the colony altogether. **Anne Hutchinson,** for example, believed in antinomianism, that God's chosen people did not have to obey God's or man's laws because they were already in God's record as predestined to enter Heaven.

Useful term to remember.

After holding prayer meetings in her home and claiming a direct revelation from God, Hutchinson was banished from the Massachusetts Bay Colony. Another dissenter, **Roger Williams**, a minister from Salem, believed that the colonists had no right to live on land that had been unlawfully taken from the Native Americans. Williams believed that an individual's conscience made the rule of civil government or church leadership irrelevant. He advocated a complete separation of church and state. Williams was ordered out of Massachusetts Bay Colony in 1636. He and his followers traveled southward and established the settlement of Providence in what later became the colony of Rhode Island.

Another small group of dissenters, the **Quakers**, believed in the power of one's "inner light," or that the power of God resided in the soul of the individual. They too were ordered to leave the Massachusetts Bay Colony. Several were executed, and several joined William Penn of England in the founding of Pennsylvania or "Penn's Woods." Later in the 17th century, the Massachusetts Bay Colony experienced trouble within its own ranks. Many young Puritans did not have a "conversion experience" and, thus, were not full members of the Congregational

Church. Therefore, the children of these people could not be baptized, and the Church was losing membership. The **Halfway Covenant** was established in 1662 to give nonconverted Puritans partial membership in the church.

THE SALEM WITCH TRIALS

In 1692, a group of young girls in **Salem**, Massachusetts, began acting strangely after hearing tales of voodoo from their West Indian servant. The girls then began to accuse older, wealthy members of the community of witchcraft, leading to mass hysteria in Salem and surrounding areas. In the end, 20 people were executed, and the prestige of the traditional Puritan clergy was damaged beyond repair.

ESTABLISHING ORDER IN NEW ENGLAND

Other New England colonies were founded by splinter groups from the original settlements of Plymouth and Massachusetts Bay. Connecticut, New Haven, and New Hampshire were all established by Puritans. The "first constitution" in colonial America—the **Fundamental Orders**—was drafted in 1639 by the citizens of Connecticut. While it modeled itself after the government of the Massachusetts Bay Colony, the document called for the power of government to be derived from the governed.

Under the constant threat of attack by surrounding Native American tribes, the New England colonies formed the **New England Confederation** in 1643 to provide for collective security. Because the English crown was embroiled in the English Civil War, the colonies were left to manage themselves. This early period of **salutary neglect** of the colonies aided in the development of colonial self-leadership and widened the distance between the ideologies of the Mother country and her colonial citizens.

Angered by what he saw as the political and economic insolence of the New England colonies, especially Massachusetts Bay, England's King James II established the **Dominion of New England** in 1686, aimed at bringing these colonies under stricter royal control. According to the king, the colonies existed purely for the economic benefit of the mother country (England). Navigation Laws were instituted by Parliament to restrict colonial trade relationships with countries other than England. The colonists reacted with distaste and quiet rebellion. Smuggling and large black markets for smuggled goods became very common during the Dominion of New England.

THE MIDDLE COLONIES

The Middle Colonies of New York, Pennsylvania, New Jersey, and Delaware were distinguished by their "mixed" nature. Economically, socially, and religiously, the Middle Colonies were much more diverse than their northern or southern neighbors.

New England | Middle Colonies | Chesapeake & Southern Colonies | Resistance | Key Terms

New York was established by the Dutch, being founded in 1623 by the Dutch West India Company as New Netherlands. New Amsterdam, now New York City, was an economic center for the trade of furs from the Hudson Valley. After fights with the surrounding Native Americans, trespassing by Swedes, and finally the expulsion of the Dutch from the colony by the English, New Netherlands became New York (King Charles II granted the land to his brother, the Duke of York). Although New York enjoyed more democracy than most other English colonies, its social structure resembled that of feudal England in terms of land distribution.

Penn's Woods, or Pennsylvania, was founded by William Penn in 1681 as a haven for Quakers. His "**Holy Experiment**" sought to explore the establishment of a liberal state while advertising to attract a wide array of potential settlers to the colony. Settlers from all walks of life and from many northern and western European nations were lured to Pennsylvania by the promise of land, religious freedom, and democracy. Quakers did not believe in the use of force or violence but rather practiced nonviolent resistance to protest. Being savvy in the ways of business, the Quakers were successful in cultivating a congenial relationship with the surrounding Native American tribes and a vast trade network, which eventually made them the fourth-largest colony.

New Jersey and Delaware, also Quaker colonies, were established in 1664 and 1703, respectively. They resembled Pennsylvania socially, politically, and economically.

THE CHESAPEAKE AND SOUTHERN COLONIES

As mentioned in chapter 3, the first British settlers arrived in what is now Virginia in 1607 under the leadership of Captain John Smith. Established first as an economic venture by the Virginia Company, the colony received its royal charter in 1624 from King James I to provide gold, God, and glory for the mother country. Another influential leader of the colony, **John Rolfe**, introduced tobacco to Virginia farmers—it soon became the number one cash crop for the region. To derive a profit from tobacco, farmers had to grow large tracts of the crop. Thus, the **plantation system** was developed.

THE HEADRIGHT SYSTEM AND SLAVERY

A high death rate due to disease and climate coupled with a low birth rate due to the lack of women in the region led to shortages of labor in the Chesapeake. To solve the labor crisis, land owners began to use the *headright system*, indentured servitude, and slavery to encourage immigration. The development of the cash crop economy was encouraged by this headright system, in which a landowner would pay the passage from England for a white *indentured servant* and receive 50 acres of land in return. These servants were bound by the indenture until their passage was paid back in the form of labor—usually a term of seven years. As indentured servants served out their contracts in greater numbers, the flood of former servants now requiring land, jobs, and money led to the need for a new labor pool.

New England   Middle Colonies   **Chesapeake & Southern Colonies**   Resistance   Key Terms

THE ROOTS OF THE AMERICAN SLAVE TRADE

Before 1660, many Africans arriving in Virginia were also deemed indentured servants and were set free after they had paid back their debt. However in 1660, the House of Burgesses passed a series of laws that made specific distinctions between whites and blacks. From this point on, current black servants and their offspring were considered lifelong slaves. White indentured servants, rapidly decreasing in number, were still freed after their contracted indenture period was over. The number of African slaves increased rapidly in the last quarter of the 17th century.

LORD BALTIMORE'S CATHOLIC HAVEN

The second Chesapeake colony, Maryland, was founded about 25 years after the Virginia Company arrived in Jamestown. As a gift of service, King Charles I graciously divided the Virginia colony in 1634 and gave a portion of that land to **Lord Baltimore** (George Calvert). Desiring more control over the administration of the colony, King Charles I used these *proprietary colonies* as a way to protect his influence in the Chesapeake region. Lord Baltimore's charge was to create a colony that would serve as both a haven for Catholics and turn a profit for the Crown. But before Lord Baltimore could set forth on his mission, he passed away, leaving the colony in the hands of his son, the second Lord Baltimore (Cecil Calvert), who then established the colony of Maryland.

Almost immediately, immigration to Maryland by Protestant farmers threatened the safety of the Catholics Calvert so desperately wanted to protect. To ensure "religious freedom" in Maryland, he persuaded the legislative assembly in 1649 to pass an "**Act of Toleration**" which would guarantee religious freedom to all Christians. The act was not tolerant of all religions, however. It provided the death penalty for any person who denied the divinity of Christ. In other words, Jews and atheists would not be tolerated in Maryland. Eventually, the majority Protestants rebelled and were successful in repealing the act. The victory was short-lived, however, as Oliver Cromwell restored the act in 1650.

THE CAROLINAS AND GEORGIA

The Carolinas were considered "Restoration Colonies," along with New York and Pennsylvania, in that they were all established after the English throne was restored to Charles II in 1660. The Carolinas originally were established to supply the sugar plantations of the West Indies with food. But soon rice became the cash crop of choice for plantation owners. South Carolina became the most aristocratic region in the American colonies, with the center of its influence in Charleston. It was in the Carolinas that the slave codes from Barbados were first imported, thus institutionalizing black slavery in America for many generations.

Georgia, the last of the British colonies, was founded and chartered in 1733 by James Oglethorpe. The colony served as a point of deposit for thousands of debtors who would be sent from

New England | Middle Colonies | **Chesapeake & Southern Colonies** | Resistance | Key Terms

overcrowded jails in London, and it served as a *buffer state* between the Spanish in Florida and the precious rice and indigo plantation economy of South Carolina.

RESISTANCE TO COLONIAL AUTHORITY

Politics in the Virginia colony most often favored large plantation owners over the former indentured servants and other poor farmers who made up the majority of citizens of the region. These poor farmers tilled land in the backwoods region of Virginia to the west and were vulnerable to attack by local Native American tribes. The governor of the Virginia colony, **Sir William Berkeley**, enraged these backwoods farmers by remaining friendly with the Native Americans and failing to protect the land and lives of those living in the western frontier. A young, newly arrived member of the House of Burgesses, **Nathaniel Bacon**, capitalized on the complaints of his fellow backwooders by mobilizing them to form a citizen's militia. In 1676, Bacon's militia engaged in a series of raids against local native villages, massacring inhabitants. The mob was successful in defeating Berkeley's forces and then set fire to Jamestown. A short time later, Bacon died of dysentery, and the rebellion was finally crushed.

BACON'S REBELLION

Bacon's Rebellion was significant in that it signaled the problems of social division, resistance on the part of colonists against royal governance, and most importantly, the difficulty of controlling former indentured servants. This led to an increase in the demand for black slaves.

Meanwhile, on the western half of the continent, the most successful uprising against Spanish authority occurred in the 1680 **Pueblo Revolt** in modern-day Santa Fe, New Mexico. In 1675, the governor of New Mexico began to persecute the Pueblo Indians by banning certain religious practices and whipping many as "witches." One of those whipped was an influential Hopi Indian who had long resisted colonial rule. He organized a revolt in response to the harsh treatment by the Spanish. On August 10, 1680, an organized attack on the Spanish occurred in which Indians killed over 400 Spaniards and destroyed every building erected by the colonials. The fleeing Spaniards landed in Santa Fe, where a brief fight drove the Native Americans back just enough to allow some of the Spanish to escape to El Paso. The Native Americans took over the governor's residence as their own and remained there to protect their land. Spain was unable to reclaim its New Mexico colony for nearly 50 years.

The year 1688 brought the "**Glorious Revolution**" to England and the overthrow of King James II. Parliament replaced James II with his daughter Mary and her Dutch husband, William III of Orange. American colonists were excited, as the removal of James II signaled the end of his repressive

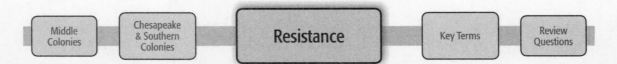

measures aimed directly at Puritans and limiting colonial self-governance. With **William and Mary** now at the helm, American colonists mistakenly believed that England would step away from the harsh policies of the Dominion of New England instituted by Parliament during James II's reign. Unfortunately for the colonists, Parliament continued restricting their ability to establish self-rule. Uprisings in several colonies arose as it became clear that they would get no respite from repression. The English governors worked quickly to quell the unrest, but damage had already been done to the relationship between the colonists and the mother country.

KEY TERMS

Names	John Winthrop
	Anne Hutchinson
	Roger Williams
	John Rolfe
	Lord Baltimore
	Sir William Berkeley
	Nathaniel Bacon
	William and Mary
Groups	The Church of England
	Puritans
	New England Confederation
	separatists
	Pilgrims
	nonseparatists
	Quakers
Events	Great Migration
	Holy Experiment
	Bacon's Rebellion
	Pueblo Revolt
	Glorious Revolution
Documents and Laws	Mayflower Compact
	Halfway Covenant
	Dominion of New England
	Act of Toleration
	Fundamental Orders
Places	Salem
Vocabulary	antinomianism
	plantation system
	headright system
	proprietary colonies
	indentured servants

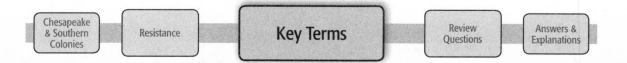

Chesapeake & Southern Colonies | Resistance | **Key Terms** | Review Questions | Answers & Explanations

REVIEW QUESTIONS

1. Anne Hutchinson and Roger Williams were expelled from the Massachusetts Bay Colony because they

   (A) did not believe in the grace of God.

   (B) felt the individual was just as important as faith.

   (C) did not wish to separate from the Church of England.

   (D) questioned the practice of antinomianism.

   (E) refused the Half-Way Covenant.

2. The Middle colonies were unique in that they

   (A) had a large number of Puritans.

   (B) lacked industry and merchants.

   (C) were harshly intolerant of many groups.

   (D) practiced democratic forms of governance.

   (E) had very few established churches.

3. The Maryland Act of Toleration

   (A) was issued by King James II.

   (B) allowed Jews to practice freely.

   (C) removed all religions but Catholic from the colony.

   (D) allowed Catholics to practice but did not allow religions that did not believe in Jesus.

   (E) was abolished by Parliament.

4. Indentured servitude in the Chesapeake increased due to

   (A) the Glorious Revolution.

   (B) the headright system.

   (C) the House of Burgesses.

   (D) the end of the slave trade.

   (E) Bacon's Rebellion.

5. Revolts by colonists in the early settlements were

   (A) motivated by greed.

   (B) very successful in establishing a sense of independence.

   (C) violent and disastrous.

   (D) only moderately successful.

   (E) crushed with fury by England.

ANSWERS AND EXPLANATIONS

1. B

Both Hutchinson and Williams believed in the power of the individual with regard to the relationship with God. Hutchinson believed that faith alone was necessary for one to reach Heaven. Williams believed that the individual should have control over his own actions rather than the Church—"liberty of conscience."

2. D

The Middle Colonies, such as Pennsylvania and New Jersey, were distinct from the New England and Chesapeake colonies in that their cities and towns were governed in a democratic manner. The other colonies were largely authoritarian, with rule coming from the landed classes or church elite.

3. D

The Maryland Act of Toleration was actually not as tolerant as the name implies. Provisions were made to give Catholics a safe haven in Maryland, but it did not allow others, such as Jews and atheists, to practice freely.

4. B

The promise of 50 acres of land in exchange for each person who was given paid passage to the Chesapeake colonies increased the number of people who entered indentured servitude. The servant would pay off the indenture (passage overseas) with seven years of unpaid service. The wealthy who paid for these indentures gained many acres of prime land and soon turned them into large plantations.

5. D

Small revolts, such as the 1649 Maryland repeal of the Act of Toleration, were usually only temporary victories. The English government was quick to restore order and deference once Cromwell was in power.

CHAPTER 5: LIFE IN THE COLONIES, 1700–1800

COLONIAL POPULATIONS

At the beginning of the 18th century, fewer than 300,000 people who inhabited the English-American colonies. By 1775, that population had climbed to almost 2.5 million people, with approximately 20 percent of those being African slaves. Mass immigration coupled with a high fertility rate—as compared to the European continent—gave rise to a burgeoning colonial society that would soon eclipse the populations of the countries they left behind. The single largest group of non-White inhabitants was the African slaves—90 percent of whom were held by Southern plantation owners.

CHARACTERISTICS OF COLONIAL SOCIETIES

The social structure of the English colonies closely modeled that of the social structure of towns in England. **Stratification** existed in the early years of the English colonies and became more apparent as the 17th century came to a close. The influx of more affluent immigrants and the further development of the plantation economy in the South further distanced the gap between rich and the poor. The Puritans in New England viewed wealth and success as a sign that one was a member of the *elect*, and in the South, social stratification had been carried over from the old feudal society of England. Led by men such as Virginia's Governor Sir William Berkeley, the royal sympathizers of the English Civil War, known as "Cavaliers," were recruited to build a society in the South that would honor the landed aristocracy.

The middle colonies did not have the same social rigidity as New England and the Chesapeake. Middling classes enjoyed the diversity, acceptance, and tolerance of the middle colonies. The *elite* in New England and the middle colonies were made up mostly of successful merchants. However, the majority (some 90 percent of colonists) were involved in agriculture—many were subsistence and/or *tenant farmers*.

[handwritten margin note: Subsistence farming — • Self-sufficient • Grow only enough to feed family]

Family was very important to both the economic and social well-being of colonial societies. On average, colonial citizens married and bore children at a much younger age than citizens of the

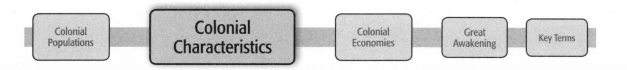

Colonial Populations | **Colonial Characteristics** | Colonial Economies | Great Awakening | Key Terms

European continent. More children meant more hands to tend the farm and, thus, more earnings for the family. The division of labor in most English colonies was clearly delineated by sex. Men were mainly responsible for labor outside the home, while women were responsible for care of the homestead and child rearing. Women had very few rights or legal recourses in colonial society; however, many were "protected" by their husbands and society as a whole from abuse.

COLONIAL ECONOMIES

The concept of *mercantilism* was a reality for the 13 American colonies, particularly after the ascension of James II to the throne and the establishment of the Dominion of England in 1686. The colonies existed solely to provide raw materials and a market of consumers for the mother country. Nevertheless, the colonists did not let the Navigation Acts keep them from developing trade markets of their own that were not sanctioned by the English crown.

THE TRIANGULAR TRADE

The most blatant of these networks was the **Triangular Trade,** in which the New England colonies provided timber, fish, and manufactured goods to Caribbean islands in exchange for molasses, which would be used to make rum in New England. The rum would make its way to Africa in exchange for African slaves. Slaves would then eventually make their way to the colonies, thus completing the triangle. Therefore, rum-running became the trade of choice for New England merchants.

The middle colonies enjoyed a mixture of agriculture and light manufacturing, the largest market for goods being the West Indies. In the Southern colonies, tobacco was the main cash crop in the Chesapeake (Virginia and Maryland), while rice and indigo were the main cash crops in Carolina and Georgia. The Southern colonies traded extensively with England and the West Indies in exchange for manufactured goods and slaves.

RELIGION AND THE GREAT AWAKENING

By the middle of the 18th century, many colonists had lost touch with traditional Calvinist teachings that had been the cornerstone of the Puritan faith. Moreover, thousands of settlers on the frontier had little to no access to churches and religious services. In the late 1630s, a wave of preachers began delivering sermons that emphasized the power of an emotional connection to and a personal inspiration from God. Religious fervor spread across the colonies, with large revivals meeting under tents in the outskirts of towns. This religious spirit was called the **"Great Awakening." "New Light"** preacher **Jonathan Edwards** is credited with starting the

Great Awakening in 1734 by giving sermons that encouraged parishioners to absolve their sins and pay penance by praying for salvation. His most famous sermon was entitled "**Sinners in the Hands of an Angry God**," which he delivered in 1741. Churchgoers were told that God was angry with the sinners of the earth and only those who obeyed God's word would be free from damnation.

Emotional sermons evolved after Edwards with other "New Light" preachers, such as English-born **George Whitefield**. Whitefield and other "New Light" preachers crisscrossed the colonies speaking to large crowds about the "fire and brimstone" eternity all sinners would face if they did not absolve their sins publicly. Whitefield also undermined the power and prestige of "Old Light" ministers by proclaiming that ordinary people could understand the gospel of the Lord without the leadership of a man of the cloth. Religious services changed drastically by the addition of emotional public admissions of sin and those sinners being "saved" right in front of the congregation.

The Great Awakening impacted the colonies in several ways. It was the first time that colonists across the 13 colonies could claim a common experience. Regardless of social class, country of origin, or occupation, the impact of the Great Awakening could be felt by all. Some historians believe this common religious experience was one of the foundations of the democraticization of colonial society that occurred after the 1740s. Secondly, new *sects* and divisions within the Protestant faith arose as a result of the religious rebirth. Baptists and Methodists, who emphasized emotion in their sermons, attracted large numbers of followers, which led to increased competition in attracting congregants. Furthermore, many universities, such as Dartmouth, Rutgers, and Princeton, were founded to educate "New Light" ministers, who were in high demand. Indeed, the old intellectual approach to faith was largely overshadowed as a new emotional and personal connection with God came to define the American form of worship.

KEY TERMS	
Names	Jonathan Edwards George Whitefield
Groups	New Light preachers
Events	Triangular Trade The Great Awakening
Documents and Laws	"Sinners in the Hands of an Angry God"
Vocabulary	stratification mercantilism

Think:
Eli from movie = There Will Be "Blood"

REVIEW QUESTIONS

1. The largest group of immigrants to the colonies in the late 17th century were

   (A) Irish.
   (B) Russian.
   (C) German.
   (D) African.
   (E) Swedish.

2. The Triangular Trade was developed in the colonies to

   (A) circumvent the Navigation Acts.
   (B) conform with mercantilism.
   (C) provide raw materials for the mother country.
   (D) save the plantation system of the South.
   (E) create a stable money supply.

3. A common feature of colonial society in the late 17th and early 18th centuries was that

   (A) women and men enjoyed the same rights and responsibilities.
   (B) religious tolerance was evident in all colonies.
   (C) there was social stratification evidenced by a small elite and large underclass.
   (D) most colonists were merchants, lawyers, and doctors.
   (E) the social structure was rigid, not allowing for movement up the social hierarchy.

4. "New Light" preachers, such as Jonathan Edwards, appealed to congregants by

   (A) encouraging people to act on their worldly impulses.
   (B) delivering emotional sermons that centered around sin and salvation.
   (C) disposing of the Bible as a source of inspiration.
   (D) venerating the traditional ministers and their teachings.
   (E) refusing to interfere with the daily lives of followers.

5. The Great Awakening was significant in that it

   (A) unified Protestants under one denomination.
   (B) further widened the chasm between rich and poor.
   (C) was a unifying experience for colonists regardless of social standing.
   (D) led to a decline in church membership across the colonies.
   (E) detracted from the demand for higher education.

ANSWERS AND EXPLANATIONS

1. D

The upsurge in the need for labor to replace indentured servants in the South led to the increase in the importation of African slaves to the colonies. German and Swedish immigrants arrived in small numbers throughout the 17th and 18th centuries. Not until the mid-19th century did Irish immigration surge due to the cataclysmic potato famine in the mid-1840s. Russian immigrants did not arrive in large numbers until after 1880.

2. A

Seeking a way to become more self-sufficient, the colonies engaged in the illegal Triangular Trade. This trade network was established to circumvent the constraints of the Navigation Acts and mercantilism.

3. C

English colonists transplanted a social system from their homeland to the colonies. A small group of elites made decisions for the majority of citizens, who were considered an underclass. Aside from the middle colonies, none of the other colonies displayed much, if any, religious tolerance. Some 90 percent of colonists farmed for a living. Opportunities did exist to move up the social ladder.

4. B

"New Lights," such as Jonathan Edwards and George Whitefield, emphasized emotion and a personal connection with God during the Great Awakening. These preachers also encouraged restraint against acting upon human impulses and fostered looking to the Bible for direct inspiration. The Great Awakening led to a decline in respect for "Old Lights," or traditional preachers.

5. C

The Great Awakening touched colonists from all walks of life, thus creating a sense of connection. Protestant churches fought for membership, and schisms developed among the faithful. Universities such as Princeton, Brown, and Rutgers were established to train the large number of ministers needed for the upsurge in religious fervor.

CHAPTER 6: THE EVE OF THE REVOLUTION, 1754–1775

THE FRENCH AND INDIAN WAR

[handwritten note: As a result, Britain was way too preoccupied to really give two shits about the American colonies; hence salutary neglect.]

A series of European wars broke out between 1688 and 1763 that would affect the American colonies politically, economically, and ideologically. The colonists found themselves fending off attacks from French, Spanish, and Native Americans. The Treaty of Utrecht in 1713 ushered in three decades of peace in Europe and another period of "**salutary neglect**," which was supported by British Prime Minister Robert Walpole. The British would protect the colonies and provide trade opportunities, but other than that, the colonists were left to their own devices. This period encouraged the colonists to develop their own systems of governance, economic networks, and ideologies.

THE FORMATION OF THE ALBANY PLAN OF UNION

The delicate peace in Europe was shattered in 1756 with the outbreak of the Seven Years' War. This conflict, called the **French and Indian War** in the colonies, had actually started two years earlier in the Ohio Valley. The French had been fortifying the Ohio Valley region to deter the British from settling further west. The British hoped to thwart the efforts of the French by driving them from the North American continent. The colonial fight began in earnest in May 1754, when the governor of Virginia sent Lt. Colonel George Washington and his men to prevent the French from putting the finishing touches on Fort Duquesne (modern-day Pittsburgh). Washington's forces proved weak in the face of a large combined French and Native American force, retreating and finally surrendering on July 3, 1754. Recognizing that this was not going to be a quick and easy victory, British officials quickly called a meeting in Albany, New York, of important colonial tradesmen to devise a defense plan. The Albany Congress, under the tutelage of **Benjamin Franklin**, constructed the **Albany Plan of Union**, which called for a confederation of colonies to provide for defense from attack by European and native foes. Franklin used his newspaper, the *Pennsylvania Gazette*, to encourage colonists to support the union plan with a political cartoon titled "Join, or Die."

French & Indian War → Salutary Neglect → British Measures → Colonial Reaction → Enlightenment & the Colonies

Unfortunately, the colonies rejected the plan because they felt it was too restrictive. Also, the British felt it allowed for too much colonial independence.

REMOVING THE FRENCH FROM NORTH AMERICA

British war efforts were ineffective in the early years of the war, until **William Pitt** took over as Prime Minister. He shifted British efforts from colonial skirmishes to the conquering of Canada, particularly Montreal, Quebec, and Louisbourg. The French surrendered Quebec in 1759 and Montreal in 1760, thus being driven to the bargaining table. The result was the monumental **Peace of Paris** (1763), where the British took control of French Canada and Spanish Florida, effectively removing the French presence in North America.

The French and Indian War was significant in many regards. The British emerged as the dominant colonial power in North America. No longer would the colonies have to worry about attacks launched by the French or Spanish or Native American tribes allied with either or both countries. However, the British had not been impressed with the colonial militias and felt that the colonists could not defend themselves adequately. The colonists on the other hand, having tasted the fruits of victory, were very proud of their ability to fend off French and Native American armies. They held the British military officers in contempt because of the poor treatment of colonial militiamen on the battlefield. More important to both the British and the colonists was the amount of debt left in the wake of war. British citizens were feeling the sting of war in their pocketbooks in the form of higher prices and skyrocketing taxes. The colonists, on the other hand, were not keen on the idea of paying for the war effort. The new Tory government of Great Britain and young King George III had other plans for the colonies.

SALUTARY NEGLECT COMES TO AN END

The long period of salutary neglect by the mother country was coming to an abrupt end by 1763. The British view that the colonists were not capable of protecting themselves was further helped along by the outbreak of **Pontiac's Rebellion** (1763). Native Americans in the Ohio Valley

French & Indian War | **Salutary Neglect** | British Measures | Colonial Reaction | Enlightenment & the Colonies

refused to hand over conquered lands to the British at the close of the war due to harsh treatment by the British. The Ottawans, led by Chief Pontiac, led an attack on the new colonial settlements from the Great Lakes region of what is now Michigan all the way to Virginia. The damage to British forts and colonial settlements was significant, with many lives lost and homes destroyed. British regular forces were sent to protect the colonies, and the rebellion was finally subdued after 18 months of fighting.

To protect the British colonies from further Native American incursion, King George III signed the **Proclamation of 1763.** This proclamation set a line of demarcation that barred American colonists from settling west of the Appalachian Mountains. The British saw this as a quick and easy way to make peace with the Native American tribes of the region. British colonists, on the other hand, were incensed by the apparent permanent interference of the crown in their ability to take land they had won in battle. Most colonists simply ignored the Proclamation Line and settled west in larger numbers than before the French and Indian War.

BRITISH MEASURES TO RAISE REVENUE

Strapped by large debt stemming from multiple wars, the British crown sought to make her colonies work to her advantage. Beginning with the Currency Act in 1764, which limited the use of colonial paper money, the British crown looked to the colonies to relieve some of the tax burden on its homeland citizens. Harsher tax collection began with the passage of the **Sugar Acts** of 1764, which raised the previous amount demanded on sweeteners (molasses and sugar) from the older Molasses Act of 1733. Britain wanted to collect the tax revenue it had been losing to the Triangular Trade by taxing molasses from the West Indies and abroad, but mainly the tax was levied to make money for the crown. In another blow to colonial autonomy, the **Quartering Act** of 1765 required colonial citizens to provide room and board for British soldiers stationed there. Nonetheless, these acts were tame in the eyes of the colonists—they were laxly enforced and rarely affected their everyday lives.

It was not until the passage of the **Stamp Act** in 1765 that colonists became truly aware of the impact of British taxation. The Stamp Tax was an attempt by Britain to collect revenues to build a new colonial army. The act required that all paper *ie: printed material* in the colonies was to have a stamp affixed, signifying that the tax had been paid. All colonial documents, from death and marriage certificates to newspapers, had to have the stamp affixed. This was the first time the colonists had been subjected to a direct tax—a tax that was paid directly by the consumer of the paper good produced in the colony—as opposed to paying an indirect tax on an imported good. The act was justifiable in the eyes of the British Prime Minister George Grenville in that colonists were only being asked to pay their fair share of the burden of war. The colonists, however, did not see things his way.

French & Indian War | Salutary Neglect | **British Measures** | Colonial Reaction | Enlightenment & the Colonies

COLONIAL REACTION TO BRITISH MEASURES

Colonials in all 13 colonies reacted to the Stamp Act with disdain. The young **Patrick Henry**, a lawyer from Virginia, expressed the sentiment of colonials when he stood in the Virginia House of Burgesses and accused the British government of usurping the rights guaranteed them as Englishmen. Supposedly coining the famous phrase "No taxation without representation," he encouraged his fellow leaders to allow Virginians to only be taxed by Virginians, not by some distant royal authority. Further north, James Otis of Massachusetts rallied representatives from 9 of the 13 colonies to meet in New York as the **Stamp Act Congress**. This body would send word to England that only colonial legislatures had the authority to tax the colonists. The colonists agreed that external taxes—levies imposed throughout the empire on traded goods—were within the rights of the crown to impose. However, they argued that internal taxes—taxes levied directly on the people of a region—were only within the rights of locally elected officials. Grenville responded by pointing out to the colonists that since Parliament governed on behalf of the entire British Empire, the colonists did indeed have representation in Parliament—*virtual representation.*

COLONIAL BOYCOTT AND THE TOWNSHEND ACT

The news did not sit well with colonials, and soon violent reactions spread. **The Sons and Daughters of Liberty**, led by Samuel Adams, intimidated tax collectors by attacking their homes, burning them in effigy, and even tarring and feathering them. The Sons and Daughters even ransacked warehouses that held stamps and burned them to the ground. It became fashionable for colonists to protest the Stamp Act quietly by participating in *boycotts* of British goods by wearing homespun clothing and drinking Dutch tea. The boycotts negatively impacted British trade, and Parliament was ultimately forced to repeal the act in 1766. In its place, however, the British passed the **Declaratory Act**, which maintained the right of the crown to tax the colonies in the future.

The new chancellor of the exchequer (treasury), Charles Townshend, decided to punish the rebellious colonies by instituting a revenue plan of his own. The **Townshend Acts**, passed in 1767, brought harsher taxes on goods such as glass, paper, and tea that were paid by the purveyors of these imported goods. In addition, a special board of customs officials was appointed to enforce **writs of assistance**. These writs allowed customs officials to search colonial homes, businesses, and warehouses for smuggled goods without a warrant from a judge. While the colonists felt that any increase in taxes signaled an abuse of Parliament, they were slow to react to the Townshend duties as they were external, rather than internal, taxes. However, John Dickinson's *Letters from a Farmer in Pennsylvania* rekindled interest in the issue of taxation without representation and inspired Samuel Adams to pen the **Massachusetts Circular Letter** in 1768. The letter argued that there was no distinction between external and internal taxes and that the Townshend Act must be immediately repealed. The letter was copied and distributed throughout the colonies, sparking the rejuvenation of boycotts of British goods. Wishing to avoid the economic troubles caused by the Stamp Act, the new Prime Minister Lord North repealed the Townshend Acts in 1770.

BOSTON RESPONDS TO TAXATION

Relative calm was experienced between the colonies and Britain between 1770 and 1772, with one noted exception. The residents of Boston were particularly angered about the enforcement of the Quartering Act. Many British regulars had been stationed in the city to protect the port and collect customs duties from imported British goods. On a cold spring day, a crowd of disgruntled Bostonians began to harass the troops guarding the customs house by throwing rocks and frozen oysters. The guards fired upon the crowd, killing five and wounding six protesters. The event became known in the colonies as the **Boston Massacre** through the propaganda spread by the Sons of Liberty.

Samuel Adams and the Sons did not let the spirit of protest die during the period of calm. Aided by the **Committees of Correspondence,** Adams and other colonials continually circulated letters of protest against British policies. A favorite event of the propagandists was the *Gaspee* incident. The *Gaspee* was a British warship commissioned to capture vessels carrying smuggled goods before they reached the colonies. The *Gaspee* ran aground the shores of Rhode Island, to the delight of some members of the Sons of Liberty. Dressed as Native Americans, the colonists boarded the ship, marched her crew to shore, and set fire to the boat. The event was celebrated and retold throughout shoreline colonial towns as a victory for the tax-burdened consumer.

The year 1773 brought renewed conflict to the British colonies with the passage of the **Tea Act**. Even though the new act actually lowered the price of tea, colonists were wary of any attempt by Britain to collect revenue and refused to purchase the tea. As a new shipment of tea sat in Boston Harbor awaiting unloading, a group of colonists, again dressed as Native Americans, boarded the ship, broke open the crates, and dumped the tea into the water. Colonists disputed whether this was to be applauded as a justified protest against oppression or if it was simply a childish destruction of property.

Lord North was not pleased by the news of the **Boston Tea Party** and decided to punish the citizens of the city. He persuaded Parliament to pass the **Coercive Acts**, which would close Boston Harbor until the tea was paid for and revoke the charter of the colony of Massachusetts. This would put the colony under the control of the crown and expand the scope of the Quartering Act, allowing soldiers to be boarded in private homes. In addition, Parliament passed the **Quebec Act** (1774), which basically allowed the former French region to be self-sufficient and expanded its borders, taking away potential lands from colonists in the Ohio River Valley. Enraged, the colonists named these the **Intolerable Acts**. They were angered more by the provision to allow Quebecers to practice Catholicism freely than by the other acts.

THE IMPACT OF THE ENLIGHTENMENT ON THE COLONIES

The ideas of political, philosophical, and social thinkers of Europe during the 17th and 18th centuries had a profound impact on the character and ideologies of many Americans. British

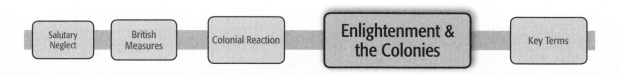

Salutary Neglect | British Measures | Colonial Reaction | **Enlightenment & the Colonies** | Key Terms

philosopher **John Locke's** theory of natural rights challenged the absolute and divine rule of kings and queens by asserting that all men should be ruled by natural laws and that sovereignty was derived by the will of those governed. Locke went on to assert that the governed have a responsibility to rebel against a government that fails to protect the natural rights of life, liberty, and property. Men such as George Washington, Benjamin Franklin, Thomas Jefferson, and John Adams either experienced Enlightenment teachings firsthand while traveling in Europe or had read the philosophies in their studies. With the addition of the writings of men such as the Baron de Montesquieu and Jean Jacques Rousseau, enlightened colonials began to emphasize the concept of reason over emotion. This shift in philosophy set the stage for a revolutionary spirit that abounded in late 18th-century America. Colonists now had justification for rebelling against a government they perceived was directly and deliberately violating their rights as Englishmen.

Arguably planted the ideological seeds of the American Revolution

KEY TERMS	
Names	Benjamin Franklin
	John Locke
	William Pitt
Groups	Stamp Act Congress
	Sons and Daughters of Liberty
Events	The French and Indian War
	Pontiac's Rebellion
	Boston Massacre
	Boston Tea Party
Documents and Laws	The Albany Plan of Union
	Peace of Paris
	Proclamation of 1763
	Sugar Acts
	Quartering Act
	Stamp Act
	Declaratory Act
	Townshend Acts
	Massachusetts Circular Letter
	Tea Act
	Coercive Acts
	Quebec Act
	Intolerable Acts
Vocabulary	salutary neglect
	writs of assistance

REVIEW QUESTIONS

1. The Albany Plan for Union was rejected by the colonies because

   (A) it did not provide protection from Native Americans.

   (B) too much control was given to a central government.

   (C) there was not enough independence for individual colonies.

   (D) it respected French claims to the Ohio Valley.

   (E) the House of Burgesses wished to maintain power.

2. In the eyes of the British, the Proclamation of 1763 was issued to

   (A) protect the colonists from Native American attack.

   (B) open up colonial settlement of the west.

   (C) instigate a war between colonists and the Native Americans.

   (D) force colonials to pay taxes.

   (E) flaunt the power of the British crown.

3. The colonists objected to taxation by Parliament because

   (A) they were paying more than their British counterparts.

   (B) the new taxes were permanent.

   (C) they desired to break away from Britain.

   (D) they viewed it as an internal tax.

   (E) colonial tax collectors were becoming rich.

4. The Committees of Correspondence

   (A) worked to smuggle tea, glass, and silk into the colonies.

   (B) kept the issue of British injustice alive in the colonies with propaganda.

   (C) led to the *Gaspee* incident.

   (D) were lauded by the British government.

   (E) encouraged colonists to pay taxes to support the war effort.

5. The Enlightenment was influential in the colonies in that

   (A) colonists felt connected with their English brothers and sisters across the Atlantic.

   (B) it united the colonies in a common cause.

   (C) religion replaced reason in the realm of political thought.

   (D) its ideas justified colonial rebellion against Britain.

   (E) a revived religious fervor spread across the colonies.

ANSWERS AND EXPLANATIONS

1. C

The British rejected the Albany Plan because it would have given the colonies too much independence, while the colonies rejected it because it didn't give them enough freedom. However, the failed Albany Plan became a significant stepping-stone for colonial unity that inspired the colonies to work together after 1765.

2. A

After Pontiac's Rebellion in 1762, the British sought to reconcile with Native American tribes by restricting colonial expansion west. The British government issued the Proclamation of 1763 to protect her colonies from Native American attack and to make peace with the tribes.

3. D

The colonists knew full well that they had not been paying their fair share of the tax burden to pay for the French and Indian War. However, they resented having to pay internal taxes that they did not choose to levy on their own. The new taxes were not intended to be long-term but were only going to last until Britain had made headway on paying off the war debt.

4. B

Citing events such as the *Gaspee* incident, the Committees of Correspondence used propaganda to keep the colonists riled up over British injustices.

5. D

The Enlightenment writings of Locke, Montesquieu, and Rousseau set the stage for colonial justification for rebellion against Great Britain. Locke emphasized the need for governments to protect the natural rights of its citizens. If these natural rights were not protected, the people had the right to overthrow the government and replace it with a new government that would preserve natural rights. The Enlightenment also emphasized reason over religion.

CHAPTER 7: THE AMERICAN REVOLUTION, 1775–1783

THE COLONIES ORGANIZE—THE FIRST CONTINENTAL CONGRESS

The Intolerable Acts (also called the Coercive Acts) led colonial leaders to organize quickly to protect themselves from further British retaliation. Representatives from 12 of the 13 colonies traveled to Philadelphia in September of 1774 to discuss acceptable forms of protest and reaction. Leaders' reactions ranged from radical (Samuel Adams) to the mild (John Jay). One thing was clear—the delegates needed to send forth a strong message to England asserting the rights of colonials by demanding the repeal of the Coercive Acts. They urged colonies to build up military reserves and organize boycotts of British goods in the meantime.

The Congress sent the *Declaration of Rights and Grievances* to the king to urge him to correct the wrongs incurred by the colonists, but it did acknowledge the authority of Parliament to regulate trade and commerce. The Congress also created the Association. The Association called for the creation of "boycott committees" throughout the colonies to bring Britain to her knees economically. Lastly, the delegates agreed to meet again in May of 1775 if their grievances had not been redressed by the crown. The king and Parliament did not respond to the demands of the **First Continental Congress**, as doing so would have legitimized its claim to wield political power. Before the Congressional delegates could meet again, war would break out between American minutemen and British soldiers.

THE FIGHT BEGINS

Lexington & Concord

Having experienced the brunt of British punishment, the citizens of Massachusetts were ready to fight. British General Thomas Gage, now the new governor of Massachusetts, ordered his men to seize armaments and arrest rebels in the town of Concord. As the large force of British soldiers marched to carry out their orders, a forewarned group of American militiamen (minutemen) assembled in nearby Lexington to try to stop the Redcoats in their tracks. "The shot heard around the world" was fired at that fateful encounter on the Lexington Green. The American Revolution

1st Continental Congress | **Fight Begins** | 2nd Continental Congress | Independence | Articles of Confederation

had begun. After losing eight men and finding themselves grossly overmatched, the American minutemen were forced to retreat, opening the way for the British to march to Concord. After the British inflicted minimal damage on Concord, the minutemen were able to force a retreat of the British back to Boston, killing about 250 of them by day's end.

[handwritten margin note: The start of the American Revolution]

[handwritten margin note: The beginning of American Revolution]

After fortifying the area around Boston, the minutemen found themselves embroiled in an intense battle for **Bunker Hill** on June 17, 1775. Even though the colonials lost the important tactical position, they celebrated the massive casualties they were able to inflict on the most powerful military force in the world. Perhaps most importantly, the king officially declared the colonies in rebellion, a proclamation that was tantamount to a declaration of war. Shortly thereafter, the king hired Hessian mercenaries from Germany, known for their ruthlessness in battle, to invade the colonies. From the point of view of the Patriots, the conflict with Mother England had always been a family affair. With the Hessians entering the picture, the colonials increasingly saw the British motive for war as one of annihilation.

At the start of the war, the odds were definitely in England's favor. With the most powerful navy in the world coupled with money and a plentiful supply of recruits, it seemed almost certain that the British would win a quick and decisive victory over the colonists. However, the colonists were able to take advantage of certain British weaknesses. The British troops were a long distance away from the mother country. Thus, orders from above, munitions, and fresh soldiers took a long time to arrive. The Americans, on the other hand, had superb military leadership and a greater understanding of the terrain of the battlefield. This is not to say that all was smooth going for the Continental Army. Infighting among colonies vying for positions of power, sinking morale of the Continental troops due to lack of wages, and shrinking war supplies threatened to sink the colonial rebels once and for all.

THE FRENCH STEP IN

Lack of funding soon became a nonissue for the Americans, as the French were waiting patiently for an opportunity to exact revenge on their longtime foes and happily provided the colonials assistance after the **Battle of Saratoga** in 1777. This proved to be a turning point in the fight for independence and opened the doors for an American victory.

THE SECOND CONTINENTAL CONGRESS

Keeping their promise to reconvene, delegates from all 13 colonies met again in May 1775 to discuss their next steps. Even with skirmishes occurring nearby, the delegates widely varied in their opinions regarding the colonial position. Those from the New England colonies tended to be much more radical—many insisted on independence. Those from the middle colonies

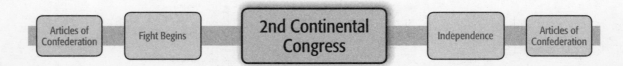

Articles of Confederation | Fight Begins | **2nd Continental Congress** | Independence | Articles of Confederation

expressed a desire to reopen negotiations with Britain. Either way, it was clear that the Congress needed to arrive quickly at consensus with regard to the colonial position. Virginia's native son, George Washington, was appointed as the head of the Continental Army, a shrewd move on behalf of Northern delegates, because the South would now rally behind the war effort. The Congress drew up the ***Declaration of the Causes and Necessities of Taking Up Arms***, which urged King George III a second time to consider colonial grievances and provided for the raising of a professional colonial military force. As a last gesture of peace and a preventative measure against total war, the Congress voted to send the **Olive Branch Petition** to Britain in July 1775. This document reasserted colonial loyalty to the crown and asked King George III to intervene with Parliament on their behalf. The king, however, refused once again to recognize the legitimacy of the Congress.

In January 1776, **Thomas Paine**, a recent English immigrant to the colonies, published a pamphlet that would shift the radical notion of independence from England to the mainstream. Titled ***Common Sense***, the pamphlet used John Locke's natural rights philosophy to argue that the citizens of the colonies were obligated to rebel against the oppression of Britain and that it would be contrary to common sense to allow the injustices to continue. Members of the Congress read the pamphlet with great interest, thereby integrating Paine's arguments into their deliberations in Philadelphia.

As a year of discussion and deliberation came to a close, the Second Continental Congress was of the mind that independence was the only acceptable decision. On June 7, 1776, Richard Henry Lee called for a resolution declaring the colonies independent of Britain. A committee was chosen to draft a declaration document that would reiterate the June 7 resolution. **Thomas Jefferson** and four other delegates quickly set to work on writing the document that came to be known as the **Declaration of Independence**. The document in its original form was a labor of love for Thomas Jefferson. It contained a preamble that heavily reflected the philosophy of John Locke regarding natural rights. Jefferson listed 27 grievances and charges of wrongdoing directed at the crown and Parliament. This declaration was the official break of the colonies from England, thus making the United States a country in its own right.

INDEPENDENCE, NOT DEPENDENCE

But the colonies could not amass a unified front against the British. Many historians believe that colonial citizens were divided roughly into thirds—one-third actively engaged in the fight for independence (**Patriots**), one-third siding with Great Britain (**Loyalists or Tories**), and the last third being uninterested or unaffected by the war altogether. Therefore, one of the major challenges for the new nation was keeping a lid on disagreement among its own citizens and educating those living in the west and removed from the turmoil. Loyalists were usually older, wealthy, educated citizens of the Middle or Southern colonies. Oftentimes, they sought to benefit from their loyalty to the crown by maintaining their social, economic, and political standing.

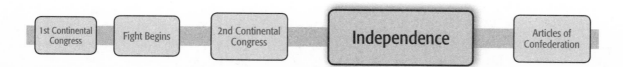

1st Continental Congress — Fight Begins — 2nd Continental Congress — **Independence** — Articles of Confederation

After the war, some 60,000 to 80,000 Loyalists chose to flee into exile rather than remain in the United States. Patriots, on the other hand, were a small force of young New Englanders or Virginians who more or less volunteered their time to the Continental Army. They would leave their homes, farms, and jobs for short tours of duty, return home for a short time, and return to the battlefield. Washington's forces were rarely paid for their services.

The war did not progress well for General Washington in the beginning. After losing New York City in 1776, Washington made a bit of headway by winning small battles in New Jersey in 1777. Other American generals can be credited with winning the most important battle of the Revolution—the Battle of Saratoga (October1777), fought by Generals Benedict Arnold and Horatio Gates. American forces were able to cut off the British charge on New England and secure the surrender of British General Burgoyne's army, thus convincing the French of America's military viability. The French had been waiting for evidence of an American success so they could justify entering the war on behalf of the revolutionaries. The entry of the French in 1778, and soon thereafter the Spanish and Dutch, on the side of the Americans turned the tide of the war in America's favor. The British were faced with the specter of another world war and had to divert their resources elsewhere.

Having survived one of the coldest winters on record at Valley Forge, Pennsylvania, Washington's forces were able to take advantage of the depleted British forces and win battles on his march to Virginia. At Yorktown in 1781, the last major battle of the Revolution was waged. Washington's men, with the assistance of French forces, secured the surrender of British General Charles Cornwallis's regiment. Tired of the strain of the war on their economy, British citizens ousted the Tory government in favor of the Whigs, who wanted to end the war with the Americans.

At Paris in 1783, the warring sides came together to deliberate and reach a peace settlement. For their part, the Americans agreed to repay debts to British merchants and promised not to punish Loyalists who chose to remain in the United States.

THE U.S. OFFICIALLY BECOMES A COUNTRY

The resulting **Treaty of Paris** (1783) included a formal recognition of the United States as a country, a boundary that stretched west to the Mississippi River, and the retention of American fishing rights in Newfoundland.

| 1st Continental Congress | Fight Begins | 2nd Continental Congress | **Independence** | Articles of Confederation |

THE ARTICLES OF CONFEDERATION

Continental leaders did not sit around idly waiting for Britain to recognize their sovereignty during the Revolution. By 1777, all but three of the colonies had drafted and ratified their own "state" constitutions. A delicate balance between law and order and the protection of natural rights needed careful attention by the fledgling state governments. Most of the new constitutions provided suffrage for landholding male citizens and the protection of basic rights.

While states were busily forming governments of their own, the delegates to the Second Continental Congress set out to create a national government. With slight alterations made to a draft national constitution written by John Dickinson, the **Articles of Confederation** were accepted and sent to the states for ratification in 1777. After a dispute between coastal states and inland states over the administration of westward lands, the Articles were finally ratified by all 13 states in 1781. The Articles of Confederation provided a template for government that the infant United States needed. They provided for a central government with a unicameral legislative branch. To amend the Articles, a unanimous vote (13 representatives) was required, while a supermajority (two-thirds) was required to pass laws. The central government under the Articles could wage war, make treaties, and borrow money to pay debts. The Articles also established clear policies regarding the settlement and statehood of newly acquired lands to the west.

[Handwritten margin notes: Essentially the precursor to the later U.S. Constitution]

[Handwritten margin notes: Enabled federal government to "learn from its mistakes" to create US Constitution]

A NEW SET OF LAWS

The Land Ordinance of 1785 required new townships to set aside a parcel of land for public education and stipulated that the sale of public lands would be used to pay off the national debt. The settlement of the Old Northwest would thus be orderly in contrast to relatively unorganized settlement in the South. **The Northwest Ordinance of 1787** established guidelines for attaining statehood, whereby territories with at least 60,000 people could apply for statehood; if accepted by Congress, the new state would have equal status with other states. Moreover, the Northwest Ordinance banned slavery north of the Ohio River, thereby guaranteeing future free states in the Midwest. While these examples show the successes of the Articles, the new central government was fraught with complications from the outset. To avoid tyranny and abuse of power by the new central government, the Articles did not allow for the taxing of citizens to raise revenue. Nor was the government given the authority to enforce its own laws. While the government could request taxes from the states, it could not enforce tax collection. This apparent weakness was deliberate; however, by limiting the strength of the central government, the states actually created more problems than they had bargained for. Since the central government could not tax its citizens for revenue, large war debts remained unpaid. This, coupled with the crippled American economy due to broken trade relationships and a depreciated currency, further drove the new nation into financial crisis. By not paying off promised debts, the new government appeared weak and vulnerable to Europeans. Therefore, the threat of an invasion by Great Britain or Spain was a possibility.

| 2nd Continental Congress | Independence | **Articles of Confederation** | Review Questions | Answers & Explanations |

SHAYS'S REBELLION AND ITS AFTERMATH

The greatest challenge to the strength of the Articles came not from abroad but from home soil. Angered by high taxes, debtors' prisons, and lack of valuable currency, **Daniel Shays** and a band of Massachusetts farmers rose up during the summer of 1786 and demanded restitution and tax relief. **Shays's Rebellion** escalated in January 1787 when the mob undertook a seizure of the state *arsenal*. At this stage, the Massachusetts militia marched in and quelled the rebellion. Although Shays' Rebellion seemed to be a minor local *insurrection*, Confederation leaders looked with concern at the implications of the event. The constitution of Massachusetts was one of the most thorough and well executed, thus Shays's Rebellion signaled a serious problem. With so much emphasis placed on the virtues of a republic, the delegates of Congress had failed to ensure that the states themselves would be able to protect faithfully the rights and liberties of their own citizens. It was clear to many congressional leaders that the Articles of Confederation needed to be overhauled.

To repair the problem of the regulation of commerce, a convention was called for Annapolis, Maryland, in 1786. Only sparsely attended (5 delegates out of 13 states), political heavyweights **James Madison** and **Alexander Hamilton** secured the calling of another convention, this time to be held in Philadelphia. Again, the focus of the meeting was to revise and repair the existing Articles of Confederation. The tenor of the meeting soon shifted, and it is now known as the **Constitutional Convention**.

[handwritten margin note: Woke government up to reality that Articles of Confederation were in serious need of overhaul.]

KEY TERMS	
Names	Thomas Paine
	Daniel Shays
	James Madison
	Alexander Hamilton
	Thomas Jefferson
Groups	First Continental Congress
	Patriots
	Loyalists
	Tories
Events	Battle of Saratoga
	Shays's Rebellion
	Constitutional Convention
Documents and Laws	*Declaration of Rights and Grievances*
	Declaration of the Causes and Necessities of Taking Arms
	Olive Branch Petition
	Common Sense
	Declaration of Independence
	Treaty of Paris
	Articles of Confederation
	Land Ordinance of 1785
	Northwest Ordinance of 1787
Vocabulary	arsenal
	insurrection

REVIEW QUESTIONS

1. The First Continental Congress was called to

    (A) discuss acceptable forms of colonial protest.

    (B) organize a military force.

    (C) demand independence from Britain.

    (D) punish colonies who failed to abide by the Quebec Act.

    (E) create a legislative assembly for new territories.

2. Which of the following contributed most to the success of the American forces?

    (A) George Washington's victory at Valley Forge

    (B) The financial and military aid of the French

    (C) The failure of the British to capture New York City

    (D) Major support of Native Americans in Canada

    (E) Encouragement from a majority of colonial citizens

3. In an attempt to reconcile with Great Britain, the Second Continental Congress

    (A) agreed to pay all back taxes.

    (B) reaffirmed colonial loyalty to the crown.

    (C) called for the disbanding of colonial militias.

    (D) allowed for British home rule of the colonies.

    (E) drafted *The Two Treatises on Government*.

4. The Treaty of Paris contained all of the following provisions EXCEPT

    (A) retention of colonial fishing rights off the Canadian coast.

    (B) British recognition of the United States as an independent country.

    (C) the Mississippi River as the western boundary of the country.

    (D) a forgiving of all colonial debts owed to Britain.

    (E) a promise by United States to honor land claims by Loyalists.

5. Ratification of the Articles of Confederation was held up by

    (A) Southern planters.

    (B) abolitionists.

    (C) citizens of coastal states.

    (D) Northern merchants.

    (E) backwoods farmers.

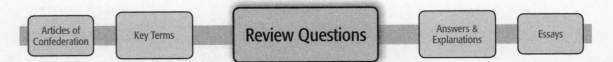

ANSWERS AND EXPLANATIONS

1. A

The delegates of the First Continental Congress were called to discuss "next steps" or acceptable forms of colonial protest in the face of British oppression. Not ready to break from Britain, the Congress was searching for ways to ask for redress of grievances, but it did not desire to engage in war or establish a militia.

2. B

After the American show of force at the Battle of Saratoga, the French decided that the Americans were worthy of their financial and military assistance. Because of this much-needed support and the diversion of British military forces elsewhere, the Patriots were able to gain the upper hand in the Revolution. George Washington's troops survived a brutal winter at Valley Forge but did not fight there. The British did capture New York in 1776. Native Americans did not support the Americans, as they stood to lose both land and trade if the British lost. Only about one-third of Americans supported the cause for independence; the other two-thirds were Loyalists or were disaffected.

3. B

In an attempt to avoid further fighting, the Second Continental Congress sent the Olive Branch Petition to the king to reaffirm colonial loyalty to him and ask again for the redress of their grievances. By no means would the colonials agree to pay back taxes they deemed unfair, nor would they allow for British home rule. Colonial militias were the only defense against British incursion; therefore, the Congress would have been remiss in asking for their disbandment. John Locke, not the Second Continental Congress, was the author of *The Two Treatises on Government*.

4. D

Great Britain expected full payment of all debts owed her by the former colonies. Fishing rights off the coast of Canada, recognition of the United States as an independent country, a western boundary of the Mississippi River, and the honoring of land claims by Loyalists were all provisions in the signed treaty.

5. C

The Articles of Confederation were not ratified until 1781 due to arguments over land claims in the west. Coastal states, such as Maryland and New Jersey, fought larger states over these lands and demanded that they be remanded to the central government. Southern planters and Northern merchants desired quick decisions be made over the incorporation of new land so they could take advantage of the land grab. Abolitionists did not amass a large enough voice until at least the 1830s, and backwoods farmers were so far removed from politics, they did not know a disagreement had taken place.

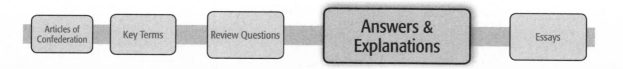

Articles of Confederation | Key Terms | Review Questions | **Answers & Explanations** | Essays

UNIT I SAMPLE ESSAYS

The following are sample Free-Response Questions that you might see on the AP U.S. History exam. Listed under each question are important terms that would greatly add to your answer. AP Readers will look for you to mention at least several of the listed people, places, and things.

1. To what extent did tolerance increase in the colonies from 1630 to 1770? Be sure to cite key individuals, events, or movements to support your answer.

   Study List
   Anne Hutchinson
   Roger Williams
   William Penn
   Quakers
   Maryland Act of Tolerance
   The Enlightenment
   Halfway Covenant
   Great Awakening
   Deists
   Masons

2. Was the American Revolution simply a revolt of citizens unwilling to pay taxes, or was it driven by principles and the desire for independence?

   Study List
   French and Indian War
   Proclamation of 1763
   Stamp Act Congress
   Common Sense
   Sons of Liberty
   Tea Act
   Colonial boycotts
   Olive Branch Petition
   Quartering Act
   Stamp Act
   Stamp Act riots
   Sugar Act
   Intolerable Acts
   Boston Tea Party
   Boston Massacre
   Writs of Assistance
   Declaration of Independence

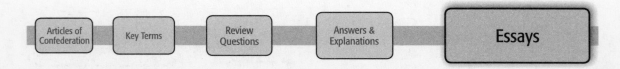

Articles of Confederation | Key Terms | Review Questions | Answers & Explanations | **Essays**

SAMPLE FRQ RESPONSES

To what extent did tolerance increase in the colonies from 1630 to 1770? Be sure to cite key individuals, events, or movements to support your answer.

The United States was founded on a desire for religious freedom, free from persecution. However, early religious groups in the colonies showed little tolerance for dissent among the members of their communities. Nevertheless, from 1630 to 1770, there was a great increase in religious tolerance in the colonies, and with the onset of the Enlightenment and the Great Awakening, new, more radical religious groups began to emerge in the colonies.

Early settlers in the colonies found little religious tolerance among their fellow settlers. In 1630, the Puritans settled in Boston, Massachusetts, fleeing religious persecution from the English King Charles I. Even though the Puritans had been persecuted for their religious beliefs, when they established their new community, they were not tolerant of other religious views. All of the laws that dealt with religious dealings, business, trade, and government were dictated by the Puritans' beliefs. One colonist, Anne Hutchinson, was tried from 1636 to 1638 for failing to agree with the religious beliefs of the group's religious leader, John Cotton. Unlike Cotton, Hutchinson did not think that leading a moral, by-the-rules life was enough to garner a person salvation; rather, she believed that God chose those that He would save. Even though a significant segment of the colonists sided with her, Hutchinson was excommunicated and forced to leave the colony. In 1631, Roger Williams immigrated to Plymouth to join another religious group who had come to America to get away from Charles I's religious persecution, the Pilgrims. He objected to the Pilgrims' practice of punishing people by law for religious transgressions. He also believed that people knew when they were "saved" by God but that no one could determine if another individual was "saved," so requiring voters to be of a certain religion was pointless. This threatened the religious and government leaders, since it basically asked for a separation of church and state. He was eventually expelled from the church and started a new settlement in Providence, where he founded the first Baptist Church in America.

Soon, however, religious tolerance began to increase in the colonies. The Maryland Act of Tolerance was passed in 1649. This act, sometimes thought to be the predecessor to the First Amendment, required that all Christian faiths be tolerated in Maryland. At this time, Maryland was the most diverse state in the Union, founded by Catholics and also home to many Protestants. There was still a political struggle for which denominations should wield power in the state, even though they had agreed to religious toleration. In 1682, William Penn founded Pennsylvania after being imprisoned in England multiple times for his religious beliefs. He wanted to create a home for himself and his fellow Quakers. The constitution of the state was based on a belief in religious tolerance.

With the onset of the Enlightenment in Europe, where great scientific thinkers like Galileo and Newton were making amazing discoveries in the fields of math and science that called

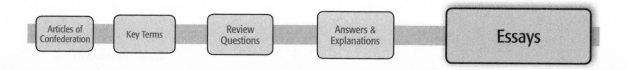

into question many of the Catholic Church's tenets, there coincided a weakening of the Puritan religious strongholds in America. Finding that fewer and fewer members were having the conversion experience required to be a full member of the Church and fearing that they were losing members, the Massachusetts government passed the controversial Halfway Covenant in 1662. This law weakened the previously rigid religious laws of the Puritans somewhat by saying that even if they hadn't had a conversion experience, individuals could still be half-members of the church and have their children baptized but couldn't take communion or vote.

The Great Awakening, which occurred from the 1730s to 1770, was the birth of American revivalism and led to an even more increased degree of religious tolerance. Many of the revivalist preachers, like George Whitefield, had little formal doctrinal training and worried more traditional ministers. Because these revivalist preachers became so popular, many old-guard religious groups like the Presbyterians split, and new religious groups like the Methodists and Baptists became popular. Through this evangelizing, religion became more accessible to the poor, new settlers, women, and blacks. Several more radical religious groups were able to gain prominence at this time. One that emerged was a radical form of Christianity called deism. Deists believed in God but not in miracles or the infallibility of the Bible. Like the deists, another group that became popular at this time, the Masons, believed in a single God but were open to diverse political beliefs among their members.

From 1630 to 1770, religious tolerance increased to a significant extent. The early settlers in the 1630s were not tolerant of other individuals' religious beliefs and even resorted to kicking dissenters out of their communities. As the 1640s dawned, however, Maryland and Pennsylvania were founded on the tenants of religious tolerance. Once the Enlightenment began in Europe, new ideas filtered to the colonies, and more religious tolerance was deemed necessary to make room for them and to maintain existing religious groups. This can be seen in the Halfway Covenant as well as in the Great Awakening, where newer, more radical religious groups became prominent.

Was the American Revolution simply a revolt of citizens unwilling to pay taxes, or was it driven by principles and the desire for independence?

It would be incorrect to say that the American Revolution was motivated by a mere refusal of the citizens to pay taxes. The citizens were not opposed to taxation. On the other hand, they were unwilling to pay taxes for the sole purpose of serving the needs of Great Britain. The desire for independence was the motive behind the Revolution, but nevertheless, the colonists would not have realized this desire without the unfair taxation. Taxes were simply the straw that broke the camel's back as just one of the mistreatments that the colonists underwent that finally forced them to fully embrace their need to become independent.

In 1756, peace was disrupted in Europe by the Seven Years' War. This war, also called the French and Indian War, actually started in 1754 by the French, who were building up the Ohio Valley region wanted to stop the British from setting further west.

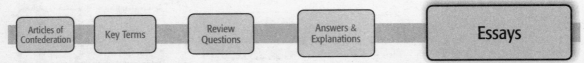

Articles of Confederation | Key Terms | Review Questions | Answers & Explanations | **Essays**

The colonists fought on behalf of Europe, and though they did experience some unsuccessful events, the pride they held for the contribution that they made did not falter. One failure included the surrender made on July 3, 1754, by Lt. Colonial George Washington. When faced with a large French and Native American army, he proved that his forces were no match for the enemies. Despite the fact that Britain thought the colonists proved incapable of defending themselves, the colonists thought themselves to be the victors. They felt that they were competent enough to defend themselves if need be. With the taste of what they felt was an act of independence, the seeds of a revolution were planted.

After the French and Indian War, the colonists lost even more confidence in Britain, as Britain was consequently left in debt. The colonists not only felt discontent toward Britain because of the way its army treated them on the battlefield, but now they were paying financially for their war. Prices and taxes began to rise. In 1764, the Sugar Act raised the prices of sweeteners. Then in 1765, there was the introduction of the Quartering Act, which required the colonists to provide room and board to the British soldiers stationed there. These taxes were not protested by the colonists because they did not affect them directly and they were not strictly enforced.

However when the Stamp Act of 1765 required colonists to have all papers stamped (thereby showing they had paid a paper tax), they were incensed. Colonists had to pay a tax on everything from newspapers to death and marriage certificates. Not only did this mean many little taxes that would end up being costly, but more importantly, this money was going to be used to fund the a new British colonial army. The colonists, being quite cooperative, still agreed to pay their fair share of losses from the war. They just wanted to pay their own share—nothing more, nothing less. On the other side of the pond, British Prime Minister George Grenville thought he was already doing what was fair.

After the Stamp Act, the colonists were fed up with Britain. They had fought and even funded their war and had endured harsh treatment by the British army when they were trying to assist them, but they were not going to sit around and be taxed further. Patrick Henry, a lawyer from Virginia, proposed that if taxes were going to be paid, they should be paid from the people to their own state—not to some long-distance royal authority.

It seems that had it not been for Britain overstepping boundaries, maybe the colonists would not have realized their full potential to become independent. The colonists already felt that they could make it without assistance after the French and Indian War. But the various forms of abuse and exploitation by Britain, including taxes, made them realize they were being used. This eventually led to a need for revolution.

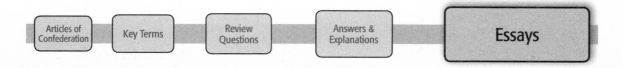

UNIT II: THE NEW NATION TO THE CIVIL WAR, 1787—1865

CHAPTER 8: THE BUILDING OF A NEW NATION, 1787–1800

IF YOU ONLY LEARN SIXTEEN THINGS IN THIS UNIT . . . .

1. Events leading to the formation of the new Constitution and the new laws it put into action

2. Differences between Federalists and Anti-Federalists and the major political figures on each side

3. The development of a post-Revolution foreign policy and roadblocks along the way

4. Jefferson's successes and struggles as president

5. Events leading up to the War of 1812 and the war's effect on policy and society

6. Financial changes and troubles: the Bank of America, taxes and tariffs, etc.

7. How advancements and changes in transportation affected the growing nation

8. Reasons behind the formation of political parties and their affect on government

9. Major players and events of the Abolition Movement

10. The formation of a new American culture leading up to the Civil War, including religion, art, literature, philosophy, and the changing roles of women

11. Effects of continued westward expansion

12. Causes and results of The Mexican War

13. Slavery's role as a major nationwide issue (Three-Fifths Compromise, Missouri Compromise, The Kansas-Nebraska Act, Harper's Ferry, Dred Scott, etc.) and how it helped lead to the Civil War

14. Lincoln's rise to power and his stance on major issues of the era

15. Major battles and events of the Civil War

16. Constitutional amendments, acts, and laws put into action as a result of the war

| Constitutional Convention | Ratification | New Republic | Foreign Policy | Internal Issues |

Treaty of Paris (1783)
- US and Britain
- Established US as independent country
- Established US borders
- US promise to repay debts to Britain

THE CONSTITUTIONAL CONVENTION

The new nation experienced many challenges in the years immediately after the Peace of Paris was signed.

POSTWAR PROBLEMS

An economic depression occurred due to the lack and depreciated value of Continental currency. Farmers were hit particularly hard under the weight of high state taxes and high ratios of debt. The *sovereignty* of the United States was also challenged by several European nations and bands of pirates from North Africa. Even though Great Britain promised to respect the sovereignty of the United States, it refused to repeal the Navigation Laws, armed Native Americans along the western frontier, and failed to remove troops from posts along the Mississippi River. The Spanish closed the port of New Orleans to U.S. trade and also armed Native Americans in the southwest. France called for prompt repayment of the war debts owed and further deepened the economic crisis by limiting the ability of the United States to trade in the Caribbean. Taking advantage of the absence of British protection of U.S. shipping in the Mediterranean, North African **Barbary Pirates** attacked merchant ships, often seizing the goods and kidnapping the crews. As a result of these problems, 12 of the 13 states agreed to send delegates to Philadelphia to improve the standing of the new nation both politically and economically by repairing the weakened Articles.

A SECRET MEETING

The meeting was to begin on May 14, 1787. However, troubles with travel and other engagements kept many delegates from arriving on time. While they were waiting for the others, the delegates from Virginia began working on a proposal that they would present to the full body once they convened. Finally, 55 delegates from all states but Rhode Island convened in secret on May 25, 1787. The meeting was comprised of young, well-educated, wealthy men who were familiar with the conventions of republicanism and democracy. Most were practicing lawyers and had taken a direct hand in the writing of their own state constitutions. Some major names did not attend the convention due to overseas business; some were not chosen due to their radical views; and one, Patrick Henry, refused to participate due to his feelings about the danger of a strong central power. From his desk in Paris, Thomas Jefferson called the meeting a "convention of demigods." After great delays caused by the perils of travel, the group decided to continue meeting in private and to keep the work of the convention secret until it had been completed.

MADISON TAKES CHARGE

In a unanimous vote, George Washington was elected as chairperson, but his was by no means the strongest voice in the statehouse. **James Madison**, a delegate from Virginia, was well read in the areas of federalism, republicanism, and Lockean theory and quickly became the leading voice of

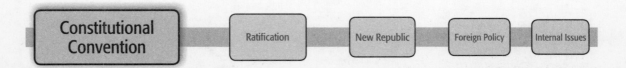

the convention. Madison provided the cornerstones for the development of what is now the U.S. Constitution. First, he expressed the need for a **central government** whose power would exceed the power of the states. Secondly, he believed in the **separation of powers**—the executive, the legislative, and the judicial branches of government would be independent of one another but would be held accountable by each. Lastly, Madison outlined the dangers of "**factions**" and the power a strong national government would have to keep these views in check. These views were somewhat radical. Many leaders, such as Thomas Jefferson and George Mason, did not believe that the national government should be supreme to the power of the states. "Early arrivals" from Virginia took control of the Convention, and soon it was clear that the Articles would be thrown out and a new document would be drafted to rebuild the national government.

A GREAT COMPROMISE IS REACHED

After the decision was made to scrap the Articles and start anew, divisive political, social, and economic issues came to light. First on the agenda was the issue of state representation in the legislative branch. Edmund Randolph and the delegates from larger states proposed a plan that favored their states called the **Virginia Plan.** This plan, presented on May 29, 1787, called for representation in both houses to be based solely on population or proportional representation. The small states, led by William Paterson, put forth their rebuttal to the large state proposal. The **New Jersey Plan** asked for equal representation, regardless of the number of citizens of a state, to a unicameral legislative body. At this point, June 9, 1787, the discussion was at a standstill, and the threat of the convention's collapsing was real. On June 11, Roger Sherman rose with this proposal: "That the proportion of suffrage in the first branch should be according to the respective numbers of free inhabitants and that in the second branch or Senate, each State should have one vote and no more." This was coined the **Great Compromise** (or Connecticut Compromise). Large states were appeased in that the lower chamber, or the **House of Representatives**, would be comprised of members who reflected the population of individual states. Small states would be appeased by representation in the upper chamber, or **Senate,** as it was comprised of membership that was equal regardless of state population. Large states stood to gain more from this compromise, as revenue bills would only go through the lower chamber, thus easing the possible tax burden that large states would more likely have to pay.

AN EXECUTIVE DECISION AND THE THREE-FIFTHS COMPROMISE

Next, the delegates needed to discuss the issue of executive leadership. All of the men present were unwilling to hand the executive branch too much power; however, they understood all too well the dangers of a weak chief. After much debate, it was decided that the president would be elected by a representative body rather than by direct popular vote. The delegates were all worried about a "**mobocracy**" in which the uneducated would choose a president who was dangerous to the stability of the nation. Thus, by allowing the **Electoral College** to cast votes as representatives of their states, they controlled democracy, and mob rule was avoided. The president was given

| Constitutional Convention | Ratification | New Republic | Foreign Policy | Internal Issues |

Major problem in determining representation in House of Reps

many more powers than the weak governors of the states. He would be commander-in-chief of the armed forces, act as chief diplomat, and have the ability to veto decisions by the legislative branch.

Just when the delegates thought the issue of representation was behind them, a conflict of geographic proportions arose. Southern delegates lived in large states, which also had equally large populations of slaves who were not considered citizens. Southerners argued that although these people could not vote, they still had to be managed by the state and should thus be counted as part of the population. Northerners, some of whom disliked the practice of slavery but knew well not to ask for abolition, agreed to the **"Three-Fifths" Compromise** in exchange for the passage of the **Northwest Ordinance**. This compromise stipulated that each Southern slave would be counted as three-fifths of a citizen. The South conceded to the end of the legal importation of slaves in 1808. Lastly, the Northern and Southern representatives decided on a compromise with regard to trade and taxes by agreeing that Congress could place taxes on imports but not exports.

Solve problem of

THE DEBATE OVER RATIFICATION—FEDERALISTS VERSUS ANTI-FEDERALISTS

"Federal"

With the document complete, the Constitutional Convention retired to their home states to campaign for *ratification*. Nine of the 13 states were required to adopt the national constitution. The discussion would rage on for almost a year. As word reached the state governments and citizens that the Articles of Confederation had been thrown out altogether, many feared a return of tyranny. States set out by selecting representatives to ratifying conventions. Several small states ratified quickly—Pennsylvania was the first large state to adopt the Constitution. Ratification debates occurred in statehouses, with those in favor of the Constitution and a strong central government called **Federalists** and those in opposition to the Constitution and in favor of strong states' rights called **Anti-Federalists**. Federalists were usually Northern merchants who had close ties with British trade networks. Anti-Federalists usually hailed from small Southern farms or western homesteads.

Typically Northerners

Typically Southerners

There were many battles to fight in order to garner the nine states necessary for ratification. Virginia was critical—it was the most populous state and had the largest concentration of Anti-Federalists, many of them concerned farmers. Soon enough, Virginia's native sons George Washington, James Madison, and John Marshall were able to persuade Anti-Federalists to ratify the document with the promise of an addition of a **"Bill of Rights"** to protect individual freedoms and state sovereignty. To encourage ratification in New York, James Madison, Alexander Hamilton, and John Jay penned a series of 85 powerful essays collectively called ***The Federalist Papers***. These papers were the *Common Sense* of the ratification period, urging ratifying conventions to set aside emotions when they considered the Constitution. Madison, Hamilton, and Jay refuted common doubts about whether a central government could effectively rule such vast territory. Soon after New York's vote to ratify, North Carolina and Rhode Island became the last states to adopt the Constitution.

Persuaded Anti-Federalists to ratify the Constitution

| Constitutional Convention | **Ratification** | New Republic | Foreign Policy | Internal Issues |

If it were not for the delay of delegates to the original convention in May 1787, Federalist Virginians might not have been able to take control of the meeting and, thus, convince the others to jettison the Articles instead of repairing them. In this respect, the new Constitution and resulting system of federalism was a victory for a very small minority. The addition of the Bill of Rights was their concession. Congress acted quickly in 1789 to prepare the first 10 amendments promised to the Anti-Federalists. Penned mostly by James Madison, the 10 amendments served to protect states and individuals from possible abuses by the central government. They were ratified by the states in 1791.

[handwritten margin note: = the Bill of Rights]

STRUCTURING THE NEW REPUBLIC

Selected unanimously by the Electoral College, President George Washington took the oath of office on April 30, 1789, in the temporary national capital of New York City. John Adams was sworn in as the first vice president. Besides being the first president of the United States, Washington set many other important precedents that shaped the office of the presidency and the federal government as we know it today. The Constitution specifically assigns the president the task of designating departments of the executive branch to assist in government functions. Washington appointed Thomas Jefferson as secretary of state, Alexander Hamilton as secretary of the treasury, Henry Knox as secretary of war, and Edmund Randolph as attorney general (appointed after the Judiciary Act of 1789). Washington called these four men his "cabinet" and met regularly with them to confer and gain advice. To this day, presidents regularly call advisory meetings of their cabinet members.

*[handwritten margin note: G. Washington's, at least
Four Components of Presidential Cabinet
– Secretary of State
– " " Treasury
– " " War
– Attorney General]*

JUDICIARY ACT OF 1789

The smallest section of the Constitution is Article III—the Judiciary Branch. This article only applies to the federal court and is vague with regard to court structure. Therefore, Congress passed the **Judiciary Act of 1789**, establishing a Supreme Court consisting of one presiding chief justice and five associate justices. The act also provided for the establishment of 13 district courts and 3 circuit courts of appeal.

HAMILTON FIXES FINANCES

As economic problems had plagued the new nation ever since the Treaty of Paris, Secretary of the Treasury Alexander Hamilton set out to repair the nation's failing financial health. His **Report on Public Credit** (1790) explained how monetary and fiscal policy should favor the rich so that their good fortune would be spent within the economy and, thus, stimulate domestic growth. His **Report on Manufactures** (1791) promoted the industrialization of the United States and advocated strong protective tariffs to protect infant industry. His overall financial plan set out to

*[handwritten margin note: Report on Public Credit (1790)
Monetary policies should favor the rich so that they keep spending]*

*[handwritten margin note: Report on Manufacturing (1971)
Advocated strong protective tariffs
Protect infant industry]*

Constitutional Convention | Ratification | **New Republic** | Foreign Policy | Internal Issues

When you think Hamilton, think BANK.

place the United States on firm ground with regard to debt repayment, a stable currency, and a strong federal banking system. Comprised of five components, the plan sought to boost national credit, create a "father/son" relationship between the federal government and the states, earn revenue by enacting heavy tariffs on imported goods and passing *excise taxes* on whiskey, and ensure stability by establishing a national bank. Each of these provisions was hotly contested, most strongly by Thomas Jefferson and the Anti-Federalists.

To Hamilton, national bank = national economic stability.

By "**funding at par**," Hamilton argued that the government should pay all debts at face value plus interest. Unfortunately for many government bond holders, the value of the bonds had dropped considerably because it was thought the new government would be unable to make good on its debts. Therefore, these original bond holders sold to speculators, who were pleased to find that the government intended to pay face value on the bonds they now held. Hamilton was criticized for not alerting Americans about his plan before they sold their bonds.

The next issue was Hamilton's suggestion that the federal government assume all state debts. Northern states who had amassed large debts due to the war were thrilled, while smaller states in the South were not pleased with this plan. To appease both sides, Hamilton acquiesced to Thomas Jefferson's request to place the nation's permanent capital on the banks of the Potomac River, which straddled the states of Maryland and Virginia. The **Revenue Act of 1789** placed an 8 percent tariff on imports, a rate much lower than Hamilton had desired. He therefore imposed excise taxes on goods such as whiskey to make up the shortfall in revenue. These excise taxes became a problem for Hamilton and the new government when the Whiskey Rebellion broke out in 1794 (see page 98).

Revenue Act of 1789 8% tariff on imports

And these huge whiskey taxes were what led to—

DISAGREEMENT OVER THE BANK OF THE UNITED STATES

The last and most contested part of Hamilton's plan was the establishment of a national bank—the **Bank of the United States (BUS)**. The federal government would hold the major financial interest in the bank, with private stock holders also contributing. The national treasury would keep its deposits in the bank, keeping the funds safe and available as loanable funds. Thomas Jefferson vehemently opposed the bank, stating that the Constitution did not provide for its creation. Jefferson was a "**strict constructionist**," one who believed in the strict interpretation of the document. Hamilton, on the other hand, had a much broader, "loose" interpretation of the Constitution. He believed the Constitution supported the creation of a national bank because of the "**elastic**" **clause**. Loose constructionists like Alexander Hamilton believed this clause granted Congress "implied powers" to pass laws that were "necessary and proper" to run the country effectively. Hamilton argued that the creation of the Bank of the United States was justified under the elastic clause and by the need to keep and collect federal monies. His arguments won over George Washington, who signed the bank into law in 1791. This issue, however, caused the rift between Hamilton and Thomas Jefferson to widen.

When you think of Hamilton, think of this. As mentioned up here.

Gave birth to ideas of strict constructionism and loose constructionism

| Constitutional Convention | Ratification | **New Republic** | Foreign Policy | Internal Issues |

RISE TO THE PARTY SYSTEM

The issues surrounding the ratification of the Constitution gave rise to a party system. Alexander Hamilton and the Federalists held fast to conservative *ideology*; the liberal states' rights and common man's viewpoint was held by the Anti-Federalists, soon to become the **Democratic-Republicans** championed by Thomas Jefferson.

Democratic-Republicans sought to limit the powers of the central government in favor of greater states' rights, while the Federalists believed in a strong national government whose powers were supreme over the states. These differences in opinion became clearer as conflict arose overseas.

[handwritten margin notes: IDEOLOGIES; DR: "power to people" (ish); larger states' rights; Feds: stronger federal government]

DEVELOPMENT OF FOREIGN POLICY

Aside from developing political stability, President George Washington and his cabinet had to respond effectively to the demands of countries around the world. Soon after the new federal government was underway, France experienced a revolution of her own. The war quickly extended beyond the borders of France and became a world war that involved Britain and the Caribbean. **The French Revolution** (1789–1793) challenged America's sovereignty, since Washington had to decide where her loyalties would lie. Giving the French revolutionaries assistance as they had done for the Patriots during the American Revolution would strain the already delicate relationship with Britain. Initially, Americans were pleased about the overthrow of the king and queen of France, as it seemed an extension of the ideals of the American Revolution. It became clear, however, that this was a very different kind of revolution that was bloody and ruthless. It did not take Americans long to become disgusted by the violence and radical nature of the French Jacobins.

Thomas Jefferson, a sympathizer to the French, urged that the United States should uphold the provisions of the Franco-American Alliance that was forged in 1778 during the American Revolution. Alexander Hamilton, on the other hand, understood the necessity of maintaining trade relationships with Britain and, thus, called for U.S. neutrality. The president decided to side with Hamilton and declared the United States to be neutral in his landmark **Neutrality Proclamation of 1793**. Jefferson was furious. The French were not happy with the decision, either. Both the French and British set out to seize American ships crossing the Atlantic, taking cargo and *impressing* sailors into military service. These seizures violated the Neutrality Proclamation, forcing Washington to send Chief Justice of the Supreme Court John Jay in 1794 to negotiate with the British to seek the recognition of U.S. neutrality.

After almost a year of negotiations, **Jay's Treaty** did not settle the issue of British seizure or impressment of American sailors, but it did call for the removal of British forts in the west. The

Ratification | New Republic | **Foreign Policy** | Internal Issues | John Adams treaty further angered Democratic-Republicans and the French, who increased their harassment of American ships.

The United States was remiss in understanding the impact of Jay's Treaty on its relationship with another foreign country with interest in North America. Spain became concerned with a possible cozy relationship between Britain and the United States and sought to clear up any possible misunderstandings regarding the boundary between Spanish Florida and the new nation. President Washington sent Thomas Pinckney to negotiate a settlement of boundary, right of navigation along the Mississippi River, and right of deposit at the Port of New Orleans. The negotiations were successful and essentially removed Spain as a threat to further American settlement in the West. Pinckney's Treaty was unanimously ratified by Congress in 1796.

Upon leaving the office of the president in 1797, Washington delivered his **Farewell Address**, in which he warned the infant nation to remain neutral with regard to European affairs, to avoid entangling alliances, and to refrain from the formation of "factions," or political parties.

Verbal form of Neutrality Act of 1793

Farewell Address (1794) synonymous with neutrality

INTERNAL ISSUES FACING THE NEW GOVERNMENT

In addition to foreign issues, the fledgling nation had to deal with domestic challenges such as the constant threat of Native American attack, insurrection by angry citizens, and the settlement of newly acquired western lands. As American settlers pushed further and further westward, tensions with Native American tribes escalated. Having been given supplies and munitions by the British, the Shawnee, Miami, and other tribes rose up against the settlers and soldiers stationed in the region. In 1794, a U.S. force led by General Anthony Wayne defeated the Native American fighters at the Battle of Fallen Timbers in the Old Northwest region of Ohio. Clearly defeated, the chiefs of the tribes agreed reluctantly to the Treaty of Greenville in 1795, whereby they surrendered tribal claims to land in what is now Ohio and Indiana. As the tribes moved west away from their homelands, they were in almost continual battle with other tribes vying for land and power.

At nearly the same time, another uprising of backwoods farmers broke out in western Pennsylvania. Backwoods farmers were hit particularly hard by the excise tax imposed on the whiskey they distilled to supplement their incomes. Much like the Sons of Liberty during the pre-Revolutionary era, some of these farmers violently protested the tax by tarring and feathering tax collectors or destroying public buildings. President Washington would not stand for such rebellion and immediately sent a militia to quell the protest. A Shays-like fiasco was averted, and the new federal government proved that it had the power to maintain peace and stop the **Whiskey Rebellion**.

NORTHWEST ORDINANCE OF 1787

Modeled after the Northwest Ordinance of 1787, the Public Land Act of 1796 set clear procedures for the settlement, sale, and distribution of federal lands.

Ratification | New Republic | Foreign Policy | **Internal Issues** | John Adams

The original 13 states had surrendered a good amount of land in the west to be administered by the federal government. The fear of losing control of this land spurred the action of Congress to act quickly.

ADAMS AS SECOND PRESIDENT

Foreign affairs and domestic troubles did not let up as the second president of the United States, **John Adams**, took office. As was provided for in the Constitution, Thomas Jefferson, runner-up in the race for president, became Adams's vice president.

THE XYZ AFFAIR AND AVOIDING WAR

Seeking to halt the incessant seizures of American vessels by the French, Adams sent a delegation to Paris in 1797 to negotiate an agreement. As the delegation arrived in France, they were approached by three French agents only named as X, Y, and Z. These agents demanded a large sum of money as a loan and an additional bribe from the American delegation just for the opportunity to speak with French officials. The delegation refused to comply, and word of the incident quickly spread across the Atlantic, where the American press dubbed it the **XYZ Affair**.

XYZ led to quasi-war

Federalists, including Alexander Hamilton, called for immediate military action. With war fever taking hold across the country, preparations for war began. An undeclared naval war, or "quasi-war," ensued. Most of the action took place in the West Indies between U.S. sailors and French vessels. From 1798 to 1800, this undeclared naval war strained trade in the Caribbean and was on the verge of escalating into a full-scale war. Adams, determined to keep the United States from engaging in total war with France, sent a team of envoys to meet with French foreign minister Talleyrand and Napoleon to negotiate a settlement. The meeting, dubbed the **Convention of 1800**, ended with the termination of the Franco-American Alliance, an agreement by the United States to pay for damages inflicted on French vessels, and the avoidance of an all-out war with France.

THE ALIEN AND SEDITION ACTS

Tension between the Federalists and the Democratic-Republicans intensified after the congressional elections of 1798. Emboldened by American anger over the XYZ Affair, Federalists swept control of Congress and began enacting laws aimed at silencing the opposition. The first of these laws were the **Alien Acts**, which increased the residency requirement for citizenship from 5 to 14 years and gave the president power to detain and/or deport enemy aliens in times of war. The second law aimed at silencing Democratic-Republicans was the **Sedition Act**. This law made it illegal to criticize the president or Congress and imposed a heavy fine or a threat of imprisonment upon violators, such as editors of newspapers. Obviously, Jefferson and the Democratic-Republicans were angered by this violation of their protected right to free speech guaranteed by the First Amendment. Republicans fought back by encouraging states to pass their own statutes to *nullify* the Alien and Sedition Acts. By invoking the "**compact theory**"—that

Think = China's stance on "freedom of speech"

Foreign Policy | Internal Issues | **John Adams** | Jefferson | Key Terms the federal government was formed because of a compact among states—Kentucky and Virginia passed resolutions overturning the Alien and Sedition Acts. However, no other states followed suit, and the issue of nullification disappeared for a short time.

"THE REVOLUTION OF 1800"—THE ELECTION OF THOMAS JEFFERSON

Due to disagreements over going to war with France, the Alien and Sedition Acts, and increasing debts, the Federalists lost much of the momentum they had gained after the XYZ Affair leading up to the election of 1800. The Federalists resorted to nasty mudslinging during the presidential election, accusing Thomas Jefferson of everything from being a thief to an atheist. These tactics backfired when the Federalists were swept from both the presidency and Congress. Although Thomas Jefferson defeated John Adams in the election, he tied in the Electoral College with his vice presidential running mate, Aaron Burr. It was then up to the House of Representatives to decide who would take the presidency. Still in control of the House, the Federalists debated for four days over the issue. At the urging of Alexander Hamilton, who hated Aaron Burr, the House chose Thomas Jefferson as the third president of the United States.

This election was significant because there was a relatively peaceful (nonviolent) transfer of power from the Federalists to the Democratic-Republicans. This peaceful transfer of power was unprecedented in world history and proved that democracy was strong in the face of adversity.

The "revolution"

Election of 1800

- "The Revolution of 1800"
- Transfer of power from Federalists to DRs
- Proved democracy's strength in face of adversity
- Mudslinging

KEY TERMS

Names	James Madison John Adams Thomas Jefferson
Groups	Barbary Pirates House of Representatives Senate Electoral College Federalists Anti-Federalists Bank of the United States Democratic-Republicans
Events	The French Revolution Farewell Address Whiskey Rebellion XYZ Affair The Convention of 1800
Documents and Laws	Virginia Plan New Jersey Plan Great Compromise Three-Fifths Compromise Northwest Ordinance Bill of Rights The Federalist Papers The Judiciary Act of 1789 *Report on Public Credit* *Report on Manufactures* Revenue Act of 1789 Neutrality Proclamation of 1793 Jay's Treaty Alien and Sedition Acts
Vocabulary	central government separation of powers factions mobocracy funding at par strict constructionist loose constructionist elastic clause compact theory

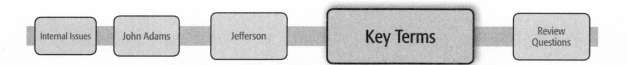

Internal Issues | John Adams | Jefferson | **Key Terms** | Review Questions

REVIEW QUESTIONS

1. During the debate over ratification, Anti-Federalists argued that the Constitution

    (A) did not protect individual and states' rights from the federal government.

    (B) needed to abolish slavery.

    (C) must specify proportional representation in the legislative branch.

    (D) required new provisions for the coinage of money.

    (E) should specify a powerful executive.

2. Which of the following became the most controversial aspect of Alexander Hamilton's financial plan?

    (A) Funding at par

    (B) Excise taxes

    (C) Protective tariffs

    (D) A national bank

    (E) Assumption of state debts

3. In his Farewell Address, George Washington

    (A) argued for increased powers for the president.

    (B) criticized Federalist views of the Constitution.

    (C) warned against alliances and factions.

    (D) urged a restoration of states' rights.

    (E) demanded an immediate alliance with Britain.

4. The decline in the strength of the Federalist party can be attributed to

    (A) the addition of the Bill of Rights to the Constitution.

    (B) the election of 1798.

    (C) the Alien and Sedition Acts.

    (D) Washington's Neutrality Proclamation.

    (E) failure to stop the Whiskey Rebellion.

5. The Kentucky and Virginia Resolutions argued that

    (A) the Constitution provided for the establishment of a national bank.

    (B) states were justified in declaring federal laws null and void.

    (C) states should be consulted before neutrality was proclaimed.

    (D) the House could settle tied votes in presidential elections.

    (E) the federal government had the right to detain enemies during times of war.

ANSWERS AND EXPLANATIONS

1. A

Anti-Federalists were very concerned over possible abuses by the federal government of individuals and states. Therefore, they complained that as it stood, the Constitution did not protect individual and states' rights and would not ratify it without the addition of provisions to provide that protection. The addition of the Bill of Rights provided the protections necessary to secure ratification and satisfy the Anti-Federalists.

2. D

Hamilton's financial plan was plenty controversial, but the issue of the creation of a national bank was the most contentious. Because the Constitution did not specifically provide for the creation of such a bank, Thomas Jefferson argued that it was therefore unconstitutional to do so. Hamilton's arguments for a strong economic base for the United States prevailed, and the Bank of the United States was chartered.

3. C

President George Washington, angered over the bickering in Congress between Federalists and Democratic-Republicans and fearful of another world war, warned of the dangers of factions and alliances as he left office. His warning would not stop political parties from forming but would shape U.S. foreign policy until World War I.

4. C

Their actions to quiet the opposition with the Alien and Sedition Acts led to the eventual downfall of the Federalist party. This, combined with spiraling debts and splits in the party over going to war with France, helped Thomas Jefferson and the Democratic-Republicans sweep the executive and legislative branches in the election of 1800.

5. B

To combat the Alien and Sedition Acts, Thomas Jefferson and James Madison each penned laws in Kentucky and Virginia, respectively, to nullify them. They argued that the federal government had broken its "compact" with the states by failing to protect the free speech of its citizens and they were therefore justified in declaring the acts null and void. However, the Alien and Sedition Acts were not officially nullified by any state, although the idea of nullification re-emerged in the sectional struggles that plagued the nation prior to the Civil War.

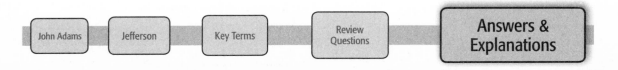

CHAPTER 9: JEFFERSONIAN AMERICA, 1800–1816

THE LOUISIANA PURCHASE

In his inaugural address, Thomas Jefferson looked to calm the fears encouraged by Washington's Farewell Address when he said, "We are all Republicans; we are all Federalists." Although he was a staunch Republican, Jefferson understood that ideology could get in the way of the decisions that needed to be made for the betterment of the nation. In this, Jefferson's presidency was somewhat of a contradiction—in some cases, he adhered to the letter of the Constitution, while at other times, he adopted a somewhat "loose" interpretation. In either case, he argued that the decisions he made were for the good of the nation he so dearly loved. He kept many of the hallmarks of the Federalist Era intact (such as Hamilton's economic system) but had the citizenship requirement of the Alien Act reduced to five years and abolished the excise tax.

NEGOTIATIONS WITH NAPOLEON

A perfect example of Jefferson's loose constructionism is his purchase of the **Louisiana Territory** from Napoleon of France. In 1800, Napoleon obtained the territory from Spain under a cloak of secrecy. The United States had enjoyed the right of deposit at the Port of New Orleans since the signing of **Pinckney Treaty** in 1795 with Spain. In 1802, the Spanish (still in control of the port) revoked the right of deposit in New Orleans. Farmers on the western frontier pleaded for government intervention, since they depended on the ability to navigate the Mississippi and deposit goods for trade in New Orleans. Jefferson, understanding the impact on the economy and the possibility of getting mixed up in European affairs, dispatched ministers to Paris to negotiate with Napoleon.

Jefferson instructed his ministers to offer $10 million for New Orleans and a strip of land that extended to Florida. If the negotiations failed, the ministers were to travel directly to London to ask for a cross-Atlantic alliance between the United States and Britain. Much to the ministers' surprise, the French ministers were offering not just New Orleans and the strip of land but the entire Louisiana Territory for the bargain price of $15 million. Napoleon had abandoned his dream of an American empire due to his failure to stop a slave uprising in Haiti and his desire to

Louisiana Purchase · Marshall Court · Jefferson · Madison · War of 1812

raise revenue to fund his conquest of Europe. The ministers jumped at the opportunity, bringing the deal home for Jefferson's approval. The president was torn. If he accepted the deal, it would be in direct conflict with his strict constructionist views of the Constitution—the document does not specifically provide for the president to negotiate for and purchase land from a foreign power. If he did not accept the deal, the Union might be in peril—the doors would open for another country to purchase the land. Ironically, it was Federalists who voiced the loudest opposition to the Louisiana Purchase by arguing that Jefferson had no constitutional authority to negotiate the deal without the consent of the legislature. The president reluctantly sent the deal to the Republican-held Senate, who quickly approved the purchase.

LEWIS AND CLARK EXPLORE THE LAND

Explored land gained by Louisiana Purchase

Direct effects of Louisiana Purchase

The Louisiana Purchase doubled the size of the United States for a mere three cents an acre. Both the French and the Spanish were removed as potential threats to U.S. sovereignty, the western frontier opened to one of the most fertile valleys in the world, and Jefferson's dream of an agricultural empire was now closer to becoming a reality. Jefferson hoped to find an all-water route connecting the Missouri River to the Pacific Ocean. To investigate this route, the president appointed a team, led by **Meriwether Lewis** and **William Clark**, to explore the vast territory beginning in 1804. The group traveled a trail that began in St. Louis, Missouri, and took them to the Pacific Ocean on the coast of Oregon. They returned back to St. Louis in 1806. By keeping meticulous field notes and drawings of the flora and fauna, as well as detailed accounts of encounters with native tribes, Lewis and Clark expanded America's knowledge of the vast new territory and warned of the hardships settlers would face moving west. However, Jefferson's most prized objective of finding an all-water route was not realized.

THE MARSHALL COURT

A few Federalists were still clinging to power during Jefferson's administration, mostly in the judicial system. In a last-minute piece of legislation before the Congress was to be turned over to the majority Republicans, the Federalists eked through the **Judiciary Act of 1801**, whereby 16 new judgeships were created. President John Adams worked through the nights of his last days in office, appointing so-called "**midnight judges**" who would serve on the bench during Jefferson's administration.

Last-minute judges appointed by the Federalist Adams to serve Supreme Court during Jefferson's presidency.

MARSHALL MAKES A DECISION

Incensed by the packing of Federalists into lifetime judicial appointments, Jefferson sought to block these men from ever taking the bench. He ordered his secretary of state James Madison not to deliver the commissions to the last-minute appointments, thereby blocking them from taking their judgeships. One of these "midnight judges," **William Marbury**, sued under the Judiciary Act of 1789, which granted the Supreme Court the authority to enforce judicial commissions.

Louisiana Purchase | **Marshall Court** | Jefferson | Madison | War of 1812

Sitting as Chief Justice of the Supreme Court was Thomas Jefferson's cousin and staunch Federalist, **John Marshall**. Marshall knew that if the Supreme Court issued a **writ of mandamus** (an order to force Madison to deliver the commission), the Jefferson administration would simply ignore the order. On the other hand, if the Court did not issue a writ, then it would seem that the court was weak compared to the other two branches. Eventually, Marshall declared that Madison should have delivered the commission to Marbury, but then he held that the section of the Judiciary Act of 1789 that gave the Supreme Court power to issue writs of mandamus exceeded the authority allotted the Court under Article III of the Constitution and was, therefore, null and void. With this decision, Marshall was able to reprimand the Republicans without compromising the stature of the Court. More importantly, Marshall had ruled a law passed by Congress to be unconstitutional, thereby establishing the precedence of **judicial review**. In this and subsequent decisions by the Marshall court, the power of the Supreme Court increased—it could check the authority of both the legislative and executive branches.

ie. the power of Supreme Court to declare laws to be unconstitutional.

AN ATTEMPT TO FLUSH FEDERALISTS

President Jefferson was determined to remove all remaining vestiges of the Federalists from the judicial branch. After the rebuke from Marshall and the Supreme Court in the *Marbury* decision, Jefferson turned his efforts to the *impeachment* of radical Federalist judges. The House successfully voted for the impeachment of Supreme Court Justice Samuel Chase due to his highly *partisan* decisions. The Senate, however, refused to convict Chase due to the absence of any evidence in regards to "high crimes and misdemeanors." Jefferson's attempt to flush Federalist judges out of the system was unsuccessful—most remained on the bench for life. The judges did tend to "behave" a bit more to the president's liking, however, as the threat of impeachment hung heavy over the judicial system. Nevertheless, this episode proved to be the last time that a Supreme Court justice would be impeached, maintaining the precious separation of powers between the legislative and judicial branches.

JEFFERSON'S CHALLENGES

Thomas Jefferson easily won reelection in 1804 and entered a much more difficult presidential term. His authority was challenged by his own former vice president, a threat from within his party, and foreign troubles.

THE BATTLES OF AARON BURR

Before Jefferson ran for his second term, the Republicans decided not to select **Aaron Burr** as the vice presidential running mate for Thomas Jefferson. In 1804, the Constitution was amended by the **Twelfth Amendment**, which called for electors to the Electoral College to specify which ballot was being cast for the office of president and which was being cast for the office of vice president. The tie vote that occurred in 1800 between Jefferson and Burr would not happen again

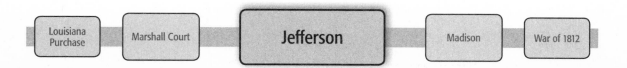

| Louisiana Purchase | Marshall Court | Jefferson | Madison | War of 1812 |

under the new amendment. Burr became very bitter due to the snubbing by his own party and the injustice he believed he had endured back in 1800 at the hands of Alexander Hamilton. Seeking retribution, Burr joined forces with a small group of radical Federalists called the **Essex Junto**. This group was plotting for a New England state *secession* from the Union and had originally asked Hamilton if he would run for governor of New York to join in their exploits. Hamilton refused the offer, so the group then asked Burr if he would run. He gladly accepted and began his campaign.

Upon hearing the news of the campaign, Hamilton leaped at the chance to crush Burr's chances of election by leading the opposition faction. Fearing what an ex-Republican would do, Federalists in New York chose not to elect Aaron Burr as governor, and the plot faded away. After hearing of a snide remark made by Hamilton about his character, Burr challenged his enemy to a duel. Refusing such a challenge would have certainly affected Hamilton's stature as a leader and a man; therefore, the duel was set. Burr shot Hamilton, fatally wounding him in 1804. Just when Americans thought Burr was gone, another secession plot arose in 1806 dubbed the **Burr Conspiracy**. His plan was to wrest Mexico from the Spaniards and join it with the Louisiana Territory to create a new country to the west. The plot was reported to President Jefferson, who called for immediate arrest and trial for treason. Chief Justice John Marshall sat on the bench of the jury trial, where the prosecution could produce no credible witnesses. Burr was acquitted and freed.

A small radical group of Republicans led by Jefferson's cousin John Randolph grew increasingly annoyed by the President's abandonment of his once staunch states' rights advocacy. The "Quids" accused Jefferson of entanglement in a faulty land deal in the western half of Georgia in 1804 (Yazoo River area, now Mississippi). Georgia had turned over her western lands to the federal government but not before granting much of it illegally to land companies. Desiring a quick end to the debacle, Jefferson and James Madison attempted to pay the land companies restitution for the illegally obtained land that the federal government was now taking. Randolph and his Quids leaped at the chance to portray Jefferson as corrupt by claiming that the president was paying off a bribe. The Yazoo Land Controversy led to a schism within the Republican party, which would further challenge Jefferson during his second term.

TROUBLES ABROAD

Foreign troubles left over from his first term plagued Jefferson through the second term. The Barbary pirates in North Africa continued to seize U.S. merchant ships as they traveled in the Mediterranean. Presidents Washington and Adams reluctantly had paid leaders of North African nations a "protection fee" to reduce the number of times U.S. ships would be seized. Once Jefferson took office, the leader of Tripoli demanded a much higher sum for protection. Jefferson refused to pay the fee and instead sent a small fleet of naval ships to stop the pirates. The U.S. Navy fought the pirates in the Mediterranean Sea for four years in what came to be called the **Tripolitan Wars** (1801–1805). While chided for their efforts, the small force was able to put a dent in the work of the pirates and gained the United States credibility overseas.

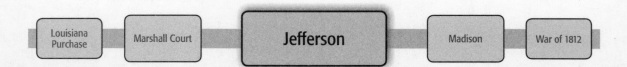

A much greater challenge to U.S. authority came with the continued escalation of the **Napoleonic War** that continued to rage in Europe. The British and French were busy punishing each other by issuing decrees that would blockade trade into one another's ports. Beginning with Napoleon's **Berlin Decree** in 1806, his attempt to cut Britain off from the rest of the world meant that American ships traveling there to deposit goods would get caught in the mess. The British quickly responded by issuing their **Orders in Council**, which retaliated against France by closing all ports under French control—any American ship traveling to mainland Europe that did not stop first in Britain would be confiscated. In 1807, Napoleon fought back by issuing his **Milan Decree**, which authorized his navy to seize any foreign ship traveling to Europe that had first stopped in Britain. In other words, American shippers could continue trade at great risk but reap great rewards in profits.

Americans were growing increasingly concerned over the British practice of impressment and the violations of U.S. neutrality. With thousands of American sailors forced into British military service on the high seas, the continued seizures of neutral ships, and a skirmish at sea with a British vessel, Jefferson was compelled to act. In 1807, the British ship *Leopard* fired upon the U.S. ship *Chesapeake* right off the coast of Virginia, killing three Americans and impressing four. Despite the war fever taking hold in the public sector, Jefferson sought to use the power of diplomacy and economic sanctions to keep the United States from engaging the British. He had no interest in going to war or getting involved in European affairs, but he hoped that the United States could hurt the British economically and, thus, force them to cease violating neutrality.

THE EMBARGO ACT

> Jefferson persuaded Congress to pass the **Embargo Act** in 1807, which would prohibit U.S. merchant vessels from anchoring at any foreign port. His hope was that Britain and France would be crippled economically by the loss of U.S. trade and would be forced to respect his country.

Unfortunately, Jefferson's plan was ruinous for the U.S. economy—most of the damage was inflicted on New England merchants and Southern farmers. A vast network of black market goods arose along the Canadian border to circumvent the embargo. This led to the passage of harsher enforcement laws that many, especially New Englanders, saw as punitive and oppressive. Congress repealed the Embargo Act in 1809 but soon replaced it with a similar bill.

MADISON PLAGUED BY EUROPEAN AFFAIRS

James Madison managed to defeat Federalist Charles Pinckney in the election of 1808 and would carry on the legacy of Republicanism that Jefferson had left behind. Still, issues overseas would

Marshall Court | Jefferson | **Madison** | War of 1812 | Ideology & the U.S.

dominate U.S. politics during his presidency. **The Non-Intercourse Act of 1809** had been passed by Congress in the last days of Jefferson's presidency to replace the Embargo Act. This law, which expired one year from its enactment, allowed the United States to trade with foreign nations except Britain and France. Congress took up the issue again in 1810 and enacted **Macon's Bill Number 2**, which sought to lift trade restrictions against Britain or France but only after they agreed to honor U.S. neutrality. Napoleon happily repealed his Berlin and Milan Decrees in the hopes of stirring up tensions between the United States and Britain. Madison issued Britain an ultimatum—remove the "orders in council" within three months, or U.S. trade restrictions would continue. Madison had been duped, however, by Napoleon, who never intended to honor his promise to remove the restrictions on shipping and trade. The British and French continued their practice of impressment and ship seizures, pushing the United States closer and closer to the brink of war.

"MR. MADISON'S WAR"—THE WAR OF 1812

A heightened sense of nationalism ushered in the first meeting of Congress in 1811. New, young Republican representatives and senators from the South and the west urged a war with Britain to secure a place in the global political structure for the United States. "War hawks," such as Henry Clay from Kentucky and **John C. Calhoun** from South Carolina, insisted that this war would finally clear Britain's influence from North America. Aside from dealing with the British at sea, the Americans were hoping to eliminate the threat of English-armed Native Americans, who continued to cause trouble for western frontier settlers.

The Battle of Tippecanoe in present-day Indiana caused many congressmen in the frontier to feel justified in their call for war. Prior to the outbreak of the War of 1812, **General William Henry Harrison** sought to break up a large native confederacy that a pair of Shawnee brothers, **Tecumseh** and **the Prophet**, had organized in the face of an American advance westward. General Harrison and his men successfully fought back a surprise attack and subsequently burned the tribal settlement at Tippecanoe. Now with the Native American threat removed in the west, the war hawks looked to conquer Canada.

The British refusal to lift trade restrictions, and immense political pressure pushed President Madison to ask Congress for a declaration of war in June 1812. Ironically, the British at that very time had repealed the "orders in council." However, by the time word traveled across the Atlantic Ocean and reached Washington, D.C., the war had already begun. Few Americans and congressmen were in favor of "Mr. Madison's War," with New Englanders voicing the greatest opposition. However, the war hawks were successful in amassing a large enough coalition to officially declare war.

"The Second War of Independence" was a small and disappointing war for the United States. The nation was not prepared to wage war—particularly not with the most powerful naval force in the world. The economy had been devastated by the Embargo Act, and America's standing military was small, poorly equipped, and under trained. The "Mosquito Fleet," or U.S. Navy, was no match for the British Navy. U.S. ships were able to outmaneuver the British in the Great Lakes region, but the American invasion of Canada was a debacle.

With Napoleon under control in Europe by 1814, the British were able to focus their attention on North America. The Americans were able to repel a British attack on New York but could not save Washington, D.C., from being burned to the ground in August of 1814. The British amassed at Fort McHenry near the city of Baltimore, Maryland, but U.S. soldiers held the fort through a night of bombing, inspiring a prisoner of a nearby British ship to write a poem about it. Francis Scott Key put words to an old drinking song to express his love for his country and called it "**The Star Spangled Banner**."

The formidable **General Andrew Jackson** led the Southern troops. He and his men were able to cut a swath through the British from Alabama to New Orleans and thwart the English attempt to control the Mississippi River at the **Battle of New Orleans**. Interestingly, the battle—while an impressive victory for the Americans—was completely unnecessary, as it was fought two weeks after the signing of the peace treaty that ended the war. Nonetheless, Jackson emerged as an American war hero.

War of 1812 = Andrew Jackson's Rise to Fame

The **Treaty of Ghent** that ended the War of 1812 was signed by American envoys and British diplomats in Belgium on December 24, 1814. The provisions of the treaty provided for the end of the fighting, the return of any conquered territories to their rightful owners, and the settlement of a boundary between Canada and the United States that had been set before the war. Essentially, the war ended in a draw—neither side gained any concessions, restitutions, or apologies. Most Americans were pleased, however, because they had fully expected to lose territory. Despite their complaints, the war did allow for manufacturing, especially in New England, to flourish. The country became a bit more independent from European markets. In effect, this was the beginning of America's industrial revolution.

IDEOLOGY DIVIDES THE UNITED STATES

A very serious ideological split divided the nation during the War of 1812—a split between the Federalists and the Republicans, essentially a split between New England and the rest of the nation. New England states were vehemently opposed to the war effort and the direction in which Republicans were taking the nation. A radical group of New England Federalists met at a convention in Hartford, Connecticut, to discuss ways to demand the federal government pay them for the loss of trade due to the Embargo Act, Macon's Bill No. 2, and the War of 1812. The group also discussed possible amendments to the Constitution, which included a one-term limit for the office of president; a two-thirds vote for an embargo, declaration of war, and admission of new states; and an end to the Three-Fifths Compromise—all aimed at Republicans. A radical, small, vocal group even suggested secession from the Union. Hartford representatives were sent to Washington, D.C., to make the demands of the Convention clear to the federal government.

However, before they could speak, news of the signing of the Treaty of Ghent and Jackson's victory at New Orleans drowned them out. With the war now over, the Federalists looked like a bunch of complainers and were labeled "unpatriotic." **The Hartford Convention** was basically the nail in the coffin for the Federalist party, which was routed by Republican James Monroe in the election of 1816. These ideological divisions would continue to intensify and become sectional as the nation moved into the 1820s and began to expand further westward.

KEY TERMS	
Names	Lewis and Clark John Marshall Tecumseh and the Prophet Andrew Jackson
Groups	Essex Junto
Events	Burr Conspiracy Tripolitan Wars Napoleonic War Battle of Tippecanoe Battle of New Orleans The Hartford Convention
Documents and Laws	Pinckney Treaty Judiciary Act of 1801 Twelfth Amendment Berlin Decree Orders in Council Milan Decree Embargo Act Non-Intercourse Act of 1809 Macon's Bill Number 2 The Star-Spangled Banner Treaty of Ghent
Vocabulary	midnight judges writ of mandamus judicial review impeachment partisan secession

REVIEW QUESTIONS

1. Jefferson contradicted his view of the Constitution when he

   (A) asked Congress for a declaration of war.
   (B) authorized the purchase of the Louisiana Territory.
   (C) repealed the Embargo Act.
   (D) enforced Macon's Bill Number 2.
   (E) signed the Alien and Sedition Acts.

2. In the case *Marbury v. Madison*, Chief Justice John Marshall established the

   (A) Judiciary Act of 1789.
   (B) rules of impeachment.
   (C) precedent of judicial review.
   (D) Embargo Act.
   (E) compact theory.

3. In the years prior to the War of 1812, Presidents Jefferson and Madison

   (A) showed little interest in engaging in a war with either France or Britain.
   (B) remained steadfast to their beliefs in regards to the Constitution.
   (C) were not prepared for the office of president.
   (D) ignored the rulings of the Supreme Court.
   (E) sought revenge against Britain and France.

4. The War of 1812 led to all of the following EXCEPT

   (A) the removal of the Native American threat in the Ohio Valley.
   (B) a heightened sense of nationalism.
   (C) the growth of American industry.
   (D) newfound respect for the United States abroad.
   (E) rising support for the Federalist party.

5. The Hartford Convention was significant because

   (A) the concept of secession was struck down.
   (B) a law passed by Congress was nullified.
   (C) Federalists gained new followers afterward.
   (D) renewed signs of sectional tension became evident.
   (E) states amassed an opposition to Jefferson's policies.

Madison | War of 1812 | Ideology & the U.S. | Key Terms | **Review Questions**

ANSWERS AND EXPLANATIONS

1. B

An ardent Republican, Thomas Jefferson held steadfastly to his strict interpretation of the Constitution and to the preservation of states' rights while a private citizen. As president, Jefferson often struggled with his ideology in the face of making tough decisions that would be for the good of the nation. One such battle for Jefferson was the decision to buy the Louisiana Territory from Napoleon. The Constitution did not provide for an executive to purchase land from foreign powers or for appropriate funding for such a purchase without the consent of Congress. This was but one of many examples of how Jefferson contradicted his private views as a public servant.

2. C

Before Chief Justice John Marshall took the bench, the judicial branch was the weakest of the three in the U.S. government. Wishing to preserve the conservative Federalist interpretation of the Constitution, Marshall successfully increased the power of the Supreme Court by declaring a law of Congress to be unconstitutional, rendering it null and void. This precedenct is now known as judicial review and makes the ruling of the Supreme Court the last word, with the exception of a constitutional amendment passed by Congress and ratified by three-fourths of the states.

3. A

Understanding the danger of entering a war with either Britain or France, Presidents Jefferson and Madison had no interest in fighting a major war. Both partial to France, the two presidents looked to diplomacy and embargoes to keep the European leaders at bay.

4. E

After their insistence on staying out of a war with Britain, the Federalists were labeled as unpatriotic after the War of 1812, thus losing a following. Americans emerged from the war more nationalistic due to victories such as the Great Lakes naval battle and the Battle of New Orleans. Native Americans were removed as a threat during the Battle of Tippecanoe and Jackson's other war campaigns. The war helped industry grow and fostered a sense of respect for the United States overseas.

5. D

The Federalists met at Hartford to protest U.S. entrance into the War of 1812, propose constitutional amendments that would protect their interests, and suggest secession if their demands were not met. After news of the Battle of New Orleans and the signing of the Treaty of Ghent, the Federalists' voices were drowned out by cheers of victory. Because the representatives at Hartford were mostly from New England and their ire was directed mostly at large, Southern states, this was a rebirth of the sectional tensions that had plagued the delegates at the Constitutional Convention.

CHAPTER 10: THE NATIONAL SPIRIT AND MARKET REVOLUTION, 1817–1850

THE ERA OF GOOD FEELING

With a renewed sense of independence and national pride, Americans elected James Monroe as their president in the election of 1816. However the "**Era of Good Feeling**" was not always as harmonious as the optimistic name ascribed to Monroe's presidency by a U.S. newspaper. The period was rife with tension regarding tariffs, slavery, and political power within the Republican party.

Due to the collapse and death of the Federalist Party, Monroe handily defeated his opponent in 1816 and easily won r-eelection in 1820. For a young American electorate giddy with enthusiasm regarding the future of the country, he ushered in an age of intense patriotism and reverence for American heroes of the past. Portraits of presidents past and present were commissioned by the federal government and private citizens. Large pieces of canvas were adorned with the likenesses of Washington, Adams, and Jefferson by artists such as Gilbert Stuart and Charles Willson Peale. Children in public schools were taught patriotic alphabets, poems, and songs through the new readers of the day.

A NEW TARIFF AND ITS OPPOSITION

Coupled with this rebirth of American culture was a desire to protect all things American, especially the burgeoning industrial economy. To deter cheap British goods from flooding the market and injuring American manufacturing, Monroe urged Congress to pass a stiff tariff to protect industry. **The Tariff of 1816** imposed a 20 percent duty on all imported goods and became the first truly "protective tariff" in American history. However, the passage of the tariff did not go over well with all sectors of the United States.

A sectional crisis emerged, with three men leading the charge for their respective *constituents*. Former war hawk John C. Calhoun spoke for the South, saying that the tariff was an attempt to line the pockets of Northern merchants at the expense of farmers and plantation owners in his region. Speaking from the North was **Daniel Webster**, who complained that New England had not developed fully enough to withstand interruptions in her ability to trade freely with Britain.

Era of Good Feeling → Missouri Compromise → Monroe Doctrine → Society & Economy → Key Terms

Lastly, Henry Clay of Kentucky argued that the tariff, along with his **American System**, would help establish manufacturing and bring in much needed revenue for internal improvements to aid those in the South.

THE BEGINNING OF INFRASTRUCTURE

Clay's American System included the recharter of the Bank of the United States; tariffs like the one passed in 1816; and the building up of American *infrastructure*, such as turnpikes, roads, and canals.

[handwritten: Protective tariffs]

Congress had already created the Second Bank of the United States and established the first protective tariff, but President Monroe had strong misgivings about the plan for internal improvements. Monroe felt strongly that the Constitution did not expressly provide for the federal government to allocate monies to fund public works projects within the states. Therefore, he repeatedly vetoed bills regarding the building of roads or canals.

TROUBLES WITH THE BANK OF THE UNITED STATES

The Panic of 1819 threatened the Era of Good Feeling that Monroe had enjoyed his first presidential term. The Second Bank of the United States (BUS) caused this financial crisis—it **overspeculated** on land in the west and attempted to curb *inflation* by pulling back on credit for state banks. Typically, countries experience inflation during wartime and then a period of recession after a war. The United States was no exception to the rule. Hit hard by the drop in demand for American agricultural goods abroad and a widening trade deficit with Britain, the BUS was forced to demand payment from state banks in hard *specie* (coin). Unfortunately, frontier banks had very limited amounts of vaulted currency due to the high number of agricultural customers who had amassed large amounts of debt in loans. Thus, these western or *"wildcat" banks* could not pay back the Bank of the United States in specie, and the amount of currency in circulation became dangerously low. The BUS demanded that western banks foreclose on farmers who could not pay back their debts, resulting in significant rise of landless farmers. Western banks were deemed "evil" by frontier farmers and poor citizens, who were hit particularly hard by the depression. Nonetheless, James Monroe was reelected for a second term in 1820.

[handwritten left margin: So that's what specie means. Coined currency]

THE MISSOURI COMPROMISE

[handwritten: Think "slavery"]

As the nation expanded westward and new states entered the Union, the debate on whether or not to allow slavery arose. New states in the Southern half of the frontier justified slavery by expressing the economic need for a large, stable workforce; those settling North had no need for slaves

Era of Good Feeling | **Missouri Compromise** | Monroe Doctrine | Society & Economy | Key Terms

(although some Northern slavery did exist). The issue reared its ugly head in 1819 as Missouri applied for statehood.

A delicate balance existed in the Senate in 1819, with 11 free states and 11 slave states represented. This balance was extremely important to the Southern states, as they had previously lagged behind the North in population growth, thus losing the sectional balance in the House in 1818. As long as the balance was maintained in the Senate, the South had the opportunity to block the passage of bills handed from the House that could hurt it. With Missouri now vying for statehood, each side had to weigh the possibility of the balance being tipped in the opposite direction. James Tallmadge of New York proposed an amendment to Missouri's bid for statehood. After the admission of Missouri as a state, the **Tallmadge Amendment** would not allow any more slaves to be brought into the state and would provide for the *emancipation* of the children of Missouri slaves at the age of 25 years. Southerners were enraged by this abolition attempt by Northern representatives and crushed the amendment in the Senate. Thomas Jefferson was quoted as saying that the argument over the issue rang out as "a firebell in the night."

Yea, not gonna happen. Tallmadge was just asking to get shut down

At this time, Henry Clay of Kentucky proposed three bills that would together make up the **Missouri Compromise** of 1820. The bills allowed for the admission of Missouri as a slave state, while also admitting Maine as a free state, to maintain the balance in the Senate. In addition, slavery would not be permitted in states admitted above the **36°30' line** (with the exception of Missouri, which lay above the line). The compromise was accepted by both North and South and lasted for 34 years. Clay, "the Great Compromiser," had temporarily resolved the intense sectional issue of slavery. However the issue of slavery would now remain on the political center stage from this point until the Civil War.

Remember that date. 1820.

Key word: "Temporarily"

THE MONROE DOCTRINE

The United States became a bit more aggressive with regard to foreign affairs as Monroe took the presidency. There were still lingering issues surrounding Canada, Florida, and the sovereignty of the United States. Back in Madison's presidency, the United States and Britain had signed a treaty to resolve issues involving Canada. **The Rush-Bagot Treaty**, signed in 1817, provided for the disarmament of the Great Lakes and frontier borders and created the longest unfortified border in the world between the United States and Canada. In addition, the United States purchased Florida from Spain in 1819 through the **Adams-Onis Treaty** and gained Spanish assurances that it would abandon its claims in the Oregon Territory.

At the same time, many Latin American countries were experiencing revolutions of their own and were leaning toward more democratic forms of government. Americans were elated, but European powers were frightened by the possibility of losing influence in the Western hemisphere due to this change in political structure. Great Britain was interested in forming an alliance with the United States to maintain a foothold in the region. Some former American leaders urged President Monroe to enter such an alliance to keep the British in check. Secretary of State

John Quincy Adams felt that the alliance was not as innocent as it looked. He believed that the alliance would serve to hinder U.S. expansion and was simply a way for the British to protect their interests. Therefore, he penned President Monroe's annual address to Congress, which included a warning to the European powers to stay out of the western hemisphere. The address, now known as the **Monroe Doctrine**, was delivered by the president in 1823. It quickly became the basis of U.S. foreign policy from that point forward. The Doctrine called for "nonintervention" in Latin America and the end to European colonization. It was more or less designed to check the power of Europe in the Western hemisphere and flex the muscles of the young nation. While the United States did not have the military means to enforce the doctrine in its early years, and a number of European countries were both amused and irritated by its contents, the United States increasingly enforced the policy throughout the late 19th and 20th centuries.

AN ECONOMIC AND SOCIAL REVOLUTION

A massive jump in America's population, along with advancements in transportation, led to the creation of a national market economy in the United States between 1820 and 1860. The development of national roads, canals, steamboats, and railroads helped bring people, raw materials, and manufactured goods to the far corners of the country like never before. While this created a national market for goods manufactured in the United States, it also began to sectionalize the regions of the country with regard to ideology and specialty. The west became known for growing the grains needed to feed a hungry nation. The east emerged as the industrial powerhouse, with textile factories dotting the landscape. The plantation economy continued to grow in the South, due to the invention of the cotton gin by Eli Whitney in 1793.

TRANSPORTATION ADVANCEMENT LEADS TO NATIONAL CHANGES

Turnpikes, or toll roads, were the first transportation advancement that served to link many towns in the eastern United States. The Lancaster Turnpike, built in the 1790s, spurred the building of many more toll roads across the United States—most importantly the Cumberland or National Road that ultimately connected western Maryland with Illinois. Most turnpikes were built with private funds, as there was much opposition to the use of federal funds for internal improvements (recall the opposition to Clay's American System).

THE CREATION OF THE ERIE CANAL

The Erie Canal, completed in 1825 with funds provided by the state of New York, linked the Great Lakes with the Hudson River. Suddenly, the cost of shipping dropped dramatically and led to the growth of port cities along the length of the canal and its terminal points.

Missouri Compromise   Monroe Doctrine   Society & Economy   Key Terms   Review Questions

Robert Fulton had helped water travel with his invention of the steamboat in 1807. Before the steamboat, river travel was done by flat or keelboat, which relied on the current of the river or the strength of the men who would push the boat upstream. With the steamboat, goods and people could be transported two ways without relying on nature or brute strength.

Finally, the advent of the railroad brought an even cheaper method of transportation to the country and further connected the regions of the United States. The railroad was not bound by water and could traverse mountains and plains quickly and cheaply. The railroad came to be the fastest, most dependable, and most convenient means of traveling and shipping freight. By 1860, the country had constructed 30,000 miles of railroads.

While these exciting changes in transportation made life easier and cheaper for the average American, there were social and political consequences. Divisions between the rich and poor became much more distinct as manufacturers and plantation owners grew in prestige. Politically, regional divisions created difficulties that would soon become the early stages of sectionalism. Naturally, the east and west were more closely connected due to the fact that eastern manufacturers aggressively pursued a linkage between the regions through improved transportation. The South was largely cut off from the rest of the United States due to the east-west railroad network, which rarely connected with the few Southern railroads that existed. This geographic division created tension between the North and the South politically and economically, which would continue to escalate through the 1850s.

IMMIGRANTS CHANGE THE NATIONAL SOCIAL STRUCTURE

Along with the change in the economic climate of the country came a shift in demographics that altered the social fabric of the United States. Since the nation had become independent, the population had doubled every 25 years due to the high birthrate of Americans. In the mid-1840s, a potato famine in Ireland and tough economic and political conditions in Germany led to an influx of immigrants to the shores of the United States. Between 1830 and 1860, Irish immigrants accounted for the single largest immigrant group; their impoverished ranks began to fill the country's cities. Boston and New York City were soon bursting with more Irish folks than lived in Ireland. The Irish were Roman Catholic, poor, and competed for jobs with native-born Americans—all traits that did not endear them to many Americans. Germans were not popular, either. Mostly displaced farmers, some 1.5 million Germans arrived at much the same time as the Irish. German immigrants often settled in the western frontier to farm and maintained some Old World customs. Members of the backlash movement against these immigrants became known as **nativists**. These Anglo-Americans believed that they were really the only true "Americans" and railed against the rights of those who had foreign blood. In 1849, an extreme wing of the nativist movement became a political party called the **American Party** or the **Know-Nothing Party**. The group opposed immigration and the election of Roman Catholics to political office. The members of the party met in secret and would not tell anyone what they stood for instead saying, "I know nothing," when asked.

Missouri Compromise | Monroe Doctrine | **Society & Economy** | Key Terms | Review Questions

As more and more foreigners arrived and advances were made in technology, transportation, and business, the nation continued to change politically, socially, and economically. These changes would challenge Americans in all walks of life and would soon place enormous burdens on those leading the country.

KEY TERMS	
Groups	American Party Know-Nothing Party
Events	Era of Good Feeling The Panic of 1819
Documents and Laws	The Tariff of 1816 Tallmadge Amendment The Missouri Compromise The Rush-Bagot Treaty The Adams-Onis Treaty The Monroe Doctrine
Places	Erie Canal
Vocabulary	The American System overspeculation nativists constituents inflation species emancipation
Names	James Monroe John C. Calhoun Daniel Webster Henry Clay John Quincy Adams

REVIEW QUESTIONS

1. Many leaders opposed Clay's American System on the basis that

   (A) the country did not have enough funding to pay for such services.

   (B) federal funds should not be used to pay for internal improvements in states.

   (C) the South was benefiting more than the North.

   (D) secret land deals threatened the authority of the federal government.

   (E) expansionists sought to keep growth controlled.

2. The development of the American Party in 1849 signaled that

   (A) many Americans were prepared to allow the federal government to start spending on public works projects.

   (B) leaders were unhappy with the economic decisions of Democrats.

   (C) some Americans were fearful of the rise of immigration.

   (D) Congress was moving toward ending slavery.

   (E) Democrats and Whigs were prepared to work together to repair the economic system.

3. The Missouri Compromise provided for

   (A) citizens of territories to decide whether or not to allow slavery.

   (B) slavery in the Oregon territory.

   (C) the abolition of slavery in the United States by 1830.

   (D) the admission of Maine as a free state and Missouri as a slave state.

   (E) excise taxes to be collected above the 36°30′ line.

4. The Monroe Doctrine

   (A) strengthened American foreign policy in regards to Latin America.

   (B) signaled an isolationist move on behalf of the United States.

   (C) was designed to quell democratic revolutions in Latin America.

   (D) encouraged the French to develop more colonies in the Western hemisphere.

   (E) was designed to frighten Britain into respecting U.S. sovereignty.

5. The Panic of 1819 was

   (A) the reason James Monroe failed in his bid for re-election.

   (B) caused many to question the efficacy of slavery in the South.

   (C) caused by overspeculation and wildcat banks in the west.

   (D) helpful to Northern merchants.

   (E) the impetus for the Missouri Compromise.

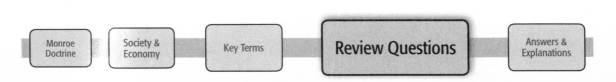

ANSWERS AND EXPLANATIONS

1. B

Tight constructionists did not think that federal funds should be used to pay for internal improvements in states and blocked all attempts at federal works projects.

2. C

The American or Know-Nothing Party was created in response to the massive influx of immigrants from Ireland and Germany. The party eventually dissolved in the mid-1850s due to its unwillingness to take a position on the issue of slavery and the meteoric rise of the Republican party.

3. D

To maintain the balance in the Senate, Clay crafted the Missouri Compromise to admit a free state in conjunction with a slave state. The Compromise also stipulated that slavery would be prohibited in newly admitted states above the 36°30' line.

4. A

Penned by Secretary of State John Quincy Adams, the Monroe Doctrine was an attempt to protect emerging democracies in Latin America from European interference. It was a bold move and certainly far removed from the isolationism preached by the first presidents.

5. C

Crazed by the availability of cheap land, many western "wildcat" banks loaned money to land buyers on the false hope that prices on that land would rise. As the bottom fell out of the U.S. financial market during the panic, these banks lost on their investments and had to foreclose on many western farms. They were unable to pay back the Bank of the United States with hard currency, and the money supply became severely restricted and economic turmoil continued. Nonetheless, James Monroe became the only president to be re-elected amidst a troubled economic period.

1820s: Regionalization

CHAPTER 11: SECTIONAL TENSION GROWS, 1820–1850

Separation of North & South into two distinct identities

THE INDUSTRIAL NORTH AND AGRICULTURAL NORTHWEST

The North included New England and the Middle Atlantic. Improvements in transportation spurred massive economic growth and served to link the populous region together. As mentioned in chapter 10, regionalization began to take hold across the country; the North was no exception. Textile factories led the way in industrial growth, followed distantly by other manufacturing, such as agricultural and consumer goods. As industry began to take hold, the region's cities experienced massive expansion in their own right. Unfortunately, the nation's urban areas were not prepared for such immediate growth and suffered from overcrowding, disease, and rising crime rates.

The North

Ohio, Indiana, Illinois, Michigan, Wisconsin, and Minnesota made up the Old Northwest region, which was closely tied to the industrial North by way of rail lines and canals. Regionalization in this area consisted of grain farming of corn and wheat. Shipping of grain products to the Northern cities of New York, Boston, and Philadelphia helped grow the river and Great Lake port cities of St. Louis, Cleveland, and Chicago.

The Northwest

KING COTTON AND THE AGRARIAN SOUTH

The regional specialty of the South was planted long before the regionalization of the 1820s settled in. The plantation/cash crop economy that is now synonymous with Southern culture was emboldened with the invention of **Eli Whitney's** cotton gin in 1793. The invention made the process of removing the seed from raw cotton much easier and faster, making cotton the number one cash crop of the region. Southern plantation owners switched from growing tobacco to growing cotton to keep up with the demand from domestic and overseas markets. The growing demand for the fiber led to the rapid increase in the demand for slaves to work the fields. King Cotton caused the "***peculiar institution***" of slavery to grow; the number of African slaves in the South increased from 1 million to almost 4 million in about 50 years. Southerners often justified and defended their dependence on slaves by citing the Bible as proof that God approved of the practice. As the numbers of slaves increased, so did the fear of whites of attack by their workers.

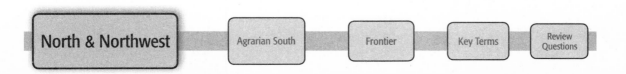

North & Northwest | Agrarian South | Frontier | Key Terms | Review Questions

Slaves were an expensive and risky investment; thus, many laws and codes were passed to protect that investment.

Slave Life

Slave life was arduous and dehumanizing but was not the same from plantation to plantation. Some slave owners treated their slaves humanely, while others beat their captives mercilessly. The goal of most plantation owners was to abase their slave population so as to drive any spirit of rebellion or humanity out of them. Slave families were split apart, marriages were either forbidden or forced, and slave women were under constant threat of sexual exploitation by their masters. Education of slaves was especially forbidden for fear of slave revolts. Many slaves found teachers in church or inside the plantation houses, where white women and children often took it upon themselves to teach slaves to read and write. Even under these oppressive conditions, African Americans forged a tight-knit community that emphasized family, faith, and oral tradition. They also were known to resist their masters through passive resistance. Slaves would refuse to work or would work slowly to protest beatings or other injustices. By 1860, there were also 250,000 free blacks in the South who had been emancipated or were the result of racial mixing (mulatto). Many worked as fieldhands, craftspeople, or house servants.

The South's social structure had been transplanted from England in the 1620s and continued into the 19th century. At the height of the pyramid was the planter aristocracy, who owned over 100 slaves and over 1,000 acres of farmable land. Next in line were the farmers who owned fewer than 20 slaves and tilled only a few hundred acres of land.

THE REALITY OF SOUTHERN SOCIAL HIERARCHY

> Contrary to popular belief, most white Southerners did not own slaves or owned only one. These people were called "white trash" by the other sectors of Southern society but held fast to their belief in slavery, as they did not wish to be the lowest rung on the social ladder.

Along the Appalachian and Ozark mountains lived a few scattered farmers and hill people, many of German decent. These "hillbillies," or mountain whites, tended not to adopt traditional Southern cultural ways and felt more at ease with their Northern neighbors.

THE FRONTIER—WESTERN LANDS

Beyond the Mississippi River lay a vast territory that many Americans either longed to settle or wanted to avoid. Besides the writings of Lewis and Clark, little was known of the western region except of the dangers that lay across the river. Native Americans who had been pushed west had settled in large numbers the Great Plains and caused great concern for white settlers moving into the frontier. Life was difficult for those who chose to venture into the vast territory. Many built log cabins or mud-thatched homes along rivers, streams, or lakes, living off of the land until farms could be established. The West was unique in that citizens tended to be more open to change than their counterparts in either the North or South. Granting women and African Americans more opportunities and having a more open governmental system were just some of the ways that the west differed from the east.

KEY TERMS	
Name	Eli Whitney
Vocabulary	peculiar institution

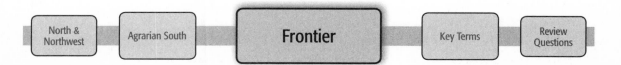

REVIEW QUESTIONS

1. Regional specialization was caused by

   (A) a drop in the demand for consumer goods.

   (B) government subsidies for farmers in the west.

   (C) railroads and overseas demand for manufactured and raw goods.

   (D) a decrease in overseas shipping.

   (E) the Embargo Act.

2. American cities during the early 19th century were characterized by

   (A) egalitarian laws for all citizens.

   (B) disease, overcrowding and high crime rates.

   (C) large African American working class communities.

   (D) advanced opportunities for women.

   (E) vast public transportation and sanitation systems.

3. Southern society was characterized by

   (A) large numbers of white slave owners.

   (B) sharecroppers and tenant farmers.

   (C) a highly educated white population.

   (D) a flexible social structure where upward mobility was easy.

   (E) an unbalanced social pyramid that had a small elite and large underclass.

4. The United States in 1850

   (A) included a free black population that lived mostly in the North.

   (B) had very few Americans still working in agriculture.

   (C) had a frontier that began west of the Mississippi River.

   (D) had few Native American tribes still in existence.

   (E) included a large working class that was protected by the federal government.

ANSWERS AND EXPLANATIONS

1. C

The British demand for cotton products, increased U.S. demands for manufactured goods, and the east-west configuration of the railroad lines created a rift that split the nation into North and South. This rift caused these regions to specialize in industries that suited their climate, geography, social structure, and economic needs.

2. B

Due to sudden and immense growth, the infra-structure of Northern cities collapsed under the weight of the burgeoning population. Overcrowding led to the rapid spread of infectious diseases and an increase in crime. Northern cities were in no way *egalitarian*, as the poor, minorities, and women were not treated with the same respect as upper- and middle-class whites.

3. E

The Southern social structure had been transplanted many years before from England, as landed gentlemen made their way to colonize the region. These rigid strata consisted of the landed aristocracy at the top and a large underclass at the bottom. Social mobility was next to impossible in the South. Southerners did not hold education as a high priority, and therefore as a whole, the South had fewer educated citizens.

4. C

Having crept further west from the eastern seaboard, the American frontier now began west of the Mississippi River. While the number of Americans involved in industry had grown, agriculture was still the number one means of earning a living. Native American tribes had diminished and moved west, but there were still many still in existence. Approximately 250,000 free blacks lived in the North, but approximately the same number chose to live in the South. The working class did not begin to enjoy the protection of the federal government until the turn of the 20th century.

Agrarian South · Frontier · Key Terms · Review Questions · **Answers & Explanations**

CHAPTER 12: JACKSON'S DEMOCRACY, 1824–1840

THE RISE OF THE SECOND PARTY SYSTEM

As the United States emerged from the Panic of 1819 and experienced the massive economic and social changes of the 1820s, the old aristocracy transplanted from England was replaced by a new democratic spirit.

CHANGES IN THE ELECTORAL PROCESS

Americans across the nation favored equality for white men. More and more men from the middle and lower classes began to become involved in the political process by voting, campaigning, and running for office. Sometimes called "the Rise of the Common Man," this era signaled a retreat from exclusive rule by the well-to-do and a shift to a more democratic society. By 1820, many states had adopted universal manhood *suffrage*, which eliminated the property-owning requirement that had once limited the voting population. These new political activists demanded leaders who more reflected their humble backgrounds—hardworking, modest, and Protestant.

Many other changes ushered in an age where the citizens of the nation had more say in the election of their leaders. The nominating caucus was replaced by nominating conventions, where large groups of people chose the party's slate of candidates. The state representatives to the Electoral College, who had once been chosen by state legislatures, were now chosen by the state's voters. New third parties, such as the **Anti-Masons** in 1832, arose to challenge the old two-party system. The popular election of electors led to the re-emergence of a new democracy, where presidential candidates now had to run national campaigns and political parties had to grow to manage the task.

THE MUDSLINGING ELECTION OF 1824

The election of 1824 pitted four candidates from the Republican Party against each other for the presidency: John Quincy Adams, Henry Clay, William Crawford, and Andrew Jackson. The campaign was ugly, with Jackson slinging mud on the reputation of John Quincy Adams and Adams slinging mud right back. In the end, Andrew Jackson won the greatest number of popular

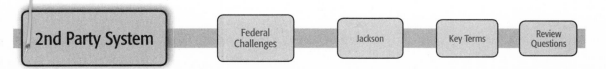

2nd Party System   Federal Challenges   Jackson   Key Terms   Review Questions

votes, but with the votes split four ways, no one man had a majority of electoral votes. It was left up to the House of Representatives to choose the president. Henry Clay, a key opponent of Andrew Jackson's, used his influence to push John Quincy Adams to the front of the pack. When President Adams then appointed Clay as his secretary of state, the Jackson camp cried "Foul!" This **"corrupt bargain"** marred the selection of the new president. By 1828, Jackson wanted to run for president again. On one side of the political fence were the Democrats who supported Andrew Jackson, while those who supported Henry Clay on the other side were called **National Republicans** ("**Whigs**" starting in 1836). The Whig ideology, which mirrored the long-lost platform of the old Federalist Party, was specifically founded to oppose Andrew Jackson. Mudslinging ensued once again, with Jackson calling Adams's wife a bastard child and Adams accusing Jackson's wife of bigamy. Thus, the second party system was reborn.

Whig Party was founded specifically to oppose Andrew Jackson

CHALLENGES TO FEDERAL AUTHORITY

Supreme Court Chief Justice John Marshall was still making his mark on American politics in the 1820s and 1830s. Still holding strong to his Federalist tendencies, Marshall continued to increase the power of the federal government over the states. The Court had to decide a case in 1819 that would challenge the doctrine of Federalism in *McCulloch v. Maryland*. Here, the state of Maryland was attempting to collect a tax from the Second Bank of the United States. In true Federalist fashion, Marshall used a "loose interpretation" of the Constitution by ruling that the federal government had an implied power to establish the Bank and that the state had no right to tax a federal institution. He argued that "the power to tax was the power to destroy" and would signal the end of Federalism. Most importantly, this ruling established that federal laws were supreme law of the land and tantamount to state laws. The Marshall court also ruled in ***Gibbons v. Ogden*** (1824) that the state of New York could not issue a monopoly to a steamboat company because it was in direct conflict with the commerce clause of the Constitution, which gives the federal government control of interstate commerce. Prior to this decision, Marshall had likewise continued to overturn laws and provisions states enacted to challenge the authority of the federal government.

McCulloch vs. Maryland

Fed law >> state law

THE DEATH OF THE BANK OF THE UNITED STATES

As a proponent of the common man, Andrew Jackson sought to separate government from the economy once and for all. His belief was that to ensure the success of every American, the government needed to stay out of economic affairs. This issue came to a head as the Bank of the United States (BUS) was set to expire in 1832. Jackson's key opponent, Henry Clay, favored the BUS and encouraged Congress to pass a rechartering bill prior to its demise. Jackson vetoed the bill and vowed to kill the BUS, which he considered a monopoly. The BUS's president, Nicholas Biddle, was successful in running the bank, but many accused him of favoring the wealthy. Upon winning re-election in 1832, Jackson came up with an elaborate scheme to kill the BUS once and for all. All federal funds were removed from the BUS and deposited in various state banks, which opponents dubbed "**pet banks**." Domestic prices for goods and land jumped dramatically and threatened to destroy the economy. Jackson then issued the **Specie Circular**, which required the payment for purchase of all federal lands be made in hard coin or "specie" rather than banknotes. This caused the value of paper money to plummet and eventually led to the **Panic of 1837**. However, Jackson did succeed in killing the BUS. The United States did not have another federal bank repository until the creation of the National Banking System during the Civil War.

THE SOUTH'S CONTENTION OVER TARIFFS

Both John Quincy Adams and Andrew Jackson found themselves in a predicament due to separate tariffs passed under their presidencies. New England merchants had been pushing for the passage of a stiffer general tariff since 1824. Already the tariff had been upped from 20 percent to over 35 percent and, through the underhanded planning of Jacksonian duties, would rise to a whopping 45 percent. New Englanders continued to push for the passage of the **Tariff of 1828** to further protect them from foreign competitors. The outspoken **John C. Calhoun** of South Carolina secretly penned "**The Southern Carolina Exposition**," outlining the anger of the South in the face of the "Tariff of Abominations." The essay expressed the Southern contention that the tariff was unconstitutional, as it severely altered trade with Europe that Southern farmers had become dependent on. Calhoun also recommended that the Southern states declare the tariff to be null and void if the federal government refused to lower the duty requirement. This time around, Calhoun was alone in his protest.

NOTE: North vs. South

WEBSTER AND HAYNE DEBATE

Senator Daniel Webster of Massachusetts and Robert Y. Hayne of South Carolina engaged one another over the particulars of the tariff on the Senate floor in 1830. Hayne proposed that Calhoun's doctrine of nullification was the only way to preserve Southern interests and that an alliance between his region and the west was the only way to persevere in the face of the tariff.

Hayne claimed that the tariff was causing the economic troubles of South Carolina and that the Union of states was a compact between the states and the federal government and could be broken. Webster, a powerful and respected orator, held the floor for two days as he decried the obvious abridgement of Union. Webster, on the other hand, argued that the Constitution was a compact between the people and the government, not to be broken by the states acting on their behalf. Ending with these impassioned words, "Liberty and Union, now and forever, one and inseparable!" Webster successfully made nullification and succession equal to treason.

Hayne claimed that Union was simply a compact and as such could easily be rendered void.

Despite Webster's passion, Calhoun would be joined by many other voices as Jackson saw the passage of the **Tariff of 1832**. To appease the South, Jackson sought to lower the tariff from 45 percent duties to 35 percent. This change did little to placate the Southerners. With Calhoun in the lead (having just resigned the vice presidency due to severe differences with President Jackson), South Carolina nullified the Tariff of 1832 and threatened to secede from the Union if Jackson attempted to collect the duties by force. Jackson did make military preparations but stopped short of sending troops to South Carolina. Instead, he encouraged Congress to pass the **Force Bill**, which gave the president the power to use military force to collect tariffs if the need arose. Amid the possibility of civil war, Henry Clay proposed a compromise that would save the day. A new tariff was passed in 1833 that slowly reduced the percentage tariff, and the "nullies" rescinded their ordinance for nullification. Andrew Jackson successfully protected the power of the federal government during the nullification crisis and averted a potentially dangerous clash of states' rights with federal power. In the end, the crisis signaled the events to come, as the North and the South would continually go head-to-head over states' rights issues.

JACKSON EXERCISES VETO POWER

Andrew Jackson was a champion of states' rights, as long as the Union was not in peril. He was also of the opinion that to protect the rights and guarantee the success of the common man, the president should exercise all due power to ensure that protection. In this respect, Jackson vetoed more bills than the previous six presidents combined. States' rights were a hot topic, from the debate over nullification between Senator Robert Hayne of South Carolina and Senator Daniel Webster of New Hampshire that lasted for nine days, to Jackson's veto of the Maysville Road Bill. Jackson vetoed the bill because he was opposed to spending federal funds for infrastructure improvements that lay totally within one state (in this case, Clay's Kentucky.) As Jackson increased the power of the presidency, he sometimes sought to expand democracy—but only when it served his interests.

JACKSON'S AMERICA—SUCCESSES AND LIMITATIONS

Jacksonians, though not necessarily Jackson himself, were successful in expanding democracy to the middle and lower classes of America. The "New Democracy" emerged in the 1820s, when many states reduced their voting requirements.

JACKSON'S GOVERNMENT OF THE PEOPLE

During Jackson's presidency, as in no time before, everyday Americans saw the inner workings of the political system. Voter turnout increased, and new civil service opportunities arose for Jackson supporters. Andrew Jackson was a proponent of the **spoils system** in which he appointed those who supported his campaign to government positions. Many felt that this practice bred corruption and tainted the political process. Nonetheless, Jackson created jobs and appointed many friends to

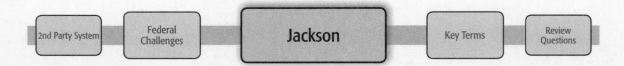

his unofficial cabinet, earning it the name "**kitchen cabinet**" from critics, who lamented that the group of advisors did not have to answer to Congress as they were not "official cabinet officers." Jackson also believed in rotating officials to discourage complacency and encourage fresh opinions. He felt that any man was as good as the next man, so there was no need for someone to hold an office indefinitely. This also opened the door for many commoners to take an active role in governmental affairs. However, this "champion of the common man" did not feel that democracy should be shared by all Americans—certainly not women, blacks, and Native Americans. Universal manhood suffrage was intended for white males only.

JACKSON VERSUS NATIVE AMERICANS

Jackson understood the positive impact continued western expansion could have on the country and wished to open up the frontier to white settlers who longed to settle. The problem was that large groups of Native Americans already lived on this land. Jackson believed that the solution was to move the Native Americans to land set aside for them west of the Mississippi in what is now Oklahoma and Kansas. The **Indian Removal Act**, signed into law in 1830, provided for the immediate resettlement of Native Americans living in Mississippi, Alabama, Florida, Georgia, and present-day Illinois. These tribes were considered "civilized"—a few of them had written alphabets, practiced democracy, and had converted to Christianity. By 1835, some 100,000 Cherokee, Chickasaw, Choctaw, Creek, and Seminole Indians had been forcibly removed from their homelands. The Cherokee Nation refused to go down without a fight and took its case against the state of Georgia to the Supreme Court. The Court ruled in ***Cherokee Nation v. Georgia*** (1831) that the tribe was not a sovereign foreign nation and, therefore, had no right to sue for jurisdiction over its homelands. In another Indian removal case, the Marshall Court ruled in favor of the tribe. In ***Worcester v. Georgia*** in 1832, John Marshall ruled that the state of Georgia could not infringe on the tribe's sovereignty, thus nullifying Georgia state laws within Cherokee territory. President Jackson was incensed and allegedly said, "John Marshall has made his decision; now let him enforce it." Jackson believed that as president, it was his duty to enforce the Constitution as he interpreted it, not how the Supreme Court interpreted it. Unfortunately for the Cherokee, the federal government did nothing to come to their aid.

THE TRAIL OF TEARS

By 1838, all the Cherokees had been forcibly removed from the state of Georgia. This trek is known as the Trail of Tears, as some 4,000 Cherokee died en route to Oklahoma.

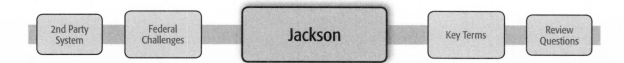

KEY TERMS	
Names	John C. Calhoun
Groups	Anti-Masons National Republicans Whigs
Events	Panic of 1837 The Southern Carolina Exposition Trail of Tears
Documents and Laws	*Gibbons v. Ogden* Specie Circular Tariff of 1828 Tariff of 1832 Force Bill Indian Removal Act *Cherokee Nation v. Georgia* *Worcester v. Georgia*
Names	Andrew Jackson Daniel Webster Robert Hayne
Vocabulary	corrupt bargain pet bank spoils system kitchen cabinet suffrage

REVIEW QUESTIONS

1. Clay's Whig Party was founded to

    (A) support immigrant rights.

    (B) encourage the expansion of slavery.

    (C) oppose the politics of Andrew Jackson.

    (D) protect the interest of farmers.

    (E) lower tariffs on imported goods.

2. Andrew Jackson's two presidential terms were marked by

    (A) the abolition of slavery.

    (B) an increase in the power of the federal government.

    (C) the demise of the two-party system.

    (D) a weakened executive branch.

    (E) large-scale Native American rebellions.

3. The "nullies" led by John C. Calhoun were concerned with

    (A) the spread of slavery westward.

    (B) the admission of free territories into the Union.

    (C) Jackson's overzealous use of the veto.

    (D) the massive influx of immigrants.

    (E) extremely high protective tariffs.

4. Andrew Jackson's Indian Removal Act was spurred by

    (A) raids on white settlements in Georgia and Mississippi.

    (B) his desire to exterminate the Native Americans.

    (C) continued white expansion into tribal homelands.

    (D) the threat of foreign nations joining forces with tribes.

    (E) a need to clear the way for the expansion of slavery.

5. Andrew Jackson's vision of expanded democracy is best illustrated by

    (A) the Force Bill.

    (B) the BUS veto.

    (C) the Indian Removal Act.

    (D) the Specie Circular.

    (E) the *Southern Carolina Exposition*.

ANSWERS AND EXPLANATIONS

1. C

Clay and Jackson were both members of the Republican Party before the mudslinging of the 1824 election, but they had gone drastically different directions by the election of 1828. The National Republicans (later, Whigs) were a party designed primarily to oppose the politics of Andrew Jackson. They favored the American System and protective tariffs and disapproved of immigration. They had little interest in agriculture and slavery issues, which would eventually lead to their downfall in the 1850s.

2. B

Andrew Jackson is known for strengthening the power of the executive branch. President Jackson used his power to veto bills he found unnecessary or unconstitutional more than any other president before him.

3. E

Southern farmers were hit particularly hard by the 35 to 45 percent protective tariffs passed by Congress during the presidencies of John Quincy Adams and Andrew Jackson. The "nullies" sought to declare the tariffs null and void and even threatened to leave the Union if the government attempted to collect the duties by military force.

4. C

President Jackson understood the strength that would be added to the United States if white settlers were allowed to move freely as far across the country as possible. Therefore, he wanted to remove the Native American tribes that stood in the way. By 1838, some 100,000 tribespeople had been forcibly removed from their homelands to the Oklahoma territory.

5. B

Jackson saw the Bank of the United States as a threat to the well-being and success of the common man. To expand democracy and end an institution he saw as corrupt, Jackson vowed to kill the BUS before it could be rechartered.

Federal Challenges | Jackson | Key Terms | Review Questions | **Answers & Explanations**

CHAPTER 13: ANTEBELLUM RENAISSANCE, 1790–1860

A RELIGIOUS REVIVAL

The "Second Great Awakening" started well before revivalist preachers began touring the United States in the 1820s. Protestant traditionalists, such as the Calvinists, created a fervor in the 1790s in response to the liberal doctrine espoused by leaders such as Thomas Jefferson and other deists. These religious figures felt that liberal religious views were a direct threat to the moral fiber of America and sought to regain a foothold in the hearts and souls of followers. Unlike their Puritan ancestors, these Calvinists had a gentler approach to moral living and the afterlife, preaching free will and abandoning the idea of predestination.

Religious revivalism did not reach its full fever pitch until the 1820s, with the preaching of Presbyterian minister **Charles G. Finney**. Like Jonathan Edwards of the first Great Awakening, Finney appealed to his audience's emotion, rather than their reason. His "fire and brimstone" sermons became commonplace in upstate New York, where listeners were instilled with the fear of Satan and an eternity in Hell. Finney insisted that parishioners could save themselves through good works and a steadfast faith in God. This region of New York became known as the "burned-over district," as Finney preached of the dangers of eternal damnation across the countryside. Aside from Finney, other preachers set out across the nation, setting up tent revivals that resembled country picnics more than church services. Methodist and Baptist ministers, such as Peter Cartwright, set out across the South and west, preaching at tent revivals and converting thousands. The Methodists and Baptists soon became the two largest denominations in the United States. As a result of this religious awakening, thousands of Americans were "saved." The new religious converts were mostly middle-class men and women, who then birthed the social reform movement that would last through to the 1860s.

PASSIONATE REFORM

Many of the new religious converts believed in **perfectionism**, or the idea that humankind could reach a level of perfection that resembled the life of Jesus. Humans could obtain this level

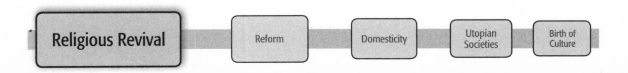

Religious Revival — Reform — Domesticity — Utopian Societies — Birth of Culture

of perfection through faith, hard work, education, and temperance. In its earliest stages, the *antebellum* social reform movement worked on a local level, seeking only to affect individual morals. But reformers soon decided that to make their work effective, they would have to influence politics on a local, state, and national level.

TEMPERANCE AND AMERICA'S HEALTH

The evils of alcohol were one of the first areas of concern for antebellum reformers. Revival preachers joined forces in the mid-1820s to form the **American Temperance Society**, whose aim was to encourage drinkers to limit their intake of alcohol and then eventually take a vow of abstinence. The consumption of hard liquor was a problem, particularly among the Old World immigrant populations of Germans and Irish but among Anglo-Americans as well. Soon state leaders would see that curbing alcohol use among their citizenry could lead to fewer on-the-job accidents and more overall productivity. Neal S. Dow led the way for the temperance movement to shift into the political arena with his **Maine Law** in 1851, which completely prohibited the manufacture and sale of alcoholic beverages in that state. Soon after, some 12 other states would pass similar laws, either severely limiting the sale of alcohol or prohibiting it altogether. The most active members of temperance societies tended to be middle-class women. When the temperance movement became overshadowed by the abolitionists in the 1850s, many of these women shifted their attention to slavery or women's rights.

A RISE IN CONCERN FOR HEALTH

Aside from drinking, Americans' overall health became the next target of the reformers. From reforming insane asylums to the food Americans ate, a wave of smaller reform movements developed to assist Americans in their path to "perfection."

Dorothea Dix crusaded for the improvement of American mental institutions to care for the nation's mentally ill population. She crusaded relentlessly until patients were removed from prisons and other deplorable conditions and given proper treatment. Connected to the asylum reform movement was the crusade to change the penal system in the United States. As a result, some prisons instituted programs that provided prisoners job skills and increased access to religious services.

To stop criminal tendencies from reaching adulthood, education reform swept the nation to raise a generation of well-behaved children. **Horace Mann** was the leader of the movement to reform the public school system in the United States. Before the 1840s, compulsory school attendance was not common. Mann was instrumental in spreading state-funded free public education for youngsters across the country.

Religious Revival | Reform | Domesticity | Utopian Societies | Birth of Culture

To cleanse the body and soul, men such as Sylvester Graham of graham flour and cracker fame and John Harvey Kellogg of the corn flake invented and espoused diets to cure "sexual excess" that led to further health problems. Dr. Kellogg practiced his diet on patients of the Battle Creek Mental Institution, where he was guardian.

THE ABOLITION MOVEMENT

The most politicized of all of the antebellum reform movements was the antislavery or abolition movement. Born from the teachings of the Second Great Awakening, abolitionists believed that slavery was sinful and, therefore, must be eliminated. In 1831, **William Lloyd Garrison** began publishing *The Liberator*, a newspaper dedicated to the end of slavery in the United States. The outspoken and often radical leader of the abolitionist movement founded the **American Antislavery Society** in 1833 to combat the pro-slavery contingent. Garrison's radicalism soon alienated many moderates within the movement when he claimed that the Constitution was a pro-slavery document. As a result, the movement split into the **Liberty Party**, which accepted the membership of women, and the **Foreign Antislavery Society**, which did not accept female participation.

Free blacks had their own leadership within the abolition movement with **Harriet Tubman**, **Sojourner Truth**, and **Fredrick Douglass**. Douglass published *The North Star*, an antislavery journal that chronicled the ugliness of slavery for readers, and argued that the Constitution could be used as a weapon against slavery. Thus, Douglass argued for legal means of fighting slavery in contrast to some other radical abolitionists, who advocated varying degrees of violence to achieve abolition. Tubman and Truth, along with many others, helped fugitive slaves flee the United States through their elaborate network called the **Underground Railroad**.

Some, however, chose to not participate in the snail's progress of politics and took matters into their own hands, often with deadly results. Virginia slave Nat Turner took it upon himself to organize a massive slave uprising in 1831. **Nat Turner's Rebellion** resulted in the deaths of over 50 white men, women, and children and the retaliatory killings of hundreds of slaves. Unfortunately for the abolition movement, rebellions like these signaled to many Americans that freeing slaves would cause massive social problems that they were unprepared to handle.

THE "CULT OF DOMESTICITY"

After the market revolution and transportation boom of the 1820s, the importance of "women's work" shifted. In many American homes, it was no longer necessary for the woman to work in both the fields and the home. The growth of industry moved men out of the fields and into factories, while women were left to tend the home and children. Children, too, became less important to the overall well-being of the family, as they were no longer required to work in the fields alongside their parents. Thus, the birthrate dropped into the 1860s among middle-

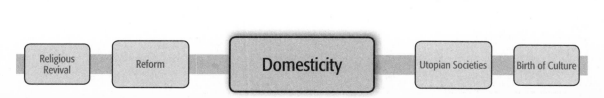

class white families. Still, in this age of moral perfectibility, women's roles were clearly defined as homemakers and mothers—hence the "**Cult of Domesticity**."

Women began to experience power within the antislavery movement and resented the second-class status even their fellow male abolitionists assigned them. A wave of female reformers left the abolitionist movement behind and started a women's rights movement to combat the "cult." Vehement abolitionists **Sarah and Angelina Grimke** voiced their opposition to male dominance within the movement in 1837, thus starting the dialogue about women's roles. Soon after, Lucretia Mott, Elizabeth Cady Stanton, and Susan B. Anthony organized a meeting of feminists at **Seneca Falls**, New York, to discuss the plight of women in the United States.

WOMEN AND FEMINISM

> Encouraged and emboldened by their convention, the women at Seneca Falls drafted the **Declaration of Sentiments**, which closely modeled the Declaration of Independence by declaring that "all men and women are created equal" and demanding true universal suffrage to include females as well as males.

Much like the earlier temperance movement, the women's crusade soon became eclipsed by the abolitionist movement and did not resurface until closer to the turn of the 20th century.

UTOPIAN SOCIETIES

The search for perfection spilled over into non-Protestant groups, who sought refuge from a society they disapproved of. Several groups, both religious and nonreligious, formed communal societies, which they hoped would be closer to the Garden of Eden in which everything and everyone was perfect.

THE BIRTH OF MORMONISM

According to Mormon tradition, the angel Moroni visited the young Joseph Smith in his western New York bedroom one autumn night in 1823. The angel told Smith of a sacred text that was inscribed on gold plates that had been buried by the fabled "Lost Tribe of Israel" nearby and revealed to him the exact location of the treasure. By 1830, Joseph Smith had translated the sacred text and formally organized the **Church of Jesus Christ of Latter-Day Saints** or, informally, the **Mormon Church**. The followers of Mormonism were chastised and ostracized by their surrounding community and left New York to head west. Smith was murdered by a mob in Illinois, where a new leader, **Brigham Young**, collected his flock and moved further west into Deseret—what is now the state of Utah. The Mormons remained outsiders due to their religious

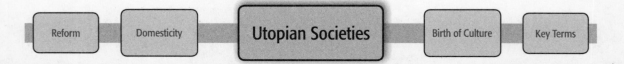

Reform | Domesticity | Utopian Societies | Birth of Culture | Key Terms

practices and beliefs, notably the practice of polygamy (having multiple wives). Only after the church agreed to forbid the controversial practice was Utah allowed to become a state.

Utah = Mormon state

THE TRANSCENDENTALISTS, SHAKERS, AND ONEIDAS

Meanwhile, Romanticism had swept over Europe, stirring emotion and an emphasis on the connection between man and nature. This romantic spirit was embraced in America through the writings of the **transcendentalists**. Close friends **Ralph Waldo Emerson** and **Henry David Thoreau** spoke throughout the country and wrote scathing essays about the state of man. Spurning materialism and embracing self-reliance, they encouraged Americans to throw off the yoke of wealth and want and embrace the beauty and truth of the natural world. Thoreau's best-known book, *Walden*, chronicled his self-initiated experiment where he excused himself from society by living in seclusion in the woods for two years.

Think: Thoreau's Walden

INSPIRATION FOR FUTURE LEADERS

Perhaps more influential was Thoreau's essay **"On Civil Disobedience,"** where he advocated passive resistance as a form of justifiable protest. His essay would inspire later social movement leaders Mahatma Gandhi and Dr. Martin Luther King, Jr.

A group of transcendentalists settled in Massachusetts in 1841 to try to live the lifestyle espoused by Emerson and Thoreau. Brook Farm, a communal effort to practice transcendentalism, collapsed in 1849 due to massive debts.

Brook Farm was just one of many *utopian* experimental communities that developed between 1830 and 1850. The **Shakers**, led by "Mother" Ann Lee, were known for their "shaking" as they felt the spirit of God pulse through them during church services. They eventually died out due to their forbidding of sexual relations. The **Oneida Commune**, founded by John Humphrey Noyes in 1848 to be the shining example of equality between all members, was controversial from the beginning. Oneida members shared everything, including spouses, which many on the outside believed to be immoral. The Oneida commune died out, but its name lives on in the Oneida Silversmith Company, which produces glass, silver, and platewares to this day.

BIRTH OF AMERICAN CULTURE

Ralph Waldo Emerson encouraged the forging of a unique American identity as he traveled across the United States delivering lectures. A distinctive American culture, divorced from European influence, had already begun to bloom before Emerson's influence. American artists, writers, and

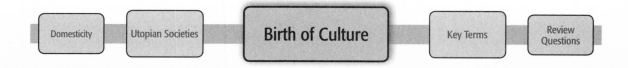

Domesticity | Utopian Societies | **Birth of Culture** | Key Terms | Review Questions

architects had started to show a unique American style that would express the growth and pride of the growing nation.

Portraits of American presidents by Gilbert Stuart and Charles Wilson Peale opened the 1820s with traditional lines and bold images. These stoic paintings faded as the Romantic era influenced Americans and large-scale landscapes took center stage. These grand landscapes, connected with artists such as Thomas Cole and Fredrick Church from the **Hudson River School** of painting, emphasized the beauty of the American landscape and rendered human interaction infinitesimal or nonexistent.

The nationalistic spirit that swept the nation after the War of 1812 continued to give fuel to American authors well into the 1850s. The **Knickerbockers** of New York, including Washington Irving, started the trend of "American" fiction by using domestic settings and character types for their stories and tales. Tales such as "Rip Van Winkle," "The Legend of Sleepy Hollow," and "Twas the Night Before Christmas" were all borrowed stories with an American twist. The tales of the west were glorified by James Fenimore Cooper, whose *The Last of the Mohicans* gained worldwide attention. Questions of religion came front and center through the works of **Nathaniel Hawthorne** (*The Scarlet Letter*) and Herman Melville (*Moby Dick*.)

American architects returned to the glory days of Rome and Greece by imitating ancient forms for landmarks, including Thomas Jefferson's home, Monticello, and the rebuilding of the nation's capital. Greek columns and Roman domes dotted the American landscape as builders expressed their pride in the Republic.

Domesticity | Utopian Societies | **Birth of Culture** | Key Terms | Review Questions

KEY TERMS

Names	Charles G. Finney
	Dorothea Dix
	Horace Mann
	Harriet Tubman
	Sojourner Truth
	Fredrick Douglass
	Sarah and Angelina Grimke
	Joseph Smith
	Brigham Young
	Ralph Waldo Emerson
	Henry David Thoreau
	Nathaniel Hawthorne
	William Llloyd Garrison
Groups	American Temperance Society
	American Antislavery Society
	Liberty Party
	Foreign Antislavery Society
	Church of Jesus Christ of
	Latter-Day Saints
	Mormon Church
	transcendentalists
	Shakers
	Oneida Commune
	Knickerbockers
Events	Nat Turner's Rebellion
Documents and Laws	Maine Law
	The North Star
	Declaration of Sentiments
	Walden
	"On Civil Disobedience"
Places	Underground Railroad
	Seneca Falls
Vocabulary	Perfectionism
	cult of domesticity
	antebellum

REVIEW QUESTIONS

1. Many abolitionists regarded William Lloyd Garrison as a radical because he

    (A) believed in the gradual abolition of slavery.

    (B) advocated the use of the Constitution as a weapon against slavery.

    (C) accepted the participation of women in his movement.

    (D) wished to send emancipated slaves back to Africa.

    (E) refused to engage in the political process.

2. The "Cult of Domesticity" referred to

    (A) a woman's role as homemaker and a mother.

    (B) the expanding influence of women outside of the home.

    (C) communal societies devoted to domestic perfection.

    (D) religious beliefs in perfectibility.

    (E) the limiting of alcohol consumption in the home.

3. Hudson River School artists portrayed the United States as

    (A) a large industrial powerhouse.

    (B) naturally immense and beautiful.

    (C) mired in urban filth.

    (D) connected with ancient Greek and Roman culture.

    (E) sympathetic to the plight of slaves.

4. Antebellum reform movements sought to

    (A) cure society's ills for the betterment of mankind.

    (B) provide individual assistance for those who needed it.

    (C) expand democracy to the disadvantaged.

    (D) create a "perfect" American society.

    (E) limit the religious freedom of splinter groups.

5. Oneida, Brook Farm, and the Mormons are all examples of

    (A) religious cults.

    (B) Protestant revival sects.

    (C) reform parties.

    (D) utopian experiments.

    (E) abolitionist societies.

ANSWERS AND EXPLANATIONS

1. C
One of the greatest arguments among abolitionists was about the equal participation of women in the movement. Garrison argued that women were vital to the success of the movement and fought vehemently for their inclusion.

2. A
After the market revolution, women were expected to stay home and raise children while their husbands went off to work. These gender roles were defined as women no longer were needed to play the larger role demanded of them as farm wives.

3. B
Hudson River School painters are known for their grandiose portraits of American landscapes. Influenced by the Romantic movement in Europe, these artists held a transcendental view of humankind's connection with nature and sought to express the beauty of the land they lived in.

4. D
While, on the surface, antebellum reformers looked as if they were simply working to foster a better society, it was a "perfect" society they were after. Middle-class Americans felt their peaceful way of life threatened by the excesses of the wealthy and the desperation of the poor and, thus, sought ways to insulate themselves from these perceived dangers.

5. D
Seeking refuge among likeminded followers, residents of Oneida and Brook Farm and the Mormons all left society behind in search for "Utopia." While Brook Farm failed due to financial troubles, the Mormon church is still thriving in today's society.

CHAPTER 14: MANIFEST DESTINY, 1830–1860

[circled: 1830–1860] ← Period of Westward Expansion *[handwritten]*

SETTLERS MOVE WEST

Journalist John O'Sullivan coined the phrase "manifest destiny" in 1845. It would soon be the cry of whites who flocked the overland trails to settle the trans-Mississippi West. In other words, it was God's will that the United States expand from sea to shining sea and all points in between. The market revolution, advancements in transportation, and lingering nationalism drove Americans to seek opportunities to spread the virtue of the United States across the continent and beyond.

[handwritten right margin: Primary causes of Americans' desire to expand West]

[handwritten: Jingoism]

By 1840, thousands had moved into what is now Texas, with a trickle braving the overland trail to Oregon. That trickle soon became a flood—by 1845, thousands more settlers had traversed the dangerous **Oregon Trail**. Caravans usually consisted of families in 10 to 20 covered wagons who traveled up to six months, covering a mere 12 to 15 miles a day depending on the weather. Many women did not wish to make the journey at all; those who did soon found their traditional roles as homemakers and mothers change shape. At the beginning of the journey, women took care of children, cooked meals, and cared for clothing. By midtrek, they were repairing wagon wheels, tending animals, and lifting the wagon covers. A sense of an established home was also lost on the journey; some women struggled to maintain some vestiges of "back home" by running prayer meetings and teaching "school."

EXPANSION AND NATIVE AMERICANS MEET

As white settlers moved west, they encountered Native American tribes who had lived in the Great Plains region for centuries. Not only were Native Americans displaced by whites but also by the **Sioux**, who were moving west to hunt buffalo. While there were no large-scale clashes between Native Americans and white settlers, stories abounded about the "ruthless savages" who lived on the plains. Aside from Native Americans stealing horses, gunpowder, or firearms, only infrequent skirmishes took place with whites.

Western Settlers | Native Americans | Territories | Mexican War | Key Terms

The Sioux, on the other hand, did much to alter the way of life for many tribes that had lived in the Great Plains. The Sioux had moved steadily westward since the mid-18th century due to the spread of guns and horses, which they used to fight for territory and hunt their prized buffalo. Outbreaks of disease often cleared the way for the Sioux as they moved west by killing off tribes that would have otherwise stood in their way. By the beginning of the 19th century, the Sioux had control over much of the Great Plains. Yet due to technological advances, destruction of the natural environment, and governmental policies, the Plains Indians did not fare as well into the late 19th century.

TROUBLE WITH TERRITORIES

The era of expansion opened up politically with Martin Van Buren elected as president in 1836 and William Henry Harrison in 1840. A benefactor of Andrew Jackson's "spoils," Van Buren had a troubled presidency. Many believed he was simply a puppet of Jackson's. Van Buren also had to oversee a terrible economic depression that stemmed from his predecessor's policies. The Panic of 1837 was caused by many of the same problems that had caused the Panic of 1819. Overspeculation on western lands, faulty loans issued by "wildcat" western banks, the absence of a national bank, and Jackson's Specie Circular all placed enormous strains on the economy.

TIPPECANOE AND TYLER, TOO AND NEW EXPANSION

Van Buren ran for re-election in 1840 against a vigorous campaign run by the Whigs, who chose Battle of Tippecanoe hero William Henry Harrison as their candidate. As in recent previous elections, the mudslinging was fierce, with the Whigs blaming "Martin Van Ruin" for the economic crisis and Democrats accusing Harrison of being a drunk. Nonetheless, the campaign was a lively one, with Whigs pushing large model log cabins and handing out hard cider in towns across America to boast of their candidate's supposed "poor" background. The **"Tippecanoe and Tyler, too"** ticket swept the elections, easily defeating Van Buren. However, Harrison fell gravely ill with pneumonia only four weeks into his term and died, leaving his vice president John Tyler to become president.

Maine, Oregon, and Texas soon became hotly sought-after pieces of real estate, as more and more Americans began settling the regions. Americans still harbored a deep-seated hatred for the British after the Revolutionary War and the War of 1812 and their continued presence along the U.S./Canadian border. This hatred came to a head when British lumber companies proposed building a road that would ease the transport of lumber and connect various regions of Canada. This road would cross sectors of land whose boundaries were still being contested by the Americans and the British. In 1838, a group of Canadian lumberjacks collided with the Maine militia as they claimed control over the Aroostook River Valley. The threatened Aroostook War was quickly averted, as Secretary of State Daniel Webster and British Foreign Minister Ashburton negotiated the terms that would settle the boundary dispute. The **Webster-Ashburton Treaty** (1838) divided

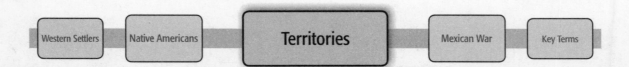

the contested territory between the United States and Britain and settled the northern boundary of Minnesota.

The conflict between the United States and Britain would not end with the settlement over the Maine issue. The British had enjoyed a profitable fur-trading business in the Oregon territory and believed that gave them claim to the region. The United States contended that it had first found and settled the region and, therefore, could rightfully stake a claim on it. The most ardent proponents of expansion demanded that the United States should take the entire territory up to the 54°40' parallel, which lay even with the southern shore of Alaska. As manifest destiny "fever" had swept the nation and the election of 1844 loomed, the Democrat **James K. Polk** sought to capitalize on the expansionist spirit with his campaign slogan "Fifty-four forty or fight!" which would make the United States border reach Russian Alaska. By the time he took office, Polk had backed down from the U.S. demand for all of the Oregon Territory by negotiating with Britain. The United States would obtain a boundary at the 49th parallel and reluctantly agreed to cede Vancouver Island and grant navigation rights on the Columbia River to the British. The Mexican War had erupted by this time, which overshadowed any concerns over the entrance of new free territories into the Union.

TEXAS JOINS THE UNION

Meanwhile, Texas was the biggest issue in the national spotlight. In 1821, Texas was officially a northern region of the newly independent Mexico. Mexico had attracted many American farmers and ranchers into the region with cheap land and relative freedom from government intrusion. By the 1830s, whites and slaves outnumbered Mexicans in the region. Mexico decided to crack down on the Texans—it decided that slavery would be banned in the region and demanded that all residents become Catholic. The Texans refused to abide by the new laws, and tensions grew. In 1834, Antonio Lopez de Santa Anna became the military dictator of Mexico and attempted to force the Texans to abide by Mexican laws. Texans, led by **Sam Houston**, staged a revolt in 1836 and declared Texas a republic independent of Mexico.

At present-day San Antonio, Santa Anna's forces attacked the Alamo, killing all the Americans stationed there, and marched to the San Jacinto River. There, a force led by Houston successfully routed the Mexican forces and captured Santa Anna. The Mexican dictator was forced to sign a decree granting independence to the Republic of Texas (the Lone Star Republic). Houston was chosen to lead the new country, and he quickly applied for annexation, or adoption as a state in the Union. His petitions were rejected early on by Jackson and Van Buren, who both feared tipping the senatorial balance to favor slave states. Despite Tyler's support for annexation, Congress rejected his bid to bring Texas into the Union in 1844. The presidential election of 1844 brought expansionism and the fate of Texas to the forefront. Outgoing president Tyler saw the election of the expansionist candidate Polk as a *mandate* to drive the annexation of Texas through Congress. A joint resolution was passed in acceptance of Texas's bid for annexation. Mexico's reaction was not joyful.

So Texas gaining independence from one country only to turn around and ask to become part of another. Okay—

"Expansionism"

| Western Settlers | Native Americans | **Territories** | Mexican War | Key Terms |

Sparked by the annexation of Texas

THE MEXICAN WAR

President Polk had to react quickly to the impending crisis between Mexico and the United States. Mexico had ended the diplomatic relationship between the countries and demanded the return of Texas. Polk sent special envoy John Slidell to Mexico City to inform the Mexican government of U.S. intentions to honor the original Nueces River boundary of Texas and its desire to purchase California. In anticipation of the Mexicans not responding positively to Slidell's proposal, Polk amassed the U.S. Army, led by Zachary Taylor, along the disputed southern border of Texas at the Rio Grande River in January of 1846. In April, a Mexican force crossed the border and attacked Taylor's men, killing several American troops. Despite a small opposition of Whigs, led by Abraham Lincoln, a large majority of Congress voted to declare war on Mexico.

THE WILMOT PROVISO SPLITS NORTH AND SOUTH

The war caused immediate dissension by many Americans who opposed the fighting on principle. Many Whigs and Northerners accused Polk of falsely claiming that American blood had been shed on American soil when the Mexican force crossed the Rio Grande. In their eyes, the southern border lay some miles to the north at the Nueces, not at the Rio Grande. Secondly, the issue of the expansion of slavery again reared its ugly head. Transcendentalists, such as Henry David Thoreau and Ralph Waldo Emerson, protested the war by refusing to pay taxes with Emerson saying, "Mexico will poison us!" The sectional tension grew in Congress, as Representative David Wilmot proposed an amendment to a bill that would forbid slavery in the new land acquired by the war with Mexico. The final bill passed in the House but failed in the Senate. More importantly, the **Wilmot Proviso** signaled the start of an even deeper crisis that would pit the North against the South over issues of slavery, states' rights, and representation.

THE MEXICAN CESSION

After quick, decisive military victories in California and Texas, the Mexican War was basically over by September of 1847. California had been declared independent as the **Bear Flag Republic** under the leadership of John C. Fremont, and Texas had been gained as the United States successfully overtook Mexico City. A peace was settled by the **Treaty of Guadalupe Hidalgo** in February 1848. The treaty granted California and most of the Southwest (current day New Mexico, Arizona, Utah, and Nevada) to the United States. The American government agreed to pay war reparations in the sum of 15 million dollars to the Mexican government. After bitter debate over the expansion of slavery, the treaty was ratified and the war officially over.

The Treaty of Guadalupe Hidalgo (1848) was essentially to Mexican War what

Treaty of Paris (1783?) was to American Revolution

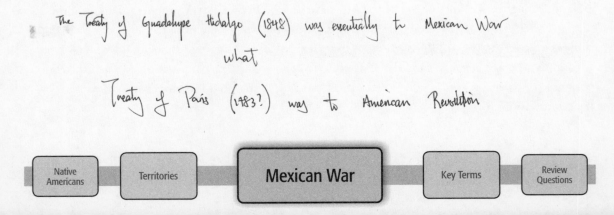

KEY TERMS	
Names	Sam Houston
	James K. Polk
Groups	Bear Flag Republic
Documents and Laws	Wilmot Proviso
	Treaty of Guadalupe Hidalgo
	Webster-Ashburton Treaty
Places	Oregon Trail
Vocabulary	mandate

REVIEW QUESTIONS

1. Believers in "manifest destiny" would have likely been

    (A) Northern Whigs.

    (B) transcendentalists.

    (C) New England merchants.

    (D) members of the Liberty Party.

    (E) supporters of Tyler and Polk.

2. Presidents Jackson and Van Buren hesitated pushing the annexation of Texas because

    (A) each needed the support of the South to further policy.

    (B) possible backlash from northern Democrats would hurt them politically.

    (C) they wished to maintain diplomatic relations with Mexico.

    (D) they had no desire to expand beyond the Mississippi.

    (E) there was no money to support the new territory.

3. The most important issue facing the country during the election of 1844 was

    (A) the Bank War.

    (B) economic depression.

    (C) the Oregon Territory.

    (D) removal of Native Americans.

    (E) removal of high tariffs.

4. The Mexican War resulted in

    (A) closer diplomatic relations between the United States and Mexico.

    (B) a decline in tensions over the expansion of slavery.

    (C) the annexation of Texas.

    (D) the U.S. acquisition of California and territories in the southwest.

    (E) increased feelings of isolationism among most Americans.

5. The Wilmot Proviso

    (A) passed overwhelmingly in both houses.

    (B) promised Mexicans payment of war reparations.

    (C) was supported by Democrats.

    (D) forbade slavery in the Mexican cession.

    (E) ended the Aroostook War.

ANSWERS AND EXPLANATIONS

1. E

Presidents Tyler and Polk both pushed for annexation of new territories, with Polk willing to engage in a war with Mexico to ensure the possession of Texas and California. Northerners, transcendentalists, and abolitionists were all staunchly opposed to territorial expansion, as they saw it as an attempt to expand slavery.

2. B

Presidents Jackson and Van Buren were both proponents of expansion. However they also understood the delicate balance between slave and free states in the Senate. Each needed Northern support for various measures and could not risk losing it by accepting a new slave territory into the Union.

3. C

"Fifty-four forty or fight!" was the cry during the election of 1844 where James K. Polk vowed to take all of the Oregon territory from the British or wage war to win it. Polk won the election on a ticket that promised a fulfillment of manifest destiny.

4. D

The Mexican government ceded California and the territory that now makes up the states of Arizona, New Mexico, Utah, and Nevada to the United States under the Treaty of Guadalupe-Hidalgo in 1848. Texas had already been annexed by the United States back in 1846. Mexicans held a deep resentment for Americans for some time after the war. As Americans were emboldened by their victory, they sought other opportunities for expansion, which further fueled the tensions over slavery.

5. D

Introduced by Northern Whig David Wilmot, the amendment to an appropriations bill passed twice in the House but failed in the Senate. As written, the bill would have forbidden slavery in any territory gained from the Mexican War. For the most part, Democrats wished for further expansion, with or without slavery.

CHAPTER 15: A TENUOUS BALANCE— ON THE BRINK OF CIVIL WAR, 1848–1860

THE MORALITY OF SLAVERY

In 1853, President **Franklin Pierce** rounded out the Mexican cession by signing the **Gadsden Purchase** with Mexico, which transferred to the United States the Mesilla Valley in the southernmost desert region of New Mexico and Arizona. As he did so, however, the controversy over the institution of slavery began to rage in Washington, D.C., and all over the nation. The discussion was political, social, economic, and for many, moral.

After the Second Great Awakening, *abolitionists* spoke out about the evils of slavery in both the North and the South. After Nat Turner's Rebellion, however, some Southerners changed their tune by expressing concern over what the nation would do with the sudden release of "uncivilized" slaves. Pro-slavery advocates in the South began to lash back at their Northern opponents by defending the "peculiar institution." Some *apologists* used passages from the Bible to justify the captivity of African Americans in bondage, while others extolled the "familylike" atmosphere slave owners provided for their slaves as being preferable to even freedom. A large movement of apologists, led by **George Fitzhugh**, spoke of the happy lives of Southern slaves who were clothed, fed, and housed by benevolent slave owners. Fitzhugh argued in his book *Cannibals All* (1857) that African-American slaves were much better off than the "Northern wage slave," who did not have basic living needs provided for him and his family.

THE FIRST ATTEMPTS AT COMPROMISE

The election of 1848 brought a third party into the political arena, encouraged by the Wilmot Proviso. The so-called "**Free-Soil**" **Party** was made up of antislavery advocates from all political parties. Its campaign slogan was "Free soil, free speech, free labor, and free men." The party held some of the same beliefs of the old Whigs (e.g., Clay's "American System"),but opposed the expansion of slavery in total. The Free-Soilers nominated Martin Van Buren as their candidate to run against the Whig Zachary Taylor and the Democrat Lewis Cass. Cass had gained national attention with his proposal of **popular sovereignty** with regard to the issue of slavery in the

Slavery — Compromise — Kansas-Nebraska Act — Lincoln — South Secedes

territories. He proposed that citizens of a territory should decide by vote whether or not slavery would be permitted. Taylor defeated Cass, as Northern Democratic votes in the crucial state of New York went to the Free Soil Party.

With the discovery of gold in 1848 and the massive influx of **49ers** into the west to find their fortune, California quickly drafted a new constitution to gain statehood. The constitution forbade slavery, which would again alter the sectional balance in the Senate. Even though Taylor was an advocate of slavery, he did understand the importance of adding California, and hopefully New Mexico, to the Union. His support of adding these free states sparked debate in Congress. Radical Southerners warned of possible secession, even going as far as meeting in Nashville to hatch their plans.

CLAY SEEKS COMPROMISE AGAIN

"The Great Compromiser" Henry Clay again came to the rescue with a plan to avert a national crisis. His compromise plan would admit California as a free state, divide the Mexican cession into the New Mexico and Utah Territories with popular sovereignty serving as the basis for determining slave status, ban the slave trade in Washington, D.C., enact a stricter **Fugitive Slave Law**, and give Texas monetary compensation for that state's willingness to forgo its claims to part of New Mexico's territory.

Debate ensued quickly, as the "Great Triumvirate" of Clay, Calhoun, and Webster led the way with impassioned speeches on the floor of the Senate, with Calhoun in opposition and Clay and Webster in support of compromise. Calhoun argued that this was a states' rights issue, not a moral issue, and the federal government had no right to intervene. Webster argued that compromise might just save the Union and urged his fellow Northerners to be more conciliatory.

However, it seemed that a compromise might not be feasible. Northern radical William H. Seward argued that slavery should be banned on moral grounds, and President Taylor turned against any talk of compromise with the South. The compromise looked to be all but moot until the sudden death of President Taylor due to cholera. Vice President Millard Fillmore took the presidency and helped to usher in the compromise bill. The young Senator Stephen A. Douglas was able to break apart the compromise bill and garner enough votes to get each piece separately passed by the Senate. As each piece was passed, President Fillmore stood by to sign it into law.

The Compromise of 1850, in effect, "bought time" for the Union. The North actually fared a bit better—it gained the political upper hand with the admission of California as a free state and time to grow economically. However the strict Fugitive Slave Law and the concept of popular sovereignty became troublesome. Many Northerners were staunchly opposed to any enforcement

Temporary fix to large problem

Early 1830s-ish

of a law designed to re-enslave those *fugitives* who had made it to freedom. In addition, the new law denied legal rights to captured blacks and sentenced whites who harbored fugitives to heavy fines or jail time. An Underground Railroad was established by abolitionists, both black and white, to assist slaves in escaping to freedom in either the Northern United States or Canada.

Catalyst in the chemical reaction
North + South → Conflict

The harshness of this new law encouraged the daughter of a Northern abolitionist to write a novel chronicling the cruelty of slavery. **Harriet Beecher Stowe** wrote *Uncle Tom's Cabin* in 1852. The novel quickly gained fame in the North and scorn from the South. In essence, the Compromise of 1850 and *Uncle Tom's Cabin* galvanized more Northerners to believe that slavery was morally wrong, while Southerners grew in their conviction to protect it.

THE KANSAS-NEBRASKA ACT

The election of 1852 brought Democrat Franklin Pierce to the office of president and the Whig party one step closer to the grave. The Whigs had decided to run a campaign that ignored the issue of slavery altogether. They discovered that the sectional crisis could not be ignored. Another factor that would serve to challenge the tenuous balance was a united government—the Democrats had control of both the executive and legislative branches.

A NEW PARTY IS BORN

Brain-father of the Kansas-Nebraska Act

Illinois Senator Stephen A. Douglas came to the forefront once again with his proposal to divide the Nebraska Territory into two regions—Nebraska and Kansas. Much as with Cass's proposal back in 1848, the slavery issue would be decided by the citizens of the territory—popular sovereignty—with Nebraska presumably becoming a free state and Kansas a slave state. Douglas's motivation was not political as much as it was economic—he desired to give his state the eastern terminus for the transcontinental railroad, which needed Southern support for its passage. Thus, he introduced a bill that would garner their support in another way. Because both Kansas and Nebraska lay above the 36° 30' line of demarcation as stipulated by the Missouri Compromise, his bill could theoretically open these lands to slavery. In effect, passage of his bill would mean the repeal of the Missouri Compromise of 1820. With his great skills of oratory, Douglas was able to push his bill through both houses. It was signed into law by President Pierce in 1854.

Main source of controversy

The Kansas-Nebraska Act actually rekindled much controversy that had been quieted by the Compromise of 1850. By repealing the Missouri Compromise, Northern Democrats believed that the Union had "sold out" to the South with regard to the slavery issue. A new political party emerged due to the renewed sectional tension whose ranks included Whigs, Democrats, Free-Soilers, and Know-Nothings, all from either the North or west. The new **Republican Party** was opposed to the expansion of slavery and the Kansas-Nebraska Act. Despite losing the election of 1856 to the Democrat James Buchanan, the Republicans made a great showing by running the exciting Californian John Fremont, who managed to win 11 of 16 free states in the Electoral College.

Parties Now
Whig
Democrat
Free-Soiler
Know-Nothing
Republican

| Slavery | Compromise | Kansas-Nebraska Act | Lincoln | South Secedes |

Essentially - conflict broke out in Kansas between pro-slavery and abolition over whether or not Kansas would be slave state

VIOLENCE IN KANSAS AND IN CONGRESS

Before the election, violence had erupted as Douglas's popular sovereignty concept was put to the test in Kansas. Little did anyone suspect that pro-slavery farmers from nearby Missouri would settle small areas along the border to vote in the election that would determine the slavery issue for Kansas. As Northerners learned of the Missourians or "**border ruffians**" setting up homesteads, they decided to fight back. Henry Ward Beecher and other abolitionists paved the way for antislavery settlers to travel and set up home in Kansas. It was not long before fighting broke out between the pro- and antislavery factions. The region earned the name **Bleeding Kansas**.

≈1856

The Missourians traveled across the border to Lecompton, Kansas, organized a pro-slavery government, and drafted a constitution that cleared the way for statehood. The constitution would only allow citizens to vote for the document with or without slavery. If citizens voted for no slavery, the rights of slaveholders in the territory were already protected. Federally, President Buchanan supported the **Lecompton Constitution**, which Douglas and others in the Senate loudly opposed. It was decided to remit the constitution back to Kansas for a revote. The antislavery factions refused to recognize the compromise re-ote by creating their own legislature in Topeka, Kansas. Unfortunately, as the politicos were busy arguing, violence escalated. In 1856, a band of armed border ruffians attacked the Free-Soil town of Lawrence, Kansas, killing two people and burning down buildings. In retaliation, fierce abolitionist John Brown and a band of followers savagely attacked a series of farms along Pottawatomie Creek, slashing five people to death.

TENSION IN CONGRESS LEADS TO VIOLENCE

All was not quiet on Capitol Hill either, as abolitionist Senator Charles Sumner spoke of the injustice in Kansas and in the process defamed the name of South Carolina Senator Andrew Butler. South Carolina Congressman Preston Brooks, who happened to be Butler's nephew, was so enraged that he beat Sumner over the head with his gold tipped cane some 30 times, nearly killing him. Even though many in the Senate were outraged by Brooks's actions, the Senate failed to censure or remove him from office.

Dred Scott case: 1857 ↑ *might be useful to remember*

DRED SCOTT DIVIDES THE NATION

The Supreme Court under Chief Justice Roger Taney added fuel to the already raging debate on March 6, 1857. In ***Dred Scott v. Sanford***, the Court ruled the 36°30' provision of the Missouri Compromise was unconstitutional and that all African Americans were not citizens, thus making them ineligible to sue in federal court. Dred Scott was a slave who had lived with his first master in Missouri and was then moved after his master's death to Wisconsin and Illinois for five years. Scott then returned to Missouri. Financed by Northern abolitionists, Dred Scott sued his master by claiming that the years he had lived in free territory made him a free man, even though he

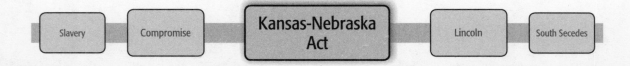

Slavery — Compromise — **Kansas-Nebraska Act** — Lincoln — South Secedes

was currently living in a slave state. In his 22-page ruling, Taney made it clear that the Founding Fathers had never had any intention of giving African Americans any protections of citizenship under the U.S. Constitution and, therefore, Scott had no right to sue in federal court. The opinion also explained that Congress had no right to infringe on citizen's right to due process—in other words, an individual's property could not be denied him under the U.S. Constitution. Therefore, the Missouri Compromise of 1820, which forbade slavery north of the 36° 30' line, was unconstitutional because it stripped slave owners of their rightful property once they moved northward. Both Democrat and Republican Northerners were horrified by the decision, while Southerners were thrilled. The decision served to create a further rift between the regions.

JOHN BROWN AND HARPER'S FERRY · figured in Bleeding Kansas

John Brown of the Pottawatomie Creek massacre again entered national headlines, as he and his followers staged a raid on the federal arsenal at **Harper's Ferry**, Virginia. Brown, claiming he was following orders from God, hoped to arm slaves in the surrounding plantations to overthrow the whites and create a free black state. In October 1859, Brown and his gang seized the arsenal and managed to hold off the Virginia militia for two days. They were finally captured, tried for treason, and hanged. In the North, John Brown was hailed by some abolitionists as a martyr due to his conviction that his actions were guided by a higher moral purpose. In the South, Brown was labeled as a dangerous psychotic who was acting at the behest of Northern abolitionists. In response, Southerners formed citizens' militias designed to counteract possible slave uprisings and became more suspicious of the North's intentions.

THE RISE OF LINCOLN AND THE ELECTION OF 1860

Republican Abraham Lincoln was not a household name until the Illinois Senate election of 1858, which pitted the country lawyer against the powerful Democrat Stephen A. Douglas for the coveted seat. Lincoln was an eloquent orator and moderate who challenged his opponent to a series of public debates, which he hoped would garner both local and national attention from the press. The most celebrated debate occurred in the town of Freeport, Illinois, where Lincoln challenged Douglas to defend the concept of popular sovereignty under the *Dred Scott* decision. In what historians call his **Freeport Doctrine**, Douglas responded that communities would have to pass and enforce laws to protect the institution of slavery for it to exist. His doctrine caused an even deeper division within the Democratic party, as Southerners felt he had not done enough to support the *Dred Scott* decision. While his popular sovereignty stance won him the senatorial seat, Douglas injured his chances of winning the presidency in the election of 1860. The debates did, however, bring the "unknown" Lincoln into the spotlight as the possible Republican hopeful for the next presidential election.

As the nominating conventions for the election of 1860 were underway, most Americans were of the opinion that the Union was on the verge of breaking apart. Most contentious was the

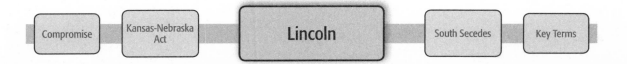

Democratic convention, where Southerners walked out in protest over the nomination of Stephen A. Douglas, whom they considered a traitor. As they tried to reconvene and reconcile, it was clear that the party would not be able to nominate a single candidate for president. In the end, the Democratic party split in two—Northerners nominated Stephen A. Douglas, and Southerners chose moderate John C. Breckinridge. The Republicans decided against the nomination of the radical William H. Seward and chose instead the moderate orator Abraham Lincoln. Aside from choosing Lincoln, the party also chose to adopt a broad platform that would appeal to a wide spectrum of voters. In addition to the nonextension of slavery into the territories, the platform also promised a protective tariff, rights for immigrants, a transcontinental railroad, federally financed infrastructure improvements for the west, and free homesteads for citizens out of publicly held land. The Southern Democrats warned that they would leave the Union if Lincoln were elected president. A fourth party also joined the election as Know-Nothings. Whigs and moderates were concerned that a Lincoln victory would mean the end of the Union. **The Constitutional Union Party** chose John Bell of Tennessee as its candidate and hoped to pull enough votes from the Republicans to keep the cotton states of the South from seceding.

Abraham Lincoln only managed to earn about 40 percent of the popular vote; Breckinridge carried the South, and Douglas and Bell earned a scattering of votes. It was Lincoln's ability to carry states with large numbers of electoral votes that won him the election. Lincoln managed to win 180 electoral votes to Breckinridge's 72. Despite the fact that the South still maintained control of both the legislative and judicial branches, it still looked as if secession was just over the horizon.

THE SOUTH SECEDES

Just four days after the election results were tallied, the South Carolina legislature voted to secede from the Union. Within the next six weeks, six more Deep South states decided to join South Carolina. A meeting of these states was called in February 1861 to form the **Confederate States of America**, with Jefferson Davis named as their president.

In a final attempt at compromise, Kentucky Senator John Crittenden proposed an amendment to the Constitution that would have protected the right of slave owners to hold their property below the 36°30' line and instituted popular sovereignty in any new states. President-elect Lincoln rejected the compromise, as it was in opposition to the Republican Party platform, which had called for the nonextension of slavery.

Crittenden Compromise

Southerners felt leaving the Union was morally and politically justified—the states had voluntarily entered into the Union to begin with and had every right to leave it. Based on the writings of John Locke and the American Revolutionaries, Southerners spoke of their responsibility and right to overthrow a government that no longer protected the rights of its citizens to life, liberty, and property. The South also drew upon the writings of Jefferson and Madison in the Kentucky and Virginia Resolutions, as well as the speeches delivered by South Carolina's John C. Calhoun with regard to nullification and the strength of Union. Southerners felt that these writings further supported their right to secede. The South was banking on the premise that the North would allow it to leave the Union quietly, since the regions were already practically independent of one another. The South did not take the strength of Union into account.

KEY TERMS	
Names	Harriet Beecher Stowe George Fitzburgh John Brown
Groups	apologists Free-Soil Party 49ers Republican Party border ruffians Constitutional Union Party Confederate States of America
Documents and Laws	Gadsden Purchase Fugitive Slave Law The Compromise of 1850 The Kansas-Nebraska Act Lecompton Constitution *Dred Scott v. Sanford* Freeport Doctrine
Places	Bleeding Kansas Harper's Ferry
Vocabulary	popular sovereignty

REVIEW QUESTIONS

1. The concept of popular sovereignty involved

    (A) squatters' rights to free land in the west.

    (B) the open sale of land in the Mexican cession.

    (C) removal of Native Americans from the Great Plains.

    (D) the enforcement of fugitive slave laws.

    (E) territorial citizens choosing whether their region would be slave or free.

2. The Compromise of 1850 was most controversial because

    (A) it overturned the Missouri Compromise.

    (B) of the stricter fugitive slave law.

    (C) it contained provisions for the slave trade in Washington, D.C..

    (D) of internal improvement funds for the west.

    (E) of popular sovereignty in the Mexican cession.

3. Aside from the violence, the effects of "Bleeding Kansas" included

    (A) the *Dred Scott* decision.

    (B) a return to the old 36°30′ line for free and slave states.

    (C) a deeper division within the Democratic Party.

    (D) the rebirth of the Whig Party.

    (E) calls for immediate emancipation of slaves.

4. Despite being made up of members from various other parties, the Republicans held firm in their belief that

    (A) slavery was morally wrong.

    (B) popular sovereignty was the proper course of action.

    (C) the South had the right to leave the Union.

    (D) slavery should not be extended into the territories.

    (E) the *Dred Scott* decision was justified by the Constitution.

5. The South's decision to secede from the Union was

    (A) precipitated by the election of Lincoln to the presidency.

    (B) expressly permitted under the U.S. Constitution .

    (C) quietly allowed by Republicans.

    (D) joined immediately by most of the Southern states.

    (E) led by Stephen A. Douglas.

ANSWERS AND EXPLANATIONS

1. E

Cass, and later Douglas, would champion the notion of popular sovereignty to obtain Southern support for a railroad bill. The concept placed the status of slavery in the hands of citizens of a territory.

2. B

Northern abolitionists were most deeply concerned over the passage and enforcement of the new fugitive slave law that was part of the Compromise of 1850. As a result, antislave literature, such as *Uncle Tom's Cabin*, and the Underground Railroad shifted more Northerners to the belief that slavery was morally wrong.

3. C

As antislave Northerners flocked to Kansas to combat pro-slavery "border ruffians," the rift between Northern and Southern Democrats began to widen. Southerners were convinced that Northerners were seeking to destroy their way of life, while Northerners felt that Southerners were messing with popular sovereignty. The caning of Charles Sumner by Preston Brooks took a further toll on the relationship of party members.

4. D

Part of the broad appeal of the Republican platform was its stance regarding the nonextension of slavery into the territories. Not all Republicans agreed upon the moral nature of slavery or the effectiveness of popular sovereignty.

5. A

Southerners warned that the election of Lincoln to the presidency would signal their departure from the Union. They were not kidding, as four days after his election, South Carolina became the first Deep South state to vote to secede. By the end of 1860, six more Deep South states had joined with South Carolina, paving the way for Civil War.

CHAPTER 16: THE CIVIL WAR, 1861–1865

TWO REGIONS AT WAR

Before the first shots were fired upon the Union stronghold of Fort Sumter near Charleston, South Carolina, in April 1861, the North and the South had already become distinctly different regions within the same continent. Now that each region was making preparations for war, it became evident that each had to take advantage of its strengths and exploit the weaknesses of the enemy.

ADVANTAGES AND DISADVANTAGES OF EACH REGION

Militarily, the Confederates only had to fight a defensive war on their own territory to a draw; thus, they required fewer troops overall. That, combined with intense troop morale, highly trained generals, and very few landlocked regions, gave the South an advantage at the beginning of the war. The Union, on the other hand, was waging an offensive war in which the goal was to destroy the South and eventually occupy the region. This required many more men and munitions that needed to be moved long distances to the front lines.

However, the sheer size of the North's population gave it an early advantage that would be bolstered by an influx of immigrants and the emancipation of slaves who would join the war effort on the side of the Union. In the 10 years between the Compromise of 1850 and the outbreak of war, the North's economy had grown in both the industrial and financial sectors. Northerners controlled the nation's banks, railroads, and factories, essentially blocking the South from the rest of the world with regard to trade. The Union still had to levy the first-ever income tax to pay for the war. It raised excise taxes, raised a previously low protective tariff, and issued *greenbacks* in place of gold as the wartime currency.

Largely *agrarian*, the South was at a distinct disadvantage with regard to access to basic resources needed to wage an effective war. As the war dragged on, Confederate soldiers were lacking basic needs such as shoes, blankets, and clothing. Because of the east-west network of railroad lines linking the North to the west, once Southern termini were destroyed by Union forces, the Confederates had limited means to transport men, supplies, or goods for manufacture. The

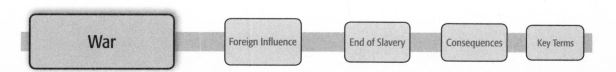

South had been banking on the worldwide demand for cotton to keep it afloat during the war and had even hoped for foreign assistance. This was not to be, however, as the French and British saw alliance with the Confederates as a liability for a future relationship with the United States, and worldwide demand for cotton plunged in the mid-1860s. As a result, the Confederates had to issue a large number of bonds to pay for the war, raise duties on farm goods, and eventually overprint their paper currency, causing rampant inflation.

FINDING SOLDIERS TO FIGHT

The largest expression of dissent among Northerners and Southerners came when it was time to raise the forces that would actually fight the war. Desertion was common on both sides of the firing lines. The Union army originally consisted of almost purely volunteers. As the pool of volunteers began to dwindle, the Union enacted the first federal *conscription* law to draft young men to military service in 1863. The draft caused dissension in many areas of the North but none so violent as the **New York Draft Riots**, sparked by angry Irish-Americans. In the end, some 500 people were killed, and whole city blocks were destroyed by fire. There were some black soldiers in the North early in the war; those numbers increased after the issuance of the Emancipation Proclamation.

The South relied on volunteers to fill its ranks, as well. With a smaller population to draw from, the Confederacy had to enact conscription a year earlier than the North. Class and regional divisions were much more evident in the South, as wealthy plantation owners were able to purchase the services of others to serve for them. Appalachian "hillbillies" refused to serve. Fear of arming slaves kept the Confederacy from using blacks until the war was almost at an end.

DISSENSION IN BORDER STATES AND CONGRESS

Abraham Lincoln was deeply aware of the tenuous relationship between the North and the Border States and the military necessity of keeping the Border States in the Union. Delaware, Maryland, Missouri, and Kentucky each decided to remain in the Union, despite their slave-holding status. This is not to say that there were not citizens in these states who were opposed to the "War of Northern Aggression." Citizen's militia groups sympathetic to the Confederate cause were active during the course of the war and had to be kept in check by Union forces. Dissent was also evident within the aisles of Congress. Speaking of the "unjust" nature of the war and their concern over the disruption of western trade routes, the **Copperheads** lashed out at President Lincoln's broad use of executive power and demanded an immediate end to the war. Despite the heated debate, Lincoln continued to flex the muscles of the executive branch throughout the war.

War   Foreign Influence   End of Slavery   Consequences   Key Terms

MILITARY ENGAGEMENT AND FOREIGN INFLUENCE

The Union hoped first to strike the state of Virginia quickly and deal the Confederacy a mortal blow. However, the Union military leadership miscalculated the tenacity and drive with which the Confederates would fight back. The first major battle of the Civil War would force the North to realize that this was going to be a long, bitter fight.

THE UNION HATCHES A PLAN

In July 1861, federal troops marched from Washington, D.C., to a position about 30 miles outside of the nation's capital. There at **Bull Run** (Manassas), Confederate troops stood at the ready for the oncoming attack. At the beginning, Union forces seemed to be gaining the upper hand. But more Confederate men led by General "Stonewall" Jackson soon arrived, sending the Union troops scrambling back to D.C. The North was now awakened to the harsh reality that this was going to be a long and bloody war. Southerners, on the other hand, emboldened by their ability to send the "Blues" scrambling back in retreat, grew complacent.

It was back to the drawing board for Union leadership, with General Winfield Scott at the helm. Scott drew up a four-phase plan to wear down the Confederacy gradually. The first phase was dubbed the **Anaconda Plan**, in which the Union Navy would blockade all Southern ports of entry, cutting them off from supplies and trade. The second phase involved splitting the Confederacy in half by taking control of the Mississippi River. Third, the Union needed to cut through the heart of the South by marching through Georgia, then snaking up the southeast coast to the Carolinas. The last phase involved capturing the Confederate capital at Richmond and routing the last of the "Grays."

THE SECOND BATTLE OF BULL RUN AND ANTIETAM

President Lincoln's patience was wearing thin, as eastern Union commander General McClellan refused to send untrained men into battle. Finally, he launched his troops into the peninsula region of Virginia in March 1862, only to be sent reeling by the military genius of Confederate General **Robert E. Lee**. As Union leadership in the east was being changed, General Lee took advantage of the lull by engaging Union troops again at Manassas in the **Second Battle of Bull Run**. This time, it was Union General John Pope who was sent scurrying back across the Potomac in retreat.

Now with two decisive victories under his belt and hopes that a third win would bring foreign aid, Lee led his men into enemy territory to Maryland. With McClellan back in command of the Union forces and advance knowledge of Confederate battle plans, Union forces were able to cut Lee off at **Antietam** Creek. The bloodiest day of the war ensued, as more than 22,000 men were lost or wounded. Lee's men, unable to break Union resolve, were forced to retreat to Virginia. However, General McClellan failed to pursue the retreating Confederates, enraging President Lincoln. Lincoln promptly relieved him from his command for the last time and replaced him with General Ambrose Burnside.

War | Foreign Influence | End of Slavery | Consequences | Key Terms

A TURNING POINT

The September 1862 fight at Antietam was a turning point of the war—it kept the Confederates from gaining much-needed foreign assistance from Britain and France. In addition, President Lincoln now had the "victory" he had been waiting for. He promptly issued his preliminary Emancipation Proclamation on September 23, 1862.

IRONCLADS ENTER THE WAR

Union General Burnside was much more aggressive than McClellan had been; however, this was not necessarily an asset for the North. At the Battle of Fredericksburg in December of 1862, Lee successfully defeated Burnside, who was subsequently replaced by General Joseph Hooker. Aside from land battles, 1862 also saw a revolution in naval warfare with the launching of the "**ironclads**." The South's CSS *Merrimac*, touted as a ship that could sink wooden naval ships with one blast, proceeded to pose a huge threat to the Union blockade. The Confederates had not, however, banked on the Union having its own version of the "ironclad," named the USS *Monitor*. In a five-hour skirmish in March 1862, the ironclads slowly shot each other to a draw. No longer would the United States depend on wooden ships in her navy.

CONTROL OF THE MISSISSIPPI AND GETTYSBURG

The war in the west was focused on the battle over control of the mighty Mississippi River. Union General **Ulysses S. Grant** was able to cut his way through Kentucky and Tennessee, fighting a bloody battle at Shiloh in April 1862. By the spring of 1863, Grant controlled the port city of New Orleans and almost all of the Mississippi River region. To complete the removal of the Confederates, Grant launched an attack on Vicksburg, Mississippi. Union forces lay siege for seven weeks to the fortified city in another turning point for the Union. It now controlled the length of the Mississippi River and the surrounding regions.

In 1863, the third year of war, Generals Lee and Jackson were still managing to keep their men fighting vigorously in the eastern United States. General Jackson's men successfully defeated Union General Hooker at Chancellorsville by flanking Northern forces. Unfortunately for the Confederates, General Jackson was killed by friendly fire in the battle. Despite the victory, the Confederates suffered great losses of some 13,000 men. In a last-ditch effort to invade the North, garner the attention of foreign supporters, and perhaps force the Union to sue for peace, General Lee launched an invasion of Pennsylvania while Union forces kept close tabs on the Confederates. The two huge armies converged at the small town of **Gettysburg** in southern Pennsylvania. The deadliest and most important battle of the war ensued from July 1 to 3, 1863, where some 53,000 men were either killed or wounded. Lee could not recover from losses at Gettysburg and retreated to Virginia once again. The Confederates would not have another victory after Gettysburg.

War   **Foreign Influence**   End of Slavery   Consequences   Key Terms

SHERMAN CONTRIBUTES TO UNION VICTORIES

General Grant chose William Tecumseh Sherman to lead Union troops through the South.
After winning the battle of Kennesaw Mountain in Georgia, Sherman's army captured Atlanta in
September of 1864, but not before the Confederates had burned the city in retreat. Marching with
some 100,000 men after winning the battle of Atlanta, Sherman cut a 60-mile swath through the
heart of the South on his way to South Carolina. Sherman's "**scorched-earth**" policy ordered troops
to burn and destroy fields, homes, and cities as they marched through Georgia. Sherman's goal was
to inflict such misery on Southerners that they would be compelled to surrender. This strategy made
the Civil War perhaps the first "modern war" in that civilians and their property became targets.
Sherman was able to capture Savannah, Georgia, in December 1864 and finally Columbia, South
Carolina, in February of 1865. By this time, Grant's forces in Virginia were on the verge of victory.

SOUTHERN SURRENDER AND AN ASSASSINATION

Lee's troop strength was wearing thin by the time his army abandoned the Confederate capital
of Richmond, Virginia, in April 1865. Knowing that the end was near, Confederate leaders
wished to negotiate with President Lincoln for peace terms. Lincoln refused anything short of an
unconditional surrender of the South and a restoration of the Union; Jefferson Davis still clung to
the dream of Southern independence. General Lee, surrounded by General Grant's forces west of
Richmond, agreed to surrender. On April 9, 1865, the Confederate Army of Northern Virginia
officially surrendered on the steps in front of **Appomattox Court House**. Tragically, President
Lincoln could only relish the Union's victory for less than a week. He was assassinated by Southern
sympathizer **John Wilkes Booth** on April 14, 1865, while sitting in Ford's Theatre.

THE END OF SLAVERY AND FREE BLACKS

Ever the savvy politician, Abraham Lincoln had been extremely cautious with regard to the issue of
slavery. As president, Lincoln was a master at gauging the pulse of public opinion and reacting to
it accordingly. Therefore, he understood that he needed to connect with Border States, prejudiced
Northerners, and all walks of American voters. He calculated the timing of his speeches and
enactments to coincide with the waves of public opinion and military victories.

In the first years of the war, the federal government passed Confiscation Acts designed to allow Union
troops to seize enemy property that could be used in an act of war. Slaves fit under the loose terms
of "property" and could, thus, be confiscated. The second of these acts freed slaves in any territory
currently in rebellion against the Union. This was the first step in the emancipation of slaves.

After the Battle of Antietam in September 1862, President Lincoln properly calculated that the nation
was ready for a shift from an "offensive war" to save the Union to a "total war" to rectify a moral wrong.
As promised after Antietam, the president issued the **Emancipation Proclamation** on January 1,
1863. The proclamation only applied to slaves living in Confederate states; slavery in the Border States
was still legal. Despite its limitations, the proclamation did much to bolster the morale of Union troops

War | Foreign Influence | **End of Slavery** | Consequences | Key Terms

and supporters at home. But it was not without its critics. Many in the North, particularly those in the Border States, felt that Lincoln had gone too far. Moreover, many Irish soldiers in the Union army felt betrayed by the proclamation, believing they had been duped into fighting a war for emancipation instead of merely for the Union's preservation. This discontent resulted in the New York Draft riots. Nonetheless, the next great step toward emancipation had been taken.

The only remaining obstacle to freedom for slaves was the Constitution. Since its ratification, interpretations of the document either ignored the slavery issue or protected the institution and slave owners. President Lincoln would need an amendment to the Constitution to realize fully the Emancipation Proclamation and offer freedom to the slaves in the Border States. The president worked tirelessly to garner enough votes in Congress to secure passage of what would become the **Thirteenth Amendment**. Sadly, President Lincoln was assassinated before he would see the amendment, which abolished slavery in the United States once and for all, ratified.

Even before the ratification of the Thirteenth Amendment, thousands of "**freedmen**" had flocked to the North in search of refuge. Many joined the Union Army, serving in segregated units, while others worked in supporting jobs along the battlefields. In fact, President Lincoln eventually credited the 180,000 African Americans who fought for the Union as having turned the tide of the war. The South simply could not compete with the overwhelming manpower of the Union Army. However, not until after the war's end were full-scale efforts were made to assimilate former slaves into American society.

SOCIAL, POLITICAL, AND ECONOMIC CONSEQUENCES OF THE WAR

No part of America was left untouched, as a war of "brother against brother" had raged on for four long and bloody years. The North and the South lost the equivalent of a generation of able young men to death and injury, a loss that would take many years to recover from. About 2 percent of the American population, or 620,000 men, had lost their lives in the war. Over a million others had been wounded.

During and after the war, the plight of poverty became feminized, as many women suddenly became heads of the household due to the death or desertion of husbands. With men away fighting, women found themselves working the fields and in factories as well as at home. Women played a critical role on the battlefield as nurses and as volunteers in veterans' hospitals. The Civil War opened doors for women and would give many the courage to fight for suffrage rights at the turn of the 20th century.

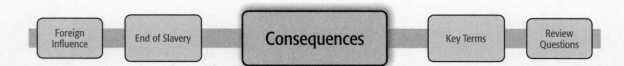

Foreign Influence   End of Slavery   Consequences   Key Terms   Review Questions

IMMEDIATE CONSEQUENCES

In 1865, the United States gained about 4 million new citizens instantly. With the ratification of the Thirteenth Amendment, these newly freed African Americans now had to find a place in the American social structure.

Southern whites came to the realization that their way of life would be forever altered and struggled to find peace among the chaos.

During the Civil War, President Lincoln exercised his power as the executive to limit Americans' civil rights and liberties to protect the Union. He suspended the *writ of habeas corpus*, which meant that the federal government could hold an individual in jail with no charges levied against him or her. For many "traitors," this meant long jail terms with no charges ever filed. Even though Lincoln suspended this guaranteed Constitutional right, he planned for it to be restored as soon as the war was over.

The major long-term effect of the Civil War was the shift of political ideology from one that protected states' rights to one that emphasized the preservation of Union and the supremacy of the federal government. The concept of "democracy" was altered, as new African American citizens were guaranteed the rights and protections of the Constitution that whites had enjoyed since 1789. Much to the chagrin of many conservatives in Europe, the American experiment of democracy had survived a major challenge and looked more powerful than ever.

Economically, the war was devastating for the South—its infrastructure and industry stood in ruins. Jefferson's dream of an agrarian empire soon faded as the energy of the country shifted into industrializing the nation. During the recovery phase, many Northerners would move into the South to help the freedmen and to organize the Reconstruction of Southern governments.

Northerners experienced an industrial boom due to wartime demands for cheap manufactured goods. Many amassed great fortunes by profiteering off of highly priced necessities, while the average factory worker saw no improvement in standard of living. The west benefited from wartime acts designed to stimulate settlement into the frontier. **The Homestead Act of 1862** granted 160 acres to any family that would agree to farm it for at least five years. **The Morrill Land Grant Act of 1862** gave federal lands to states for the purpose of building schools that would teach agriculture and technical trades. Perhaps most significantly, the **Pacific Railway Act of 1862** approved the building of a transcontinental railroad that would utterly transform the west by linking the Atlantic Ocean with the Pacific.

While the Civil War left behind devastating losses in population, wealth, and land, the reunified United States would have a harrowing journey ahead, as the task of rebuilding the nation was at hand.

Foreign Influence | End of Slavery | Consequences | Key Terms | Review Questions

KEY TERMS	
Names	Robert E. Lee Ulysses S. Grant Abraham Lincoln John Wilkes Booth
Groups	Copperheads freedmen
Events	New York Draft Riots Bull Run Second Battle of Bull Run Antietam Gettysburg
Documents and Laws	Anaconda Plan Emancipation Proclamation Thirteenth Amendment The Homestead Act of 1862 The Morrill Land Grant of 1862 The Pacific Railway Act of 1862
Places	Appomattox Court House
Vocabulary	greenbacks ironclads scorched-earth writ of habeas corpus agrarian

REVIEW QUESTIONS

1. President Lincoln hesitated to free the slaves during the Civil War because

   (A) he believed in the institution of slavery.

   (B) he did not wish to drive the South to secede.

   (C) his party was discouraging emancipation.

   (D) he needed the support of the Border States.

   (E) many feared the arming of freed slaves.

2. The Emancipation Proclamation

   (A) immediately freed all slaves.

   (B) only freed slaves in Border States.

   (C) limited the executive's power of confiscation.

   (D) was well received by all Northerners.

   (E) shifted Northern war aims to a moral cause.

3. The Battle of Gettysburg was critical in that

   (A) General Lee was captured.

   (B) the Confederates would never again have a victory.

   (C) Ulysses S. Grant was able to take control of the Mississippi River.

   (D) the Confederates successfully crossed the Potomac River.

   (E) the port of New Orleans was closed to trade.

4. General Lee hoped to earn foreign assistance by

   (A) successfully invading the North.

   (B) emancipating the slaves.

   (C) keeping the cost of cotton low.

   (D) keeping Lincoln from re-election.

   (E) forming a strong central government.

5. Copperheads were

   (A) Northern merchants who sympathized with the South.

   (B) Northern Democrats who protested against the "unjust war."

   (C) Southern abolitionists.

   (D) British nationals who secretly assisted the Confederates.

   (E) Republicans who wished for a permanent split of North and South.

ANSWERS AND EXPLANATIONS

1. D

Abraham Lincoln understood the necessity of keeping the Border States within the Union for both political and military reasons. By not freeing the slaves too soon, Lincoln was able to obtain the passage of the Thirteenth Amendment, which legalized his Emancipation Proclamation, giving full emancipation to the nation's slave population.

2. E

Understanding the effect that the "victory" at Antietam would have on the Northern public, Lincoln chose to issue his Emancipation Proclamation to build on that sentiment and free all slaves in Confederate territory. This effectively made the Northerners feel as if they were fighting to right a moral wrong in addition to maintaining the Union.

3. B

Unfortunately for General Lee and his Confederate compatriots, the bloody Battle of Gettysburg signaled the end of their winning streak. Suffering great losses and unable to launch a strong enough flanking move, Lee was forced to retreat to Virginia.

4. A

Robert E. Lee hoped to gain foreign assistance after he attempted to invade the North through Pennsylvania at Gettysburg. As shown in question 3, Lee was not successful in his invasion and did not get the much-needed foreign aid.

5. B

Northern and western Democrats in Congress who wished for an end to what they deemed an "unjust war" were called Copperheads, after the poisonous snake of the same name, due to the "venom" they spit as they spoke. They did not approve of President Lincoln's broad use of executive power and called for an immediate end to the Civil War.

UNIT II SAMPLE ESSAYS

The following are sample free-response questions that you might see on the AP U.S. History exam. Listed under each question are important terms that would greatly add to your answer. AP Readers will look for you to mention at least several of the listed people, places, and things.

1. How did changes occurring due to the Market Revolution in the 1830s impact the social climate of the United States by 1840?

   Study List
   Jacksonian democracy
   Rise of the Common Man
   post–War of 1812 nationalism
   emerging "American" culture
   utopian societies
   Oneida
   Brook Farm
   Shakers
   Second Great Awakening
   rise of cities
   urbanization
   increase in immigration
   movement west

2. Historians disagree on whether the Civil War was "inevitable." Using your knowledge of the period 1820–1860, assess whether or not the Civil War could have been averted.

   Study List
   Missouri Compromise
   Compromise of 1850
   Kansas-Nebraska Act
   Ostend Manifesto
   filibustering expeditions
   Free-Soil Party
   manifest destiny
   popular sovereignty
   fireeaters
   Republican Party
   Wilmot Proviso
   Dred Scott decision
   abolitionism
   Liberty Party
   Abraham Lincoln
   Lincoln-Douglas debates
   nullification

SAMPLE FRQ RESPONSES

How did changes occurring due to the Market Revolution in the 1830s impact the social climate of the United States by 1840?

The Market Revolution of the 1830s was a time of great change in the American economic landscape. These economic changes led to significant social changes by 1840, especially in the areas of urbanization, religion, and an emerging "American" sociopolitical culture.

The Market Revolution led to technological and economic changes that affected all areas of the country. Improved transportation and immigration to the Northeast and Midwest led to the demise of the previous individuated artisan and yeoman economy and to the rise of cash-crop agriculture and manufacturing. Manufacturing spawned the rise of cities and an increase in urbanization, especially in the Northeast. The South's plantation-based economy was revitalized by a boom in the cotton industry. This led to increased settlement in the South. In the West, an increase in immigration was also seen, as more land was taken from Native Americans and Hispanics and turned over to new white settlers.

After the successful Second War of Independence against Britain in 1812, there was a distinct rise in nationalism. Through his victorious leadership in the Battle of New Orleans, Andrew Jackson (or "Old Hickory") became a well-known war hero and was elected president from 1829 to 1837. With the Market Revolution in the 1830s came a fear from those men not of the elite class that the economic boom would only benefit the minority of wealthy landowners and bankers. Jackson, a self-made man, came to power by championing the class concerns of the Common Man. He advocated that government be cleansed of elite cronyism and that more jobs be held as rotating positions. He also did not support large private bank monopolies. He wanted to dispose of the elitist Electoral College and championed equal rights for all white men and limited government. His everyman agenda tapped into the emerging American ideal that hard work would equal success in life and led to a greatly increased participation in politics by the common man, even as it led to opposition by 1840 from the newly formed Whig party.

The increased movement of people caused by the Market Revolution led to a destabilization of households and people looking for a new community to call home and a new faith to believe in. Out of this uncertainty, the Second Great Awakening, a period of skyrocketing interest in new religions and a proliferation of evangelism, was born. The religious groups of this time often founded what they considered utopian societies, where the members lived and worshiped communally. One new religious group was the Shakers, so named because they were seen shaking during their religious services. They believed in celibacy and communal living and became famous for the unique crafts their community produced. Another group was founded by John Humphrey Noyes, the leader of what he named in 1840 the Putney Association. This group was communist and believed in communal living and "complex marriages," where all men were married to all women in the community and vice versa. Women and men held equal levels of power

in the committees that governed the group. After being indicted for adultery, Noyes decided to establish a community for his followers in Oneida, New York. A third notable religious group was formed by George Ripley, a transcendentalist who established his utopian community at Brook Farm. They believed in engaging in physical activity, particularly manual labor, as a way to be closer to God. These new religious communities mark a notable change in American religious culture by 1840, where Americans were creating new faiths indigenous to America.

The Market Revolution in the 1830s did not solely affect the United States economically. With the economic changes it caused in Northeast and Midwest industry, Western expansion and settlement, and Southern cotton production came great population movement, rapid urbanization, and class-consciousness. Individuals like President Andrew Jackson used these changes to forge a political ideology that spoke to and excited common people and veered away from the elitist views often seen previously in government. Groups like the Shakers found that, through the new interest in religion the Second Great Awakening spawned, they could find followers and form new utopian societies that were different from the societies they had grown up in and were more of a reflection of their new world.

Historians disagree on whether or not the Civil War was "inevitable." Using your knowledge of the period 1820–1860, assess whether or not the Civil War could have been averted.

It was hard to believe in the mid-1800s that the United States was a country formed from the same source, a "united" force that had banded together to break apart from a mother country to form an independent nation. In the years leading up to the Civil War, the country was not a Union—it was cleanly and clearly divided into North and South, two areas with two wildly different ideologies. By 1860, tensions had risen to a boiling point, most notably over the issue of slavery. Due to a variety of laws and decrees, a highly contested court case decision, and the leadership of Abraham Lincoln, war was the only option for a nation under such stress and strain. Metaphorically, the balloon was blown up so tightly, it simply had to burst. The country's burst was the Civil War.

Of course, slavery was the main issue of contention between the North and the South. The agrarian South physically needed the manpower to work the fields in order to produce and maintain crops that were its main source of income. The North, on the other hand, had no real need for slaves. They saw the practice as cruel and unjust; the South saw slaves as their right. Perhaps their disagreement would not have been such a problem had westward expansion not been an issue. The South needed ensure that slavery was not blocked in any way through Congress. As long as the vote was split, this wasn't a problem. With new territories being added at a rapid pace, both North and South wanted to have claim over the type of government that would reign in these states. Missouri is the premier example, as it entered statehood at a time when the government was in balance. The answer to the North/South mini-fight over the state, Henry Clay's Missouri Compromise, called Missouri a slave state as long as Maine was a free state. The Compromise also outlawed slavery above the now-famed 36° 30′ line. Such a delicate

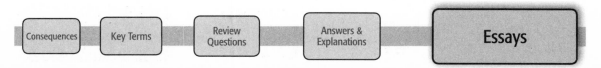

agreement paved the way for the possibility of more disagreements in the future. Missouri was an easy area of land to "agree to disagree" over. When the area expanded, so the scope of disagreement had to, as well.

Another government decision that began to pick at the unraveling threads of the Union was the Wilmot Proviso and the war with Mexico. Northerners were angry at possible false accusations that more blood had been shed than was truthful. The Proviso, which would have forbidden slavery in the land acquired in the war, angered Southerners, even when it was not passed. From the Wilmot Proviso forward, every iota of politics was saturated by slavery and its morality (or lack of). The Compromise of 1850 again attempted to balance government with the admittance of California as a free state and the proposal of popular sovereignty for the Mexican cession (among other stipulations). All seemed calm until the Kansas-Nebraska Act, which demanded the practice of popular sovereignty, even though the states lay above the 36° 30′ line. Issue after issue ruffled feathers, then was calmed, creating a dangerous cycle that could not go around and around forever. (Bleeding Kansas is an example of a mini-explosion that foreshadowed the Civil War). Furthermore, slavery for many seemed to exist more as a catchphrase and an idea rather than an actuality.

Dred Scott finally gave the intangible notion of slavery a face and a name, escalating the antislavery sentiments of the North so much that they were compelled to take action. His court decision was the point where war began to become inevitable. The notion that (a) the Missouri Compromise of 1820 was overturned and (b) an individual, because he was African American, had no right to protection and no right to sue (and was considered property) incensed Northerners.

Finally, the election of 1860 was the fight for president that easily led into the fight between North and South. Lincoln was brilliant, outspoken, and in his platform called for nonextension of slavery in the territories and rights for immigrants, in addition to many other progressive changes. Southern Democrats basically said that they would not live as members of a country where Lincoln was president, thus pushing further on the teetering union that threatened to fall. Lincoln won the electoral college, and days after, South Carolina led the movement to secession. Lincoln, as much as Dred Scot, put a face on every ideal that the South hated about the North. The North proudly wore Lincoln's face and ideals as their badge.

The righteousness that had led to a victory over the mother country the century before was still with proud Southerners. This was their country and this was how they wanted to run it. They learned from their ancestors the century before that if you are unhappy with something, work to change it. If things cannot be changed within the society where you exist, start a society of your own. Although ultimately unsuccessful, the South simply wanted to live life the way they wanted it. The States were a proud union based on self-motivation and initiative. These traits never disappeared, and so a war to determine the way their country was to be run was inevitable, given the various events of the mid-1800s.

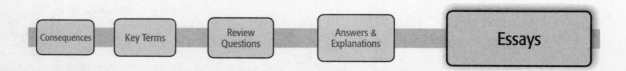

Consequences   Key Terms   Review Questions   Answers & Explanations   **Essays**

UNIT III: RECONSTRUCTION TO THE GREAT WAR, 1863–1919

CHAPTER 17: THE TRIALS OF RECONSTRUCTION, 1863–1877

IF YOU ONLY LEARN THIRTEEN THINGS IN THIS UNIT . . . .

1. How the federal government attempted assimilation of former Confederate states and their citizens into the Union

2. The many troubles African Americans faced upon freedom from slavery (a struggling Freedman's Bureau, Jim Crow laws, etc.)

3. Continued westward expansion, development of the frontier, and violent dealings with Native Americans

4. Development of a railroad system and changes in economic policy and business due to industrialization

5. The increasing division of wealth and the development of an active working class and labor unions

6. The effects of immigration on the United States

7. Economic woes and debates over gold and silver

8. The evolving roles of women in politics, education, and the workforce

9. How Progressivism affected society—changes in government and voting policies, Theodore Roosevelt's Square Deal, controversies over journalism

10. Overseas expansion and continued involvement in foreign affairs (the Spanish-American War, the Panama Canal, the Open Door Policy, etc.)

11. The events leading up to World War I and U.S. involvement (the *Lusitania*, the Sussex Ultimatum, etc.)

12. Wilson's Fourteen Points and the United States's role in the Great War

13. Peace negotiations post–World War I and the war's immediate effects on society

Reconstruction — Southern Gov't — Freedmen — 1877 Compromise — Reconstruction Impact

PRESIDENTIAL AND RADICAL RECONSTRUCTION

As the Civil War came to an end, the federal government had to figure out what to do with the former Confederate states that were buried under the weight of economic and physical destruction. Questions abounded about the treatment of Confederate leaders, the readmittance of former Confederate states into the Union, and the assimilation of 4 million freedmen and freedwomen into the social fabric of the nation. Standing in the way of any decision-making process were the traditional American views of government and democracy roles. As before the Civil War, most Americans feared a large, powerful federal government. However, without the federal government leading the way to rebuild the nation, **Reconstruction** would be over before it started.

Traditionally, Americans believed that to reap the benefits of a democratic society, all one needed to do was work hard. Thus, when it came time to assist the former slaves begin their lives anew, Americans were reluctant to provide too much assistance—they felt African Americans should work just as hard as they had. The enormous burden of reconciling North and South fell upon the shoulders of President Andrew Johnson and Congress.

ASSIMILATING FORMER SOUTHERN STATES AND SLAVES

Before his assassination, President Lincoln had formulated some provisions for the rebuilding of the Union. His **Proclamation of Amnesty and Reconstruction** was set in 1863 as a way to bring Southern states back under the wing of the federal government. The re-entry process would begin by the re-establishment of state governments, which would gain legitimacy by having at least 10 percent of their voting populace having swear an oath of loyalty to the United States and the Constitution. Secondly, the president was prepared to grant complete *pardons* to any former Confederate, as long as he also took the oath of allegiance and agreed to the elimination of slavery. Fellow Republicans were not thrilled with Lincoln's plan and decided to pass legislation of their own that would create a few more obstacles to full incorporation of former rebellious states. The **Wade-Davis Bill** was passed in 1864 by both houses. It required that 50 percent of Southern state voters take the oath of loyalty and allowed only those citizens who had not been active members or supporters of the Confederacy to approve of the new state constitutions. Exercising his executive power, President Lincoln pocket-vetoed the bill by refusing to sign it until after Congress had gone on recess.

To manage and assist the newly emancipated slaves of the nation, the federal government created the **Freedman's Bureau** in 1865. The bureau provided assistance in the form of food, shelter, and medical attention to both African Americans and Southern whites. Eventually, the bureau would establish schools across the South and educate large numbers of former slaves. The Freedman's Bureau struggled as President Johnson refused to increase its funding, finally expiring in 1872.

THE UNEASY RULE OF ANDREW JOHNSON

After Lincoln's assassination, it looked as if President Johnson would continue his predecessor's basic Reconstruction plan, with some added burdens on former Confederates. Keeping Lincoln's

Reconstruction   Southern Gov't   Freedmen   1877 Compromise   Reconstruction Impact

10 Percent Plan, Johnson added the disenfranchisement of former Confederates, namely those who had been in leadership positions or who had assets of $250,000 or more. Johnson retained his right to grant full pardons to these former Confederates, which he exercised freely among the planter elite of the South. As a result, many former Confederate leaders and wealthy plantation owners were back in Congress as early as the end of 1865.

Johnson was no friend of Republican congressmen, who felt that he was too friendly with the old Confederate guard and were angered by his continual refusal to support African Americans. With the election of 1866 just around the corner, Johnson decided to travel the country to bash his congressional foes and gain votes. Johnson took to the road in his "swing around the circle" tour, lodging attacks on his opponents who were running for congressional re-election. They did not sit by and allow Johnson to beat them to the punch, instead countering with accusations of alcoholism and anti-Unionism. Republicans running for office resorted to emotionalism by "waving the bloody shirt," or invoking the pain of the Civil War for Northern voters in an attempt to turn them against Democrats they hoped to tie to the "South" for eternity. Their tactics worked beautifully against President Johnson—the election yielded a Republican victory, with moderates and radicals gaining more than a two-thirds majority in both houses.

The Republicans in Congress felt they had better ideas when it came to Reconstruction. Fearing a return of the Southern Democratic contingency, Republicans became more and more radical in their views as the election of 1866 forced them to work with Johnson, who was already in the White House.

THE BLACK CODES

> While Congress was on hiatus, Southern legislatures adopted **"Black Codes"** to restrict the actions, movements and freedoms of African Americans. Under these codes, African Americans could not own land, so they were tied instead to small plots leased from a landowner.

This began the system of **sharecropping**, in which African Americans were bound to the land under the crop-lien system. *Sharecroppers* would "lease" land and borrow supplies to till their plots, while giving a significant portion of their harvest to the landowner as payment for the "lien" or "loan." Never able to harvest quite enough to pay the landlord and feed their families, generations of African Americans remained tied to their plot of land until the Civil Rights Movement of the 1950s and 1960s. Having refused to sign legislation that would revive the dying Freedman's Bureau and protect African Americans from the "Black Codes," President Johnson assured himself a fight with Congress as he served out the remainder of his term.

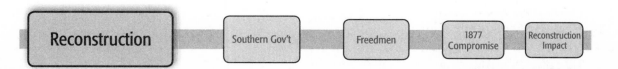

Reconstruction | Southern Gov't | Freedmen | 1877 Compromise | Reconstruction Impact

THE FOURTEENTH AMENDMENT

Congressional or Radical Reconstruction occurred as many former Confederates took office. Republicans were furious that these former "rebels" were being allowed to rejoin Congress and were further angered by President Johnson's backtracking with regard to civil rights. After they modified the bill that would restore the Freedman's Bureau, Radical Republicans set out to protect the civil rights of African Americans. The **Civil Rights Bill of 1866** was designed to destroy the Black Codes by giving African Americans full citizenship. As expected, President Johnson vetoed the bill, and Congress simply overturned his veto. Many Republicans were concerned that a return of a Democratic majority in the future might mean the end of the bill they had worked so hard to pass. Therefore, they needed a more permanent solution to the civil rights problem. Proposed by Congress in 1866 and finally ratified in 1868, the **Fourteenth Amendment** protected the rights of all U.S. citizens and required states to adhere to the due process and equal protection clauses of the Constitution. Furthermore, radical Republicans added some provisions aimed directly at the former Confederacy, which disallowed former Confederate officers from holding state or federal office and would decrease the proportional representation of any state that denied suffrage to any able citizen.

MORE TROUBLES FOR JOHNSON

Even with this victory, the fight was far from over for President Johnson. Radical Republicans took aim directly at him when they outright rejected Presidential Reconstruction, passed the Military Reconstruction Act of 1867, and sought to remove him from office in 1868 by impeachment. The **Military Reconstruction Act** divided the South into five districts that would be managed by military forces stationed there—in other words, martial law was in effect. The Act further tightened the requirements for the readmission of former Confederate states by requiring petitioning states to ratify the Fourteenth Amendment and provide for universal manhood suffrage.

The impeachment crisis began when congressional Republicans passed the **Tenure of Office Act,** disallowing the executive to discharge a federal appointee without the express consent of the Senate. The Act was an attempt by Republicans in Congress to protect their numbers from the angry hand of Johnson. The president chose to ignore the act and fired Secretary of War Edwin Stanton, who happened to be a Republican. The House of Representatives promptly submitted articles of impeachment to the floor by charging Johnson with 11 counts of "high crimes and misdemeanors." He was duly impeached by the House, but the Senate failed to convict Johnson by only one vote.

THE FIFTEENTH AMENDMENT

Needless to say, Johnson did not run for the presidency in 1868. The Republican bid went to the Civil War hero Ulysses S. Grant, who squeaked out a win by gaining a large boost from the African American vote. During his tenure, Radical Republicans such as Congressman Thaddeus

Reconstruction   Southern Gov't   Freedmen   1877 Compromise   Reconstruction Impact

Stephens and Senator Charles Sumner continued pushing for the protection of civil rights from states. Realizing how precious the African American vote was to the future success of their party, Republicans quickly drafted another constitutional amendment that would protect suffrage rights for blacks. The **Fifteenth Amendment** barred any state from abridging a citizen's right to vote on the basis of race, color, or previous servitude. The last of the Reconstruction-era civil rights acts was passed in 1875. This act made it a crime for any person to deny full and equal use of public places, such as hotels, railcars, restaurants, and theaters. Unfortunately this last act had a major shortcoming—it lacked any wording that would provide for enforcement of the law. The law was simply ignored by the majority of states, both Northern and Southern. It would take another 90 years before Congress penned an enforceable civil rights act.

DREAMS, SUCCESSES, AND REALITIES— SOUTHERN GOVERNMENTS

Despite being under federal martial law, Southern states hoped to return to statehood and quickly regain some semblance of stability. In the eyes of the Republicans on Capitol Hill, how quickly these state governments were recognized as legitimate depended on how soon the federal government's demands were met. African Americans soon realized the power of the vote, taking control of the lower house in South Carolina and seating several black congressmen and senators in Congress. However, whites still maintained majority control of all other upper and lower houses and the governorships in all Southern states.

The Democrats remained the party of choice for Southerners, although the Republican Party did gain some strength through freedmen and Northerners who moved south. Southern Democrats named Southern Republicans *scalawags*, a derogatory term that meant they were pirates who sought to steal from state governments to line their own pockets. Northern Republicans who moved south to seek their fortunes were called *carpetbaggers*, a term that came from the stereotype of the Northerner who packed all of his worldly possessions in a suitcase made from carpet. White Southerners resented any incursion by Northerners, even if they were only in the South to aid in the rebuilding process.

Although tensions ran high during the military Reconstruction period, Southern governments did manage to piece together several successes. Never a haven for solid public education, Reconstruction Southern legislatures created a system to provide state-funded public education. Southern infrastructure was given a boost as well, with the public rebuilding and improvement of roads, rail lines, and waterways. Hospitals and prisons were also modernized. Republican legislatures funded these improvements through better tax codes and collection services.

All was not perfect, however, as Southerners continued to suspect wrongdoing among the Republican do-gooders. There were accusations and instances of Northerners taking advantage of the weak Southern system by siphoning off monies. Many legislators arranged for government contractors to give them gifts of money in return for contracts. Others received bribes from

Reconstruction | Southern Gov't | Freedmen | 1877 Compromise | Reconstruction Impact

companies and individuals who sought to bilk the system. Washington scandals in the Grant administration did not help Republicans shake the label of "thief."

As the ire of Southern Democrats began to rise due to the corruption, a new movement began in reaction to the greed and meddling of Northerners. Radical Democrats formed a secret society aimed at ridding the South of Northern Republicans and returning the region to its glory days before the war. The **Ku Klux Klan** was an underground society of whites who ruthlessly and successfully used terrorist tactics to frighten both white and black Republicans in the South. Congress sought to abolish the KKK with the **Force Acts** of 1870 and 1871, which authorized the use of federal troops to quell violence and enforce the Fourteenth and Fifteenth Amendments. While these were moderately successful in calming the KKK's activities, the group continued to exist, resurfacing in the 1920s in response to the influx of southern and eastern European immigrants.

The Deep South experienced a resurgence of Democratic power in state legislatures through **Redeemers**, who hoped to revitalize the South through industry and rid state legislatures of corrupt Republicans. They succeeded in convincing voters that they were right for the job by wresting away the remaining Republican seats in all Southern statehouses. Their campaigns focused on issues important to Southern whites: low taxes, small government, and white power. By the mid-1870s, the Republican Party was dead in the South and would remain so until the 1970s.

FREEDMEN IN THE POSTWAR SOUTH

The Reconstruction was a very confusing time for African Americans in the South—many were never told they had been emancipated. Slaves would be freed by Union armies marching through their region and then re-enslaved as soon as the soldiers left. Other plantation owners simply refused to recognize the Thirteenth Amendment and kept their "property." For their part, slaves themselves varied in their response to their newfound freedom. Some joyfully ran from the plantation looking for a new life. Others remained loyal to their slave master in a sort of "parent/child" relationship. Yet others reacted with violence when freed by ransacking the main house or burning the fields. Eventually, all slaves in the South were freed, particularly under federal martial law.

Once free, many went in search of a new life or to find family members and friends. Encouraged by a former slave named Ben Singleton, as many as 25,000 former slaves uprooted their families and moved toward Kansas between 1878 and 1880. These migrants called themselves **Exodusters**, because they believed that somewhere in the west lay their promised land. Word of their travels, as well as rumors about the federal government "setting aside" the entire state of Kansas for former slaves, spread through the vast church networks that connected black families across the South. The church became the central focus for most African Americans during the postwar period. It was here that one could receive comfort, food, and advice all under one roof.

"Forty acres and a mule" were supposed to make it into the hands of former slaves from confiscated Confederate land as per the provisions in the Freedmen's Bureau. However most of that land was returned to white ownership with leasing contracts available for black tenants.

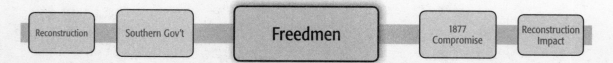

Reconstruction — Southern Gov't — **Freedmen** — 1877 Compromise — Reconstruction Impact

CREATION OF THE FREEDMEN'S BUREAU

Created in 1865 to assist in the assimilation of former slaves into American Society, the Freedmen's Bureau acted as a pseudo-welfare agency in the early postwar years. Given the task of feeding, clothing, housing, and educating freed slaves and poor whites in the South, the Freedmen's Bureau struggled to stay alive throughout Reconstruction.

COMPROMISE OF 1877

The election of 1876 brought Republican Rutherford B. Hayes to the White House but not without a fight. When the polls closed and the votes were counted, Democrat Samuel Tilden was the clear front-runner. There was a problem with the votes in three Southern states however, where Tilden would need an electoral vote from each state to take the presidency. A federal commission was appointed to investigate and decide who should take the contested votes. The commission was made up of both Republicans and Democrats, who were supposed to be impartial in their investigation. Much to the chagrin of the Democrats, the majority Republicans on the committee concluded that Hayes should get the electoral votes, declaring him the winner of the election.

The Democrats were in a rage and threatened to *filibuster* the proceedings to certify the results, which would send the decision to the House. Democrats maintained a majority in the House, so the Republicans had to act fast. **The Compromise of 1877** provided that Rutherford B. Hayes would become president only if he agreed to remove the federal troops stationed in South Carolina, Florida, and Louisiana. The end of martial law in the South signaled the end of Reconstruction in the United States.

THE IMPACT OF RECONSTRUCTION

Historians today still cannot agree on the overall impact and effectiveness of the Reconstruction. It is agreed, however, that white Southerners emerged from the Civil War and Reconstruction embittered and angry. They believed that their way of life had been forever altered and that they would not in their lifetimes see the South reclaim the glory of prewar days. Southerners were angry about Northern interference in their politics and daily lives and the protections provided to African Americans by the federal government. As a result, average white Southerners turned radical in their resentment of freedmen and Northerners.

It is evident that President Lincoln, President Johnson, and Congress had no clear plan to deal with the postwar South. Republicans as a whole seemed to enter Reconstruction with rose-colored glasses of idealism and left worn out. By offering pardons and "quick" readmittance for former Confederate states, Presidential Reconstruction hoped that the South would jump at the chance to rejoin the Union without much of a fight. Republicans in Congress, however, wished to protect

Freedmen | 1877 Compromise | **Reconstruction Impact** | Key Terms | Review Questions

the rights of African Americans while also advancing their own political agenda. Unfortunately for African Americans, it was the political agenda of Republicans that would ultimately stand in their path to realizing full rights and protections. In the end, African Americans were no longer held as involuntary servants, but they soon found themselves lost in a cycle of poverty due to the sharecropping system and without the rights and privileges guaranteed them in the Fourteenth and Fifteenth Amendments. In many respects, the prewar South was revived by the actions of Republicans who had sought to dismantle it once and for all.

KEY TERMS

Groups	Freedmen's Bureau scalawags carpetbaggers Ku Klux Klan Redeemers Exodusters Rutherford B. Hayes
Events	Reconstruction
Documents and Laws	Proclamation of Amnesty and Reconstruction Wade-Davis Bill 10 Percent Plan Civil Rights Bill of 1866 Fourteenth Amendment Military Reconstruction Act Tenure of Office Act Fifteenth Amendment Force Acts The Compromise of 1877
Vocabulary	Black Codes sharecropping pardons sharecroppers scalawags carpetbaggers filibuster

REVIEW QUESTIONS

1. The postwar Southern economy

    (A) was destroyed by the war.

    (B) was not effected by the loss of slave labor.

    (C) was relatively stable.

    (D) experienced a rebirth of the plantation system.

    (E) revealed a narrowing of the gap between rich and poor.

2. The Freedmen's Bureau is best known for

    (A) its ability to give land to former slaves.

    (B) the schools it built and ran to educate former slaves and poor whites.

    (C) aiding in the search for lost family members.

    (D) assisting large groups of former slaves in a move to the North.

    (E) lasting through Reconstruction until 1877.

3. Lincoln's 10 Percent Plan included

    (A) laws designed to punish former Confederate leaders.

    (B) suffrage rights for at least 10 percent of the former slave population in the South.

    (C) provisions for the quick readmittance of former Confederate states.

    (D) a plan to redistribute confiscated land to the poor.

    (E) creation of the Freedmen's Bureau.

4. Black Codes were instituted by Southern legislatures to

    (A) protect the rights and freedoms of African Americans.

    (B) tie former slaves to the land they leased to keep them working.

    (C) assist in the voting process.

    (D) place large taxes on goods manufactured by blacks.

    (E) aid in the migration of blacks into other regions of the South.

5. The impeachment of President Johnson was precipitated by his

    (A) campaign tactics in the election of 1866.

    (B) pardoning of many former Confederate leaders.

    (C) veto of the bill to restore funding to the Freedmen's Bureau.

    (D) "Waving the Bloody Shirt."

    (E) refusal to abide by the Tenure of Office Act.

ANSWERS AND EXPLANATIONS

1. A

Unfortunately for the South, its fragile agricultural economy was devastated by the Civil War. The loss of slave labor, rampant inflation, and the destruction of thousands of acres of farmland meant disaster for the South. However, the rich remained at the top of the economic ladder, with the gap between them and the lowest rung of poor citizens growing ever greater.

2. B

Despite lack of proper funding and attempts by President Johnson to kill it off, the Freedmen's Bureau was successful in educating thousands of former slaves and poor whites in the South during Reconstruction. The Bureau took its last breath in 1872, when it finally lost the federal funding it needed to stay afloat.

3. C

Hoping to rebuild the Union quickly after the end of the Civil War, President Lincoln optimistically crafted his 10 Percent Plan to provide for the easy readmission of former Confederate states by asking for 10 percent of the voting citizens of a petitioning state to take an oath of allegiance to the Union and U.S. Constitution.

4. B

To ensure a stable labor supply that would continue to till the land of the South, the Black Codes sought to bind former slaves to the land they leased. Known as sharecroppers or tenant farmers, many of these families would still be tied to the land well into the 20th century.

5. E

Members of Congress acted quickly to save themselves from President Johnson's line of fire by enacting the Tenure of Office Act, which would forbid the president from removing any federal appointee from a post without the consent of Congress. President Johnson ignored the act when he dismissed Secretary of War Stanton from his post, thus prompting the House to charge Johnson with 11 counts.

1877 Compromise | Reconstruction Impact | Key Terms | Review Questions | **Answers & Explanations**

CHAPTER 18: THE CLOSING OF THE FRONTIER, 1865–1900

THE THREE WESTERN FRONTIERS: MINING, CATTLE, AND FARMING

"The existence of an area of free land, its continuous recession, and the advance of American settlement westward explain American development." These words, taken from "The Significance of the Frontier in American History," a lecture delivered by historian Frederick Jackson Turner at the World's Columbian Exposition in Chicago in 1893, would become known as **Turner's "Frontier Thesis."** Turner argued that the American character was shaped by the existence of the frontier and the way Americans interacted with and developed the frontier. But as the Civil War ended and Manifest Destiny was complete, the frontier was closing. There was no longer any part of the continent that Americans had not touched. This was a dangerous time for Americans in Turner's eyes; he felt the frontier encouraged individualism and democracy. Without that "free land," would democracy and the American way close as well?

49ERS AND IMMIGRANTS IN SEARCH OF GOLD

With the discovery of gold in California and silver in Nevada, the spread of cattle ranching, and the flood of "homesteaders" rushing into the west, it was clear that this region would be uniquely American. After the initial gold strike at **Sutter's Mill** in central California in 1848, thousands rushed to the region to pan the rivers and mine the hills to find their fortunes. The cities of San Francisco and Sacramento evolved practically overnight by the influx of "**49ers,**" a rough group of young men who loved adventure.

California also experienced a flood of Chinese immigrants who came in search for the fabled "Mountains of Gold." Many Chinese immigrants had no intention of staying in the United States, but were hoping to find enough gold to live like kings once back in China. In one year, more Chinese left the country than came in. Those that did remain found no "mountain of gold" but did find discrimination and poverty. Mostly young men, they either worked on the building of the transcontinental railroad, acted as house servants for the few wealthy women in the city, or eventually opened up laundries for the miners and their wives who could not do their own wash.

Western Frontiers — Plains Indians — New South — Farmer's Plight — Key Terms

There were other gold strikes across the west in Colorado, Arizona, and South Dakota, and the Comstock Lode in Nevada was discovered in 1859 with both gold and silver ores. The discovery and mining of gold and silver had an impact on the economy—the value of both metals fluctuated as more was discovered, which became a national issue in the last part of the 19th century. More importantly, the mining had an adverse effect on the western environment. Panning for gold soon led to the deep-core mining that gored mountainsides and destroyed lakes, rivers, and streams.

CATTLE TAKE CONTROL

Miles and miles of open grassland were soon converted into vast cattle ranches in Texas, Kansas, and Nebraska. Additional rail lines were added in Kansas, Nebraska, Colorado, and Wyoming, which made the transport of beef more viable. Soon the Texas Longhorn was the most prized cattle in the United States. Trails were created for transporting the cattle on "**long drives**" from deep inside Texas to the rail junctions of Dodge City, Abilene, Denver, and Cheyenne. Cowboys and Mexican *vaqueros* drove and grazed thousands of heads of cattle along these trails, to the immense profit of the ranch owners. Before long, however, the lush grassland became the haven for new settlers—homesteaders and sheepherders, who built barbed-wire fences and small farms, breaking the way of the long drives. In addition, the overgrazing by cattle along the trails eventually made the long drive something of the past. Cattle ranchers turned to enclosing their herds, selectively breeding, and hiring only local ranch hands to tend their cattle.

FARMLAND TURNS UNFARMABLE

The **Homestead Act of 1862** provided a settler with 160 acres of land if he promised to live on it and work it for at least five years. At one point, public lands were basically being given away to encourage Americans to settle and improve the frontier. About 500,000 families took advantage of the Homestead Act, while many more actually bought land from private purveyors. Unfortunately, the promised 160 acres on the Great Plains were often not farmable due to the lack of rain and hard-packed soil, forcing many homesteaders to leave the land behind and return home. Those who remained were often called "**sodbusters**," as they attempted to farm the land that they were given. Life was difficult on the Plains. Families lived in houses built out of the sod they dug up. Drought was always a problem. Plagues of insects were a constant nuisance. About two-thirds of the original homesteaders had to leave the Great Plains, draining the region of half of its population by the turn of the 20th century.

REMOVAL OF THE PLAINS INDIANS

In 1865, some 400,000 Native Americans lived freely in the trans-Mississippi west. Some tribes had lived in the region for thousands of years, while others had been progressively forced westward from ancestral homelands by the push of white settlement. Plains Indians were largely nomadic, traveling by horse to hunt buffalo and wage war on neighboring tribes.

AN ATTEMPT AT A RESERVATION SYSTEM

Sioux Indians were able to control much of the upper west due to devastating diseases that had removed potential resistance. The Sioux were able to wipe further resistance away through their aggressive warring tactics. The Pawnee pleaded to the federal government for assistance, as the Sioux were attempting to wipe them out. In response, the federal government created boundaries throughout the west that designated the land held by each tribe. These first attempts at a "**reservation**" system failed, as the white leaders in Washington, D.C., were ignorant of the nomadic nature and paternal tribal leadership system of most Native Americans.

NATIVE AMERICANS AND WAR

More and more Native American tribes were becoming aggressive against one another and against the incoming white settlers. From the end of the Civil War to 1890, there was constant warfare. At Sand Creek, Colorado, in 1864, a U.S. militia slaughtered 400 unarmed Native Americans who had been promised protection. Colonel **George Custer** marched into the Black Hills of South Dakota, a section of the Sioux Indian reservation, and proclaimed the discovery of gold. As a result, the hills soon were flooded with gold seekers, which enraged the Sioux.

CUSTER'S DEFEAT

To quell a possible Sioux uprising, Custer marched his column of men deep into Sioux territory, only to discover some 2,500 Sioux warriors waiting for them at the Little Big Horn River. Custer and his men were cut down by the Native American warriors, who were soon hunted themselves by white reinforcements.

Many other tribes (such as the Nez Perce led by Chief Joseph and the Apache led by Geronimo) were forced to fight for their land and lives throughout the end of the 19th century.

STRIPPING NATIVES OF THEIR RESOURCES AND IDENTITY

Warfare was not the only factor to affect the Native Americans living on the Great Plains. Plains tribes depended on the buffalo for meat, clothing, and fuel. As the railroad made its way across the west, mass killing of the buffalo ensued. Buffalo coats became fashionable, and the buffalo hunt became a favorite pastime. As a result, the American buffalo became an endangered species, with only a few surviving in the nation's zoos and preserves.

The 19th century did not end on a happy note for the Indian tribes of the Great Plains. Even though Helen Hunt Jackson's book *A Century of Dishonor* (1881) sparked debate over the government's treatment of Native American tribes, it seemed that no one could decide what to do now that the damage had been done. Many believed that the tribes needed to be assimilated into American society by being stripped of their culture and traditions. A new ritual was born in 1870 that promised a rebirth of Native American tradition and a repelling of white incursion. This "**Ghost Dance**" so frightened whites living near the Dakota Sioux that it was outlawed. The U.S. army was called in 1890 to stop the Sioux from performing the dance, which led to the Battle of Wounded Knee. Two hundred men, women, and children were slaughtered over the ritual.

In an attempt to "civilize" the Native Americans, the federal government enacted the **Dawes Severalty Act of 1887**, which stripped tribes of their official recognition and land rights and would grant individual Indian families land and citizenship in 25 years if they "behaved." Former reservation land was sold, and the proceeds would fund "civilizing" ventures for Native Americans, such as Indian schools that taught Indians how to dress and behave like whites. This forced-assimilation policy remained the federal government's way to deal with Native Americans until 1934. The Dawes Severalty Act served to destroy tribal organization and strip Native Americans of the land they had been legally deeded by the U.S. government.

THE NEW SOUTH

Slow economic progress was a reality for the South after the Civil War. However, soon the South was back on her feet with the resurgence of tobacco as a cash crop. The South was also able to outperform the North in the textile industry due to an abundance of cheap labor and ready raw cotton supplies. The emergence of a modern, viable railroad network further assisted the South in regaining and eventually surpassing her prewar financial status.

SOUTHERN FARMERS STRUGGLE

But for the most part, Southern citizens still remained some of the most impoverished in the nation. The unprecedented postwar economic recovery came with strings attached; the North had financed a major portion of the South's war debt. Therefore, Northerners owned the lion's share of the industry that was being revived in the South. The majority of Southerners, both black and white, subsisted from day to day as sharecroppers and farmers. Due to the South's steadfast belief in the plantation

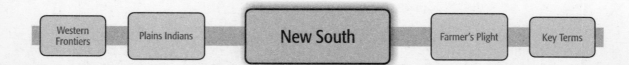

Western Frontiers   Plains Indians   New South   Farmer's Plight   Key Terms

economy and lack of value placed on education, economic recovery, growth, and innovation moved more slowly than in the North. Thus, the average Southern citizen did not reap any reward from even modest growth of the region, remaining below the poverty line.

As in the antebellum economy, cotton remained a major cash crop for the South—more and more farmers converted land to till cotton. They eventually glutted the worldwide marketplace with the fiber, driving the price to an all-time low in the 1890s. As a result, many small farmers lost their land due to their inability to pay back debts. Many tenant farmers were driven off land by landowners, who then needed to till it themselves. Most farmers, tenant or otherwise, remained tied to the land due to the use of crop-liens in which farmers paid for goods on credit to be paid back with the harvest of their next crop. A poor harvest drove farmers deeper into debt.

PLESSY V. FERGUSON AND JIM CROW LAWS

Southern "**redeemers**," who sought to return the South to its antebellum glor,y gained support from many white Southerners. After the North removed troops and any other support for African Americans, white Southerners sought to enact policies that would separate the races to create two distinct societies as before the war—one black and one white. By using fear as a political tactic, the redeemers were successful in gaining power and diverting attention from the economic problems of poor whites.

The Supreme Court aided the South's ability to discriminate through several decisions that more or less dismantled any Reconstruction protections of African American civil rights. In the Civil Rights Cases of 1883, the Court decided that Congress had no jurisdiction to bar private citizens from practicing discrimination. In 1896, the landmark case of *Plessy v. Ferguson* was brought before the Court. In this case, a mulatto man who was seven-eighths white and only one-eighth African American refused to give up his seat on a "whites-only" railcar in the state of Louisiana and was arrested. He sued, claiming that his civil rights had been violated. Justice Henry Brown delivered the opinion of the court, which ruled that because a car was provided for passengers of color, the state of Louisiana had not violated the Fourteenth Amendment. The justices used the "separate but equal" doctrine to justify their decision. The South had now been given permission by the U.S. Supreme Court to discriminate on the basis of color in all public places. *Jim Crow laws*, which segregated public facilities from drinking fountains to hotel rooms, were immediately adopted by cities across the South.

FURTHER FORMS OF DISCRIMINATION

Discrimination did not end with Jim Crow. Southern states worked to disenfranchise African American voters through the use of *literacy tests*, *poll taxes*, and **grandfather clauses**.

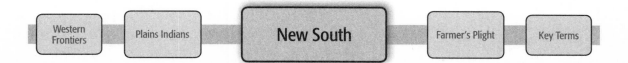

Grandfather clauses would allow a man to vote only if his grandfather had voted in an election before 1865—that is, before Reconstruction. African Americans were not allowed to serve on juries and were subject to harsher penalties when convicted of crimes than their white counterparts. A new form of justice called *lynching* took the place of trial by jury. Lynching was the unauthorized execution of a person by a mob. Often the lynching would be publicized in advance so crowds of whites could gather to witness the event. In response, African Americans could do little but leave the South for similar discrimination in the North. Self-educated former slave Booker T. Washington advocated the education of African Americans to make them more economically viable and indispensable to the economy. His Tuskegee Institute was founded to instruct African Americans in the industrial arts and the ability to "work within the system." With the turn of the 20th century, more radical views would take umbrage at Washington's stance of "assimilation."

THE FARMER'S PLIGHT

Falling farm prices and changing demand in the domestic and international markets crippled an already troubled sector of the U.S. economy. Farmers were dwindling in number due to the mechanization of the agriculture business and the growth of industry across the country. The beginnings of "**agribusiness**," large-scale cash crop farms, were growing, with small family farms falling by the wayside. Soil preparation, planting, and harvesting no longer required the same number of workers as before with the invention of better and faster machines to do the work. As a result, small farmers could not keep up with their large competitors in both buying expensive equipment and bringing goods quickly to market.

In the spirit of Jackson's "Frontier Thesis," Midwestern farmers decided to fight their dilemma by organizing together. In 1868, Oliver H. Kelley organized the **National Grange of Patrons of Husbandry** as a kind of fraternity of brothers and their families. Soon the social atmosphere of the Grange meetings was replaced by a more political zeal. The Grange sought to break the hold of railroad owners and middlemen who kept raising the price of farming by pocketing the profits. By the mid-1870s, there were Grange meetings across the country. Grangers organized farm cooperatives (member-owned businesses that sold farm products directly to the buyer), cutting out the middleman. The railroads and silo owners were under watch of the Grangers, due to the exorbitant prices they charged for the shipping and storage of grain. Due to the Grangers' political clout and expert lobbying, Granger laws, which regulated the rates farmers could be charged for shipping by rail or using grain elevators, were passed in many states.

The Supreme Court stepped into the controversy in the case *Munn v. Illinois* (1877) by ruling that a state had the right to regulate the practices of a business if that business served the public interest. Since railroad transportation was very much in the public's interest, according to the Court, state regulation of rates was appropriate. Despite these successes on the state level, farmers

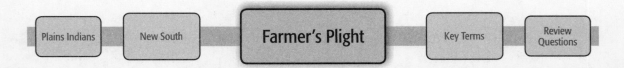

still had many of their laws overturned due to federal laws protecting interstate commerce and railroad companies raising their long-haul rates to offset the losses on short hauls. Congress responded by passing the **Interstate Commerce Act** in 1887 and creating the **Interstate Commerce Commission (ICC)**, which would regulate and investigate railroad companies that participated in interstate rail trafficking. However, the ICC lacked enforcement powers and remained essentially a "paper tiger." Farmers did not gain much from the formation of the ICC, as they lost most of these cases. Nonetheless, farmers kept up the fight up through the end of the 19th century as currency issues and railroad trusts made tough times even tougher.

KEY TERMS

Names	George Custer
Groups	49ers sodbusters National Grange of Patrons of Husbandry Interstate Commerce Commission
Documents and Laws	Turner's Frontier Thesis Homestead Act of 1862 Dawes Severalty Act of 1887 *Plessy v. Ferguson* Jim Crow laws Interstate Commerce Act *A Century of Dishonor*
Places	Sutter's Mill
Vocabulary	long drives Ghost Dance grandfather clauses agribusiness

REVIEW QUESTIONS

1. Mining for gold and silver

   (A) forced Native Americans off of the Great Plains.

   (B) destroyed large cities in the west.

   (C) brought law-abiding citizens to California.

   (D) encouraged great numbers of fortune seekers to move west.

   (E) pushed the United States off of the gold standard.

2. A major problem faced by homesteaders on the Great Plains was

   (A) lack of land.

   (B) shortage of rainfall.

   (C) continued Indian attacks.

   (D) the high price of land.

   (E) too many settlers crowding the region.

3. Plains Indians were systematically eliminated by all of the following EXCEPT

   (A) disease.

   (B) lack of food.

   (C) fighting.

   (D) the federal government.

   (E) white settlement.

4. Jim Crow laws were designed to

   (A) segregate blacks from whites.

   (B) open up land purchase to poor Southerners.

   (C) curb northern immigration.

   (D) create schools for former slaves.

   (E) increase the number of black voters.

5. "Granger Laws" did which of the following?

   (A) Raise tariffs on farm goods

   (B) Decrease interest rates on credit

   (C) Create farm cooperatives

   (D) Eliminate debtors' prisons

   (E) Allow for regulation of shipping rates

ANSWERS AND EXPLANATIONS

1. D

The promise of fortunes hidden in the hills of the west brought adventurers to California, Nevada, and other western states to mine for gold and silver. Large mining cities popped up within miles of lode discoveries; inhabitants tended to be lawless and rough.

2. B

The broad, sweeping plains were dry, as rainfall was scarce. Homesteaders soon discovered that their sweet land deal was sour—they could not afford to pay for the equipment necessary to irrigate the land.

3. D

The federal government sought to protect Native Americans by setting up the first stage of the reservation system, which would forcibly separate the warring tribes from one another. Disease, the killing off of the buffalo, war, and white settlers all served either to drive Native Americans from their land or kill them off slowly.

4. A

Southern whites sought to return to the antebellum days when blacks and whites lived in virtually separate societies. After the Supreme Court ruling of *Plessy v. Ferguson*, Southerners had the blessing of the federal government to continue discriminatory practices.

5. E

The Grange was successful in lobbying state legislatures to pass laws that would regulate railroads and grain silo operators with regard to the rates they charged farmers. The "Granger Laws" were the first step in the federal government playing a role in the protection of farmers and eventually breaking up businesses that unfairly took advantage of Americans.

CHAPTER 19: THE RISE OF INDUSTRY, 1865–1900

RAILROAD TYCOONS AND ROBBER BARONS

After the Civil War, the federal government sought to build railroads through undeveloped, barren sections of the United States to encourage the growth of cities along the rail lines. To make this happen, the U.S. government subsidized the building of the **transcontinental railroad** and gave huge land grants to rail companies who sought to construct rail lines throughout the west.

VANDERBILT'S RAILROAD AND A TRANSCONTINENTAL SUCCESS

The railroad industry already had a foothold in the east, with men such as **Cornelius Vanderbilt** leading modernization of older rails. Vanderbilt had amassed a fortune in the steamboat business before venturing into rail. He invested his fortune in the conversion of eastern lines to common gauge steel rails and consolidated many smaller rail lines under one name—the New York Central Railroad. Before Vanderbilt's domination of the industry, there were dozens of small rail lines with varying widths of rail, mostly constructed of iron. Steel rails were safer because they did not rust and were stronger, allowing for trains to carry heavier loads. By connecting and consolidating the smaller lines, Vanderbilt linked of major cities on the East Coast and Midwest.

The western half of the **transcontinental railroad** was constructed by the congressionally appointed Union Pacific Railroad and Central Pacific Railroad companies. The federal government gave the railroad companies generous land grants and federal loans for each mile of track that was laid as they progressed west. **The Central Pacific Railroad**, led by Leland Stanford, set out to build the most treacherous stretch of rail from Sacramento, California, through the Sierra Nevada mountains and then eastward. The **Union Pacific** began building its portion of the transcontinental railroad starting in Council Bluffs, Iowa, and moving westward. The rail lines of the Central Pacific and Union Pacific finally met in May 1869 at **Promontory Point**, Utah, just above the Great Salt Lake. Chinese labor ("Coolies") had been largely responsible for building the Central Pacific's line while Irish workers ("Paddies") built the Union Pacific. The completion of the transcontinental railroad ranks as perhaps the greatest American technological achievement of the 19th century. It linked the nation from sea to sea by both rail and telegraph. Furthermore, the vast railroad helped speed along the development and eventual closure of the frontier.

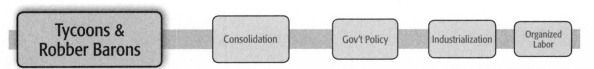

Tycoons & Robber Barons — Consolidation — Gov't Policy — Industrialization — Organized Labor

RAILROAD CORRUPTION

Wishing to reap the rewards of land and money, some railroad owners overbuilt their lines or simply defrauded the federal government. Men such as Jay Gould earned the nickname "**Robber Barons**," as they artificially inflated the value of their company's stock, sold the stock to the public, and pocketed the profits. The company would then go bankrupt, leaving the stockholders with nothing. Competition among rail lines was fierce, leading to dishonest businesses practices. Many companies offered rebates or kickbacks to certain high-volume customers, while charging exorbitant rates to smaller shippers, namely farmers. Another system the railroad tycoons invented was the *pool*, whereby competing rail companies would secretly agree to divide up business territories, artificially fix shipping rates, and split the profits among pool members.

The federal government largely kept out of the affairs of big business, with the exception of *Munn v. Illinois*, which the Supreme Court overturned with its decision in *Wabash v. Illinois* (1886). In this case, the Court broadly interpreted the Fourteenth Amendment (equal protection under the law) by deeming corporations to be "citizens" under the Constitution. This interpretation basically insulated corporations such as railroad companies from regulation by the federal government.

INDUSTRIAL CONSOLIDATION AND MONOPOLIZATION

The hands-off mentality of the federal government toward big business helped to fuel the growth of other large-scale manufacturing ventures after the Civil War. The United States experienced a "second industrial revolution," as it shifted from light manufacturing to heavy industry with steel, oil, and heavy machinery now predominant.

ANDREW CARNEGIE AND THE BIRTH OF A STEEL INDUSTRY

The continued growth of the railroad industry after the Civil War served as a stimulus to the steel industry, since new rails and locomotives were constructed with steel, rather than iron. Thus, steel was the heart of the rise of heavy industry in the postwar period. Henry Bessemer revolutionized the production of steel when he discovered a way to produce it faster and make it stronger. What once took a week or more now could be completed in as little as three hours. A young Scottish immigrant named **Andrew Carnegie** saw a future in the production of steel as he worked his way up in the railroad business in the 1860s. Carnegie emerged as one of the nation's wealthiest men by the late 1880s through his Carnegie Steel Company. By using the Bessemer process to produce steel to sate the appetite of U.S. businesses, Carnegie soon was responsible for supplying over half of the world's steel. Steel production alone was not the recipe for Carnegie's success, however. Carnegie used a business tactic called *vertical integration*, in which he single-handedly controlled every aspect of the production process for steel from the mining of the ore, to the distribution of the final product, to the customer. Carnegie lived out the rest of his life as a philanthropist, giving away much of his immense fortune to establish universities, endow libraries, and infuse culture in cities across the United States.

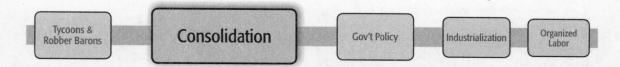

RISE OF J. P. MORGAN

> Eventually, Carnegie retired from the steel business and sold his company to J. P. Morgan, who then created U.S. Steel, the country's first billion-dollar corporation. Still headquartered in Pittsburgh, Pennsylvania, U.S. Steel today remains one of the world's top producers of steel products.

ROCKEFELLER'S BUSINESS STRATEGIES

Meanwhile, the discovery of oil in the Pennsylvania hills in 1859 would revolutionize many other industries throughout the world. Kerosene soon emerged as the fuel of choice for lighting, and the combustion engine would make work such as mining and farming faster. Another young businessman saw the potential in this "black gold" and soon joined Carnegie as one of the nation's wealthiest men. **John D. Rockefeller** turned a small petroleum company into a massive monopoly by his business strategy of *horizontal integration*. Much more damaging to competition than Carnegie's vertical integration, Rockefeller's style was to control one aspect of the production process of oil, in this case the refining stage. His **Standard Oil Company** eventually controlled 95 percent of the refineries in the United States by the process of consolidation. Rockefeller offered an opportunity for stockholders in competing oil companies to enter a *trust* in which they would sell him their shares of stock and control in exchange for trust certificates. The board of trustees would then control the business transactions of the now consolidated companies, driving other competitors out of business. Rockefeller was able to undercut his competition by cornering the market and driving prices dramatically downward. As a result, Americans were buying Standard Oil products whether they wanted to or not, as smaller companies were either aggressively taken over or driven out of business altogether. Taking the cue from Rockefeller's success and the government's "blind eye," other American industries developed trusts, creating a ruthless, Darwinian business environment in the country.

The Panic of 1893 threw several overstretched railroads into financial ruin, threatening the industry and the economy as a whole. J. P. Morgan and several other Wall Street financiers rushed to wrest control of the failing rail lines and merge them into single companies. The system ran more smoothly, and shipping rates were consistent across the country. However, the governing boards of these companies were dominated by a few powerful men, namely J. P. Morgan. Morgan created "**interlocking directorates**," or regional monopolies, which controlled almost two-thirds of the rail traffic in the United States.

Tycoons & Robber Barons | Consolidation | Gov't Policy | Industrialization | Organized Labor

GOVERNMENTAL POLICY TOWARD CAPITALISM

Hoping to allow states to control trusts on their own, the federal government was reluctant to intervene in the progress of big business. Standing by the doctrine of *laissez-faire* articulated by economist Adam Smith in his treatise *The Wealth of Nations*, American lawmakers believed that natural market forces, not governments, should regulate the marketplace. It soon became clear, however, that a new breed of businessman had been born. Natural competition was being ruthlessly choked out. Heavy influence from the "old moneyed" and middling classes pushed Congress to act.

Congress passed the **Sherman Antitrust Act** in 1890 in an attempt to break up the massive monopolies that were dominating the American economy. The act forbade the creation of trusts that were designed to restrain trade. However, the act failed to specify the difference between trusts that were beneficial to customers and those that were harmful. More importantly, the act failed to include any real method of enforcement. The Supreme Court further weakened the act in its ruling of **United States v. E. C. Knight** (1895), where it interpreted the commerce clause of the Constitution to exclude manufacturing, thus rendering Congress incapable of regulating that sector of the economy. In essence, the Sherman Antitrust Act had no teeth, and businessmen found ways to skirt its penalties.

IMPACT OF INDUSTRIALIZATION ON AMERICAN SOCIETY

The economic divide between the rich and the poor grew steadily wider as the 19th century drew to a close. America's new class of elite, called the "**nouveau riche**," disgusted the old upper class and was detested by the middle and lower classes. The new rich felt that science and God were on their side and justified their newfound status.

OPINIONS ON WEALTH

Americans were quick to apply Charles Darwin's theory of evolution and the notion of "survival of the fittest" to the economic and social sectors of the country. **Social Darwinists**, such as Yale's William Graham Sumner, argued that wealth belonged in the hands of those who were fittest to manage it. Many of Sumner's followers also believed that giving assistance to the poor was only prolonging lives that were altogether worthless. John D. Rockefeller followed a more Puritanical path, decreeing that it was God who gave him his wealth. The "Puritan work ethic" was invoked by many of the nouveau riche as they sought to justify their success.

In the end, 90 percent of America's wealth was controlled by only 10 percent of the population by the turn of the 20th century. Many lower-class Americans subscribed to the "rags-to-riches" myth propagated by novelist **Horatio Alger**, whose titles such as *Ragged Dick* were intended to inspire young street urchins to become wealthy industrialists like Andrew Carnegie. In reality, even though opportunities for incredible success were available, the odds were slight that a street waif would become another Andrew Carnegie.

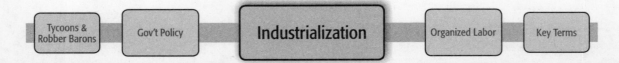

TRICKLE-DOWN THEORY AND THE ACQUISITION OF WEALTH

Andrew Carnegie wrote *The Gospel of Wealth* to explain that wealth was God's will and that, in turn, the wealthy had an obligation to give money away to better society. In addition, Carnegie subscribed to the **"trickle-down"** theory that wealth would benefit the lower classes via the spending and good nature of the rich and would, therefore, benefit society as a whole.

A GROWING MIDDLE AND WORKING CLASS

As Americans moved from farms to factories, the middle class expanded as the cities grew to accommodate them. Managerial positions abounded—factories required people to make sure that human capital was working efficiently to increase profits. As the middle class grew, so did the professional service industry in the areas of medicine, law, and education.

The sector of the American society with the greatest growth was the working class. Blue-collar workers who often toiled 10 to 12 hours a day for barely enough money to scrape by, made up nearly two-thirds of the population of the United States by the end of the 19th century. In smaller numbers, women joined the workforce as clerical help but earned significantly less than their male counterparts. For the most part, factory work was reserved for men. Long hours, occasional 24-hour shifts, and unsafe conditions made factory jobs a death sentence for many Americans.

ORGANIZED LABOR FIGHTS BACK

This industrial revolution was dramatically different from the one that occurred after the Revolutionary War. No longer were skilled artisans in demand; machines now took their place in the lines of production. A worker would not see a product through from start to finish, instead being relegated to oversee just one aspect of production. Craftsmanship became a thing of the past, as Americans and those abroad demanded cheap goods that were made quickly. The increase in demand for manufactured goods meant longer and harder hours for the American factory worker. Laborers often worked 24 hours straight as they moved from a day to a night shift. Factory owners would bar or paint windows shut to keep workers from "daydreaming." Conditions were dangerous in steel mills, where white-hot molten steel was poured day and night by men who had been on the job for upwards of 12 hours or more. Soon enough, American laborers had enough and decided to organize for safer work conditions and better wages.

The first attempts at protest were often met with indignation or even violent resistance by factory owners. Cheap replacement laborers, or *scabs*, were easy to come by when laborers went out on strike. Factory owners would often hire private police forces, which would inflict violence on strikers as they attempted to protest. Locking out workers from their jobs could stop a strike

| Gov't Policy | Industrialization | Organized Labor | Key Terms | Review Questions |

before it started. Blacklisting could keep workers with "difficult" dispositions from being hired. Factory owners sometimes would force prospective employees to sign a *yellow-dog contract* or "ironclad oath" in which the worker agreed not to join a union as a condition of employment.

THE GREAT RAILROAD STRIKE

Unfortunately for organized labor, the federal government was reluctant to help, due to laissez-faire policies and the sway of public opinion against organized labor. Factory owners were successful in taking advantage of the government's stance by obtaining court orders to ban strikes or gaining permission to fire all striking workers. One of the earliest attempts by labor to protest also became one of the most violent. **The Great Railroad Strike** of 1877 occurred when rail companies cut wages by 10 percent in the wake of an economic *depression*. This was the second time in four years that the railroads had cut workers' wages. The strike began in the east, but quickly became a nationwide strike that paralyzed rail traffic across the United States. In addition, workers from other industries joined the strike, further injuring the economy. President Rutherford B. Hayes authorized the use of federal troops to break the strike. In the end, over 100 men died in the fight, and workers gained little from employers in return.

UNIONS ATTEMPT TO PROTECT RIGHTS

Early labor unions often succumbed to their own idealistic vision of the future as they sought to include all workers under one organization. The first union, the **National Labor Union**, was founded in 1866 to urge better working conditions, higher wages, shorter hours, and the inclusion of women and African Americans. After the violent Railroad Strike of 1877, the National Labor Union fell by the wayside.

EMERGENCE OF KNIGHTS OF LABOR

> Meeting in secret so as to not lose their jobs, the **Knights of Labor** finally emerged in 1881 under the leadership of Terrance Powderly. The union was inclusive—all workers, women and minorities included, were invited to join.

Much like the National Labor Union before them, Powderly and his followers advocated both economic and social reforms, such as the development of labor cooperatives modeled after the Grangers, an eight-hour work day, government regulation of business, and *arbitration* to settle disputes between labor and management rather than violent strikes. Unfortunately for the Knights, a pivotal event would mark their demise. On May 4, 1886, a Knights of Labor protest in Haymarket Square in Chicago turned violent. Police were sent to break up the public meeting. Someone in the crowd threw a bomb, killing eight policemen and leading to chaos. It was alleged that an *anarchist* with ties to the Knights had thrown the bomb in an attempt to begin the

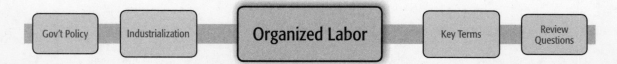

overthrow of the government. Americans, many of them middle class, believed that the Knights were an anarchist movement that intended to take over their country violently. By the end of the 19th century, the once 700,000-member-strong Knights of Labor had faded to a membership roll of just 100,000.

Many of the former Knights had left to join Samuel Gompers and his **American Federation of Labor** (AFL) founded in 1886, a union that became the country's largest with over a million members. The Federation was a practical union (as opposed to a politically ideological union such as the Knights) that chose to concentrate on "bread-and-butter" economic issues—such as the eight-hour work day and higher wages—rather than mire itself in social commentary. Because the AFL was made up of skilled rather than unskilled laborers, Gompers was able to negotiate with employers more effectively, as his men were not as easily replaced by "scabs" if a strike was called. Gompers utilized the tactic of *collective bargaining* to make modest gains for workers, particularly through the establishment of *closed shops*, or businesses where all employees had to be a member of the union.

A STRIKEBREAKING GOVERNMENT

The end of the 19th century was difficult for organized labor, as the government time and time again sided with big business. One facet of that support was the practice of strikebreaking. Andrew Carnegie's manager of his Homestead Steel mill found himself in deep water with organized labor when he announced a 20 percent cut in worker wages in 1892. To stop a strike before it occurred, Henry Clay Frick locked out the members of the steelworkers union. As scabs attempted to enter the plant, the strikers became violent, scaring potential replacement workers away. To remedy the situation, Frick ordered hundreds of private Pinkerton police to surround the plant and rid the area of strikers. Violence erupted, with 16 dead and over 150 wounded. The governor of Pennsylvania ordered the state militia to assist the entrance of the replacement workers, and the strike was given its final death blow. This union had been crushed by Carnegie and the state of Pennsylvania.

In response to the Great Railroad Strike of 1877, the **Pullman Palace Car Company**, which manufactured sleeping cars for the railroads, constructed a "model town" for its employees. When management announced a wage cut and fired the leader of their union, Pullman workers chose to stop working. With their homegrown union without a leader, the group sought assistance from the American Railway Union under the leadership of Eugene V. Debs. Rail workers across the nation joined the Pullman strikers by refusing to load, link, or carry any train that had a Pullman car attached. In effect, all rail traffic came to a screeching halt. To push the federal government to intervene, the rail owners began linking U.S. mail cars to Pullman cars. This way, they could claim that the strikers were impeding the flow of mail and, thus, violating the laws protecting interstate commerce. President Grover Cleveland encouraged the filing of an injunction to demand the workers stop striking and to get the flow of mail running once again. Debs and his union refused to abide by the court's ruling and were eventually arrested and jailed.

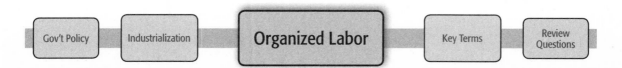

Gov't Policy | Industrialization | **Organized Labor** | Key Terms | Review Questions

Organized labor was given yet another blow when the Supreme Court ruled in *In re Debs* (1895) that the use of court injunctions to break strikes was justified in the support of interstate commerce. In effect, the federal government had given employers permission to destroy labor unions.

KEY TERMS	
Names	Cornelius Vanderbilt
	Andrew Carnegie
	John D. Rockefeller
	Horatio Alger
Groups	robber barons
	U.S. Steel
	Standard Oil Company
	scabs
	National Labor Union
	Knights of Labor
	American Federation of Labor
	Pullman Palace Car Company
Events	The Great Railroad Strike
Documents and Laws	Sherman Antitrust Act
	United States v. E. C. Knight
Places	Central Pacific Railroad
	Union Pacific Railroad
	Promontory Point
Vocabulary	transcontinental railroad
	vertical integration
	horizontal integration
	interlocking directorates
	laissez-faire
	nouveau riche
	social Darwinism
	trickle-down theory
	yellow-dog contract
	closed shops
	scabs
	depression
	arbitration
	collective bargaining

REVIEW QUESTIONS

1. Railroad "pools" were formed in the mid-19th century to

   (A) protect farmers from costly shipping rates and middlemen.

   (B) bloat the market value of stock shares to reap more profit.

   (C) extend better services to farther outlying rural areas.

   (D) "divide and conquer" the rail business by sharing profits and customers.

   (E) offer more competitive rebates to lure new customers.

2. The federal government responded to the Pullman strike by

   (A) ordering each side to attend binding arbitration.

   (B) issuing an injunction ordering the end of the strike.

   (C) supporting the goals of the strikers.

   (D) hiring Pinkerton police to break the strike.

   (E) forcing the state government to intervene in the crisis.

3. In his *Gospel of Wealth*, Andrew Carnegie believed all of the following EXCEPT

   (A) the rich were predetermined by God to be wealthy.

   (B) money was intended to be spent at will.

   (C) the wealthy had an obligation to better society.

   (D) those that worked the hardest deserved the best rewards.

   (E) those that were fittest were rightfully the wealthiest.

4. John D. Rockefeller amassed his fortune by

   (A) discovering oil.

   (B) using the Bessemer process.

   (C) horizontal integration.

   (D) vertical integration.

   (E) being a merciful businessperson .

5. A major flaw of the Sherman Antitrust Act was its

   (A) inability to go after labor unions.

   (B) narrow interpretation of the commerce clause.

   (C) applicability only to states.

   (D) lack of enforcement provisions.

   (E) precise language.

ANSWERS AND EXPLANATIONS

1. D

Railroad "pools" were designed to combine the customer base of several competing companies so that their shipping rates were fixed (and lower) than those of lines that operated in surrounding areas.

2. B

President Grover Cleveland ordered federal troops into the Pullman town to enforce the court-ordered injunction to end the strike. Using the pretense of the stoppage of the flow of the U.S. mail and the interference of interstate commerce, the injunction effectively broke the strike and ended the American Railway Union.

3. C

An ardent philanthropist, Andrew Carnegie believed that even though God had made wealth possible, it was the duty of those with money to use it to better society. By the end of his life, Carnegie had personally given away almost $350 million, with his endowment still in existence today.

4. C

Rockefeller used a new system of corporate ownership—the trust—to build his oil empire through horizontal integration. By controlling one aspect of the production of oil, in his case refining, Rockefeller controlled 95 percent of America's oil refineries by 1890.

5. D

The Sherman Antitrust Act was so vague as not to be effective at all. It had no major provision to allow for its enforcement. It subsequently was used against labor unions instead of trusts.

Industrialization   Organized Labor   Key Terms   Review Questions   **Answers & Explanations**

CHAPTER 20: FROM A RURAL TO AN URBAN AMERICA, 1865–1900

FLOOD OF IMMIGRANTS AND THE LURE OF THE CITY

Both push and pull factors brought millions of new immigrants to the shores of the United States in the years 1880 to 1924. Poverty, overcrowding, and religious persecution pushed immigrants from southern and eastern Europe. Stories of opportunity and freedom pulled them to cities such as New York, Chicago, and Boston. Clipper ships gave way to large ocean liners, which could carry both freight and passengers across the Atlantic relatively quickly. Cheap "steerage class" tickets could be purchased for as little as 20 dollars. For some families, this was a life's savings; nonetheless, "new immigrant" families from Italy, Poland, and Russia gathered as much money as they could to send their young sons on the one-way trip to America.

A BACKLASH AGAINST IMMIGRANTS

These "new" immigrants were markedly different from the "old" immigrants who had come to the United States in the 1820s and 1830s. Southern and eastern European immigrants were often Catholic, Jewish, or Greek Orthodox Christians, and many were poor and illiterate; the "old" immigrants were predominantly literate English Protestants, although large numbers of Irish and Germans had begun to arrive in the mid-1840s. On the West Coast, Chinese and Japanese immigrants continued landing in Los Angeles and San Francisco, prompting the passage of the **Chinese Exclusion Act** of 1882 to restrict Asian immigration to the United States. Soon, Congress passed a rush of acts aimed at restricting the tide of immigration flooding American cities. **Nativists**, much like the old "Know-Nothings" during the first wave of immigration, feared domination by a population loyal to the Pope (Roman Catholics). Labor unions feared a loss of jobs to an eager immigrant work pool. In response, the American Protective Association was formed in 1887 to oppose directly the election of any Catholic to public office. The Reverend Josiah Strong echoed the sentiments of many Americans in his book *Our Country* (1885), in which he derided cities as dens of hell and immigrants as the reason for the downturn of urban America. The tide could not be stemmed, however—by the turn of the century, one out of every three New Yorkers was foreign-born.

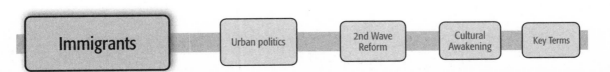

Immigrants — Urban politics — 2nd Wave Reform — Cultural Awakening — Key Terms

MAKING A NEW HOME IN AMERICA

Immigrants flocked to America's cities, where they could find cheap housing and abundant factory jobs. Ethnic *ghettos* popped up in New York, Chicago, and Philadelphia, eclipsing the old Irish sections of town. To handle the massive influx of bodies, landlords converted once-lavish homes to apartment complexes. The city of New York held a contest in 1879 for the best building design for urban dwellings. E. Ware won the contest with his "dumbbell *tenement*," which conformed to a law requiring windows for every dwelling. The design included an "airshaft" that was supposed to aid in the distribution of fresh air through the apartments but in the end only served to aid in the spread of infectious diseases, as more and more people were crammed into the buildings. New apartment buildings were built up rather than out, as land was at a premium and steel made skyscrapers possible.

RISE OF THE EARLY SUBURBS

With the change in the inner-city populace, affluent and middle-class white Americans fled to burgeoning suburban neighborhoods, aided by the expansion of trolley cars and subway services that could still take them to their jobs in the city.

Ethnic groups often formed tight community bonds through common language, customs, and foods. Even though immigrants found themselves living in deplorable conditions, these urban ghettos began to feel more like home and provided a haven where many of the newest arrivals could get on their feet in America.

URBAN POLITICAL MACHINES

Politics in America's large cities was mired in corruption and collusion. Large, consolidated political groups called "machines" controlled party politics in cities such as New York, Chicago, and Baltimore.

THE TWEED RING OF TAMMANY HALL

The most famous of these machines, **Tammany Hall** in New York City was led by **"Boss" Tweed**. Tweed and his fellow Irish gave aid to small businessowners, immigrants, and the poor in exchange for votes. *Political machines* provided coveted city jobs to those who promised to vote for their candidates. They also found housing for newly arrived immigrants and doled out various forms of support to needy families throughout the city, like turkeys at Thanksgiving, clothes, and job search assistance.

Not all members of the machine were honest in their intentions. George Washington Plunkett, a lower boss in Tammany Hall, would pocket large sums of taxpayer money in what he called "honest graft." Plunkett would gain advance notice of a city project from an insider sitting on the planning board. He would buy the land for the proposed project and then sell it to the city for as much as three times its original price. By 1870, the Tweed ring had bilked New York City taxpayers of over $200 million. Urban citizens did not complain, however, as the political machines took care of them and threatened harm to protesters.

The end of the Tweed ring began in 1871 when a story ran in the *New York Times* alleging fraud, bribery, and graft by the political machine. **Thomas Nast**, a political cartoonist for *Harper's Weekly*, became Tweed's archenemy as he began drawing scathing commentaries regarding the machine's corruption and greed. Tweed's immense stature and distinct facial features graced the pages of the magazine, to the delight of readers and law enforcement. Having escaped serving jail time on a number of occasions, Tweed fled to Spain in 1876, where he was captured by Spanish police who recognized him from the Nast cartoons. They turned over someone whom they believed to be a child molester to U.S. authorities. Tweed finally was sent to jail, where he died of heart failure in 1878.

A SECOND WAVE OF REFORM

The deplorable living conditions of immigrants caused by urban crowding and the greed of political machines spurred a new wave of reform, though it would not fully take hold until the turn of the 20th century. Nonetheless, these reformers were by and large middle-class Americans who were more concerned about a possible violent uprising of the poor and working class than they were about the well-being of the less fortunate.

THE SOCIAL GOSPEL AND THE HULL HOUSE

One of the most influential reform movements of this era was the **Social Gospel** movement. Leaders such as Walter Rauschenbusch believed that Christians had an obligation to improve the lives of those less fortunate, such as the citizens of the rough Hell's Kitchen area of New York City with whom he worked. In many ways, it was the work of Rauschenbusch that encouraged many middle-class Protestants to join the reform effort and bring on the Progressive movement.

Akin to the Social Gospel movement was the settlement house movement, brought on by young, college-educated, middle-class women. In this age when women were expected to adhere to a strict ideal of femininity, young female activists sought to better society through volunteerism if they could not become involved in the political process. The most famous of all of the settlement houses was **Hull House** in Chicago (1889). The goal of its founder, **Jane Addams**, was to invite immigrants and the poor to live among college-educated people in order to teach them how to manage life in the city. Settlement house guests were taught courses in English, hygiene, and cooking. Addams and others also pioneered some of the first instruction in child care. Many other settlement houses modeled themselves after Hull House as the 19th century came to a close. Moreover, settlement houses soon became a meeting place for young women activists.

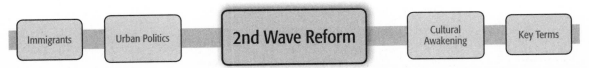

Immigrants | Urban Politics | **2nd Wave Reform** | Cultural Awakening | Key Terms

THE TEMPERANCE MOVEMENT

The Victorian ideal of strict moral decorum and the concern over Catholic influences led to the revival of the *temperance* movement (which had been overshadowed by the abolitionist movement in the antebellum years). **Francis Willard** and the **Woman's Christian Temperance Union (WCTU)** gave the movement new life in 1874 by lobbying for laws to prohibit the sale of alcoholic beverages. They believed prohibition would cure society of a variety of ills, particularly poverty. **The Anti-Saloon League** followed in 1893, gaining more success as states across the country agreed to shutter bars. Having suffered personally from two failed marriages, one due to the death of an alcoholic, the Kentucky-born **Carrie A. Nation** traveled across the United States, smashing bars with her trademark hatchet. Nation believed she was doing the work of God as she wreaked havoc across the Midwest. She was arrested over 30 times and lost her second husband because of her zeal to stop the evils of alcohol. Nation also crusaded against the evils of smoking tobacco, fought for women's suffrage, and railed against the restrictive and sometimes dangerous women's fashions of the day.

THE CHANGING ROLES OF WOMEN

Nation was just one of the women who publicly fought for the rights of women. The industrial age brought women more independence—and more difficulties. Women married later in life (if at all) and bore fewer children. Divorce became more common. Despite newfound freedom, women still did not have a voice in politics. The women's movement had split during Reconstruction—the issue of African American suffrage had taken precedence over women's suffrage. Understanding the need to revive the cause, some broke off from the WCTU and formed women's suffrage organizations from the 1870s to the 1890s. Activists **Elizabeth Cady Stanton** and **Susan B. Anthony** formed the **National American Woman Suffrage Association** in 1890, combining the once rival National Woman Suffrage Association and American Woman Suffrage Association to fight for a woman's right to vote. While gains for women were slow to come, a number of western states did have provisions for women to vote by 1900.

CULTURAL AWAKENINGS

As America's urban centers grew by leaps and bounds, cultural and intellectual endeavors were also given new life.

CHANGES IN EDUCATION

Publicly funded high schools and compulsory elementary attendance laws increased the literacy rate of Americans to almost 90 percent by the beginning of the 20th century. Higher education, already improved by the Morrill Land Grant Act of 1862, was supplemented by the Hatch Act of 1887 and the philanthropy of men such as Carnegie, Rockefeller, Stanford, and Vanderbilt. American universities began to apply the scientific method to social subjects, and "social science"

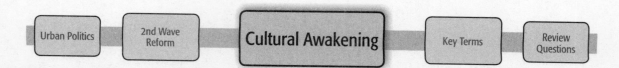

emerged. Universities also professionalized the areas of medicine, law, and sociology by requiring research and practice to obtain a degree. "Normal" schools (teachers' colleges) were established across the country to train new educators to keep up with the new demand for qualified instructors.

ACHIEVEMENTS IN THE ARTS

Reacting to the romanticism of the antebellum and Civil War eras, realist writers and artists sought to reflect the actual conditions industrialized Americans were facing. One of the most famous and prolific of the realists was **Mark Twain** (Samuel Clemens), who captured the ruggedness of the frontier and South with humor and satire. It was Twain who coined the term **"the Gilded Age"** for this era. Bret Harte entranced Americans with his stories of the gold rush and Wild West. As the era wore on, authors turned to stories of human nature and emotion in novels such as *Red Badge of Courage* by Stephen Crane and *Sister Carrie* by Theodore Dreiser. Many visual artists, such as Winslow Homer, remained tied to the romantic spirit of the Hudson River School with lush American landscapes and marine scenes, while others broke away from tradition and redefined the American art scene. James Whistler and Mary Cassatt changed the perception of color and composition in their works, which were heavily influenced by their time spent in Europe. Architects also reacted to the world around them as they designed buildings and landscapes that would reach the sky but remain functional for everyday life.

BEAUTIFICATION OF CITIES

Many cities sought to beautify their surroundings by bringing some wilderness to the urban landscape.

Men such as **Frederick Law Olmsted** focused on bringing nature to the city by designing vast parks that were densely planted and meticulously planned. His Central Park in New York City set the standard for future urban beautification projects and with his use of winding trails, arched bridges, and open spaces that were nestled among the hustle and bustle of city life.

The music scene was altered as African American music traveled from the Deep South to Northern cities such as Chicago. Early jazz, known as ragtime, was soon the rage, as dancers across the nation moved to the "Maple Leaf Rag" of **Scott Joplin**. Ragtime would evolve into distinct sounds as it moved from city to city.

Informing and entertaining the masses was now big business in cities such as New York and Chicago. Daily newspapers like **Joseph Pulitzer**'s the *New York World* and **William Randolph Hearst**'s *New York Journal American* fought over circulation numbers in the city with their sensationalized stories and rock-bottom prices. Magazines also hit the newsstands in search of readership. *Ladies Home Journal, McCall's*, and *Vogue* all sought to reach women through glittery advertisements and fashion tips.

City dwellers searching for a diversion looked forward to the big tent shows that came rolling into town. The Barnum and Bailey Circus promised not only animals and tightrope walkers but a museum of "oddities," ranging from the bearded lady to the fishboy, that patrons could walk through. William "Buffalo Bill" Cody traveled across the United States with Annie Oakley and his Wild West Show, thrilling audiences with sharpshooting, real "Indians," and bronco busting. Professional sports such as boxing, basketball, and baseball were popular with young men, who would use their leisure time to bet on the results and hope for a win. Live vaudeville variety shows brought humor, drama, dance, and song to city dwellers. In the South, minstrel shows, in which whites would don black face paint and act as they imagined African Americans would, were popular among both whites and blacks.

KEY TERMS

Names	"Boss" Tweed
	Thomas Nast
	Jane Addams
	Francis Willard
	Carrie A. Nation
	Elizabeth Cady Stanton
	Susan B. Anthony
	Mark Twain
	Frederick Law Olmsted
	Scott Joplin
	Joseph Pulitzer
	William Randolph Hearst
Groups	Nativists
	Woman's Christian Temperance Union
	The Anti-Saloon League
	National American Woman Suffrage Association
Events	The Gilded Age
Documents and Laws	Chinese Exclusion Act
	Our Country
Places	Tammany Hall
	Hull House
Vocabulary	Social Gospel
	ghettos
	tenement
	political machines
	temperance

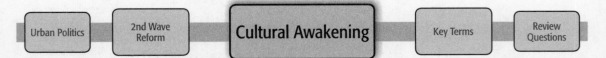
Urban Politics · 2nd Wave Reform · **Cultural Awakening** · Key Terms · Review Questions

REVIEW QUESTIONS

1. One of the greatest lures of the city for immigrants was

    (A) abundant high-standard housing.

    (B) factory jobs.

    (C) advertising.

    (D) lack of discrimination.

    (E) the ease of life in the city.

2. The settlement house movement led the way for

    (A) the temperance movement.

    (B) the realist movement.

    (C) the professionalization of law, medicine, and sociology.

    (D) the nativist movement.

    (E) the suffrage movement.

3. Realists such as Mark Twain and Stephen Crane hoped to

    (A) expose the greed of the Tweed ring to the country.

    (B) explain the division between rich and poor.

    (C) describe the closing of the frontier.

    (D) obtain suffrage rights for women.

    (E) portray life as it happened in the United States.

4. The growth of popular entertainment in the late 19th century can be attributed to all of the following EXCEPT

    (A) reduced hours on the job.

    (B) the impact of Victorian values.

    (C) increased advertisements.

    (D) ease of transportation.

    (E) growth of urban culture.

5. Reformers of this era were typically

    (A) middle-class white Protestants.

    (B) former Southern slaves.

    (C) upper-class white Catholics.

    (D) northern and western European immigrants.

    (E) Western frontier settlers.

ANSWERS AND EXPLANATIONS

1. B

The majority of European immigrants were lured to the cities of America by the large number of available factory jobs. Once in the United States, they soon found substandard living conditions, rampant discrimination, and a difficult adjustment period.

2. E

Buildings such as Hull House provided a meeting place for young feminists, who would then branch out to demand the right to vote.

3. E

Reacting to the Romanticism of the previous era, realists such as Twain and Crane sought to depict the real lives of Americans through their struggles with other people and the world around them.

4. B

To escape the restrictive Victorian values of the late 19th century, Americans—particularly young males—sought ways to spend their extra time. This involved watching professional sports or attending jazz performances. Such events were widely advertised and covered by local newspapers, broadening their mass appeal.

5. A

Much like the earlier antebellum reformers and the later Progressives, these "do-gooders" were mostly white middle-class Americans who sought to better the world around them. While there were a few black reformers at this time, they focused mostly on issues of civil rights rather than society as a whole.

CHAPTER 21: POPULISTS AND PROGRESSIVES, 1890–1919

THE "FORGETTABLE" ADMINISTRATIONS

Politics in the post-Reconstruction years was marked by lackluster performances by presidents many Americans have never heard of. Rutherford B. Hayes, James Garfield, and Chester A. Arthur all served one term apiece from the years 1876 to 1884, but none did much to earn a place in the collective memory. After the "big" government of the Reconstruction era, many in Washington, D.C., sought to limit the role of the federal government. This was not due so much to ideology but rather to the concern over job security. The *spoils system* got a makeover during the **Gilded Age**, as bigwigs in both parties played the game of party *patronage* much as the political machines did in large cities. The Republican party was known for its special relationship with certain patrons named **Stalwarts**, whereas the opposing faction was called **Halfbreeds**. Sitting in the middle, neither supporting or against the Republican patrons, were the **Mugwumps**.

The presidency was not immune from the patronage that plagued the parties at the national level. After a less-than-stellar term by the Republican Hayes, the party chose to run the Halfbreed James Garfield for president, with Stalwart Chester A. Arthur as his running mate. After winning the election, Garfield quickly set to work appointing party loyalists to coveted civil service positions. In true Halfbreed fashion, Garfield appointed his friends and ignored the strong Stalwart contingency. As Garfield prepared to leave for his vacation in 1881, an irate civil service job seeker shot the president in the back. Garfield hung on for nearly three months, finally succumbing to infection from the wound.

Arthur began to separate himself from his Stalwart pals as he took the presidency. Unfortunately for him, the party chose another candidate for the next election, Senator James Blaine. Blaine did not succeed in winning the election of 1884, as his image had been tarnished by his connection to the Credit Mobilier and other scandals. Instead, Democrat Grover Cleveland became the first of his party to take the executive office since before the Civil War.

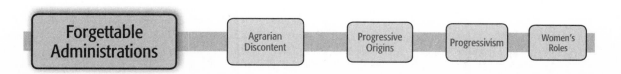

Forgettable Administrations → Agrarian Discontent → Progressive Origins → Progressivism → Women's Roles

ECONOMY AND CURRENCY ISSUES

There were some hallmarks in the "forgotten" administrations, such as the passage of the **Pendleton Civil Service Act of 1881**, which reformed the corrupt patronage system of obtaining civil service jobs. No longer could political cronyism secure government positions—all potential civil service employees had to take an exam to prove their worthiness. The economy became a hot-button issue in the Gilded Age. The money supply was tied to the gold standard, which limited circulation of liquid cash assets. As the country rebounded from panic after panic, it was clear to those who needed cash the most—farmers and other debtors—that the nation would have to adopt a bi-metal standard or use paper currency in place of limited hard coin. Some argued for the unlimited coinage of silver to loosen up the money supply. Others, such as those in the **Greenback Party**, looked to paper money not backed by hard specie as the answer to the country's economic woes. Currency issues, coupled with debate over the high protective tariff, carried over into the next election in 1888.

AGRARIAN DISCONTENT

Grover Cleveland did not win a second term in 1888 due to his support for a lower tariff that would benefit Southern and western farmers. The Republicans were able to rally the votes of Northern business owners to gain the upper hand in the Electoral College. The new president, Benjamin Harrison, presided over a unified government for two years, with Republicans also in control of the legislative branch. The unification was short-lived, however, as midterm elections brought Democrats back in control of Congress.

THE BIRTH OF THE POPULISTS

Republicans had a run for their money from a rising third party as well. Taking the cue from the earlier Grange movement, farmers joined forces in several states across the country to form the **Farmers' Alliance**. The Alliance gained membership, successfully seated senators and governors in several Midwestern states, and eventually morphed into the **Populist** (People's) **Party**. Having drafted their political platform in Omaha, Nebraska, in 1892, the Populists advocated for the following: the unlimited coinage of silver; a graduated income tax; public ownership of railroads, telegraph, and telephone; government subsidies to assist in stabilizing agricultural prices; an eight-hour workday; the direct election of U.S. senators; and increased voter power with the use of the initiative, referendum, and recall.

Even though the Populists made an impressive third-party showing by garnering almost 1 million popular and 22 electoral votes, they failed to win the election. Vying for office were President Harrison and former president Cleveland. The Democrat Cleveland became the only president in history to win a second term after leaving the office for a term in between.

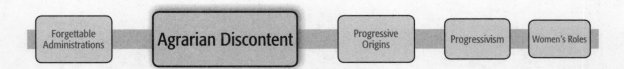

Forgettable Administrations | **Agrarian Discontent** | Progressive Origins | Progressivism | Women's Roles

PANIC AND PROTEST

The victory celebration would be short, however, as the country soon was gripped with an economic depression, triggered by the **Panic of 1893**. Again, railroads and overspeculation by investors artificially inflated the price of stocks, which took a tumble and did not recover for almost four years. Investors began trading in their cache of silver bars for the more valuable gold bars, depleting the already dangerously low supply of the metal. To mitigate the crisis, Cleveland brokered a loan from wealthy investment banker J. P. Morgan for a sum of $65 million and repealed the Sherman Silver Purchase Act. While this temporarily solved the gold shortage, it did much more to damage the president in the eyes of the American public, which already was wary of Washington's dealings with big business. The depression brought protesters to Washington under the leadership of Populist **Jacob Coxey**, whose "army" of the jobless and the homeless proposed federally funded public works projects to employ those who needed work. The government did not listen but rather arrested the "army" for trespassing. Coxey's radical ideas would soon become the cornerstone of policy for a future president who looked to emerge from an even greater depression.

GOLD VERSUS SILVER IN THE 1896 ELECTION

With the economic crisis, currency, and tariff issues still raging, candidates traveled across the country to tout their remedies for a renewed nation before the election of 1896. The Democrats were split due to the gold and silver controversy, with "**Gold Bugs**," such as Cleveland on one side and pro-silver advocates without a leader on the other. The young William Jennings Bryan of Nebraska wowed the crowd at the Democratic National Convention with his famous "**Cross of Gold**" speech, which made him the spokesperson for the pro-silver advocates. In essence, the Democrats adopted the old Populist platform, and they nominated Bryan as their candidate for the 1896 election. Cleveland and his "Gold Bugs" were disgusted with the new party direction and left to form their own run for the presidency. The Republicans nominated William McKinley, a friend to labor and a proponent of the gold standard, as their candidate. With the Democratic ticket split and McKinley's modern use of the media, the Republicans easily took the presidency. Fortunately for McKinley, the country was finally on an economic upswing, and world events would soon turn American's attention away from domestic issues.

ORIGINS OF PROGRESSIVISM

The assassination of President McKinley amid his second term brought his spirited, progressive vice president **Theodore Roosevelt** into office. Reform movements had already established firm roots in local and state politics, but with the executive office now in the hands of the young Roosevelt, the spirit of change had a national audience. The **Progressive Era** began with the swearing in of Theodore Roosevelt in 1901 and lasted until the beginning of U.S. involvement in the Great War in 1917.

Roosevelt marked beginning of Progressive Era

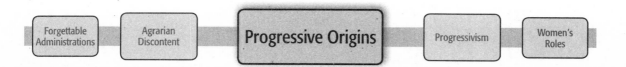

Much like the reformers of earlier times, Progressives were largely white, middle-class Protestants who hoped to better society and preserve the lifestyle they were accustomed to living. They gained inspiration from earlier reformers such as Walter Rauschenbusch and the Social Gospel movement. The nation was changing at an alarmingly rapid rate, and thus reformers sought to preserve moral values while altering the social, economic, and political fabric of the country at the same time.

This reform movement did differ from past ones, however, as diverse groups such as women, African Americans, and organized labor gained voices as never before. But it was still the white, middle-class sector of the movement that gained the most legislation and attention.

JOURNALISTS AND AUTHORS STIR CONTROVERSY

Just as newspaper giants Pulitzer and Hearst sought to entertain their readers with sensational stories, a new breed of author hoped to awaken the reformist spirit. Authors and journalists who wrote articles, essays, and books aimed at exposing scandal, corruption, and injustice were disparagingly called "**muckrakers**" by Theodore Roosevelt, who felt that they took sensationalism a bit too far. Nonetheless, the muckrakers were successful in gaining an audience and stirring up concerns among their readers. Magazines such as *McClure's* and *Collier's* were the first weapons of the muckrakers. **Ida Tarbell's** series of articles titled *The History of the Standard Oil Company* (1902) caused a stir, as she detailed the ruthless business tactics of John D. Rockefeller. Starting his career in magazines, **Lincoln Steffens** moved into writing books with his *The Shame of Cities* (1904), which chronicled the corruption and greed of big-city political machines. To show the conditions of New York's tenements in Hell's Kitchen, Danish photojournalist **Jacob Riis** shocked the nation with his book *How the Other Half Lives*, published in 1890. Muckraking moved into fiction with the works of Theodore Dreiser (*Sister Carrie*) and Frank Norris (*The Octopus*) and became wildly popular through the early 1900s. However, as the era progressed, it became increasingly difficult for muckrakers to best their previous story. Soon the sensational became commonplace, as every newspaper, magazine, and novel had an "exposé." The muckrakers were successful in opening the eyes of many American readers and were moderately successful in gaining the attention of lawmakers and big business.

Essentially nit-pickers

STATE, LOCAL, AND PRESIDENTIAL PROGRESSIVISM

Progressivism took hold in local and state politics long before it reached the national level. As early as 1888, voters in Massachusetts were using a "secret ballot" to vote in elections. Under the leadership of Wisconsin governor and later U.S. Senator "Fighting Bob" **Robert La Follette**, the state became the model for increased voter power at the ballot box. Wisconsin was the first state in the Union to institute *direct primaries* in which state voters nominated their own slate of candidates, as opposed to the prior selection of the party ticket by the state legislature. The **Wisconsin Experiment** set the pace for other states to adopt reform laws with regard to taxes, representation, and commerce regulation.

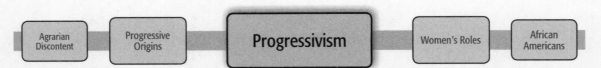

Wisconsin and other states adopted the *initiative, referendum,* and *recall,* once touted by Populists as the answer to the nation's ills, to increase the power of the voter in state and local politics. The initiative allowed voters to propose a law without the legislature; the referendum was the way in which voter-proposed laws were placed on the ballot; and recall allowed voters to remove an elected official from office through the ballot box. States also led the way in adopting the direct election of U.S. senators, with the federal government making it the **Seventeenth Amendment** to the Constitution in 1913.

City governments looked to right the wrongs inflicted by political machines and overall complacency with massive reforms during the Progressive Era. Public entities, such as electric power, water, and transportation were privatized in an effort to release the stranglehold of the powerful and corrupt political machines. Much like Wisconsin, the city of Galveston, Texas, became a model of reform when it became the first municipality in the nation to appoint a city planning commission.

ROOSEVELT AS A MODERN PRESIDENT

Theodore Roosevelt soon became known as the Progressive's president as he worked on issues ranging from labor disputes to land conservation. His **Square Deal** involved busting up harmful trusts, increasing government regulation of big business, giving labor a fair chance, and promoting conservation of the natural environment.

Theodore Roosevelt is often called the first "modern president" in that he actively set an agenda for Congress and expected that it listen to his suggestions. Roosevelt's first test was a coal miners' dispute in which the fate of a nation on the cusp of a very cold winter hung on his decision. Past presidents had all sided with business owners at the expense of labor, so America held its breath as Roosevelt made his move. Surprisingly, the young president decided to intervene by holding a private audience in the White House between labor and management. When it was clear that neither side was willing to budge, Roosevelt threatened to take over the mines and run them with federal troops. Reluctantly, the mine owners agreed to lift the lockout, offer a 10 percent pay raise, and give in to a nine-hour workday. Roosevelt's willingness to step in on the side garnered him enough support to get him re-elected in his own right in the election of 1904.

Next on his agenda was the busting up of the **Northern Securities Company**, which Roosevelt considered a "harmful" trust. The railroad monopoly fought the president by taking its case all the way to the Supreme Court. The Court, however, upheld the president's actions. Roosevelt's victory gave him a reputation as a champion trust buster. However, this was somewhat misleading, as President Taft prosecuted twice as many trusts as Roosevelt did and in half the time. Nevertheless, this success gave the president reason to seek ways to regulate the railroad industry. Congress passed the **Elkins Act** in 1903, which gave the Interstate Commerce Commission more power to prohibit rail companies from giving rebates and kickbacks to favored customers. The **Hepburn Act** in 1906 allowed the ICC to regulate the price level of shipping rates railroad lines could charge, ending the

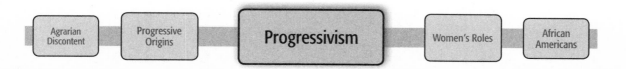

Agrarian Discontent | Progressive Origins | Progressivism | Women's Roles | African Americans

long-haul/short-haul price gouging that had been the bane of the farmer. Along with targeting the rail industry, Roosevelt also sought to destroy other "harmful" trusts, such as Standard Oil.

LITERATURE CAUSES NATION WIDE HEALTH PANIC

President Roosevelt did react to a piece of muckraking literature that had the nation in a virtual panic. Author Upton Sinclair wrote *The Jungle* to expose the filthy conditions in which several meatpacking plants were churning out their products.

Roosevelt had firsthand experience with the dangers of food borne bacteria, as more soldiers died of food poisoning during the Spanish-American War than did by fighting. To calm Americans and provide more consumer protections, Roosevelt worked to get the **Pure Food and Drug Act** and the **Meat Inspection Act** passed in 1906.

The fourth piece of Roosevelt's "Square Deal" was conservation of the environment. An ardent outdoorsman himself, Roosevelt sought to protect the nation's natural resources from industrialization and human habitation. Roosevelt could name among his friends the naturalist John Muir, and he visited the Yosemite Valley in California often during his presidency. Under Roosevelt's administration, millions of acres of land were protected after the creation of natural reserves and the National Conservation Commission.

TAFT'S PRESIDENCY

The next Progressive president came into the White House in 1909 after serving as Roosevelt's secretary of war. William Taft continued his predecessor's policies of dismantling trusts and protecting natural resources. The **Mann-Elkins Act** of 1910 placed the regulation of communication directly under the ICC. More importantly, Taft saw the ratification of the **Sixteenth Amendment** to the Constitution during his presidency, which authorized the federal government to collect an income tax.

 see pg. 195

Taft's presidency was not enjoyed by some, however. Unfortunately for him, these naysayers were within his own party. Progressives were angry at Taft's support of a higher tariff bill, his firing of the popular conservationist Gifford Pinchot after he criticized another cabinet member, and his open support of conservative Republicans for the midterm elections. As a result, the Republican party was split, with liberal progressives on one side and conservative "Old Guard" Republicans on the other. Taft further angered his predecessor, Roosevelt, by ordering the prosecution of an antitrust violation by U.S. Steel—a merger that Roosevelt himself had approved. Roosevelt took the case as a personal attack by Taft. The feud would encourage Roosevelt to seek presidential re-election under a new banner flying for the splinter sect of the Republican party in 1912.

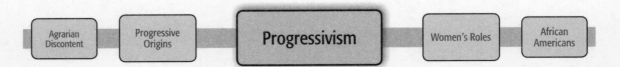

The election of 1912 saw Taft as the Republican candidate, Theodore Roosevelt as a Progressive Republican (or "Bull Moose"), and political newcomer Woodrow Wilson as the Democratic contender. The Socialists hoped to make a dent in the election again, with Eugene V. Debs again running for president. Taft was already faltering with low approval ratings, and Debs was not an option for most Americans due to his radical views. Therefore, Roosevelt and Wilson sparred for the Oval Office. Roosevelt introduced his vision of "New Nationalism," under which government would take a larger role in business regulations, women would be given the right to vote, and federal welfare programs would be offered to the poorest Americans. Wilson countered with "New Freedom," which promised a smaller, reformed government, decreased big business influence, and support for entrepreneurs and small businesses. Due to the split in the Republican Party, Wilson enjoyed an easy win but not enough to claim a mandate. Americans in large part supported the Progressive Party, a clear indication that the new president needed to take heed.

WILSON INTRODUCES NEW POLICIES

Woodrow Wilson was a deeply religious man who was always concerned about morality and justice. Wilson sought to break what he saw as the "triple wall of privilege": high tariffs, unfair banking practices, and monopolies by trusts. In 1913, he persuaded Congress to pass the **Underwood Tariff Bill**. Hoping to restore power to consumers, Wilson demanded reduced tariffs to keep the price of manufactured goods low. To offset the loss of federal revenues from the lower tariff, the Underwood Bill imposed the first permanent federal income tax on the well-to-do. The income tax had a strong constitutional basis, since the Sixteenth Amendment in 1913 had made federal income taxes legal. From this point on, tax revenues for the government would exceed tariff revenues.

In light of the recent Panic of 1907, Wilson was deeply concerned about the financial health of the nation. He looked to Congress to address the problem of the money supply. Congress passed the monumental **Federal Reserve Act** in 1913, which created the **Federal Reserve System**. The new banking system consisted of 12 regional banks that were publicly controlled by the new Federal Reserve Board but privately owned by member banks. The system would serve as the "lender of last resort" for all private banks, hold or sell the nation's bonds, and issue Federal Reserve Notes—otherwise known as dollar bills—for consumers to purchase goods and services. This was the first time since Andrew Jackson killed the Second Bank of the United States that the country would have a national bank.

The third of Wilson's goals was to curb the power of monopolies. His first step was to gain passage of the **Clayton Antitrust Act** in 1913, which finally gave some teeth to the weak and ineffective Sherman Antitrust Act of 1890. The Clayton Act strengthened provisions for breaking up trusts and protected labor unions from prosecution under the Sherman Act. American Federation of Labor leader Samuel Gompers hailed the bill as the "Magna Carta of Labor." Wilson's second step in controlling monopolies was the creation of the **Federal Trade Commission** in 1914. This

Agrarian Discontent — Progressive Origins — **Progressivism** — Women's Roles — African Americans

regulatory agency would monitor interstate business activities and force companies who broke laws to comply with government's "cease and desist" orders. Wilson's progressive legislation after 1914 would soon be eclipsed by gradual U.S. involvement in the Great War.

WOMEN'S ROLES: FAMILY, WORK, EDUCATION, AND SUFFRAGE

Progressive politicians were not so liberal as to accept that women should have a voice in politics. Still, women's roles in the United States continued to shift as industrialization took hold in more parts of the country. No longer was it necessary for a family to have many members to care for the family farm. Very few urban families had more than two children; thus, the role of the women as mother and homemaker decreased.

More and more women entered the workforce as factory jobs opened up. Women were mainly involved in the textile industry, working in spinning mills or large garment factories. Other women found work as telephone or telegraph operators, secretaries, or typists. As men moved out of these jobs, the pay was decreased for the "lesser sex." Some women entered the world of academia, as women's universities opened across the nation. Mount Holyoke, Wellesley, and Barnard all offered women the opportunity to learn in a liberal arts environment that they were not afforded anywhere else.

Not all women could afford to attend college; they had to enter the workforce to keep their families alive. Some even broke through the male-dominated organization of the labor unions to promote better working conditions for females. The International Ladies' Garment Workers Union (ILGWU) organized women who worked in sweatshops in cities like New York and Chicago by planning pickets and walkouts. On March 25, 1911, the unspeakable happened in a New York City sweatshop. **The Triangle Shirtwaist Factory** was housed in the top floors of the Asch building, where women, some as young as 15 years old, were crammed in. Windows, doors, and fire exits were completely blocked by people, machines, and trash cans. That night, just before closing, a fire broke out on the ninth floor. With no way to escape, many of the young women died in the building, while others jumped from windows to the pavement below. After the flames were finally tamed, the fire had taken 146 of 500 employees' lives. The ILGWU organized protest rallies to inform others around the country of the tragedy. As a result, the state of New York made massive reforms in the conditions of its garment factories. This victory was bittersweet, however, as the owners of the factory were later acquitted of any wrongdoing, even though they knew the exits and fire escapes were all locked.

Active among the railroad workers and coal miners, female activist **Mother Jones** traveled the country protesting and lobbying for the rights of all workers. Even as she lost her ability to write and walk without assistance, Mother Jones continued to fight for labor rights up until her death at the age of 94 in 1930.

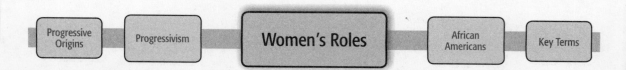

College-educated women were emboldened by the successes of their male Progressive counterparts and looked to improve their standing in the United States as well. The **National American Woman Suffrage Association** (NAWSA) gained a new president in 1900 with the election of **Carrie Chapman Catt**. Catt was an outspoken advocate of women's suffrage. She believed that women could only guarantee protections for themselves and their children through voting. The NAWSA would soon have some inner conflict, as more aggressive members of the group wanted to push for more immediate action. Led by **Alice Paul**, this splinter group left the NAWSA to form the **National Woman's Party** in 1913. The women in this group often picketed important sites, such as the White House and the Capitol, to demand the right to vote. Arrests occurred, and the women were known for going on hunger strikes while in jail. President Woodrow Wilson was disgusted with the militant protesters, who would chain themselves to the White House gates, yell insults at the president, and carry signs intending to embarrass the executive. He did, however, listen to Carrie Chapman Catt, who skillfully used the American mobilization for entrance into the Great War as her rallying cry. She claimed that armed with the vote, American women would support their president and country as it entered the world-wide crisis. Her message, delivered on the eve of the congressional vote on women's suffrage, hit home. President Wilson gave his public support for the amendment.

Due to the efforts of women such as Catt, the **Nineteenth Amendment**, which granted women the right to vote, was signed into law in 1920. Catt formed the **League of Women Voters** to assist the new voters, while Paul continued working with the National Woman's Party and shifted her focus to the Equal Rights Amendment (ERA), which repeatedly failed passage and finally succumbed in the early 1980s.

AFRICAN AMERICANS AT THE TURN OF THE CENTURY

As mentioned before, the Progressives were largely white, middle-class citizens who were interested in preserving their way of life from the wickedness of poverty, drunkenness, and corruption. African Americans were basically ignored by Progressive agendas at the local, state, and national levels. Progressive President Woodrow Wilson even issued an executive order to segregate federal buildings and named the racist silent film ***Birth of a Nation***—which glamorized the history of the Ku Klux Klan—as one of his personal favorites. Since the end of Reconstruction, the protection of African American civil rights had decreased as the legislative and judicial branches failed to take a stand against segregation, disenfranchisement, and lynching. It was up to the African Americans themselves to fight for their own rights.

Having risen to prominence during the late 1890s, **Booker T. Washington** continued to argue that African Americans needed the skills necessary to work within the white world. In essence, he claimed that blacks needed to make themselves successful economically before they could become equal to whites. This view came to be known as "**accommodation**." On the other side of the fence was Harvard-educated **W. E. B. Du Bois**, who disagreed vehemently with Washington. Du Bois believed that African Americans should demand nothing less than social and political equality with whites; only then would blacks gain economic success. In 1905, Du Bois held a meeting in Niagara Falls to discuss possible forms of protest and to formulate a plan of action. This group, called the **Niagara Movement**, joined forces with other concerned African Americans and whites to form the **National Association for the Advancement of Colored People (NAACP)** on February 12, 1908. Originally called the National Negro Committee, founding members W. E. B. Du Bois, Ida Wells-Barnett, Henry Moscowitz, Mary White Ovington, Oswald Garrison Villiard, and William English Walling answered what they deemed the "Call" to end all racial discrimination, segregation, and disenfranchisement. The NAACP became one of the largest and most active civil rights groups in the country. It was so influential that it pushed President Wilson to make a public statement condemning lynching in 1918.

The activism of the NAACP and Booker T. Washington was spurred by the increase in discriminatory practices throughout the country. In the period between 1910 and 1930, a "**Great Migration**" of millions of African Americans moved from the South to Northern cities in search of jobs and a better life. Just as the cities lured European immigrants during the 1880s, the promise of factory work and less discrimination brought blacks to urban centers. Unfortunately, the stories filtering to the South were fairy tales. Blacks experienced horrible living conditions, low-paying jobs, and racial unrest with both whites and other ethnic groups in the city's large ghetto neighborhoods. African Americans would find the fight against discrimination just as difficult in the North as it was in the South.

KEY TERMS	
Names	Jacob Coxey
	Theodore Roosevelt
	Ida Tarbell
	Lincoln Steffens
	Jacob Riis
	Robert La Follette
	Samuel Gompers
	Mother Jones
	Carrie Chapman Catt
	Booker T. Washington
	W. E. B. Du Bois
	Alice Paul

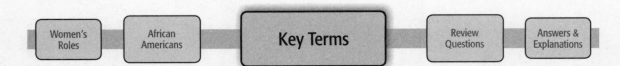

Women's Roles | African Americans | **Key Terms** | Review Questions | Answers & Explanations

Groups	Stalwarts
	Halfbreeds
	Mugwumps
	Greenback Party
	Farmers' Alliance
	Populist Party
	Gold Bugs
	muckrakers
	Northern Securities Company
	Federal Trade Commission
	National American Women Suffrage Association
	National Women's Party
	Niagara Movement
	League of Women Voters
	Advancement of Colored People (NAACP)
Events	Panic of 1893
	"Cross of Gold" speech
	Progressive Era
	Wisconsin Experiment
	Great Migration
Documents and Laws	Pendleton Civil Service Act of 1881
	Seventeenth Amendment
	Square Deal
	Elkins Act
	Hepburn Act
	The Jungle
	Pure Food and Drug Act
	Meat Inspection Act
	Mann-Elkins Act
	Sixteenth Amendment
	Underwood Tariff Bill
	Federal Reserve Act
	Federal Reserve System
	Clayton Antitrust Act
	Nineteenth Amendment
	Birth of a Nation
Places	Triangle Shirtwaist Factory
Vocabulary	initiative, referendum, and recall
	accommodation
	spoils system
	patronage
	direct primaries

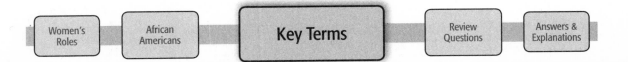

Women's Roles | African Americans | **Key Terms** | Review Questions | Answers & Explanations

REVIEW QUESTIONS

1. The Progressives were largely

   (A) working-class Americans fighting for labor rights.

   (B) minority groups seeking social justice.

   (C) middle-class whites looking to preserve their way of life.

   (D) conservative Republicans reacting to Mugwumps.

   (E) Midwest farmers seeking revenge against big business.

2. The major issue of the 1896 election was

   (A) the free and unlimited coinage of silver.

   (B) the lowering of high tariffs.

   (C) veterans' pensions.

   (D) civil service reform.

   (E) welfare for the poor.

3. President Roosevelt named journalists "muckrakers" because

   (A) he thought they were helpful in cleaning up corruption.

   (B) they aided in his fight against trusts.

   (C) their essays liberated the urban poor.

   (D) he thought they had gone too far with sensationalism.

   (E) of their attacks on Congress.

4. Progressive Republicans supported Theodore Roosevelt in the 1912 election because

   (A) Populists were poised to take a number of votes from the party.

   (B) Taft had abandoned them during his term.

   (C) conservative Republicans were going to run Eugene V. Debs.

   (D) Taft refused to intervene in a coal strike.

   (E) Roosevelt promised to keep the United States out of war.

5. An example of the limits of Progressivism is

   (A) the abandonment of the gold standard.

   (B) the creation of the Federal Reserve.

   (C) the implementation of the income tax.

   (D) the enactment of the Clayton Antitrust Act.

   (E) Wilson's executive order to segregate federal buildings.

ANSWERS AND EXPLANATIONS

1. C

Middle-class, white Americans were frightened by the changes rapidly occurring around them. To protect their way of life, the Progressives sought to rid society of ills such as monopoly, poverty, alcohol, and corruption that would possibly threaten their Victorian, moralistic lifestyle.

2. A

Farmers, with the help of William Jennings Bryan's "Cross of Gold" speech, made silver the main issue of the 1896 election.

3. D

Theodore Roosevelt was a bit annoyed with the journalists and authors he called "muckrakers." The president felt that the group had sunk to the level of pandering by sensationalizing everyday events as more dramatic than they were.

4. B

Progressives grew increasingly angered at President Taft as he continually ignored their needs and desires to side with the conservative "Old Guard" wing of the Republican Party. Thus, they broke away and created their own ticket for the election—the Progressive or "Bull Moose" Party.

5. E

President Woodrow Wilson proved just how narrow "progress" was when he issued an executive order that would segregate federal buildings such as post offices. Wilson was not very fond of giving women the vote until he saw the need to have their support for U.S. entry into the Great War.

CHAPTER 22: FOREIGN POLICY, 1865–1919

NEW IMPERIALISM VIA POLITICS AND ECONOMICS

With the closing of the western frontier, many Americans felt that Manifest Destiny had still not been fulfilled. That, coupled with the increase in population, wealth, and industry, led many to believe that the time was ripe to expand beyond the contiguous United States.

SEWARD'S FOLLY

First on the new map was Alaska, a region held by Russia on the northwestern edge of North America. Secretary of State William H. Seward brokered a deal to purchase the icy land from Russia for a sum of $7.2 million in 1867. Seward was seen by many as a laughingstock, and Alaska was nicknamed "**Seward's Folly**" or "**Seward's Icebox**." Not until the 20th century would Americans realize the sweet deal they had received when oil drillers found that Alaska was rich with fossil fuel.

OVERSEAS EXPANSION

Survival of the fittest: wealth flows naturally to those with the best capacity to manage it

Charles Darwin had not realized the extent to which people throughout the world would take his theory of evolution and mold it to fit their specific needs. Industrialists had used it to justify their wealth with "social Darwinism," and imperialists would alter the theory to justify their expansionism in the late 19th and early 20th centuries. After the ease with which Americans had removed the Native American population from the west, it seemed natural to remove other native populations overseas from the way of "progress." *Imperialism* was not a new idea. European nations had been gathering their fair share of new colonies as early as the mid-1800s in places such as Africa and Asia. It was this early expansion that led President Monroe to deliver his Monroe Doctrine to Congress in 1823. This "new" imperialism was spurred by the concept of *jingoism* (extreme *nationalism* that encourages a very aggressive foreign policy stance), the need to find new markets in which to sell American goods, and Darwinism.

American industry began to produce more than it was selling, needed more customers

Might be a good word to use in exam

One proponent of overseas expansion was U.S. Naval Captain Alfred Thayer Mahan. His influential book *The Influence of Sea Power upon History* (1890) focused on the idea that the

| New Imperialism | Great War | War at Home | Versailles Peace | Postwar Society |

United States needed to pour money and resources into the building a powerful, world-class navy to become a major world power broker. To do this, Mahan contended that the United States would need to occupy sites around the world to establish refueling stations and naval bases. The most logical areas for such bases were Hawaii and Cuba. Mahan also advocated the building of a canal across the Isthmus of Panama to provide a quick route from the Pacific to the Atlantic. Thus, the focus for early expansion was on Pacific islands and Central America. American Minister to Hawaii John Stevens perfectly illustrated the U.S. view of the islands when he said, "The Hawaiian pear is now fully ripe, and this is the golden hour for the United States to pluck it." He uttered these words as an unauthorized battalion of U.S. troops landed on the islands to assist a planter revolt, led by the pineapple exporter Sanford B. Dole. The revolt began when a new, nationalist queen named Liliuokalani took the throne and began to work on expelling whites from the islands. Dole and a small band of planters revolted against the queen and her people and demanded assistance from the United States. But by the time word had reached President Cleveland, the damage had been done. A treaty to authorize the *annexation* of the islands had already reached Congress. Cleveland was outraged by the debacle and refused to sign the treaty, instead demanding the reseating of the queen on the throne and the immediate removal of American troops. He was unsuccessful in his bid, however, as Dole and his followers declared Hawaii an independent republic in 1894. Hopes of annexation faded until 1898, when Dole was appointed to serve as provincial governor of the islands.

United States' imperialism characterized by objectification

THE SPANISH-AMERICAN WAR

The debate regarding overseas expansionism moved to the Caribbean, as trouble reared its head on the Spanish-held island of Cuba. Americans had moved to Cuba after the Civil War to establish large sugar plantations on the lush, tropical island. Cuban natives had been growing more and more irritated by the presence of foreigners, American and Spanish, amassing huge fortunes while they toiled on the plantations and subsisted from day to day. The Spanish sensed the seeds of revolt and set to nip a revolution in the bud by "**reconcentrating**" the Cuban natives into central locations under direct Spanish control. Many Cubans died as a result of this effort to rid the country of revolutionaries.

Americans heard of the atrocities, real and sensationalized, from the American popular press. Papers such as Hearst's *Journal* and Pulitzer's *World* radically altered the truth of stories coming out of Cuba in the effort to sell papers. This kind of writing was dubbed "**Yellow Journalism**," after a popular color comic strip called "Yellow Kid" that ran exclusively in Hearst's paper. As a result, many Americans and Cuban immigrants in the United States grew increasingly concerned over the events in Cuba. American jingoism also contributed to concerns over the island. Presidents Cleveland and McKinley did not favor this position, however. It would take a supposed attack on the United States to make war an option for McKinley.

New Imperialism — Great War — War at Home — Versailles Peace — Postwar Society

The popular stance on Cuba began to shift toward war when, in 1898, a letter was leaked to Hearst's *Journal*. In this letter, Spanish Minister to the United States Dupuy de Lome insinuated that President McKinley was corrupt. Americans immediately took this as a direct insult from the Spanish. The next event made war inevitable in the eyes of most Americans. On February 15, 1898, the U.S.S. *Maine* exploded in Havana Harbor under mysterious circumstances. The ship had arrived in the Cuban harbor to provide protection and act as an escape vessel for the Americans currently living on the island. The ship exploded while anchored in the harbor, killing 260 sailors and injuring many more. The Spanish immediately responded to accusations by denying any role in the tragedy. The Americans sent down a crew to investigate the wreckage and declared that a submarine mine had sunk the ship. Hearst and Pulitzer took to the story and blamed the Spanish for the tragedy, further fanning flames of anger. Americans now cried "Remember the *Maine*" to push President McKinley to declare war on Spain. The president was reluctant to issue the war decree without some caveats. The **Teller Amendment** was added to the war declaration to assure Cuba and the world that the United States intended to grant Cuba her independence once the war ended.

Accident. Spanish had nothing to do with it, but effectively sparked the war.

The Spanish-American War officially began on April 11, 1898. Fighting did not begin in Cuba but rather in the Spanish colony of the Philippines. U.S. Naval Commodore George Dewey was sent with his fleet to Manila Bay and opened fire on May 1. The naval battle was short-lived— the U.S. Navy was able to rout the Spanish fleet in a matter of days. But as the battle made landfall, it was not quite as easy. Many Filipinos fought to oust both the Spanish and American forces. The United States was able to convince the Filipino revolutionary Emilio Aguinaldo to assist in the fight against the Spanish in exchange for independence after the war's end. As a result, the American and Filipino fighters were able to take Manila by August.

Essentially caused by increased tension between Spanish and Americans.

The fight in Cuba would be much more difficult—not due to better Spanish fighters but due to tropical diseases and the inexperience of the American forces. Most American causalities, some 5,000, were attributed to diseases and food poisoning, with just 10 percent due to actual combat. The most celebrated American battle was for the high ground of San Juan Hill. Theodore Roosevelt and his volunteer force of college students, cowboys, and adventurers called the "**Rough Riders**" were able to take the Hill with the heavy assistance of the Fourteenth Regiment Colored Calvary.

Convinced President Roosevelt to pass Pure food & Drug Act

U.S. INVADES PUERTO RICO

After the United States claimed victory in Cuba on July 1, it invaded the Spanish colony of Puerto Rico. Unable to fight any longer, the Spanish signed a cease fire with the United States in August 1898.

Not, by any means, a very long war. Hardly feels like a war, in fact.

New Imperialism | Great War | War at Home | Versailles Peace | Postwar Society

The resulting peace treaty signed in Paris gave the United States the Pacific island of Guam and the Caribbean island of Puerto Rico. The most difficult decision was what to do with the Philippines. President McKinley was between a rock and a hard place. On one hand, he could give the Philippines their independence as promised and risk either the possibility of a radical dictator taking over the islands or a European power taking control. Or he could take the islands and face the court of world opinion. He decided that the United States would take the Philippines and deal with the independence issue at a later date.

PROBLEMS WITH THE NEW EXPANSION

The debate over imperialism only intensified with the end of the Spanish-American War. Anti-imperialists such as **William Jennings Bryan**, even formed an organization to oppose U.S. expansion publicly. Citizens living in newly conquered territories brought cases regarding their constitutional rights to the U.S. Supreme Court. In 1901, the Court ruled in the **Insular Cases** that the Constitution and its protections did not follow the flag. In other words, a citizen in a conquered territory did not necessarily have the protection of the Constitution. It was up to Congress to decide the rights of the peoples in the newly conquered territories. As Cuba set to draft its constitution, the United States grew unsure of the Teller Amendment and its promise to give Cuba independence with no strings attached. Thus, the United States issued the **Platt Amendment** in 1902, which Cubans would now have to write into their new constitution to gain freedom. The provisions of the Platt Amendment were that Cuba had to have all treaties approved by the United States before signing, the United States had the right to interfere in Cuban affairs both politically and militarily, and the United States would be given access to naval bases on the island. In essence, the Cubans had not gained their independence at all.

The United States had to put out other fires throughout the world after it dealt with Cuba. The Filipinos, under the leadership of the once-American ally Aguinaldo, broke out into a revolt against the American presence. Horrible guerrilla warfare broke out between the Filipino revolutionaries and Americans in the jungles of the islands in 1899. Aguinaldo and his fighters were finally subdued by the Americans in 1901, when the leader was captured. The Philippines did not gain their independence until 1946.

China was another area of concern for Americans, especially investors. Japan and European nations had already carved China up into *spheres of influence* in which they basically controlled the economic dealings of the regions. Hoping to get a piece of the action, Secretary of State John Hay issued his answer to the problem in 1899. This was called the "**Open Door Policy**." Under the Open Door, China and her surrounding regions would be open and free to trade with any nation. The policy was wildly popular in the United States but received a cold shoulder abroad. In 1900, a young group of Chinese nationalists revolted against the Open Door Policy and foreign intervention. The **Boxer Rebellion** sought to remove all foreigners from China by force. The rebels killed some 200 whites, and a multinational force, including U.S. forces, was sent to Peking

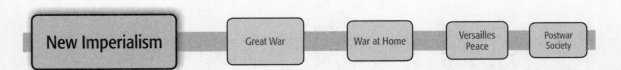

New Imperialism → Great War → War at Home → Versailles Peace → Postwar Society

to end the rebellion. It was clear that the Chinese were not interested in foreign intervention in their political and economic affairs.

THE PANAMA CANAL

The canal that Mahan had suggested became a reality, as Americans and Europeans sought to build it across the Isthmus of Panama. The canal was already under construction by Ferdinand de Lesseps, who had constructed the Suez Canal. Unfortunately, the construction effort was plagued with setbacks—workers fell to disease and engineering troubles ensued due to the tropical climate and geography, respectively. The United States was more than willing to take over the building of the canal, but several issues remained in the way. First, the United States needed to secure the right to build the canal from Colombia, since the canal would go right through the country. The Colombian government did not agree to the **Hay-Pauncefote Treaty**, in which the British granted full construction rights to the Americans. The nation of Panama would have to be created, and quickly.

Under secrecy and with the aid of the French, President Theodore Roosevelt raised a revolutionary force to fight for Panamanian independence from Colombia. The "revolution" ended as quickly as it began; Roosevelt immediately recognized the new nation. It came as no surprise that the Panamanian government quickly signed an agreement to allow the United States to build the canal exclusively in 1903. The building was completed in 1914. Critics of Roosevelt's policy regarding Panama branded his actions "**gunboat diplomacy**." Latin American countries were becoming increasingly alarmed at the way the "Colossus of the North" was flexing its muscles throughout the region.

The United States of America.

THE ROOSEVELT COROLLARY CHANGES RELATIONS ABROAD

President Roosevelt had his own style of imperialism aside from the Panama Canal. The president was growing increasingly concerned over problems with the nation of Venezuela and attempts by Britain and Germany to collect debts from the country. In an attempt to protect the Latin American nation from European intervention, President Roosevelt amended the Monroe Doctrine to come to the aid of Latin American neighbors. This new policy, called the **Roosevelt Corollary**, stated that the United States would come to the aid of any Latin American nation experiencing financial trouble. In essence, the United States became the police officer of Latin America through the Corollary.

Under this new reality, the United States used force to "protect" the Dominican Republic and Cuba from political chaos. Roosevelt also intervened in the Russo-Japanese War of 1904. Russia and Japan were feuding over land and ports in Korea and Manchuria. Roosevelt did not want either nation to win control over the region and approached Japan to assist in the settlement of the war. The **Treaty of Portsmouth** was signed in 1905 to end the war. A year later, Theodore Roosevelt won the Nobel Peace Prize for his role in mediating the treaty.

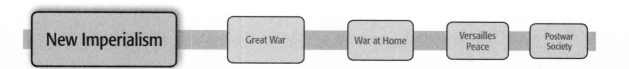

New Imperialism   Great War   War at Home   Versailles Peace   Postwar Society

NEGOTIATIONS WITH JAPAN

U.S.-Japanese relations were not perfect after the end of the war, however. An influx of Japanese immigrants flooded the city of San Francisco to escape the financial crisis of their homeland and to start life anew. White San Franciscans were terrified of the possibility of the Japanese taking over their city, and they began passing restrictive laws aimed directly at the incoming immigrants, such as banning Japanese children from attending public school. The Japanese were enraged at the discrimination, and Theodore Roosevelt decided to step in. The president was able to craft a "**Gentleman's Agreement**" between the San Francisco School Board and the Japanese government. The school board would allow Japanese students to enter public school if the Japanese government would help stem the tide of immigrants coming to California. Not wanting the Japanese to think that the United States had given in to their wishes as a show of weakness, Roosevelt sent the U.S. Navy, nicknamed the **Great White Fleet**, around the world as a show of power. From this point on, U.S.-Japanese relations were amiable but strained.

TAFT AND WILSON ON IMPERIALISM

President Taft used a different tactic to deal with foreign relations—his was much more an economic system than militaristic. Taft's **Dollar Diplomacy** encouraged Wall Street investors to send their dollars to foreign countries, such as those in Latin America, to weaken European bonds and strengthen ties with the United States. However, when these American investments were endangered, Taft on several occasions sent U.S. forces to invade Latin American countries and protect American interests. These actions further alienated the United States from Latin America.

President Wilson, in contrast, believed imperialism was immoral. Yet he also believed in the superiority of American democracy and thought it was his duty to spread that ideal to protect nations under threat of totalitarianism. This policy became known as **Moral Diplomacy**. As a result, Wilson invaded Nicaragua and the Dominican Republic and purchased the Virgin Islands. Wilson also intervened in the Mexican Revolution to capture the revolutionary Pancho Villa after he had killed Americans in the towns of Santa Ysabel, Mexico, and Columbus, New Mexico. The United States was finally forced to withdraw from the civil war in Mexico in 1917. However, another, dramatically larger war was in progress that would soon trouble President Wilson.

THE GREAT WAR AND INITIAL NEUTRALITY

Initially, President Wilson sought to keep the United States out of the affairs of Europe. However, military and political alliances all over Europe, militarism, and extreme nationalism made war inevitable after the assassination of the **Archduke Francis Ferdinand** of Austria-Hungary by a Serbian nationalist in 1914. For the United States, there was no desire to enter the war. Many Americans were anti-German and did not feel that U.S. national security was in danger.

| New Imperialism | Great War | War at Home | Versailles Peace | Postwar Society |

Yet Americans did not stay completely out of the war in the early years. The outbreak of war in Europe had devastating effects on the American economy. A deep recession was spurred by the drain of hard specie, as European nations looked for debt repayment in the form of gold and silver. There was also a loss of profitable overseas markets for U.S. products. Thankfully, by 1915, Britain and France looked to the United States to supply them with munitions of war, giving the economy a much-needed boost. Also, the demand for U.S. foodstuffs became a boon to the American farmer.

DEBUT OF THE GERMAN U-BOAT

U.S. neutrality was severely tested after both Britain and France imposed naval blockades against the Germans. The Germans had a new weapon that they would use to terrorize shipping traffic across the Atlantic. The German **U-Boat** (submarine) would strike ships as they crossed the Atlantic, whether civilian or military.

The Germans claimed that these ships might be carrying munitions of war for Britain or France and must be stopped. By September of 1915, German U-Boats had sunk 90 ships in the Atlantic and surrounding waters. One such ship was the British luxury liner *Lusitania*. Almost 1,200 lives were lost (about 130 of those American) as the ship was sunk off the coast of Ireland. Wilson, still not wishing to enter the war, issued a stern warning to the Germans to cease submarine warfare on unarmed ships. After the sinking of another liner that cost the lives of two Americans, the Germans finally agreed to stop this type of attack.

arabic

The promise was short-lived. In March 1916, the Germans attacked the French passenger liner *Sussex*, killing four Americans. Wilson issued the **Sussex Ultimatum**, where he warned the Germans to stop submarine warfare or the United States would break all diplomatic relations with Germany. This move clearly signaled America's willingness to go to war. Germany again agreed to stop submarine warfare but only if the United States convinced Britain to lift its deadly blockade. In the meantime, Wilson just   waited.

In January 1917, an announcement came from Germany—it would again start unrestricted submarine warfare and would sink any ship violating the war zone, including American ships. Wilson immediately broke relations with Germany. He also had another trick up his sleeve but waited for the right moment to bring it out. On March 2, 1917, Wilson received word that a British agent had intercepted and decoded a letter from the German Foreign Secretary Zimmerman to the German ambassador to Mexico. The letter contained a promise from the German government to the Mexican president that if his country assisted Germany in a possible war against the United States, Mexico would be given back the territory lost in the Mexican-American War after Germany's victory. Wilson had the ammunition he needed—the security

Zimmerman
—telegram

| New Imperialism | **Great War** | War at Home | Versailles Peace | Postwar Society |

of the United States had been directly threatened. After the news of the telegram and the German sinking of four unarmed American merchant vessels, the United States was now poised to enter the "**Great War**."

IMPACT OF THE WAR AT HOME

The United States was woefully unprepared to enter the war in Europe. Woodrow Wilson's idealism, stubbornness, and belief in American exceptionalism led the country through the crisis. Wilson truly believed that the Great War was the "war to end all wars." He also believed that the American way of life, including democracy, was better than any other system in the world and that it was his duty to "make the world safe for democracy." In preparation for his postwar vision, Wilson delivered his **Fourteen Points** speech to Congress on January 8, 1918. Wilson's points provided for the abolishment of secret treaties, freedom of the seas, economic freedom, reduction of arms, the end of colonialization, the freedom of *self-determination* of all peoples to choose independence, and the formation of an international organization for collective security. This last point was the most important to Wilson, but it would also be a thorn in his side as the war ended.

The United States mobilized for war reluctantly. The country was aided by the formation of the **Committee on Public Information**, headed by George Creel. This department was given the task of informing Americans of the war through a massive propaganda machine. Posters, speeches, and "liberty leagues" throughout the country encouraged Americans to buy war bonds and support the war effort. Herbert Hoover headed up the Food Administration, which encouraged Americans to have "meatless" Mondays, to grow "victory gardens," and to limit the amount of food they ate. Americans also stopped eating "German" foods, such as frankfurters (liberty sausages) and sauerkraut (liberty cabbage). Americans ceased playing German music, and the German language was no longer taught in the schools. American factories soon found themselves under the **War Industries Board**, headed by Bernard Baruch, which sought to control production, wages, and prices of manufactured goods.

Propagandists

Raising the army was another difficult task for the government, as allies were begging for fresh men to fight the Germans. In response, Wilson urged the passage of the **Selective Service Act** (1917), which authorized the conscription of American males into military service. Within months of its passage, the army had enough men to relieve the allied forces overseas.

Americans experienced a curbing of their civil liberties during wartime. Mostly aimed at Germans and antiwar protesters, the **Espionage Act** of 1917 and **Sedition Act** of 1918 curbed the right to free speech. *Socialists* such as Eugene V. Debs were targeted and arrested. In the pivotal ruling of ***Schenck v. United States***, the Supreme Court, with Justice Oliver Wendell Holmes writing the majority opinion, upheld the Espionage Act by stating that Congress could limit the right of free speech if it represented a "clear and present danger" that would bring about "evils" that the government was seeking to stop. Unfortunately, the war years were an ugly time for civil liberties—many Americans served time well into the 1920s and 1930s for wartime "crimes."

New Imperialism — Great War — **War at Home** — Versailles Peace — Postwar Society

NEGOTIATING PEACE AT VERSAILLES

As the fighting ended and it was time to negotiate peace, President Wilson hoped to further his Fourteen Points in the treaty talks at **Versailles**, located just outside of Paris. The president had lost some pull at home, however, as the 1918 midterm elections brought a narrow Republican majority to Congress. Wilson infuriated the legislative branch when he traveled without any Republicans to Versailles to negotiate the peace terms with the European powers. This would later haunt him when he worked to get the treaty ratified by Congress.

The peace conference began on January 18, 1919, with the "**Big Four**"—Woodrow Wilson, Georges Clemenceau of France, Vittorio Orlando of Italy, and David Lloyd George of Great Britain—meeting at Versailles Palace. Germany and Russia were conspicuously absent from the meeting. Being a rather stubborn idealist, Wilson was determined to see his Fourteen Points to fruition, especially his fourteenth point (the call for the creation of a League of Nations). The other European leaders were interested in exacting revenge from Germany, which they believed was responsible for the war. This made Wilson's job rather difficult—he had to compromise to see his ideas become a reality. One of the first areas of compromise was the idea of "mandates," in which conquered territories would not become the property of the conquering nation but would rather be under the trusteeship of the League. Wilson would rather have left the conquering countries free to determine their fate, but the Balkan and Baltic States were given independence.

[handwritten margin note: well duh. Actually not really.]

Eventually, Wilson would have to compromise on most of his Fourteen Points and give in to the desires of the European powers to assign full blame of the war and its consequences on Germany. Woodrow Wilson did get his **League of Nations and Article X** of the League's charter, which called for members to stand at the ready if another member nation's sovereignty was being threatened.

It was Article X, along with the other mistakes Wilson made in the eyes of the Republicans, that would derail ratification of the Versailles Treaty in the United States. One of the most outspoken opponents of the president and of the treaty was Republican Senator Henry Cabot Lodge. Those who were opposed to ratification of the treaty fell into two camps, the **reservationists** and the **irreconcilables**. Lodge and his reservationists would only agree to ratify the treaty if "reservations" such as the ability to leave the League and international acceptance of the Monroe Doctrine were added to the League's Covenant. The irreconcilables, led by Senators Hiram Johnson and William Borah, refused to ratify the treaty under any circumstances. Wilson had to act quickly to save the treaty and the League of Nations.

President Wilson got on a train and traveled the United States to speak directly to the American public about the treaty and its importance. While in Colorado, the president collapsed of exhaustion. A few days later, he suffered a stroke, which left him partially paralyzed and unable to meet with his executive cabinet for seven months.

The Senate voted on the treaty twice in 1919, both times failing to ratify. Eventually, the fight over the treaty turned on whether or not it would be accepted with or without reservations. Democrats

| Great War | War at HIme | **Versailles Peace** | Postwar Society | Key Terms |

were split: some voted with the reservationists; loyal Wilson supporters voted to reject the treaty rather than accept it with reservations. The election of 1920, in Wilson's eyes, would be a "solemn referendum" on the treaty, as he hoped Americans would give his Democratic party a majority in Congress and continued control of the White House. It was the Republicans, however, dominated the election. The United States did not officially end the war with Germany until 1921 and never ratified the Treaty of Versailles. As a result, the United States did not join the League of Nations, thus weakening the organization.

POST–WORLD WAR I AMERICAN SOCIETY AND ECONOMY

Returning from war was difficult for American "Doughboys." The federal government did not have any plans for helping war veterans re-establish themselves in civilian life. The realities of trench warfare and the horrors of war left many veterans scarred both physically and mentally. Many American veterans returned from Europe with missing limbs, facial disfigurements, and "shell shock" (now called post-traumatic stress disorder). While most war veterans found work quickly when they returned to the States, they displaced thousands of women and African Americans who had held these jobs during the war years.

TROUBLES ABROAD

Tensions rose as society shifted from wartime to peacetime. Aside from the end of the war, other developments in Europe frightened Americans and caused social unrest as the country entered the 1920s. The 1917 **Communist Revolution** in Russia frightened middle- and upper-class Americans, as the Bolsheviks overthrew the Provisional Government of Russia and pledged to destroy capitalism. Socialists and anarchists in the United States had been persecuted throughout the war, and their problems intensified as fears over communism rose. Attorney General A. Mitchell Palmer fanned the flames of unrest after a series of bombings, one that occurred in his neighborhood and was attributed to anarchist groups. Palmer immediately ordered the rounding up of suspected anarchists, socialists, aliens (usually Russian), and agitators and started what is known as the **Red Scare**. Some 6,000 people were arrested in a two-month period, and 500 were deported on "Soviet Arks," which sent the passengers back to Europe.

LABOR AND RACE ISSUES

Fears of socialist or communist takeover spilled over into labor conflicts, which peaked in 1919. Organized labor felt the need to protect workers as the nation fell into a recession. Many companies had to lay off employees and drastically cut wages. As labor strikes grew increasingly violent, many Americans began to believe the labor unions were being infiltrated and funded by communist groups. As a result, the federal government began to take a hard-line stance with regard to strikes, especially in cases where the public safety was at risk.

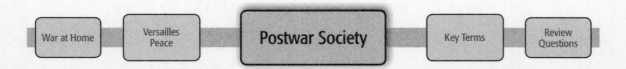

One of the most notable strikes occurred in Boston, when police officers refused to work because they wanted the right to organize collectively and a wage increase. Governor of Massachusetts Calvin Coolidge felt that the police had no right to strike because doing so would place the public safety at risk. As a result, Coolidge sent in the National Guard to break the strike, making him an instant hero in the eyes of many Americans.

Racial issues also came to the surface as the nation moved into the new decade. Having been fired in favor of war veterans returning from Europe, African Americans in many cities began to voice their anger with whites. Racial riots broke out in Chicago, Baltimore, and Omaha, where African Americans burned and looted as they expressed their anger and resentment toward discrimination and poverty.

KEY TERMS

Names	William Jennings Bryan
	Archduke Francis Ferdinand
Groups	Rough Riders
	Great White Fleet
	Committee on Public Information
	War Industries Board
	Big Four F I B U
	League of Nations
	Socialists
Events	Seward's Folly or Seward's Icebox
	Spanish-American War
	Boxer Rebellion
	Gentlemen's Agreement
	Great War
	Communist Revolution
	Red Scare
Documents and Laws	Teller Amendment
	Insular Cases
	Platt Amendment
	Open Door Policy
	Hay-Pauncefote Treaty
	Roosevelt Corollary
	Treaty of Portsmouth
	Sussex Ultimatum
	Fourteen Points
	Selective Services Act
	Espionage Act
	Sedition Act
	Schenck v. United States
	Article X

Places	Versailles
Vocabulary	jingoism
	reconcentrating
	yellow journalism
	gunboat diplomacy
	Dollar Diplomacy
	Moral Diplomacy
	U-boat
	Lusitania
	mandates
	reservationists
	irreconcilables
	imperialism
	nationalism
	spheres of influence
	self-determination
	reparations

REVIEW QUESTIONS

1. The cartoon shown above illustrates

   (A) the acceptance of the Roosevelt Corollary by Panama.

   (B) Roosevelt traveling to meet the Rough Riders.

   (C) American involvement in the Panamanian Revolution.

   (D) America going to assist Colombia in fighting the British.

   (E) the opening of the Panama Canal.

2. American foreign policy at the end of the 19th century can be characterized as

   (A) supportive of the ideal of self-determination.

   (B) largely isolationist.

   (C) concerned about the rise of communist dictatorships in Latin America.

   (D) primarily interested in gaining economic markets.

   (E) driven by morality and Christian values.

3. Which of the following does NOT describe the United States as it entered World War I?

   (A) The U.S. military was in desperate need of new recruits.

   (B) The nation was 100 percent behind the decision to enter the war.

   (C) The United States had remained partially isolationist before entering the war.

   (D) The U.S. economy had rebounded due to British and French orders for war munitions.

   (E) The U.S. military was woefully unprepared to enter the war.

4. Herbert Hoover and the Food Administration gained success by

   (A) imposing harsh rationing of meat, sugar, and milk during the war.

   (B) using yellow journalism to appeal to Americans.

   (C) giving government subsidies to farmers for plowing under crops.

   (D) issuing war bonds to help finance the war.

   (E) relying on volunteerism to conserve food and energy in the United States.

5. The most damaging weakness of the League of Nations was that it

   (A) could not enforce mandates.

   (B) did not have the United States as a member nation.

   (C) did not include Germany.

   (D) was not financed by the World Bank.

   (E) did not provide collective security.

ANSWERS AND EXPLANATIONS

1. C

In a covert operation, Theodore Roosevelt intervened in the revolt of Panamanian rebels against Colombia. By sending military aid and funding the French and Panamanians, the United States was able to secure exclusive rights to build the Panama Canal after the successful revolt.

2. D

American manufacturers were experiencing problems with overproduction and needed to find markets overseas for their goods. As a result, American presidents sought to gain territory overseas or open other markets for trade with the United States.

3. B

Many Americans, such as William Jennings Bryan, were opposed to the war effort and spoke out publicly against President Wilson and U.S mobilization. Other groups, such as Populists, Progressives, and Socialists, also argued that U.S. involvement was unjustified.

4. E

A strong believer in private charity and the heart of Americans, Hoover was able to appeal to citizens to limit their consumption of meat, sugar, and energy without having to impose mandatory rationing. This was known as "voluntary compliance."

5. B

Due to the inability of the United States to ratify the Treaty of Versailles, the founding nation of the League failed to join the organization. This severely weakened the League and affected its ability to become a powerful force in the world.

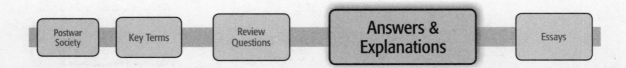

UNIT III SAMPLE ESSAYS

The following are sample free-response questions that you might see on the AP U.S. History exam. Listed under each question are important terms that would greatly add to your answer. AP Readers will look for you to mention at least several of the listed people. places, and things.

1. Compare and contrast the expansion that occurred during the 1840s with the expansion of the 1890s. Be sure to discuss the political, moral, and economic factors of each time period in your answer.

   Study List

   slavery

   popular sovereignty

   manifest destiny

   American nationalism

   Monroe Doctrine

   Oregon

   Mexican War

   President Polk

   Texas

   transcendentalism

   Josiah Strong

   Alfred Thayer Mahan

   Spanish-American War

   Teller Amendment

   Platt Amendment

   Roosevelt Corollary

   Dollar Diplomacy

   Guam

   Puerto Rico

   Hawaii

   Cuba

   Philippines

   Open Door Policy

   Anti-Imperialist League

   Insular Cases

2. How did the Progressive reformers significantly impact the lives of TWO of the following groups? Include local, state, or federal laws or court decisions to illustrate your answer.

Women

African Americans

White males

Study List

Nineteenth Amendment

Carrie Chapman Catt

Alice Paul

League of Women Voters

W. E. B. Du Bois

NAACP

Booker T. Washington

Tuskegee Institute

lynching

Jim Crow laws

secret ballot

direct primaries

direct election of senators

initiative, referendum, and recall

city councils

prohibition

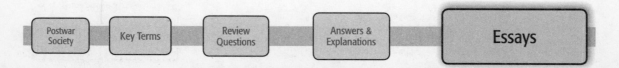

SAMPLE FRQ RESPONSES

Compare and contrast the expansion that occurred during the 1840s with the expansion of the 1890s. Be sure to discuss the political, moral, and economic factors of each time period in your answer.

In the 1840s the United States was attempting to keep other countries from conquering more of the continent. The focus shifted in the 1890s to the imperialist desire of the United States to rule other nations as Europeans did. Both the U.S. expansion in the 1840s and in the 1890s had roots in moral justifications for economic and political gains, but while the 1840s saw an expansion within North America by increased settlement West and the gain of lands previously held by Mexico, the expansion in the 1890s was focused on Latin America and East Asia.

President James Monroe's 1823 speech presenting the Monroe Doctrine became a key tenant of the United States's attitude toward expansion in the West, declaring that the Americas were no longer to be colonized by European countries and making way for U.S. increased settlement in the 1840s. Andrew Jackson, president from 1829 to 1837, had been a strong believer in settling the West and had battled Native Americans to help attain that goal. He was succeeded in 1844 by President James Polk, who wanted Mexican-held California and Oregon for white settlers. In 1846 Polk signed a treaty with Britain that gave them what is now western Canada, and in exchange the United States got what are now Oregon, Washington, Idaho, and part of Montana. Then America began the two-year-long Mexican War, winning California and a border set between Texas and Mexico that moved out to the Rio Grande. Polk, and many Americans, believed in Manifest Destiny, the theory that it was American settlers' God-given right to spread West, bringing democracy with them. This term also worked to aggrandize their settlement scheme, ignoring the fact that much of the motivation for growing the country Westward was financial greed. Transcendental religious teachings of the time encouraged people to believe that individuals held universally known truths, like the value of being kind to one's neighbor, rather than worshiping the institutions of the traditional Christian church. This new attitude of independent, democratic faith also encouraged settlers to go out on their own.

As settlers moved West in the 1840s, one key issue was whether or not the areas they were settling would become free states or slave states. Established states on either side were concerned that there remain a balance of free and slave states for political purposes. Some politicians believed in popular sovereignty, the term created by Stephen A. Douglas to define the idea that settlers should decide early on, on their own, which way they would go. Others believed that settlers should wait and vote as a collective when they were ready to form a state. Southern slaveholders and Northern abolitionists wanted settlers to decide earlier.

In the 1890s expansionism was still going strong, but this time it was focused on lands not part of the continental United States. Manifest Destiny had evolved into

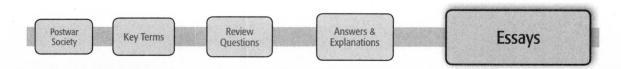

nationalistic, imperialist jingoism, an egotistical belief that America's superior belief system should be spread to other countries, making the country a superpower on par with European nations. This movement was led by leaders like Josiah Strong and Alfred Thayer Mahan, and was it justified by missionaries who felt it was the "white man's burden" to spread Christianity and by businessmen who saw a ripe financial opportunity.

From April to July of 1898 the United States engaged in the Spanish-American War, prompted by the warmongering of yellow journalists pushing images of the defeated U.S.S. *Maine* and decrying the cruelty of the Spanish toward their colony in Cuba, which concluded in an American victory and our ceding of lands in the Carribean and the Pacific: the Phillipines, Puerto Rico, Guam, and Cuba. The government had passed the Teller Amendment in April, promising to give Cubans their freedom once the Spanish were defeated. However, in 1901 the less generous Platt Amendment was passed, giving the conditions on which the United States would leave, which included ceding the naval base Guantanimo Bay to the United States and requiring that Cuba would not cede any land to or make any treaties with any country but the United States. Also in 1901 President Roosevelt's Roosevelt Corrolary to the Monroe Doctrine was passed, stating that Latin America was an agency for U.S. economic expansion, introducing an era when the United States used its economic influense to police Latin America. In 1896 Hawaii had became a state, after a U.S.-funded governement coup of the isolationist Queen Lili'uokalani in favor of the American fruit business interests there. The United States then began a campaign of "dollar diplomacy," using American business interests in Latin American and east-Asian countries to exert control on those nations and to keep them out of the hands of European nations. The United States pursued an Open Door Policy with nations like China, which made the United States the prefered economic trading partner there, further exerting economic control in the East.

The settlement of the West in the 1840s was justified by many through Manifest Destiny and spurred on by the competition between slave states and nonslave states for political control of the nation. The focus was on keeping lands geographically acessible to the United States from European control and gaining untapped economic opportunities. With this accomplished, in the 1890s the country began an era of imperialism, mimicking European nations and again justifying their desire for political and economic gain through the espoused belief that the United States's superior democratic system and religious beliefs should be spread to other lands.

How did the Progressive reformers significantly impact the lives of TWO of the following groups? Include local, state, or federal laws or court decisions to illustrate your answer.

> Women
> African Americans
> White males

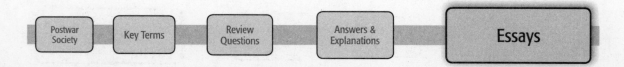

The Progressive Era began when Theodore Roosevelt was sworn into office in 1901. He was known as the Progressive's president, as he worked on many issues that ranged from providing social programs for the poverty stricken to breaking up the Northern Securities Company, which he regarded as a "harmful trust." Even though the Progressives had good intentions to better society, they still had their own private agenda. The Progressives were mostly white, male, middle-class Protestants who wanted to maintain the comfortable lifestyle they were accustomed to living. This selfish agenda excluded the rights of African Americans and women. It will become evident that the impacts made on the lives of African Americans and women were made by the two groups themselves.

African Americans were ignored on the local, state, and national levels of politics. It was no surprise, as lynching, segregation, and discrimination continued to occur following the decrease of protection granted to African Americans after the end of the Reconstruction era. Lack of progress was made evident as President Woodrow Wilson encouraged Jim Crow Laws by issuing an executive order to segregate federal buildings. He publicly announced that the silent film entitled *Birth of a Nation*, which celebrated the history of the Ku Klux Klan, as one of his favorite movies. With no one to lead them, the African Americans decided to lead themselves.

W. E. B. Du Bois believed that African Americans should demand nothing less than social and political equality with whites. At Niagara Falls in 1905, Du Bois held a meeting to form plans to achieve this goal. This group was called the Niagara Movement. Then in February of 1918, this group, together with other African Americans and whites, joined together to create the National Association for the Advancement of Colored People (NAACP). The NAACP made such an impact that President Wilson made a public statement in 1918 condemning lynching. This was a far cry from his declared love of his favorite Ku Klux Klan movie. This was also a big step, as lynching was the norm and raised no eyebrows at the time.

Women, too, unfortunately held little standing in politics during the Progressive Era. Still women could not be held down. With the rise of industrialization, women proved that they were able to take over the jobs that men vacated to take on new responsibilities. These jobs included factory work in spinning mills and the textile industry. There were also administrative positions such as secretaries, typists, and telephone operators. Some women even entered into the education field as universities for women opened up. When women entered the workforce, their salaries were lower (for the same positions), as they were considered the "lesser sex." Working conditions were unacceptable, as proved by the fire in March 1911 at the Triangle Shirtwaist Factory in New York. Women, including young women in their teens, died that day as a fire broke out the ninth floor. There was no way for these women to escape. The windows, doors, and fire exits were blocked by machines, trash cans, and of course the women who were crammed into this small space. The International Ladies' Garment Workers Union, who were key players in the pickets and walkouts of the

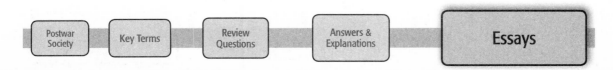

Chicago and New York sweatshops, organized protest rallies to inform other countries about the 146 women (out of 500) who died in the fire or who died trying to escape. Consequently, New York made major changes in the conditions of its garment factories.

Another great achievement that women gained for themselves was the signing of the Nineteenth Amendment into law in 1920. The Nineteenth Amendment, which allowed women to vote, was the result of efforts made by women such as Carrie Chapman Catt. Catt became the new president of the National American Women Suffrage Association (NAWSA) in 1900. She was an outspoken woman who believed that women could only create a better political system for the future by teaching their children, the future politicians, progressive ideas…and of course also through voting. She got her wish in 1920 and she created the League of Women Voters afterwards to assist new voters at the polls.

It took underrepresented minorities with drive and passion to make changes during the Progressive Era. It might have been a time for massive "progression" and change, but if the government had its say, this change would only have been for middle-class white males who already had rights, jobs, and respect. Progressive reformers like the ones mentioned above made sure that ALL citizens had some part in the progression of Americans during the era.

CHAPTER 23: A NEW ERA, THE 1920s

IF YOU ONLY LEARN ELEVEN THINGS IN THIS UNIT . . . .

1. Post-WWI changes in business and the emergence of a new prosperity (high wages, a mass-consumption society, etc.)

2. The string of Republican presidents (Harding, Coolidge, Hoover) and their split from Progressive politics

3. Post-WWI changes in foreign policy (the Dawes Plan, the Good Neighbor Policy, etc.)

4. Post-WWI cultural events (the Roaring Twenties, changes in the arts, the Harlem Renaissance, etc.) and reactions from conservative society

5. Minorities' continuing struggle for equality

6. Events leading to the Great Depression and how it affected the country

7. The complexities of FDR's New Deal and how it changed society; opponents of the New Deal

8. Events leading up to world involvement in WWII; events leading up to U.S. involvement in WWII

9. Major battles and groundbreaking decisions of WWII (Pearl Harbor, "Little Boy" and "Fat Man," D-Day, etc.)

10. WWII's changes on U.S. soil—the roles of women and minorities during the war, internment of Japanese Americans, etc.

11. The effects of WWII on the United States and postwar recovery actions

American Business — Republicans — Modern Culture — Conservative Reaction — Equality Struggle

AMERICAN BUSINESS AND CONSUMERISM

Big business continued to enjoy the protections of *laissez-faire* policies as the country entered the 1920s. Presidents Harding, Coolidge, and Hoover all sang the praises of the wealthy businessmen of the nation and insulated them from litigation. A booming economy, after the brief recession in 1921, complemented this attitude. The country emerged from World War I as a creditor nation, and American industrial production rose dramatically in response to the appetite for manufactured goods. Despite the strikes of 1919 and the losses that labor endured in 1920 and 1921, workers' wages actually were higher than they ever had been.

This did not mean the work of organized labor was over. The labor movement suffered setbacks due to the prosperity of the 1920s. Business owners demanded the end of the "closed shop" in which all employees had to become members of the union, sinking union membership to an all-time low. Although the standard of living for the average American was higher than in any other nation in the world, not all Americans enjoyed such prosperity. The very poor, including many rural tenant farmers, struggled to make ends meet on pay that was well below the poverty level. Farmers also suffered from a drop in the price of crops and heavy debt burdens.

FORD AND CHANGING CONSUMERISM

Manufacturing fully enjoyed the prosperity of the new era. American productivity was greater than ever due to advances in electric power and the management systems of men like **Frederick W. Taylor** and **Henry Ford**. Many applied Taylor's principles of **scientific management** to make factory production faster and more efficient. Henry Ford applied Taylor's ideas to the assembly line in his automobile factories. By specializing the work that employees were hired to complete, cars could be turned out of Ford's factory at a speed previously unthinkable. Overall, American labor was producing 70 percent more than before the war.

This new prosperity, coupled with massive production of low-priced goods, led to the growth of a mass-consumption society. Ford's goal was to create an automobile that would be priced so an average American family could purchase one. His increase of wages in return for "thrifty habits" led to his being labeled a "traitor to his class" by other industrialists. By 1929, there were about 30 million automobiles in the nation, compared to barely 1 million before World War I. The car revolutionized American life economically and socially. Because of the increased demand for this product, related industries like steel, rubber, petroleum, and construction experienced booms. Rail was no longer the method of choice for shipping goods on the short haul, as trains gave way to trucks. The way Americans viewed their country was altered; it was now possible to see other regions by driving rather than taking a train. One could stop and see the sights and then stay in a place far away from home. Suburbs grew, because it was now possible for middle-class families to move outside of the city limits and still commute to work in the city. Courting was also changed by the car, as young people could drive alone together to hidden spots in the privacy of their Model T.

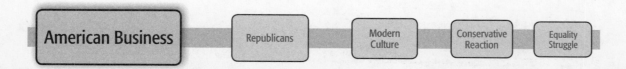

American Business | Republicans | Modern Culture | Conservative Reaction | Equality Struggle

New inventions that took advantage of the increasing availability of electric power became the must-have products of Americans looking to keep up with the new standard of living. Refrigerators, vacuum cleaners, electric stoves, and clothes irons were soon in vogue, as American housewives looked to keep up with their neighbors. All of these must-have products needed to be purchased, and many consumers did not have enough cash to pay up front; therefore, the credit industry boomed.

REPUBLICANS TAKE THE HELM

Hoping to leave the stubborn, idealist presidency of Woodrow Wilson behind, Americans elected Republican Warren G. Harding in 1920. Harding promised Americans a return to "normalcy," a word he invented to assure citizens that his administration would renew an interest in domestic prosperity and leave intervention in world affairs behind. The Progressive agenda was now a memory.

A SCANDALOUS PRESIDENCY

Harding's election began 12 years of conservative Republican rule. A poker-playing, handsome gent from Ohio, Harding was a change from the moralistic Wilson. At the outset, Harding understood that he needed to surround himself with men who were capable and powerful to assist with running the country. His cabinet, dubbed the **Ohio Gang** or the **Poker Cabinet**, was made up of old friends from the president's home state who were specialists in the areas in which they served. Some positions were filled by powerful men: Wall Street financier Andrew Mellon was secretary of the treasury, Supreme Court justice Charles Evans Hughes was secretary of state, former head of the Food Administration Herbert Hoover was secretary of commerce, and former president William Taft was a justice to the Supreme Court. Some of his friends did more harm than good, however, as Harding's presidency soon became mired in scandal. It was discovered in 1923 that two of Harding's pals, Secretary of the Interior Albert Fall and Attorney General Harry Daugherty, had illegally leased government oil fields near Teapot Dome, Wyoming, in exchange for bribes of cash and cattle. Fall was charged with fraud and served one year in prison. He was the first cabinet official in history to be charged with a federal offense. As a result, Harding's administration would be labeled as dishonest and eventually gained the reputation among some historians as one of the worst presidencies in American history. While on a goodwill tour of the Pacific Northwest, President Harding fell ill and died of pneumonia on August 1923, leaving his vice president, Calvin Coolidge, to take over.

HARDING'S FOREIGN POLICY

Aside from dodging scandal, Harding ignored domestic issues and renewed the isolationist spirit. After refusing to join the League of Nations, the United States worked to avoid having the delicate postwar peace disturbed by other countries. A naval arms race had been brewing since the end

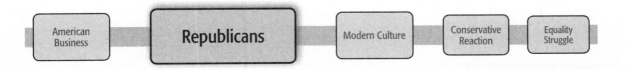

American Business | **Republicans** | Modern Culture | Conservative Reaction | Equality Struggle

of World War I among the United States, Britain, and Japan. To keep the relationship amiable, Secretary of State Hughes organized the **Washington Disarmament Conference** in 1921 and 1922 to address security issues. Several treaties were signed among the countries present— Belgium, China, France, Portugal, Japan, Italy, the Netherlands, and the United States—to limit the expansion of arms and build territorial respect among all present. The United States also sought to provide aid to Germany so it could pay war reparations to Britain and France, thus freeing those nations to repay the United States for war debts. In 1924, Director of the Budget Charles Dawes crafted a loan program that would give money to Germany, thus lessening the financial crisis in Europe. **The Dawes Plan** was successful until the program ended with the U.S. stock market crash in 1929.

COOLIDGE AND HOOVER TAKE OFFICE

After taking the oath of office as president of the United States in his parent's farmhouse in Vermont, Calvin Coolidge set out to continue the Republican ideal of limited government. Less than a year after taking the oath, Coolidge won the presidency in his own right in the election of 1924. "Silent Cal" was a man of few words who worked very little as president. Where Woodrow Wilson would often put in 12- to 15-hour days, Coolidge would rarely work more than 4. Aside from the growth of big business aided by Coolidge's inaction, he is mainly known as a president who refused to pay World War I veterans their promised bonuses and twice vetoed the **McNary-Haugen Bill**, which would have assisted farmers who badly needed price supports. His announcement that he would not seek re-election did not surprise the Republican party, who had Herbert Hoover waiting in the wings to run for office in 1928.

Running against Democrat Alfred Smith, a New York, Catholic "wet" (meaning he opposed Prohibition), Hoover won relatively easily on a conservative platform that promised a continuation of prosperity and progress. Unfortunately for the new president, economic disaster loomed just eight months from his inauguration. Hoover believed in the strength of the American businessperson. He abided by the idea of "**rugged individualism**," where anyone could become a success if he or she worked hard enough.

At the end of Coolidge's term, isolationism gained strength with the signing of the **Kellogg-Briand Pact** in 1928, which made offensive wars illegal throughout the world. Unfortunately, the pact did not have any teeth—it did not prohibit defensive warfare or provide punishment to countries that disobeyed the pact. Hoover did intervene in a mild way after Japanese aggression towards Manchuria in 1931. The **Hoover-Stimson Doctrine** of 1932 declared that the United States would not recognize territorial gains made by nations who violated the Kellogg-Briand Pact. Hoover also initiated the **Good Neighbor Policy** with Latin America, withdrawing American forces from the region to establish more normalized relations.

American Business | **Republicans** | Modern Culture | Conservative Reaction | Equality Struggle

BIRTH OF MODERN CULTURE

America's new mobility—aided by the automobile and later by air travel—and the rise of radio and film as forms of mass communication helped spawn a new American sensibility, which would excite some and frighten others.

THE ROARING TWENTIES

> Often called the **Jazz Age** or the **Roaring Twenties,** the era from 1920 to 1929 experienced a cultural explosion similar to that of the antebellum period. African American ragtime music began to change as it moved from the Deep South into Northern cities like Chicago and Philadelphia. Jazz became the music of choice for the young and "hep" urbanites.

American families had more leisure time and looked to entertainment to fill their afternoons and weekends. Commercial radio began in 1920 with the first broadcast of limited range by KDKA in Pittsburgh and expanded to the National Broadcast System (NBC) in 1924, which reached some 5 million homes across the country. A radio listener in California was oftentimes listening to the same program as someone in New York City. A common cultural identity was established, as Americans listened to comedy, drama, and sports from all corners of the nation. Movies became wildly popular; Americans flocked to the theaters to see these "moving pictures." Early films were silent, with text at the bottom of the screen for the actor's dialogue and a live orchestra playing the film's score. The release of the *Jazz Singer* in 1927 began the age of the "talkies," so now audiences could listen to actors converse onscreen. Hollywood, California, became the glamorous entertainment capital of the country, housing stars such as Rudolph Valentino and Lillian Gish. Radio and movie altered the standard for the "true American hero"—movie stars, radio personalities, and professional athletes took the place of presidents and world leaders. Professional sports also gained attention. Big boxing matches between Jack Dempsey and Gene Tunney mesmerized fans, the legendary Babe Ruth continued hitting home runs out of Yankee Stadium, and Gertrude Ederle swam the English Channel.

Some Americans were not as pleased by the newly materialistic and mass-consumption society of the 1920s. A group of authors and artists, increasingly concerned by the influence of money and conservatism on society, began to express themselves. The "**Lost Generation**" was made up of authors and poets such as F. Scott Fitzgerald, Gertrude Stein, Ezra Pound, and Ernest Hemingway. Artists such as Georgia O'Keeffe and Thomas Hart Benton reacted to the impact of technology and business by painting realist or early surrealist works that portrayed American themes without the glitter of consumerism.

American Business   Republicans   **Modern Culture**   Conservative Reaction   Equality Struggle

Harlem, a neighborhood of New York City, became the center of African American life and culture in the 1920s. Largely through white patronage, African American artists, poets, and musicians gave birth to a movement now called the **Harlem Renaissance**. Deeply critical of white society in many respects, writers such as Countee Cullen, Langston Hughes, and Zora Neale Hurston wrote poems, essays, and novels expressing the joy and pain of being an African American. Art by such names as Sterling Brown and Augusta Savage brought African American and African culture to life and into the homes of many white New York socialites. Jazz musicians like Louis Armstrong and Duke Ellington became wildly successful as they traveled the country playing concerts for whites and blacks. Musicians were the only artists to prosper once the stock market crash hit and white patronage died away. The Harlem Renaissance had little impact beyond New York City, where most Americans never realized any cultural rebirth had occurred.

A CONSERVATIVE REACTION

The 1920s stereotype of flappers and *speakeasies* does not reveal the underlying struggle between the conservative right and the modernist left. Many Americans were frightened by the changes occurring around them and sought to protect their communities from moral degradation. Fundamentalists, prohibitionists, and nativists all hoped to stop these changes from impacting American lives.

A FIGHT OVER EVOLUTION

Fundamentalist Christians had new fuel for their fight when the American Civil Liberties Union (ACLU) found a Tennessee science teacher willing to become its test case regarding a state statute that barred teaching the theory of evolution. **John Scopes**, a biology teacher in Dayton, Tennessee, was arrested and brought to trial in 1925. The ACLU appointed lawyer Clarence Darrow to represent Scopes, while the State of Tennessee chose the outspoken Christian fundamentalist **William Jennings Bryan** as its counsel. The trial was a spectacle. Newspaper and radio press dubbed it the "Monkey Trial," swarming the town of Dayton. Darrow got Bryan to fumble and contradict himself as he tried to use the Bible to justify the statute while testifying as a religious expert. In the end, however, Scopes was found guilty. The conviction was later overturned.

PROHIBITION AND ORGANIZED CRIME

Prohibitionists continued to protect their precious amendment, although it was ineffective and largely unenforced. **The Volstead Act** of 1919, the enforcement arm of the Eighteenth Amendment, had many Americans finding ways to skirt the law. The young and fashionable in America's cities visited secret clubs called "speakeasies" where visitors needed to know the password and whisper it or "speak easy," to gain entrance. Even President Harding defied the law by serving alcohol in the White House to guests and dignitaries. The underground or "bootleg"

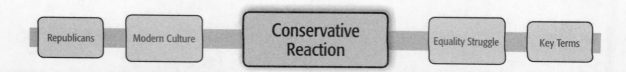

Republicans | Modern Culture | **Conservative Reaction** | Equality Struggle | Key Terms

network of illegal alcohol began first with small-time distillers, who would brew "bathtub gin" for sale to local clients. Soon organized crime took a hold of the bootleg industry and grew in numbers, influence, and violence. The infamous Chicago crime boss Al Capone ran a network of illegal activities that began with alcohol and soon connected with drugs, prostitution, and illegal gambling. Violent turf wars between rival gangs and assassinations of informers made Chicago one of the most dangerous cities in the United States. Soon many called for the repeal of the Eighteenth Amendment, as it looked as if the "noble experiment" engendered more disgust than respect for the law.

IMMIGRATION RESENTMENT AND RACISM CONTINUE

Meanwhile, European immigrants and African American migrants continued to swell American cities well into the 1920s, causing a resurgence of the nativist feelings that the Know-Nothing Party had embraced in the 1850s. In response, Congress passed several laws aimed at curbing the tide of immigrants coming from European countries. The **Quota Act**, or **Immigration Act**, of 1921 set a 3 percent limit on individuals from each nation of origin based on the 1910 census. The second was the **National Origins Act** of 1924, which set the limit at 2 percent based on the 1890 census; this act was directed at southern and eastern European and Asian immigrants.

The once-powerful racist organization of the Ku Klux Klan experienced a rebirth during the 1920s with an ire directed not just at African Americans but at Jews, Catholics, and communists. The KKK used the terror tactics it had used in the Reconstruction era, such as cross burnings, whippings, and lynchings. Klan members included government officials and police in many Southern and Midwestern cities. In 1925, a former Grand Dragon of the Klan was convicted of murder, and the public nature and membership of the Klan dipped significantly.

The case of Nicola Sacco and Bartolomeo Vanzetti best illustrates the grip of fear and the injustice of nativism. A robbery and murder of a paymaster in South Braintree, Massachusetts, resulted in the arrest of two Italian anarchists, Sacco and Vanzetti. The evidence of the case was contradictory and confused. However, the two were convicted and sentenced to death by electric chair. Many Americans came to their defense—such as Albert Einstein and the Italian-American community—but to no avail. After multiple appeals, Sacco and Vanzetti were executed in 1927.

THE CONTINUING STRUGGLE FOR EQUALITY

Immigrants were not alone in their struggle for a place in American society. African Americans and women continued to fight for basic civil rights and equality. Some had radical solutions to the problems of inequality, while others chose to work within the system to better their lives.

Amidst the Harlem Renaissance, a young Jamaican immigrant named Marcus Garvey had formed the **United Negro Improvement Association** and encouraged African Americans to form a separate community from white society. He eventually advocated a "Back to Africa" movement

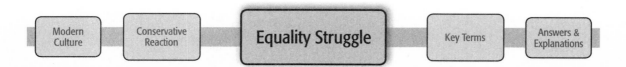

Modern Culture | Conservative Reaction | **Equality Struggle** | Key Terms | Answers & Explanations

in which African Americans would board his ships and set up a new life and a new country. Unfortunately for the movement, Garvey was arrested and convicted for tax fraud regarding his Black Star Steamship company. Garvey was deported back to Jamaica in 1929, and the "Back to Africa" movement collapsed. Other African Americans, such as W. E. B. Du Bois and the NAACP, continued to fight for justice and equality as the number of lynchings increased in the South.

The "cult of domesticity" continued to be a reality for American women, particularly those of the middle class. New inventions, such as the vacuum cleaner and dishwasher, only left many American women wondering what to do with their time. But this leisure time was not experienced by all women, as poor and minority women had to work outside of the home to make ends meet. Young women liberated by the works of **Sigmund Freud** and his view of human sexuality began to break away from the Victorian style, to the disgust of their elders. The "**flappers,**" so named because they were not unlike baby birds flapping their wings and leaving the nest, cut their hair into short "bobs," wore short skirts, rolled down their stockings to reveal their knees, drank alcohol, and danced the Charleston. Their numbers were few, but their behavior was very public and raised concerns in America's Christian community. Also of great concern to America's Christians was the increase in divorce during the 1920s. Now that women were voting, legislators had to listen to their concerns. One was maintaining the ability to divorce. As a result of more liberal laws regarding divorce, women were leaving their marriages in much greater numbers than before. Women also benefited from new laws making attendance in school compulsory until age 16. This opened doors for many women to gain a college education. By 1929, the illiteracy rate dropped to a low of 6 percent, making it one of the lowest in the world. Margaret Sanger made trouble when she advocated the use of birth control, founding the American Birth Control League in 1921. Sanger encouraged young women to discuss openly issues ranging from menstruation to the prevention of pregnancy and to help put a stop to poverty, abuse, and premature death of young women.

KEY TERMS

Names	Frederick W. Taylor Henry Ford William Jennings Bryan Sigmund Freud John Scopes
Groups	Ohio Gang Poker Cabinet the Lost Generation United Negro Improvement Association flappers
Events	Washington Disarmament Conference Jazz Age Roaring Twenties Harlem Renaissance
Documents and Laws	Dawes Plan McNary-Haugen Bill Kellogg-Briand Pact Hoover-Stimson Doctrine Good Neighbor Policy Volstead Act Quota Act Immigration Act National Origins Act
Vocabulary	scientific management rugged individualism laissez-faire speakeasies

REVIEW QUESTIONS

1. The "Red Scare" was spurred by

   (A) the "Great Migration" of African Americans into the North.
   (B) the rebirth of the KKK.
   (C) the repeal of Prohibition.
   (D) increasing labor unrest and violence.
   (E) the death of President Harding.

2. The National Origins Act of 1924 limited immigrants based on

   (A) religion.
   (B) health requirements.
   (C) number of children.
   (D) job prospects.
   (E) nationality.

3. The trial of John Scopes illustrated the battle over

   (A) immigration and quotas.
   (B) fundamentalism and modernism.
   (C) prohibition and morality.
   (D) women's suffrage and divorce.
   (E) labor strikes and collective bargaining.

4. Prosperity in the 1920s led to

   (A) all Americans experiencing a better life.
   (B) labor unions gaining membership.
   (C) the elimination of the wealth gap.
   (D) massive consumer debt due to buying on credit.
   (E) the reduction of white-collar jobs.

5. Coolidge's presidency protected the interests of

   (A) farmers and workers.
   (B) big business.
   (C) minorities and women.
   (D) immigrants.
   (E) modernists.

Conservative Reaction | Equality Struggle | Key Terms | **Review Questions** | Answers & Explanations

ANSWERS AND EXPLANATIONS

1. D

Americans were terrified by the increasing violence of labor strikes in 1919 and 1920. Likening them to the Bolsheviks, who had just overthrown their government in Russia, Americans were afraid that the same fate would befall them if labor unions weren't kept in check.

2. E

The Quota Act of 1924 was also known as the National Origins Act. The act specifically limited immigrants from specific areas of the world, such as southern and eastern Europe and Asia.

3. B

At issue in the Scopes trial was the teacher's instruction of students in the theory of evolution in Tennessee schools. The state of Tennessee had a statute barring the teaching of evolution in its schools and arrested Scopes for violating the law.

4. D

American consumers looked to purchase all of the new goods that would make their lives easier and better. Not having the cash to pay outright, consumers purchased goods with credit, eventually becoming entrapped by their consumption.

5. B

Coolidge once stated, "The chief business of the American people is business." Calvin Coolidge was a champion of big business and protected it to the detriment of other groups throughout America.

CHAPTER 24: THE GREAT DEPRESSION AND THE NEW DEAL, 1929–1938

CAUSES OF THE GREAT DEPRESSION

The United States had experienced economic crises every 20 years or so, usually labeled "Panics," from the years 1819 to 1907. Most of these depressions were short-lived and corresponded with the natural business cycle. By 1929, the New York Stock Exchange had reached an all-time high, with stocks selling for more than 16 times their actual worth. This "**bull market**" was a façade, however, as Americans ignored the signs that a serious economic crisis was on the horizon. Millions of Americans sought to "get rich quick" by gambling their life savings in the stock market. Until late September 1929, this seemed a worthwhile risk. In October, however, the "bubble" would burst, and the stock market crumbled before investors' eyes.

"**Black Tuesday**," October 29, 1929, signaled a selling frenzy on Wall Street—days before, stock prices had plunged to desperate levels. Investors were willing to sell their shares for pennies on the dollar or were simply holding onto the worthless certificates. The signals of impending doom were clear well before the crash. Americans had spent themselves far into debt by purchasing stocks with loans (*buying on margin*). Investors also artificially drove stock prices sky-high by overspeculation, gambling that the value of the stocks would continue to rise. Big business was ruled by the classical economic model of supply-side theory, in which the supply of a good naturally created its own demand. This led to an overproduction of manufactured goods, both consumer and industrial, that flooded the American marketplace. When it became apparent to manufacturers that consumer purchasing was slowing down, especially in the realm of durable goods, they laid workers off or cut wages to maintain profit levels. Farmers too suffered, as the demand for agricultural goods never rose back to World War I levels. To keep up with innovations in agriculture, farmers had purchased new equipment like tractors on credit, which drove them further into debt. The new equipment added another dimension to their problems, as improved methods led to overproduction.

The American banking system suffered as a result of its own risky policies. Overspeculating on property and issuing risky personal loans led to defaults and foreclosures. Bank customers' deposits were not protected from poor banking practices; as the stock market failed, many of these people lost the money they had secured in checking and savings accounts.

Depression Causes | Hoover | FDR & New Deal | Organized Labor | New Deal

Republican policies through the 1920s did not help the situation, as laissez-faire and classical models reigned supreme. High tariffs such as **Hawley-Smoot**, passed in 1930, hurt American farmers and resulted in retaliatory tariffs from other nations around the world, which then hurt manufacturers. Globally, economic depression was just around the bend—heavy debt burdens, war *reparations*, and the suspension of loan programs to assist the rebuilding of Europe drove countries such as Germany and Britain deeper into recession.

HOOVER'S REACTION

Initially, President Hoover believed that Europe was the force behind the economic crisis. In response, Hoover made a grave mistake in hopes of protecting American business from further injury by signing the Hawley-Smoot Tariff into law. The tariff on imported goods increased from 30 percent to almost 50 percent and spurred the retaliation of foreign governments, who passed protective tariffs of their own. Hoover also called for a worldwide debt moratorium to ease the struggle of nations paying back loans and reparations from World War I. Hoover's foreign policy was not his downfall; his stubbornness in ignoring domestic issues caused most Americans to blame him for their despair.

A staunch believer in "rugged individualism" and volunteerism, Hoover was reluctant to give direct aid to Americans who were suffering under the weight of the depression. When it seemed that something had to be done, Congress created the **Reconstruction Finance Corporation** (RFC) in 1932. Too little, too late, the corporation was given authority to issue loans to assist railroads, banks, and municipalities to prevent them from collapsing. Hoover held fast to his belief in "trickle-down" economics, where the wealthy are given more to spend so eventually they stimulate the economy and the benefits reach the poor. Therefore, the RFC continued to benefit only the wealthy instead of those truly in need. Hoover continually refused to provide any kind of government assistance to those who were being crushed under the weight of the economic crisis. Much as during his leadership of the Food Administration during World War I, he believed that private charity groups should be responsible for assisting the needy.

This solution was not enough for a group of World War I veterans who marched on Washington in 1932 to demand early release of bonuses Congress had promised to pay in 1945. The **Bonus Army** arrived in the nation's capital and set up a makeshift encampment around the Capitol. Many Americans who had become homeless had set up similar makeshift camps, which they named "Hoovervilles" as a jab at the current administration. Eventually, the original "Army" was joined by thousands more veterans and their families, who protested and marched around the Capitol building and the White House. The Bonus Bill was not passed by Congress, and a clash between the remaining veterans with local police resulted in the deaths of two marchers. President Hoover called in the U.S. Army to quash the ensuing riot, which used tear gas and tanks on the unarmed protesters. The U.S. Army also burned the encampment, driving the veterans from Washington, D.C. Across the nation, Americans looked on in horror. Many saw Hoover as a heartless coward.

All in all, Hoover actually did more than his Republican predecessors in staving off a much more serious economic crisis. He did encourage states and cities to institute public works projects to

Depression Causes | Hoover | FDR & New Deal | Organized Labor | New Deal

stimulate the economy and to give work to the unemployed. However his staunch conservatism stood in the way of his becoming a hero. If he had bent, he might have been able to help stop the deepest years of the Great Depression.

FRANKLIN DELANO ROOSEVELT AND THE NEW DEAL

The election of 1932 took place during the deepest year of the depression. The Democratic party looked for a household name to run for president and chose the governor of New York, **Franklin Delano Roosevelt** (FDR). The candidate promised Americans a "new deal" and criticized the Hoover administration for massive government spending that had led to a large budget deficit. FDR also promised the repeal of the Eighteenth Amendment. Americans responded and overwhelmingly elected FDR to office. The president-elect had made a name for himself through a career in politics that had begun in state politics during World War I and then took him on the path of his cousin, Theodore Roosevelt. FDR almost left politics permanently when he was stricken by polio in 1921, which paralyzed him from the waist down. If not for the tenacity of his wife, Eleanor Roosevelt, who encouraged her husband to health and campaigned for him when he was ill, he would have never become president.

The "new deal" FDR promised as he campaigned was a mystery to Americans—and the president himself—as he entered the Oval Office. Roosevelt knew that he had three goals, which he labeled the "**three Rs**": relief, recovery, and reform. But aside from this, the president really had no real plan of action to get the country out from under the grips of depression. To start, FDR appointed a group of economists, professors, and politicians he would dub the **Brain Trust** to advise him on matters of economic and political policy. Within the first three months of taking office, FDR had managed to get Congress to pass an unprecedented amount of new legislation, which would revolutionize the role of the federal government from that point on. This "**First Hundred Days**" saw the passage of bills aimed at repairing the banking system and restoring American's faith in the economy, starting government works projects to employ those out of work, offering subsidies for farmers, and devising a plan to aid in the recovery of the nation's industrial sector.

The period of 1933 to 1935, called the first **New Deal**, began with a banking holiday. FDR ordered all financial institutions to close for two days; only those banks that were solvent could reopen their doors on the third day. The other banks' assets were taken over by the federal government. To inform Americans of the **Emergency Banking Relief Act** passed on March 9, 1933, that reopened solvent banks, the president gave the first of his "**Fireside Chats**." FDR delivered these weekly radio addresses to inform and soothe an American public that was still weary from the pain of unemployment and poverty. To restore the nation's Federal Reserve, the president also took the United States off of the gold standard and recovered all of the gold held by private banks and individuals in exchange for Treasury notes (dollar bills). The **Glass-Steagall Act** paved the way for the Federal Deposit Insurance Corporation (FDIC), which would protect Americans' banking deposits up to $5,000 per deposit. Now Americans could bank with confidence, knowing that the government was standing by in case of a banking collapse.

Depression Causes   Hoover   **FDR & New Deal**   Organized Labor   New Deal

Several acts designed to assist in the "relief" effort were also passed in this period. Beginning what was called an "alphabet soup" of government agencies, the first hundred days saw the birth of such programs as the **Public Works Administration** (PWA), designed to employ thousands of Americans to rebuild the country's infrastructure; the **Civilian Conservation Corps** (CCC), which employed young college- and high school-aged young men to reforest America; and the **Tennessee Valley Authority** (TVA), which worked to electrify the impoverished Tennessee Valley with hydroelectric power. The **National Recovery Administration** (NRA) started industrial relief. The "blue eagle" of the NRA was displayed in the windows of businesses that adhered to the regulations of the agency, which included fair labor standards, price ceilings and floors, and temporary "monopolies" between companies joining forces to increase production. Before long, however, the blue eagle would be shot down—the Supreme Court, under the leadership of Charles Evans Hughes, ruled it unconstitutional in the "Sick Chicken Case" of *Schechter v. United States*. This would be the first in a long series of battles between the president and the Supreme Court over his New Deal policies. The next program, the Agricultural Adjustment Administration (AAA), was also deemed unconstitutional by the Supreme Court in 1935, but not before it aided many of America's farmers. The AAA paid farmers subsidies to destroy or plow under fields so as to create artificial scarcity, thereby increasing the price of foodstuffs.

A SECOND NEW DEAL

The **Second New Deal**, which ran from roughly 1935 to 1938, focused more on relief and reform. Another round of congressional acts continued to increase the federal government's role in the lives of Americans. To encourage more public works projects and the employment of "nontraditional" workers, such as artists, writers, and young people, the **Works Progress Administration** (WPA) employed Americans to build bridges, refurbish parks, write plays, and paint murals. The **Social Security Act** (SSA), passed in 1935, guaranteed benefits for retirees, the disabled, and the unemployed. Monies were collected from a worker's pay on a monthly basis, to be paid back monthly after the worker turned 65. Unfortunately, the law was biased—it did not apply to millions of service workers, such as domestics, nannies, and janitors, who were largely African American. Nonetheless, the SSA provided a guaranteed pension to shield America's most vulnerable from abject poverty.

Watching the American economy from overseas was the British economist John Maynard Keynes. Keynes called into question the classical economic model of supply-side economics and argued that it was actually demand that determined the health of the economy. Even though Roosevelt was willing to experiment with government policies, he was both unwilling and uninterested in messing with fiscal and monetary policy. Keynesian theory posed that instead of attempting to balance the budget and imposing new taxes on an already "taxed" system, the government should spend that which it did not have—in other words, resort to deficit spending. By the government increasing spending, it would "prime the pump" by spurring an increase in investment and eventually increase the need for employees. Roosevelt had to do something, because the "**Roosevelt Recession**" had

Depression Causes · Hoover · **FDR & New Deal** · Organized Labor · New Deal

impacted the economy in 1937 and 1938 due to the fact that the president had decided to "pull back" on government spending. Reluctantly, FDR initiated an increase in spending on public works projects and other programs, which almost magically increased investment and employment. It should be noted, however, that even during the best times of recovery during the Great Depression, the unemployment rate never dipped below 16 percent. It took *mobilization* for World War II to finally get the country out of the economic doldrums.

ORGANIZED LABOR GAINS

The **National Industrial Recovery Administration** (NIRA) passed during the "first" New Deal was the most proactive legislation to date in preventing the abuse of labor and capital by big business. The NIRA was comprised of a board of trustees responsible for setting policy for industry in the United States. The board set maximum work hours, minimum wages, and price floors. It was also responsible for setting production quotas and inventories to prevent overproduction or price gouging. Most importantly for organized labor, **Section 7a** of NIRA formally guaranteed organized labor the right to collectively bargain and organize. No longer was the old "yellow-dog contract" or "iron clad oath" an issue; unions could actively recruit members in American factories and workplaces. Finally, organized labor had gained legal acceptance and could come out of the shadows of secrecy to gain a voice.

To further the gains of labor, the **National Labor Relations Act** of 1935—also called the Wagner Act after the senator who penned the bill—strengthened the language of Section 7a of NIRA. Even though all labor unions fought for the protections of workers, not all agreed on who should be protected. The American Federation of Labor (AFL) was comprised mainly of white skilled workers who did not agree that the union should protect all workers. Members of the AFL who wished to extend membership to all workers broke away and joined other union members to form the **Congress of Industrial Organizations** (CIO) under the leadership of John L. Lewis of the United Mine Workers. The CIO focused on unskilled laborers in America's heavy industrial sector such as steel, automobiles, and mines. By 1938, the CIO was completely independent of the AFL. During the Second New Deal, the **Fair Labor Standards Act** was passed to establish a federal minimum wage and maximum hours for interstate businesses and ensure an end to child labor.

This is not to say that labor was entirely happy throughout the New Deal. Some industries were reluctant to allow unions to set up shop. To drive a point home to General Motors in Flint, Michigan, the CIO's Lewis organized a "sit-down strike" of assembly-line employees in the plant in 1937. When the government refused to intervene between labor and management, the companies reluctantly went to the bargaining table and officially recognized the **United Auto Workers** (UAW) as an official party with which to negotiate contracts. The UAW did not fare as well at the Ford plant, however, as workers were driven away violently before they could strike. The steel industry was also slow in its wholehearted recognition of unions, with most finally folding at the arrival of World War II.

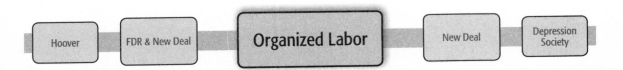

NEW DEAL SUPPORTERS AND CRITICS

The New Deal was largely supported by Democrats, who stood by their charismatic president from the day he took office. Organized labor became an ally of both FDR and the Democratic Party, as the administration continued to support workers and workers' rights throughout the New Deal. African Americans also became hearty supporters of the Democrats and FDR as the New Deal continued. President Roosevelt, at the urging of his wife Eleanor, appointed more African Americans to cabinet positions than any president before him. His "**Black Cabinet**" worked on issues ranging from the repeal of Jim Crow laws in the South to anti-lynching legislation. Unfortunately for African Americans, FDR needed to maintain the support of Southern Democrats and did not sign the legislation designed to end either of the practices the "Black Cabinet" fought against.

CHANGING PARTY POLITICS AND ANTI-FDR SENTIMENTS

The Republicans and Democrats both experienced changes in the makeups of their parties as the role of government changed. Southern Democrats struggled with FDR's seemingly liberal values with regard to race and gender relations, and many considered fleeing to the "party of Lincoln." The Republicans were experiencing an influx of conservative Northerners and Southerners who had been lifelong Democrats but disagreed with FDR's handling of the Great Depression. All in all, supporters argued that the New Deal had been successful in relieving millions of Americans from the clutches of poverty, had cleansed the capitalist system of greed, and had renewed the spirit of self-preservation, all without a revolution.

FDR had critics both inside and outside his party. It seemed that in many respects FDR could do nothing right. Extremists on both ends of the political spectrum charged that the president was either not doing enough or doing too much. Socialists argued that the administration needed to do more with regard to the "forgotten man," otherwise known as the taxpayers, minorities, and the poor. Conservatives were frightened by the increasing role of the government in every aspect of Americans' lives. Claiming that the New Deal was "socialism," Republicans and conservative Democrats joined to form the **American Liberty League** to promote the concerns of big business and small government. They were so convinced that the New Deal and FDR were bad for America that they sought to unseat FDR as he ran for president in 1936.

Some of FDR's critics used the airwaves to reach Americans, much as the president did in his Fireside Chats. Playing to the fears of the average citizen, Catholic priest Father Charles E. Coughlin attacked the New Deal as a benefit to only the well-to-do and big business. He was extremely popular; almost 40 million Americans tuned in to his radio show every day. Father Coughlin eventually digressed into *anti-Semitic* and *fascist* tirades before the Catholic Church pulled him from the air. Before the passage of the Social Security Act, **Dr. Francis Townsend** advocated a federal tax that would provide $200 a month for every retired American over the age of 60. His Old Age Revolving Pension plan gathered millions of supporters, who agreed that if retirees were given this pension and required to spend it all within a month, it would help to stimulate the economy.

FDR &
New Deal   Organized Labor   New Deal   Depression
Society   Key Terms

Roosevelt decided that he would opt for a much less radical plan, which became the Social Security Act. After its passage, Townsend criticized the president for not pushing for more.

From within Congress, Roosevelt found a critic in the senator from Louisiana, **Huey P. "Kingfish" Long**. Long had long advocated a "Robin Hood" plan to take from the rich and give to the poor called "Share Our Wealth." His plan would impose heavy taxes on inheritance and estates to fund a minimum salary of $5,000 a year for every American. Long was very popular among voters in his home state, but he did use some controversial political tactics. Long controlled all government offices in Louisiana, both state and local. He argued that the New Deal was not enough to aid the country's most severely depressed. Felled by an assassin's bullet in 1935, Long could have given Roosevelt a run for the Democratic nomination in 1936.

The Supreme Court offered another challenge for Roosevelt as he continued to drive more and more legislation through Congress and further increase the power of the executive and legislative branches. Fed up with decisions that had effectively killed two important pieces of New Deal legislation (the NRA and the AAA), Roosevelt decided that he was going to reorganize the makeup of the Supreme Court with the hope that his legislation might find a more sympathetic audience. His **Judicial Reorganization Bill** (1937) would allow the president to appoint one justice for every seated justice over 70 years old. At the time, the bill would have given FDR the ability to seat 6 justices on the court, bringing the number to 15. Conservatives and Republicans immediately smelled a rat and dubbed the bill a "court-packing scheme." Neither side would back down, but the bill finally died when some of FDR's biggest supporters refused to back it. It may have been the threat of the reorganization or a softening of the Court, but by the time the "court-packing" bill was killed, the Court was backing down from its previous hard-line stance. Roosevelt eventually was able to make nine appointments to the Supreme Court during his presidencies, leaving a liberal legacy on the bench. By 1938, the once strong New Deal seemed out of touch and off course. After the "Roosevelt Recession" in 1937, the economy had only modestly rebounded, and many problems such as high unemployment and poverty remained. Americans voiced their concerns during the midterm elections of 1938, where more Republicans and moderate Democrats replaced Roosevelt's army of followers. This, coupled with worldwide attention moving to Hitler's actions, signaled an end to the New Deal.

AMERICAN SOCIETY THROUGH THE DEPRESSION

The Great Depression had a profound impact on those who survived it. Many of these Americans were insecure about the economy well into the 1940s and 1950s, despite new prosperity. Americans from all walks of life had to "make do" with what was available to them. Depression cookbooks would include recipes for dishes such as "dandelion soup" made with water, a potato, and dandelion greens that could be picked from the lawn. Desperate businessmen would turn to selling apples on the street for a nickel to avoid having to accept charity. Even with the ingenuity of Americans, soup kitchens and bread lines became an everyday sight across the country as citizens looked for a hot meal. Many proud Americans were not happy about having to take a hand-out and would rather die than take charity.

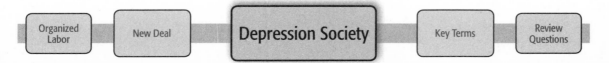

Organized Labor   New Deal   **Depression Society**   Key Terms   Review Questions

THE ROLE OF WOMEN AND THE DUST BOWL

Certain groups of Americans faced special challenges during the depression. Women were left with the burden of caring for children, as many were left behind by their husbands; many men deserted their families out of shame because they could not find work to support a wife and child. Women entered the workforce when possible to supplement meager incomes brought in by husbands, other family members, or children. Scraping together enough money to keep the family fed, clothed, and housed was a daily dilemma for women during the depression.

That plight was even more difficult for the wives of farmers in the Great Plains region. A severe drought hit the Great Plains, killing all of the crops. The topsoil turned to a fine, powdery dust that blew away with the severe, hot winds that wreaked havoc on the farmers who remained. The area was called the **Dust Bowl**, as Plains farmers saw their land literally blow away. With no opportunity to save their land from foreclosure, many of these families packed their belongings onto makeshift trucks and sought a new life in the west. Californian picking companies blanketed the Dust Bowl region with flyers promising jobs, money, housing, and fields of beautiful produce. As a result, the farmers and their families flocked to the region and earned the name "**Okies**," as many came from the panhandle regions of Oklahoma or Texas. If they survived the journey, upon arrival many of these migrants realized that they were not in the "Promised Land." Bouncing from migrant camp to migrant camp, Okies experienced discrimination, abuse, and humiliation. Nonetheless, many remained in California, finally settling in the Central Valley region to begin a new life.

MINORITIES IN THE DEPRESSION

American minority groups fared much worse than whites during the depression. African Americans struggled to survive, as there was no work available for them at all. Any available job was given to a white person before it would ever be given to a black person. Due to discrimination all across the nation, many African Americans were not given assistance from their states or cities. Despite FDR's need for the Southern white vote, African Americans did find a friend in Eleanor Roosevelt. Several New Deal programs openly accepted African Americans, and after the threatened march on Washington organized by Rail Porters Union President A. Philip Randolph, the **Fair Employment Practices Committee** (FEPC) was developed to assist African Americans in finding employment in the defense industry. Native Americans were accepted in several federal programs that not only employed them but also improved their communities. Most significantly, the **Indian Reorganization Act** of 1934 repealed the Dawes Act of 1887 by returning federal reservation lands to the tribes and giving support to Native Americans to reestablish and preserve tribal culture. Mexican Americans were more or less displaced by Okies flooding the Southwest and as a result faced discrimination in areas where they had lived for years. The federal government was of no assistance, and many Mexican Americans chose to go to Mexico. In addition, many Latinos were forced back to Mexico, even those with American citizenship. They were rounded up and dumped on the border because the United States believed they should not have jobs when "native-born" Americans were without.

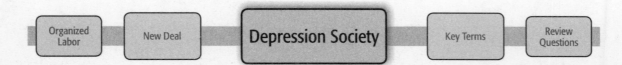

KEY TERMS

Names	Dr. Francis Townsend
	Huey P. "Kingfish" Long
	Franklin Delano Roosevelt
Groups	Reconstruction Finance Corporation
	Bonus Army
	Brain Trust
	Congress of Industrial Organizations
	United Auto Workers
	Black Cabinet
	American Liberty League
	Okies
	Fair Employent Practices Committee
Events	Black Tuesday
	First Hundred Days
	New Deal
	Gentlemen's Agreement
	Second New Deal
	Roosevelt Recession
Documents and Laws	Hawley-Smoot Tariff
	Emergency Banking Relief Act
	Glass-Steagall Act
	Public Works Administration
	Civilian Conversation Corps
	Tennessee Valley Authority
	National Recovery Administration
	Section 7a
	Works Progress Administration
	Social Security Act
	National Industrial Recovery Administration
	National Labor Relations Act
	Fair Labor Standards Act
	Judicial Reorganization Bill
	Indian Reorganization Act
Places	Dust Bowl
Vocabulary	bull market
	the three Rs
	fireside chats
	margin
	repatriation
	mobilization
	anti-Semitic
	fascist

REVIEW QUESTIONS

1. The Hawley-Smoot Tariff of 1930 resulted in

   (A) retaliation by foreign governments.

   (B) a reduction of the tax paid by foreign exporters.

   (C) a dramatic rise in agricultural goods.

   (D) the drop in the value of gold.

   (E) the easing of the debt burden of European countries.

2. President Roosevelt's "New Deal" campaign promise consisted of

   (A) the nationalization of the country's financial sector.

   (B) deficit spending.

   (C) high tariffs.

   (D) traditional economic policies.

   (E) mysterious plans.

3. The Glass-Steagall Act

   (A) limited the work hours and pay of laborers.

   (B) allowed for organized labor to collectively bargain.

   (C) created the Federal Deposit Insurance Corporation.

   (D) took the United States off the gold standard.

   (E) encouraged the use of deficit spending.

4. Senator Huey P. Long advocated

   (A) an end to racial discrimination.

   (B) an old-age pension.

   (C) subsidies for American farmers.

   (D) a guaranteed salary for all Americans.

   (E) the creation of farm cooperatives.

5. The Wagner Act of 1935 was a milestone for the American labor movement because it

   (A) gave labor the right to organize and bargain collectively.

   (B) created the NIRA.

   (C) provided guaranteed pensions for retirees.

   (D) opened up the AFL to unskilled labor.

   (E) forced employers to have "open shops."

ANSWERS AND EXPLANATIONS

1. A

European nations were angry at the passage of such a high protective tariff and retaliated by enacting high tariffs of their own. As a result, American farmers and industry suffered, as European markets stopped purchasing American goods.

2. E

FDR himself did not really know what he was going to do to "fix" the country. While his "new deal" campaign promise was a mystery, it was clear to Americans that this candidate was willing to try anything to get the country out of depression and on to recovery.

3. C

To protect Americans' banking deposits, the Glass-Steagall Act created the FDIC, which still serves today to protect deposits in private U.S. banking institutions. It provided another assurance from the federal government that Americans could trust the financial industry.

4. D

The "Kingfish" advocated a Robin Hood-type system where the wealthy would be taxed at a heavy rate to establish a fund for every American to get a guaranteed salary. His "Share Our Wealth" plan was wildly popular in his home state of Louisiana.

5. A

The Wagner Act solidified previous legislation that had legalized labor unions. In the NIRA Section 7a, unions were already protected. However, after the "Sick Chicken Case" ruling by the Supreme Court, which killed NIRA, Congress enacted the Wagner Act to strengthen the language, giving organized labor the right to negotiate with management to establish work standards, wages, and hours.

CHAPTER 25: THE ROAD TO THE SECOND WORLD WAR, 1929–1945

WORLD PROBLEMS AND AMERICAN NEUTRALITY

Americans were not keen on getting involved in another world crisis, since the country had fought in the Great War just two decades earlier. Americans were intensely immersed in domestic affairs regarding the Great Depression, even as Germany's Adolf Hitler continually violated the provisions of the Treaty of Versailles. President Herbert Hoover ushered in the 1930s using diplomacy instead of fighting to stave off potential threats around the world. With his diplomatic intervention into the crisis in Manchuria (see the Hoover-Stimson Doctrine in chapter 24) and the initiation of the Good Neighbor Policy with Latin America, it was clear that Americans were interested in maintaining their distance through isolationism. It was Franklin Delano Roosevelt who gave a name to the relationship with Latin America, promising to be "good neighbors" by staying out of their affairs. At the **Montevideo Conference** in 1933, the president personally pledged that the United States would never again intervene in the region.

Economically, FDR looked to rid the world of the high protective tariffs that had crippled world economies throughout the Depression. To open up new trade markets, FDR formally recognized the Soviet Union as a sovereign nation in 1933 and declared the Philippines independent in 1934, with the Philippines becoming free and clear in 1946. But even FDR, occupied with getting the United States out of the depths of the Great Depression, could not ignore the crisis that was worsening across the Atlantic and Pacific Oceans.

TROUBLE BREWS ABROAD

Totalitarian regimes had gained power in Europe and Japan during the 1920s and early 1930s due to the impact of the worldwide economic depression. The grim reality of being blamed wholly for the Great War caused many Germans to feel betrayed by their new government. They looked for someone to relieve them of their pain. Faced with runaway inflation caused by the printing of German marks to pay the massive war reparation debt, Germans saw Adolf Hitler as a beacon of hope to return them to the days of the Holy Roman Empire and German Empire. Italians, too, felt that their government had "sold them out" to other world powers during the Versailles

American Neutrality — Road to War — Two-Front War — Diplomacy — Wartime Mobilization

conference, as they lost valuable war-gained territories and prestige. They found hope in the words of "**il Duce**"—the leader of the Fascist movement, **Benito Mussolini**. Faced with a trade imbalance that would cripple their island nation, the Japanese looked for a return to the glory days of the shoguns as a military dictatorship rose in the 1930s. Again, the United States watched from afar, not wishing to become involved again in a nasty foreign war. Several neutrality acts were passed from 1935 to 1937, each enacted in the face of another potential threat to American security. The United States sat and watched as her allies in Europe and Asia fumbled with diplomatic policies aimed at keeping the dictators at bay. Even as Hitler and Mussolini used the Spanish Civil War as a testing ground for their military tactics, the United States stood by silently.

FDR BEGINS TO PREPARE

For his part, President Roosevelt did not make the same idealist mistake as his predecessor Woodrow Wilson. FDR started by increasing military spending in 1938 to begin the preparation for war. Part of his "pump priming," this increase in government spending ultimately took the country on the road to full economic recovery. Even as early as 1940, FDR was realistic about the potential of U.S. involvement in a war; he pressured Congress to pass the **Selective Service Act**, which provided for all American males between the ages of 21 to 35 to register for compulsory military service. This was the first time a peacetime military draft had been initiated, signaling that the president's stance was shifting from isolationism to interventionism.

THE ROAD TO WAR

Mussolini and Hitler understood the fragility of the League of Nations and hoped to take advantage of its weaknesses in their bid to take over all of Europe. Mussolini first sent in troops to invade the African country of Ethiopia in 1935; the League condemned his actions but did nothing to intervene. Hitler invaded the demilitarized region between France and Germany, the Rhineland, in 1936 thus violating the Versailles Treaty. The year 1937 brought the Japanese invasion of China and a potential U.S.-Japanese war as the Japanese "accidentally" sank an American ship on the Yangtze River.

European leaders were at a loss as to how to handle Hitler's increasingly aggressive demands. He claimed a strip along the country of Czechoslovakia called the **Sudetenland** in 1938. In a bid to keep war at bay, the British Prime Minister Neville Chamberlain and French President Edouard Daladier met with Hitler to negotiate a settlement over the disputed territory. Surprisingly, Czechoslovakia was not invited. At the conference, held in Munich in 1938, the policy of "**appeasement**" was born. Hitler would be allowed to take the Sudetenland in exchange for his promise to not invade any other territories. Hitler agreed, and Chamberlain and Daladier were pleased that they had dodged another bullet.

American Neutrality — **Road to War** — Two-Front War — Diplomacy — Wartime Mobilization

THE WAR BEGINS

The calm was short-lived, however, as Hitler invaded the rest of Czechoslovakia six months later and set his sights on Poland. Stalin had reason to want to keep Poland a neutral "buffer zone" between Germany and Russia. His country had been invaded through Poland many times throughout history; he hoped to occupy the region to keep his people safe. The world was surprised when it was announced that sworn enemies Stalin and Hitler had signed a secret non aggression pact in 1939, basically freeing Germany to invade the western half of Poland with no resistance; the Soviets would take the eastern half. The British and French pledged their support of Poland by stating they would declare war on Germany if the invasion took place. Then, on September 1, 1939, Hitler's forces rolled over Poland and started World War II.

Even as American allies Britain and France were now engaged in a war with Germany and Italy, the United States took measures to maintain its neutrality while supplying munitions of war. **The Neutrality Act of 1939** again proclaimed U.S. neutrality but only in name—not in deed. The act provided for the sale of U.S. weapons to European allies on a "**cash-and-carry**" basis only. In other words, countries such as Britain and France would have to pay cash and provide their own transport for whatever war munitions they bought. This would eliminate the need for war loans to allies that would cause problems in a postwar economy and keep U.S. merchant ships out of the war zone. September 1940 would bring yet another change in U.S. involvement in the war. The new prime minister, Winston Churchill, pleaded for more assistance in the face of continual bombings of his country by the German air force (the *Luftwaffe*) and the threat of U-boats in the Atlantic and English Channel. The two sides brokered the **Destroyers-for-Bases** deal, whereby the United States would provide Britain several older U.S. naval ships in return for the right to establish U.S. military installments on British-held Caribbean islands.

RE-ELECTION FOR FDR AND PLANS WITH CHURCHILL

With the election of 1940 looming, President Roosevelt broke the precedent set by George Washington by running for a third term. Running against Republican Wendell Willkie, Roosevelt was able to convince Americans that electing him again was choosing a voice of experience in the face of war. He won the election with 54 percent of the popular vote.

Growing more and more concerned over the fate of U.S. allies, President Roosevelt believed that his re-election was a mandate from the American people to end isolationism and become more involved in the war. He still emphasized diplomacy over war, but it was clear to many that the president was not unwilling to enter the war if necessary. In his January Address to Congress in 1940, the president offered his vision of U.S. involvement. FDR argued that offering Great Britain loans to buy U.S.-made munitions of war would further stimulate the economy and aid in the protection of the "**Four Freedoms**": Freedom of Speech, Freedom of Religion, Freedom from Want, and Freedom from Fear. His proposal was to end the "cash-and-carry" program and institute the **Lend-Lease Act** (March 1941), which would allow Britain to borrow U.S. war materials. FDR arranged a secret meeting with Prime Minister Churchill to discuss postwar aims

in response to the secret nonaggression pact signed by Hitler and Stalin. The two men drew up the **Atlantic Charter**, which declared that the self-determination of peoples and free trade would be the cornerstones of a world free of fascism.

ATTACK ON PEARL HARBOR

As Hitler continued to conquer Europe, with Paris falling in June 1940, the United States struggled to maintain amiable relations with Japan. Japanese forces remained in China and were poised to take French Indochina, which prompted FDR to cut Japan off from U.S. raw materials. As an island nation with few natural resources, the Japanese relied heavily on the import of oil. Hoping to negotiate the removal of Japanese troops from China and Indochina by the promise of lifting the oil embargo, FDR sent Secretary of State Cordell Hull to settle with the Japanese government. Amidst the negotiations, the new Japanese leader General Hideki Tojo changed course unexpectedly and backed out. Little did Hull know that the general was planning a secret attack on the Pacific fleet that he hoped would cripple the United States.

On December 7, 1941, the entire U.S. Pacific fleet was attacked at **Pearl Harbor**, Hawaii, in the early morning hours. The surprise attack killed 2,400 American sailors and wounded 1,200. Eight battleships were either sunk or severely damaged, including the USS *Arizona*, which lost 1,100 sailors. Ten other ships were damaged and almost 200 planes destroyed in the attack. Immediately, FDR asked Congress to declare war on Japan, with legislators responding with all but one dissenting vote. Three days later, Germany and Italy responded by declaring war on the United States.

A TWO-FRONT WAR

By the time the United States entered the war, the focus had shifted from the western front to the east, as Hitler broke his promise to Stalin and invaded Russia through Poland in late 1941. The Soviet leader joined the Allies in an act of desperation, making the "Big Three" of Roosevelt, Churchill, and Stalin. The three agreed to focus on getting rid of Hitler before turning to Japan.

FOCUS ON GERMANY

In the European "theater," the Allies concentrated on ridding the seas of German U-boats and the skies of the German *Luftwaffe*. The new British invention of radar turned the tide of war against the Germans, as the Royal Air Force was able to down German planes and the U.S. Navy was able to sink U-boats. In the south, the Allies struggled to rout the Germans from the North African theater as they cut their way northward under the leadership of tank commander German General Erwin "the Desert Fox" Rommel. Operation Torch, led by U.S. General Dwight D. Eisenhower and British General Bernard Montgomery, successfully flanked Rommel in Tunisia in May 1943. Next, the Allies looked across the Mediterranean Sea to the island of Sicily, which they invaded in September 1943. Facing fierce resistance from both Italians and Germans, the United States finally took the island in May 1945.

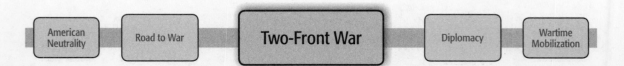

American Neutrality — Road to War — **Two-Front War** — Diplomacy — Wartime Mobilization

Understanding the need to liberate France, the Allies began planning an invasion of the beaches of Normandy. Operation Overlord, now known as the **D-Day** invasion, was an amphibious landing that required the utmost secrecy and favorable weather conditions. The perfect opening arose on June 6, 1944. General Eisenhower led a multinational force to storm the beaches at Normandy. Despite enormous losses of men, the invasion proved to be a success, as the Allies liberated Paris by the end of August. The final Allied push into Belgium was met with a final defensive attack by the Germans in December 1944 at the **Battle of the Bulge**. Even after suffering losses in the battle, the Allies were able to recover and continue their push toward Germany. The British and U.S. air forces were successful in crippling Germany by bombing her urban centers. With German defeat imminent, Hitler took his own life in April 1945, and Nazi forces surrendered on May 7. As Allied troops marched further into Nazi-held territory, they came upon unspeakable horrors. Massive concentration camps were discovered throughout Germany, Poland, Austria, and Czechoslovakia, where much of Hitler's *genocidal* "**Final Solution**" of the Jews and other groups had been carried out.

Focus on Japan

The second front was in the Pacific—after **V-E Day** (Victory in Europe Day), the Allies could focus on the Japanese. By the end of 1942, the Japanese had extended their sphere of influence far beyond China and Indochina, occupying the Korean peninsula, the Philippines, Indonesia, and many Pacific islands. This theatre was different from the one in Europe—the Allies had to rely heavily on naval supremacy and the destruction of the Japanese air force to win.

Early in the Pacific war, two naval battles served as turning points for the Allies. In the Battles of Coral Sea and Midway (May 1942 and June 1942, respectively), the Allies were able to stop a Japanese aircraft carrier from reaching Australia. They also broke the Japanese code to intercept and destroy four more aircraft carriers. U.S. Admiral Chester Nimitz soon adopted the strategy of "island hopping," in which the U.S. Navy would focus only on strategic Pacific islands and surround Japanese-held islands to engage the enemy. Eventually, this tactic would lead the Allies to the southernmost Japanese islands.

The Japanese were not about to back down, however, as several other bloody battles raged between 1943 and 1945. By 1945, the United States had come close enough to the Japanese mainland to launch air raids on major cities, such as Tokyo. As the Japanese grew more desperate, sending suicide bombers called **kamikazes** into U.S. aircraft carriers, it was clear to new president Harry Truman that the only way to end the war would be to invade Japan. (President Roosevelt had died in April 1945, thus leaving the power of the presidency in the hands of Vice President Truman.) Not wishing to launch an invasion that would more than likely cost many thousands of American lives, Truman decided instead to use a new secret weapon on Japan. On August 6, 1945, "Little Boy," an atomic bomb, was dropped from the *Enola Gay* over the industrial city of Hiroshima, killing 80,000 people instantly. With the Japanese still unwilling to submit to an unconditional surrender, a second bomb, "Fat Man," was dropped on August 9 on the island of Nagasaki. Another 60,000 were killed immediately. Soon after, Japan surrendered on September 2, 1945.

American Neutrality | Road to War | **Two-Front War** | Diplomacy | Wartime Mobilization

DIPLOMACY AND CONFERENCES

Throughout World War II, the Big Three met to discuss wartime concerns and postwar desires. Meetings in Casablanca, Tehran, Yalta, and Potsdam all yielded agreements and concessions among Britain, the United States, and the USSR that would shape the course of the war and impact the coming of the Cold War.

Casablanca in 1943, the first of these war meetings, only included Roosevelt and Churchill—Stalin declined the invitation. Here the world leaders decided to invade Sicily and settle for nothing less than "unconditional surrender" from the Axis powers. November 1943 brought Roosevelt, Churchill, and Stalin together in Iranian city of Tehran. The seeds of the D-Day invasion were sown here, and Stalin agreed to enter the war against Japan. It was here that the first disagreements between the Soviet leader and the Western powers came to light. Stalin claimed the right to Eastern Europe to create a buffer zone between his country and Germany. Churchill, on the other hand, demanded a free Europe and the preservation of a unified Germany after the war's end. Roosevelt mediated between the two by promising peace through the proposed United Nations.

The Big Three met once again at Yalta in February 1945 to finalize the plans for postwar Europe. Here, Stalin agreed to enter the war against Japan within three months of Germany's surrender and signed an agreement to create a free and liberated Eastern Europe with free elections. Additionally, the Yalta conference yielded a skeleton for the United Nations and the division of Germany into four occupied military zones.

Sadly, the Big Three suffered a loss with the death of President Roosevelt on April 12, 1945. The president struggled with failing health while in Yalta. Worn down and exhausted, he died suddenly while resting at his vacation home in Georgia. A shocked nation soon learned that Vice President Harry S. Truman had taken the oath of office and, in doing so, had tkaen on awesome duties with war raging around him. The Big Three further changed, as the British had elected a new prime minister, Clement Attlee. The three leaders decided to demand an unconditional surrender from Japan, hold war-crimes tribunals after the war, and organize the occupation of Germany. The meeting was contentious—all three men disagreed on just about every issue. It was evident that this group was on the brink of a breakup.

WARTIME MOBILIZATION

The Selective Service System, having already instituted the draft in 1940, expanded to include all 18- to 65-year-old males when the United States declared war on Japan. In addition, some 260,000 women enlisted as members of the **Women's Army Corp** (WACs), **Women Appointed for Voluntary Emergency Service** (WAVES), and **Women's Auxiliary Ferrying Squadron** (WAFs). These women supported the war effort by flying supply missions, decoding codes, and repairing machines. By the war's end, almost 16 million men and women had served in some capacity in the war effort.

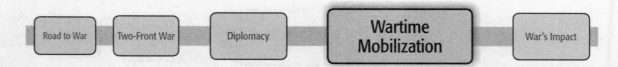

Road to War Two-Front War Diplomacy **Wartime Mobilization** War's Impact

The Office of War Mobilization took over from the earlier War Production Board to shift the country from a peacetime to a wartime economy. Soon outproducing the Axis powers, U.S. manufacturers split their time between making consumer goods and war supplies. Unemployment, the scourge of 10 years prior, had all but vanished, as Americans went to work to fuel the war machine. **The Office of Price Administration** (OPA) and **Office of Economic Stabilization** set forth to keep the wartime economy under control by setting price floors and ceilings, regulating the tax code, and instituting rationing. Rationing stamps were issued to every American family for goods such as sugar, coffee, and gasoline. Rationing made these goods available to troops overseas and freed up manufacturers to supply war munitions rather than consumer goods. Because of the lack of consumer goods for sale, American families sunk the money they made during the war into savings, which would impact the postwar economy through their increase in consumer spending.

Americans were asked to sacrifice and save voluntarily in addition to enforced rationing. Women saved bacon fat for the manufacturing of artillery shells, and children donated their bicycle tires for recycling. Like no time before, it seemed the entire country was willing to sacrifice to win the war.

WW II AND THE ECONOMY

World War II saw the national debt rise by some $200 billion, as the government increased spending to manage the needs of war. All Americans were required to pay a federal income tax for the first time, with some workers' funds deducted directly from their paychecks. The federal government borrowed more money from Americans in the form of war bonds, which would be repaid after the war was over. Organized labor had to compromise, as measures were taken to stop strikes before they occurred.

THE WAR'S IMPACT ON AMERICAN SOCIETY

The war effort impacted Americans from all walks of life. Citizens could not escape war propaganda as they walked to work, listened to the radio, ate their meals, and went to the movies. **The Office of War Information** (OWI) produced radio shows and news reels to keep Americans apprised of the events overseas. Many sat riveted as USO shows from overseas featuring Bob Hope and Francis Langford were broadcast across the nation. Movies of the day often glorified American war involvement, reaching audiences of millions each and every day. Posters and cartoons were created to encourage the adherence to rationing, the saving of grease, and the purchasing of war bonds. OWI aimed to keep American morale high and to increase war production.

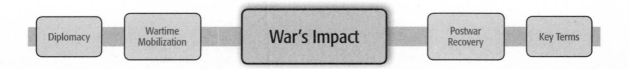

Diplomacy | Wartime Mobilization | War's Impact | Postwar Recovery | Key Terms

WOMEN AND MINORITIES DURING WARTIME

Women were specifically targeted by OWI propaganda. As many as 5 million women joined the workforce during the war in response to propaganda that glorified women's work. "**Rosie the Riveter**" was typified in songs, posters, and movies as an American heroine and everyday woman, able to work all day and still manage to run the household. Despite the urging of women such as Eleanor Roosevelt to make women's pay equal to that of their male counterparts, female workers typically earned just two-thirds of a male salary.

America's ethnic minorities also experienced changes in their lives due to the war. African Americans flocked again to industrial centers in the North and the Southwest to seek jobs in factories as they had during World War I. Just as before, race riots broke out as African Americans released pent-up frustrations by looting and damaging their communities. The summer of 1943 saw dozens of deaths in cities such as Detroit and Baltimore. The NAACP experienced a surge in membership during the war, encouraged by the inclusion of African Americans in Roosevelt's "Black Cabinet" and Eleanor Roosevelt's insistence on the desegregation of the armed forces. (However, only after the war would the armed forces be integrated.) Mexican Americans, many of whom had been displaced during the Great Depression, were encouraged to return to the United States as migrant farm laborers in the *bracero* program. Both former U.S. residents and Mexican nationals freely crossed into the United States to work during harvest season; many remained north of the border to live permanently. Tensions between East Coast sailors stationed in Los Angeles and Long Beach awaiting deployment to the Pacific theater and young Mexican American men reached a boiling point in the summer of 1943. The **Zoot Suit Riots** occurred when the sailors roamed the streets of Los Angeles and Long Beach looking for young "zooters"—Mexican American teens who wore long coats, flashy colors, and long hairstyles. The sailors beat the young men, ruined their clothes, cut their hair, and even raped their female companions. A special commission headed by Earl Warren discovered that the riots were not caused by the Mexican Americans but rather by discrimination from sailors and police.

Native Americans served the country by enlisting in the armed services and working in thousands of factories across the United States. Most famous were the **Navajo Code Talkers**, who translated U.S. code into the Native American language so that enemy forces could not decipher the content.

WARTIME TREATMENT OF THE JAPANESE

The individuals most affected by the war domestically were the thousands of Japanese Americans living along the West Coast. Some 100,000 Japanese American citizens were ordered to leave their homes for internment camps located in horse tracks, fairgrounds, and government plots of land far from the coast. President Roosevelt issued **Executive Order 9066** in reaction to the paranoia of the War Department that American citizens of Japanese ancestry might turn against their adopted country to aid Japan in an invasion of the West Coast. Of the 100,000 Japanese Americans interned, only 30 percent were actually foreign-born. These citizens were given less

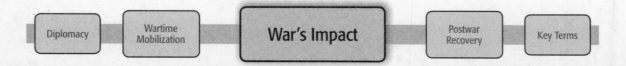

Diplomacy | Wartime Mobilization | War's Impact | Postwar Recovery | Key Terms

than 48 hours to vacate their homes and businesses. Carrying only what they could in a few suitcases, the internees arrived in dusty camps and lived in tarpaper shacks until the war's end. Once the families returned to their homes, they found their property, land, and homes taken over by other families. Japanese Americans lost millions of dollars in potential income, property, and land. The Supreme Court upheld the decision to intern the Japanese in the case *Korematsu v. United States* (1944), stating that in times of war, the curbing of civil rights was justified and that the Court could not second-guess military decisions. The federal government finally agreed in 1988 to apologize formally for internment, paying surviving families $20,000.

POST–WORLD WAR II RECOVERY

World War II had certainly made its mark on the United States. The war cost the country 400,000 men and over 800,000 causalities, more than all other U.S. wars combined, excluding the Civil War. Monetarily, the war cost some $360 billion and led to the largest budget deficit in U.S. history. Approximately 55 million people died worldwide, and 38 million were either wounded or missing. To aid in the repairs of a war-torn world, the **United Nations**, chartered in October 1945, set to work to combat nationalism and aid countries under threat of invasion.

Hoping to avoid the mistakes of World War I regarding returning veterans, Congress acted quickly to create a plan to aid those that returned from war to begin life as civilians. In 1944, Congress passed the **GI Bill** (Servicemen's Readjustment Act), which provided funding for a college education and low-interest home and small business loans. With 15 million soldiers returning from war, the GI Bill provided the opportunity for veterans to begin life with a career and a home in the near future. Returning GIs married sweethearts and had babies, leading to a "baby boom" that lasted from 1945 to 1963.

The war opened doors of opportunity to many groups, forever changing the United States. Women and African Americans felt a sense of hope, as they enjoyed steady jobs and an increased role in the economy. President Truman hoped not only to continue the New Deal programs of Roosevelt but to improve upon them by insisting on striving for full employment and increased rights for African Americans. Congress passed the **Employment Act of 1946** in an attempt to keep the United States at full employment at all times. Like most postwar economies, the United States experienced inflation as rationing and price regulations were lifted. Workers struggled to earn wages that kept up with inflation, even though the standard of living for the average American was higher than ever before. With regard to civil rights, President Truman rebuffed Southern Democrats by ending racial segregation in the federal government and armed forces.

Sensing trouble with Democrats at the helm, Americans elected enough Republicans to give the GOP a majority in Congress during the midterm elections of 1946. Under their leadership, the Constitution was amended to avoid the repeat of a four-term president (FDR) by limiting a president to two terms. In addition, Congress passed the **Taft-Hartley Act** in 1947 in an attempt to throw more support to big business. The bill, which was vetoed by Truman but enacted by a

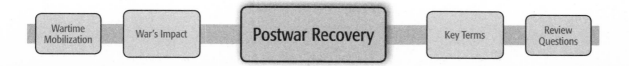

congressional override, outlawed the "closed-shop" union shops by states who wished to do so and boycotts by other unions and allowed the president to demand a "cooling-off" period of 80 days before the beginning of a strike. In Taft-Hartley, organized labor had lost some of the ground it had gained during the New Deal.

The population of the country shifted to *sun belt* states, such as Florida, California, Texas, and Arizona, with families fleeing the former *Rustbelt* of Michigan, Ohio, and Illinois. Suddenly once prosperous Northern and Midwestern states were strapped with the loss of tax revenues and sagging economies as families fled to warmer climates. Wartime technologies gave way to consumer conveniences, such as plastics and increased public air travel. But it was the political realm that would impact Americans most, as fears of fascism soon gave way to fear of annihilation from a nuclear weapon.

KEY TERMS

Names	Il Duce Benito Mussolini Rosie the Riveter Roosevelt Churchill Stalin *Luftwaffe*
Groups	kamikazes Women's Army Corps Women Appointed for Voluntary Emergency Service Women's Auxiliary Ferrying Squadron Office of War Mobilization Office of Price Administration Office of War Information Navajo Code Talkers United Nations
Events	Montevideo Conference D-Day Battle of the Bulge V-E Day Zoot Suit Riots
Places	Sudetenland Pearl Harbor

Documents and Laws	Selective Service Act
	Neutrality Act of 1939
	Destroyers-for-Bases
	Lend-Lease Act
	Atlantic Charter
	Executive Order 9066
	GI Bill
	Employment Act of 1946
	Taft-Hartley Act
Vocabulary	appeasement
	cash-and-carry
	Four Freedoms
	bracero
	genocide

REVIEW QUESTIONS

1. Roosevelt issued Executive Order 9066 because Japanese Americans

   (A) had publicly supported the Japanese regime.

   (B) had offered asylum to Japanese sailors fleeing Hawaii.

   (C) were not protected under the U.S. Constitution.

   (D) blamed the president for the attack on Pearl Harbor.

   (E) were believed to be loyal to Japan instead of the United States.

2. Tensions arose between the "Big Three" at Potsdam with regard to

   (A) war loans and repayment.

   (B) postwar Eastern Europe and Germany.

   (C) the date when the USSR would enter the war.

   (D) treatment of Holocaust victims.

   (E) the closing of the second front.

3. In *Korematsu v. United States*, the Supreme Court decided that

   (A) the shipping of grain to Japan should immediately cease.

   (B) the government was responsible for reimbursing Japanese Americans for lost wages.

   (C) the internment of Japanese Americans was justified.

   (D) Japanese men of age must serve in the armed forces.

   (E) Asian immigration needed to be curbed.

oop!

4. Wartime America during World War II can be characterized by all of the following EXCEPT

   (A) increased national debt.

   (B) a large number of women in the workforce.

   (C) racial riots in American cities.

   (D) lack of overall support for the war effort.

   (E) decrease in unemployment.

5. President Truman justified the dropping of the atomic bomb on Japan by

   (A) claiming that America was at risk of being invaded.

   (B) arguing that communists would abuse the technology if they found it first.

   (C) explaining the monetary cost of the project to build the bomb.

   (D) estimating loss of American life in the millions if Japan was invaded.

   (E) limiting its use to barely inhabited islands.

Postwar Recovery | Key Terms | **Review Questions** | Answers & Explanations | Essays

ANSWERS AND EXPLANATIONS

1. E

Paranoia gripped Americans living on the West Coast, spurring FDR to issue the order to remove Japanese Americans from their homes. Despite the fact that many had taken oaths of loyalty to the United States and were full U.S. citizens, some 100,000 Japanese Americans were rounded up and sent to government internment camps for the duration of the war.

2. B

Stalin's postwar vision was very different from that of Roosevelt and Churchill. He wished to have control over Eastern Europe and parts of Germany to ensure that the USSR would never again be invaded through the region.

3. C

The Supreme Court ruled in the *Korematsu* case that internment of Japanese Americans was justified due to a wartime threat posed by these people. Never was an act of treason or espionage attributed to the thousands of Japanese Americans living in the United States during the war. Actually, many Japanese Americans faithfully served the United States in the armed services during World War II, despite their treatment.

4. D

Americans were unified as during no other time in history during World War II. Voluntarily saving, rationing, and purchasing war bonds, Americans from all walks of life supported the war effort wholeheartedly.

5. D

Knowing that Americans were growing weary of fighting in World War II, President Truman looked to end the war with Japan quickly and to avoid a land invasion by dropping the atomic bombs on the manufacturing cities of Hiroshima and Nagasaki. Some 140,000 people were killed instantly, and 1 million were injured after the bombs' blasts.

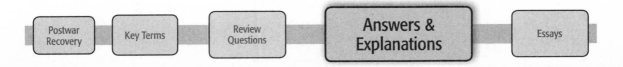

UNIT IV SAMPLE ESSAYS

The following are sample free-response questions that you might see on the AP U.S. History exam. Listed under each question are important terms that would greatly add to your answer. AP Readers will look for you to mention at least several of the listed people. places, and things.

1. The lives of American women have shifted dramatically since 1940. Analyze how THREE of the following factors have changed the status of women in the United States through the year 2000.

   Growth of mass consumption

   Medical advances

   Economic growth

   Governmental actions

   Study List

   television

   household appliances

   rise in standard of living

   supermarkets

   advertisements

   birth control pill

   hormone replacement

   advanced tests for breast cancer

   heart disease

   pregnancy and birth

   change in the workplace

   women going to college

   entrepreneurs

   two-income families

   day care issues

   Roe v. Wade

   Equal Rights Amendment

   equal pay for equal work

   National Organization of Women

   Betty Friedan

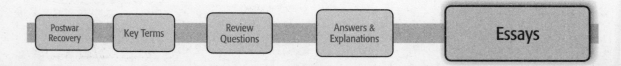

Postwar Recovery | Key Terms | Review Questions | Answers & Explanations | Essays

2. Discuss the impact of World War II conferences on the eventual foreign policy decisions of the United States between 1945 and 1975.

Study List

Montevideo Conference

Geneva Convention

Cuban Missile Crisis

Bay of Pigs

Yalta

Potsdam

Vietnam War

Truman Doctrine

Marshall Plan

Warsaw Pact

D-Day

Pearl Harbor

National Security Act

Eisenhower Doctrine

SAMPLE FRQ RESPONSES

The lives of American women have shifted dramatically since 1940. Analyze how THREE of the following factors have changed the status of women in the United States through the year 2000.

Growth of mass consumption

Medical advances

Economic growth

Governmental actions

From 1940 to 2000, America evolved from World War II rationing into a country with great wealth and prosperity. With economic growth, the growth of mass consumption, and new governmental actions, the lives of American women and what the country could expect from them changed greatly.

During World War II, women first went into the workforce in great numbers, filling in at work for their male counterparts at war overseas. Once the men returned, some women had to vacate those positions, but they had experienced working away from the home. With the end of the war came an economic boom. During the 1950s, the housewife ideal still

reigned. However, with the more liberal 1960s and the onset of the feminist movement came new ideas about what a woman's role was. In 1963, Betty Friedan's book *The Feminine Mystique* voiced the belief of many contemporary women that traditional gender roles were frustrating, unsatisfying, and limiting. No longer were women happily relegated to jobs as school teachers, librarians, and nurses, if they worked at all. They wanted to have the same educational and employment opportunities as men. By the 1980s, more women than men were attending college. With greater education came greater job opportunities and the rise of two-income families; as the economy tightened, it often became necessary for both parents in a family to work. These economic shifts led to complex issues for modern women, including having to use day care for their children and figuring how to work and manage their status as a mother at the same time.

The economic growth that began post–World War II led to a growth in mass consumption. Television, introduced at the World Fair in 1939, became commercialized in 1947. As television use spread, its programming evolved to show portrayals of what Americans culture was, including a standard of beauty portrayed in TV programming that has had lasting effects on American women's self-image. Television also shaped societal mores about how women should behave and live their lives. A host of new technology was soon invented to assist women workers. Frozen dinners became popular as women joined the workforce and had less time to cook. Dishwashers, vacuums, washing machines, and dryers were all created to eliminate the extra time women spent on household tasks. With the advent of supermarkets, women no longer had to go from the butcher shop to the drug store to the bakery; they could buy everything in the same place.

With economic and technological changes came changes in government policies. Feminist organizations like the National Organization of Women (NOW) came to prominence in the 1960s, bringing to the government's attention the need for equal rights for women including equal pay between men and women for equal work, and the need to fight violence against women. Many laws have since been passed by our government in the last 30 years to protect the rights of women. In the landmark case of *Roe v. Wade*, the Supreme Court ruled that women had the right to abortions. This landmark case, ruled upon in 1973, stated that a woman's right to an abortion fell under her constitutional right to privacy under the Fourteenth Amendment. From 1972 to 1982, women's rights groups spearheaded by NOW and organized labor lobbied for the Equal Rights Amendment, trying to get states to ratify it. After a long battle the effort failed.

The lives women were able to live in American society changed greatly from 1940 to 2000. Economic growth led to an increase in women's participation in the workforce and to a higher status for them in the workforce, even as they still weren't totally equal. This economic boom also brought with it a growth in mass consumption, making it easier for women to take care of their families and work and/or attend college. This led to changes in how women chose to raise their families. New media technology like television changed

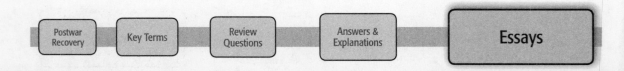

the perception of what women's roles should be in society. Changes in social mores also changed government policies, and groups like NOW were able to successfully agitate for more protection of women's rights.

Discuss the impact of World War II conferences on the eventual foreign policy decisions of the United States between 1945 through 1975.

The Yalta and Potsdam Conferences of 1945 were held with the purpose of organizing relations among the participating countries—England, the United States, and the Soviet Union—after World War II concluded in Europe. The ensuing postwar events were not what were agreed upon at the two conferences, resulting in many significant American foreign policy decisions over the next 30 years.

One of the primary issues discussed at the Yalta conference was what would happen to countries liberated from the Nazis. According to the Yalta conference, free and democratic elections should be held, which would allow each country to create a new government. In Eastern European countries occupied by the Soviet "Red Army," postwar elections were rigged to heavily favor communist parties controlled by Moscow. Because these actions were in direct opposition to what Stalin agreed to at the Yalta conference, and later reaffirmed at the Potsdam conference, and due to an aggressive insistence by Stalin during the Tehran conference in 1943 that resulted in nearly half of Poland being ceded to the Soviet Union after the war, the United States leaders had deep-seated suspicions and distrust for the Soviet Union and for communism in general.

Fearing a spread of communism, the U.S. President Truman issued the Truman Doctrine, stating that the United States would support free peoples who were fighting against armed minorities and outside pressures, namely communism. Originally a political response to Soviet policy in Eastern Europe, it also contributed to U.S. involvement in both the Korean and the Vietnam Wars.

The Marshall Plan, enacted in 1947, followed along the same lines as the Truman Doctrine. Under the Marshall Plan, Western European countries, including West Germany, received billions of dollars in economic and technical aid from the United States. The plan was intended to bring economic prosperity to postwar Europe, and it achieved its designed goal in almost every country. Eastern European countries, as well as the Soviet Union, were invited to participate in the plan; however, Stalin refused to allow any of his satellite countries to participate. These actions furthered the divide between the U.S. and the Soviet Union and re-enforced suspicions that the Soviet Union had no intentions of following the official agreements of the Yalta conference concerning the free will of Eastern European peoples.

In the 1950s, the U.S. moved toward a policy of "brinkmanship." The basic philosophy was to bring both the U.S. and the Soviet Union to the brink of war in order to force

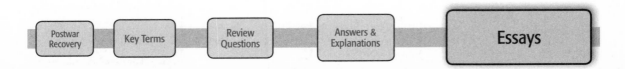

concessions from the Soviets. This policy was founded upon the distrust of the Soviet Union that had been building since the end of the Potsdam Conference. Brinkmanship resulted in an arms race that created thousands of nuclear bombs and kept the world paralyzed with fear during the Cuban Missile Crisis in 1962.

The late 1960s saw a move in U.S. foreign policy from "brinkmanship" to "containment." In 1965 the U.S. began to send the first waves of troops to Vietnam. Using a foreign policy based on the Truman Doctrine, the U.S. fought an eight-year campaign to "contain" the spread of communism in Vietnam and prevent it from spreading to the rest of Southeast Asia. The resulting pullout of troops and the fall of Saigon in 1975 were a definite blow to the U.S. policy of containment.

The Potsdam Conference, the culmination of the Casablanca, Tehran, and Yalta Conferences, should have been followed by an official peace conference to end World War II. This peace conference would have defined borders, opened lines of communication, and allowed for many peoples in formerly occupied countries to speak out on the conditions they lived in. Instead those questions were left largely unanswered. In Eastern Europe, where many of the most terrible atrocities were committed, many questions would be left unanswered for decades as the Soviet Union and it's satellite nations descended into a shroud of secrecy. During the same time, the United States, already distrusting of communism, was forced to act accordingly.

UNIT V: THE COLD WAR TO THE NEW MILLENNIUM

CHAPTER 26: THE COLD WAR, 1945–1963

IF YOU ONLY LEARN TWENTY-ONE THINGS IN THIS UNIT . . . .

1. Events leading up to the Cold War—Truman's stance on communism, the Marshall Plan, the Warsaw Pact, etc.

2. The emergence of communism in Asia; U.S. involvement in Korea; the Geneva Convention

3. U.S. involvement with Cuba—Bay of Pigs, Castro, the Cuban Missile Crisis

4. How the United States prepared itself for future war (National Security Act, CIA, SEATO, etc.)

5. McCarthyism and the effects of the Red Scare on the United States (Sputnik, NASA, etc.)

6. The major causes and effects of the Civil Rights Movement (*Brown v. Board of Education*, Little Rock Nine, Rosa Parks)

7. The effects of Civil Rights unrest in nationwide political involvement and protests—Martin Luther King, Jr., Malcolm X, Freedom Summer, etc.

8. Sociological changes in the mid-century—the effects of television and radio, beatniks, *The Feminine Mystique*

9. Kennedy's presidency, his New Frontier, and his assassination

10. LBJ's Great Society and its effects

11. Events leading up to the Vietnam War domestically and abroad

12. U.S. reactions to the Vietnam War

13. The effects of Vietnam, socially and politically (War Powers Act)

14. Nixon's presidency, stagflation, and the effects of Watergate on the U.S. mindset

Cold War Origins — Containment Policy — Cold War in Asia — Eisenhower & Kennedy — 2nd Red Scare

15. Carter's presidency and attempts at peace agreements in the Middle East

16. The Reagan Revolution and a changing society under Reagan's presidency (Iran Contra, Star Wars)

17. Events leading to the end of the Cold War (détente, *glasnost*, etc.) and the collapse of the Soviet Union

18. Changing times of present-day society—the graying of America, technology advancements, healthcare discoveries, environmental concerns, etc.

19. Nationwide racial tensions and their effect on society (Rodney King, affirmative action debates, etc.)

20. The presidency of Bill Clinton and his changes to economic policy

21. The events leading to 9/11; the country's "war on terrorism" and its effects on society

ORIGINS OF THE COLD WAR

It was clear to Roosevelt and Churchill, and later Truman and Atlee, that Joseph Stalin was focused on carving out spheres of influence in Eastern Europe. The "shotgun marriage" between the Soviets and the United States during World War II would soon crumble as it became clearer that Stalin could not be trusted. The Soviets' refusal to sign a plan eliminating atomic weapons and to join the World Bank also caused Western powers to grow increasingly alarmed about Stalin's intentions. Despite his agreement to free elections in Eastern Europe at the Yalta Conference, when time came for the elections, Stalin refused to allow them in Poland and other Eastern European countries. From 1946 to 1948, communist leaders were installed by Moscow, with the Soviets finally taking the countries under their wing as "satellite" nations. This was a clear violation of the agreements of the war conferences, where the world powers set forth to protect the self-determination of peoples.

In another turn of events, as the United States, Great Britain, and France looked to unify Germany once again as a sovereign nation, the Soviets turned East Germany into a communist state. By tightening control over its sector, the USSR hoped to keep Germany crippled enough to avoid another world war. It also sought to force the other three world powers to give up their sectors of the capital city of Berlin, since it lay within the Soviet-controlled region of East Germany. In March 1946, Winston Churchill delivered a speech in Fulton, Missouri, where he said, "An iron curtain has descended across Europe." The "iron curtain" he spoke of was communism.

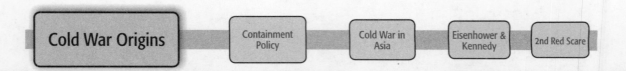

Cold War Origins | Containment Policy | Cold War in Asia | Eisenhower & Kennedy | 2nd Red Scare

THE POLICY OF CONTAINMENT

← Truman Doctrine, (1947) *← Later developed "domino theory" in Eisenhower Doctrine*

Heavily influenced by his top advisors, Secretary of State George Marshall, Undersecretary of State Dean Acheson, and Soviet expert George Kennan, President Truman was interested in "containing" communism from spreading. Kennan had recently penned an article in which he outlined his predictions of Soviet domination if the United States and United Nations did not act to stop their advance. The containment policy was first implemented in reaction to a communist threat in Greece and Turkey.

THE TRUMAN DOCTRINE

In March 1947, President Truman asked Congress for funding to assist these countries in repelling a possible communist takeover. Now known as the **Truman Doctrine,** the president's speech explained that the United States had a duty to give financial assistance to free nations under communist threat. The Truman Doctrine passed its first test, as both Greece and Turkey successfully thwarted communism.

THE MARSHALL PLAN

In rebuilding war-torn Europe, the Truman administration wanted to act quickly to avoid the same troubles that had besieged the region after World War I. History was on the side of extremist parties, who stood poised to take advantage of the hungry, tired, and poor. One of these parties consisted of hard-line communists, who were building momentum in France and Italy. To curb the success of the communists, the Truman administration needed to supply funding to rebuild the economies of Western European nations and get citizens back on their feet.

In June 1947, Truman's secretary of state, George Marshall, masterminded a plan to give Western Europe massive amounts of financial assistance and political support for rebuilding democratic forms of government. Congress readily approved the **Marshall Plan**, which would supply $3 billion in aid over a four-year period. Historians debate the impetus behind the Marshall Plan. It was offered to the Soviet Union and other Eastern European countries, but they did not wish to take "dirty capitalist" money and be forever indebted to the United States. Many saw the plan as a way to aid a faltering region and prevent another worldwide war. Others saw it as a direct slap in the face of the Soviets, who had to scramble to come up with an aid plan of their own. The Marshall Plan was an economic miracle for Western Europe. By the end of the era, the region was entirely self-sufficient, and communism had been contained away from vulnerable countries.

THE BERLIN AIRLIFT AND THE WARSAW PACT

It looked as if the Cold War was about to get hot in June of 1948. Stalin had grown tired of U.S. intrusion into European affairs. The last straw was when Western powers sought to create

Cold War Origins | **Containment Policy** | Cold War in Asia | Eisenhower & Kennedy | 2nd Red Scare

a stabilized currency for the western sector of Germany. Again, not wanting to take part in any capitalist economic system, Stalin angrily cut off the city of Berlin from Western contact. All land routes into and out of the city were blockaded by Soviet troops. Not wishing to provoke the unstable Soviet leader, Truman decided to fly supplies into the city's citizens by air. **The Berlin Airlift** delivered supplies to the city, day after day, for 11 months. The world held its breath while the possibility of a world war loomed, but neither side budged, and Stalin finally reopened the city.

President Truman broke a tradition dating from Washington's Farewell Address—he joined an alliance with European countries. Stalin responded by forming the Warsaw Pact in 1955, which provided the same military protection but at a cost—once a country was a member, it could never leave the alliance. These alliances created an atmosphere in which each side attempted to one-up the other by building up arms and superior large-scale weapons. After the Soviets exploded their first atomic bomb in 1949, the atomic race was on. By 1952, the United States had developed and tested its first hydrogen bomb, which was at least one thousand times stronger than the bombs dropped on Hiroshima and Nagasaki.

THE NATIONAL SECURITY ACT AND NSC-68

Domestically, President Truman urged the passage of the **National Security Act** in 1947, which created the **Department of Defense** (formally the Department of War), the **National Security Council**, and the **Central Intelligence Agency** (CIA). To keep the country always at the ready, a permanent peacetime draft was enacted in 1948. As a boost to Truman's belief in the need for increased defense spending, a secret document labeled NSC-68, written by the National Security Council, was released just after China fell to communism and the Korean crisis was about to begin. The document detailed the Soviet's plans for worldwide domination and encouraged an immediate buildup of the nation's military. Where the Truman Doctrine had provided for financial support in preventing the spread of communism, NSC-68 now provided for the use of U.S. troops to achieve containment.

COLD WAR POLICY IN ASIA

Containment in Asia was not as easy as containment had been in Europe. To keep Japan on a straight path, the United States occupied the islands until 1951. The new constitution, written with the assistance of General Douglas MacArthur, retained a ceremonial emperor and a limited military. Americans assisted Japan in rebuilding economically and politically after the war's end. Other regions in Asia would not take to democracy so easily.

CHINA FALLS TO COMMUNISM

A corrupt regime had taken control of China with the support of the United States during World War II. The **Nationalists (Kuomintang)**, under the leadership of Chiang Kai-shek (Jiang Jieshi), received financial aid from the United States to keep the country from falling prey to the Japanese.

| Cold War Origins | Containment Policy | Cold War in Asia | Eisenhower & Kennedy | 2nd Red Scare |

Once that support was removed after the war, the Nationalists and the Communists, under the leadership of **Mao Tse-Tung** (Mao Zedong), re-engaged in a war that had been brewing since before World War II. Many Chinese citizens began to turn to Mao and the Communists as they became more and more disgusted by the corruption, inflation, and inequality they experienced under Chiang. President Truman sent George Marshall to mediate between the two parties but to no avail. More money was sent to the Nationalists, but much of it never made it into their hands. China finally fell to the Communists by 1949; Chiang and the Nationalists fled to the nearby island of Formosa, now Taiwan. Americans were taken aback by the initiation of millions of new communists in the world and blamed the Truman administration for its lack of strength. Another blow came in 1950, when Joseph Stalin and Mao Tse-Tung signed a pact that linked the two large nations in one communist bloc.

WAR IN KOREA

Soon the former Japanese colony of Korea seemed ripe for the picking to the Soviets. They withdrew from the northern region of the peninsula, leaving it in the hands of the communist Kim Il Sung, while the United States left the southern half to Syngman Rhee. Supplied with Chinese and Soviet weapons, the North Korean army invaded the South over the 38th parallel in June 1950. President Truman reacted immediately by urging the United Nations Security Council to intervene on behalf of the South Koreans. Luckily, the Soviet Union—a permanent member of the council—had boycotted the UN, opening the door for a quick decision. The Security Council and U.S. Congress authorized a "police action" of military force to liberate South Korea. Congress did not declare war.

The fighting in Korea was a fiasco, as the North Koreans cut their way easily to the heart of the South. General MacArthur was able to push the North Koreans back across the 38th parallel with a surprise landing of UN forces at Inchon, near the border of the two Koreas. MacArthur pushed the enemy back almost to the Chinese border. Gloating with his success, MacArthur was taken by surprise as Chinese forces crossed the border and forced the UN troops to retreat back across the 38th parallel. At this point, MacArthur was convinced that if he had more resources, he could win the war and possibly take China as well. Truman had already called for a "limited war" and sternly told MacArthur that he was not to make any statements that were critical of American policy in Asia. In a letter that was later leaked to the press, the general said that "there is no substitute for victory," and alleged that the president was weak.

MacArthur then ignored Truman's wishes and demanded an unconditional surrender of the North Koreans. Upon hearing this news, Truman immediately removed General MacArthur from his command and had him return to the United States in April 1951. He returned to a hero's welcome, as most Americans had never experienced a U.S. military loss and could not understand the objectives of containment. Nonetheless, Truman's action signified that civilian rule in the United States was supreme; it was the military's responsibility to follow the president's orders, not make them. In the end, the Korean conflict ended in a stalemate, with the original division at the

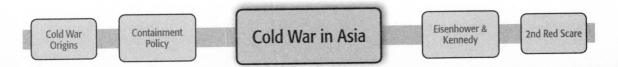

38th parallel remaining—communists in the North and nationalists in the South. Now that the United States had "lost" two Asian nations to communism, Republicans were beginning to claim that the Democrats did not have what it took to rid the world of the "Red Menace."

EISENHOWER AND KENNEDY

World War II hero General **Dwight D. "Ike" Eisenhower** took the reigns of the presidency in 1952 with the anti-communist-crusading Richard M. Nixon as his vice president. Eisenhower chose John Foster Dulles as his secretary of state. Dulles advocated a departure from Truman's Cold War policies as a "new look." American foreign policy would now actively support nations who sought liberation from communism through his idea of "**brinksmanship**"—the United States would push the aggressor nation to the brink of nuclear war, forcing it to back down in the face of American superiority. The other portion of the "new look" regarded the military. Dulles believed that the United States needed to place more emphasis on nuclear and air power and less on conventional troops and weapons. This led to his concept of "**massive retaliation**," whereby the United States would unleash its arsenal of nuclear weapons on any nation that threatened it. This did not address the problem of small countries under communist threat.

THE GENEVA CONVENTION AND TROUBLES IN VIETNAM

As colonial governments collapsed in Asia, the Pacific, and Africa, the United States struggled to keep up with the need to close the opportunity for communist takeover of these vulnerable countries. Along with brinksmanship and massive retaliation, Dulles also championed the use of covert action to fight the Cold War quietly. In 1953, the CIA staged a coup that led to the return of the corrupt and ruthless Shah of Iran. Similarly, the CIA aided in the overthrow of a left-leaning government in Guatemala in 1954.

The French were losing control of their colonies in Indochina, with the final ouster at the Vietnamese city of Dien Bien Phu in 1954. Without American assistance, the French were forced to give up the colony entirely. At the **Geneva Convention** (1954), the region was divided into three nations: Vietnam, Cambodia, and Laos. The convention also decided to divide Vietnam at *[handwritten: Not a permanent split]* the 17th parallel, with the communists led by Ho Chi Minh in the North and anti-communists led by Ngo Dinh Diem in the South. It was further decided that elections to reunite Vietnam would occur in two years. Fearing a communist win in the elections, Ngo Dinh Diem never allowed them to occur and became increasingly dictatorial. Eisenhower, fearing what he called the "domino theory" (where one Asian nation would fall to communism and the rest would follow), urged Dulles to action. He created the **South East Asian Treaty Organization** (SEATO), which resembled NATO, to give mutual military assistance to member nations and hold up Diem's crumbling regime.

Containment Policy | Cold War in Asia | **Eisenhower & Kennedy** | 2nd Red Scare | Living in Fear

EISENHOWER AND THE MIDDLE EAST

Aside from Iran, other Middle Eastern countries provided their fair share of trouble for Eisenhower. When the Egyptian leader Nasser asked the United States for assistance in building the **Aswan Dam**, he was assumed the deal was an easy one. The United States refused, however, as Egypt seemed to threaten the security of the new Jewish state of Israel. Nasser took this rebuke very seriously and seized the foreign-held Suez Canal. The free flow of oil from the Middle East to Europe and the United States was now cut off. Unbeknownst to Eisenhower, Britain, France, and Israel launched a surprise attack on Egypt and regained control of the Suez Canal. An angry Eisenhower called upon the UN Security Council to denounce the surprise action and call for the immediate removal of the multinational forces. The UN complied. Britain and France fell from their role as world leaders.

THE EISENHOWER DOCTRINE

> Eisenhower seized this opportunity to become more of a presence in the Middle East by proclaiming the **Eisenhower Doctrine**. Much like the Truman Doctrine, Eisenhower's document was pointed at the Middle East.

THE SOVIET UNION AND HUNGARY

The relationship between the United States and the Soviet Union would continue to plague Eisenhower just as it had Truman before him. In some respects, Eisenhower's approach to the USSR was somewhat restrained in comparison to Truman's, but things did heat up sporadically. After Stalin's death in 1953, many looked for relief from Cold War tensions, and signs existed that this was a possibility. Agreements to "open skies" and the end to some postwar occupations gave some unwilling members of the Warsaw Pact a glimmer of hope. One such member was Hungary, who in 1956 successfully overthrew a Soviet puppet government. The new government demanded Hungary's removal from the Warsaw Pact. The new Soviet Premier, Nikita Khrushchev, had heard enough and ordered Soviet troops to crush the resistance. Protesting students rushed to their radios and telegraph machines to send urgent messages to the United States—"**S.O.S.**"—but there was no response. Eisenhower feared that sending in U.S. troops would signal the beginning of World War III. The USSR brutally crushed the Hungarian resistance, killing many.

SPY PLANES OVER BERLIN

Berlin was again in the news when in 1958 Khrushchev demanded the removal of Westerners from the city within six months. Eisenhower called an urgent meeting with the Soviet premier, where they agreed to hold off on any decision until they could meet again in Paris in 1960.

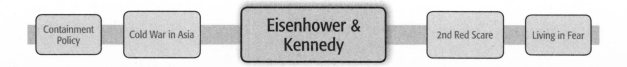

Unfortunately, this meeting would never occur, as a U.S. U-2 spy plane was shot down over the Soviet Union two weeks prior to it. It was then discovered that the United States had been flying regular spy missions over the USSR since 1955. Khrushchev called off the Paris talks.

CASTRO COMMUNIZES CUBA

Communism found a new home just 90 miles off the coast of the United States on the Caribbean island of Cuba. The brutal dictator Batista had been overthrown by the revolutionary Fidel Castro in 1959. Cuban exiles living in the United States rejoiced, as it looked as if their nation was now free from oppression. The "honeymoon" with Castro soon faded, as he nationalized businesses owned by Americans and introduced massive land reforms. After Eisenhower cut diplomatic relations with Castro, the leader looked to the Soviets for help. Castro then set about building a communist state on the lucrative island. Before he left office, Eisenhower approved of a covert plan to invade Cuba and overthrow Fidel Castro. However, Eisenhower would not see the plan through.

Bay of Pigs That didn't work out at all

BAY OF PIGS AND THE BERLIN WALL

John F. Kennedy was the next president in line to deal with Cold War politics. The young president would agree to allow an invasion to take place in April 1961 at the **Bay of Pigs** (Bahia de Puerco). Using faulty intelligence, the CIA operatives landed on the beach and were immediately surrounded by unhappy Cubans. The invasion was a failure and an embarrassment for the new president. Kennedy had little time to rest, as he was scheduled to meet with Khrushchev soon in Vienna. The Soviet leader used this opportunity to threaten President Kennedy with regard to Berlin. Kennedy did not back down, refusing to remove U.S. troops from the city. The Soviets responded by building a wall around West Berlin to stem the flow of East Berliners escaping the communist regime. The president did not stop the building of the wall, but he did travel to West Berlin in 1963 to proclaim U.S. support for its citizens.

THE CUBAN MISSILE CRISIS

The nation was gripped with fear as Fidel Castro and Khrushchev joined forces to threaten U.S. national security. U.S. spy planes discovered the building of nuclear missile sites on the island of Cuba in October 1962. These medium-range and long-range nuclear missiles decreased the existing warning time of a nuclear attack on the United States from 30 minutes to 30 seconds. The missiles in Cuba also left no spot on the North American continent safe from nuclear attack (except the Pacific Northwest region near Seattle). Kennedy ordered the immediate removal of the missiles, but Castro and Khrushchev balked. JFK was left with a grave decision and enlisted a group of advisors to assist him. Headed by his brother, Attorney General Robert Kennedy, the group decided that a naval blockade would be the least dangerous option. After several days of Soviet ships being turned back in the Atlantic Ocean and tense talks back and forth, Khrushchev decided to remove the missiles from Cuba, as long as the United States promised never to invade

Containment Policy | Cold War in Asia | **Eisenhower & Kennedy** | 2nd Red Scare | Living in Fear

[handwritten: Signified beginning of and of Cold War]

Cuba again and removed its own missiles from Turkey. As close as the two nations were to nuclear war, the **Cuban Missile Crisis** was effective in opening up the channels of communication between Washington, D.C. and Moscow. A direct "**red phone**" or hotline was installed so that the world leaders could have immediate contact in the instance of an emergency.

Upon entering the presidency, Kennedy did not believe that Dulles's "new look" military would be effective in a world where colonial governments continued to fall in small Asian and African nations. His "flexible response" military looked to use conventional tactics and elite special forces units to root out communists in nations such as Vietnam and Congo.

THE SECOND RED SCARE

[handwritten: McCarthyism]

To root out potential "disloyals" from the inner workings of the federal government, Congress, against the wishes of President Truman, drafted several acts aimed at communists and other subversives. Some methods had been around since before the United States entered World War II. **The Smith Act** of 1940 was designed to arrest people who were advocates of overthrowing the government, even if they had no intention of ever doing so. The **House Un-American Activities Committee** (HUAC), established in 1939 to look for former Nazis who had made it to the United States, was reactivated in the postwar years to find communists.

AMERICAN ESPIONAGE AND SENATOR MCCARTHY

Paranoia about a potential communist takeover swept the nation in the 1950s, much as it had after World War I. Fueling this fear were actual cases of espionage in which American spies were handing U.S. secrets to the Soviets. The HUAC made headlines in 1948 when American communist Whittaker Chambers testified in the case of a State Department employee who had supposedly leaked secrets to the communists. Young lawyer Richard M. Nixon linked Whittaker's testimony to that of a man who had assisted President Franklin Roosevelt during the Yalta conference. The employee, **Alger Hiss**, denied any connections to the Communist Party or any spy networks. Nonetheless, he was convicted and sent to prison for perjury; Hiss had falsely testified under oath that he had never been a member of a Communist Party.

[handwritten right margin: One of many trials of actual cases of communist infiltration that fueled Second Red Scare and subsequently McCarthyism]

The FBI successfully discovered a spy network that led to the arrest of a husband and wife duo, Julius and Ethel Rosenberg. The married couple was accused of delivering atomic bomb secrets to the Soviets. The trial was a press spectacle, and a conviction was finally handed down in 1951. Convicted of treason and espionage, the Rosenbergs were sentenced to death and executed by electric chair.

[handwritten: "I have in my hand..."]

Republican Senator Joseph McCarthy started raising suspicions that communists besides Alger Hiss were still working in the State Department. Using the media to his advantage, McCarthy widely cast his anti-communist net as he accused many within the Truman administration and other well-known Americans. The middle class were drawn to his down-home, direct comments on television, which were very different from the "limited war" stance that many felt had lost the Korean War. While his accusations were mostly false, Republicans did little to stop him, as he helped their chances in the upcoming presidential election. McCarthy painted himself into a corner however, when in 1954, his ruthless tactics were shown on television. The Senate committee hearings regarding communism in the army portrayed McCarthy as an unfeeling beast as he questioned those on the stand. Soon, fellow members of Congress decided that "**McCarthyism**" had gone far enough and voted for censure to silence the senator.

LIVING IN FEAR—AMERICANS AND THE COLD WAR

Americans were hoping for some peace after World War II, but they traded fear of Hitler and Tojo for fear of nuclear war. It seemed that every time they turned around, U.S. citizens were faced with images of nations falling to communist rule, American spies, and nuclear threat. Businesses focused on the protection of American lives boomed during the Cold War, as upper- and middle-class families flocked to trade fairs to learn of the latest and greatest ways to keep their families safe. After the launch of the Russian space satellite *Sputnik* in 1957, Americans were convinced that they had better get moving if they were to keep up with the "Ruskies." Congress responded by allocating millions of dollars to schools and universities across the nation to prepare students in mathematics, science, and foreign language. Eisenhower also saw the creation of the **National Aeronautics and Space Administration** (NASA) in 1958 to get the United States back in the running with the Soviets.

[handwritten margin note: Led to greater emphasis on maths and sciences in the American education system.]

Bomb shelters were big business in the United States, with Americans spending upwards of $5,000 to protect their families. These buildings, constructed underground, had provisions for a family of four to survive after a nuclear attack. Children in schools practiced "duck and cover" drills in which they would fall out of their seats, hide under desks, and remain until the "all clear" signal sounded. Americans purchased canned goods, bottled water, and Geiger counters to fill their homes and bomb shelters. Once novelty items, "spy gear" became popular as Americans hoped to be able to outsmart neighbors who might be Russian double agents. **The National Highway Act** of 1956, which created the nation's interstate freeway system looked as if it was intended solely to improve the county's infrastructure, but the 42,000 miles of road were also meant to provide for the quick evacuation of large urban centers, the emergency landing of planes, and the transport of missiles.

The Cold War had a profound effect on the entertainment industry, as well. Comic characters such as Captain America and movies like *The Invasion of the Body Snatchers* fueled the American thirst for "commie hunting." Eisenhower himself played into Cold War fears as he warned the nation of the negative impact of the Cold War on America in his farewell address. Eisenhower warned of the "military-industrial complex," whereby the nation would be driven by the needs of the arms race and war machine.

KEY TERMS	
Names	Mao Tse-Tung Dwight D. Eisenhower Fidel Castro Alger Hiss Joseph McCarthy
Groups	Department of Defense National Security Council Central Intelligence Agency (CIA) Nationalists (Koumintang) South East Asian Treaty Organization (SEATO) House Un-American Activities Committee (HUAC) National Aeronautics and Space Administration (NASA)
Events	The Geneva Convention Cuban Missile Crisis
Documents and Laws	Truman Doctrine Marshall Plan Warsaw Pact National Security Act Eisenhower Doctrine The Smith Act National Highway Act
Places	Aswan Dam Bay of Pigs
Vocabulary	Berlin Airlift brinksmanship massive retaliation S.O.S. red phone McCarthyism *Sputnik*

REVIEW QUESTIONS

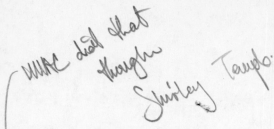

HUAC did that though
Shirley Temple.

1. President Truman's containment policy was first tested in

   (A) Cuba.
   (B) Greece.
   (C) Iran.
   (D) Egypt.
   (E) Vietnam.

2. The Marshall Plan called for

   (A) military aid for Europe.
   (B) economic assistance for Western Europe.
   (C) the occupation of Japan.
   (D) the protection of Greece and Turkey.
   (E) the end of nuclear testing.

3. Prior to the Korean conflict, Truman's insistence on increased military spending was boosted by

   (A) the release of NSC-68.
   (B) the launching of *Sputnik*.
   (C) MacArthur's return to the United States.
   (D) the North Korean invasion of South Korea.
   (E) the Hungarian uprising.

4. Senator Joseph McCarthy gained publicity by

   (A) testifying before the HUAC in the Hiss case.
   (B) accusing Hollywood directors and actors of being communists.
   (C) claiming that Eisenhower was involved in a spy ring.
   (D) demanding evidence to support the Korean War.
   (E) alleging that communists were still working for the State Department.

5. Kennedy's "flexible response" strategy

   (A) drastically cut the number of nuclear weapons in the United States.
   (B) brought back the conventional military in conjunction with nuclear weapons.
   (C) relied solely on special forces to root out communists.
   (D) angered Fidel Castro, driving him to ally with the USSR.
   (E) drove Ho Chi Minh to forbid elections to reunite Vietnam.

ANSWERS AND EXPLANATIONS

1. B

In response to a potential communist threat in Greece and Turkey, President Truman sought economic assistance to aid the nations in defending themselves against takeover. The Truman Doctrine, which looked to give financial assistance, hoped to contain communism where it existed in Europe.

2. B

In a bid to stave off communist influence and avoid the mistakes of the Versailles Treaty, the Marshall Plan provided $12 billion in aid to Western European countries to rebuild.

3. A

The National Security Council document NSC-68 furthered Truman's bid for increased spending on defense by warning of Soviet intentions of world domination.

4. E

Hoping to gain re-election to his Senate seat, Wisconsin Senator Joseph McCarthy grabbed the spotlight in 1950 when he claimed he had inside information regarding at least 200 communists working in the U.S. State Department. Eventually becoming wildly popular, McCarthy continued accusing government officials of wrongdoing until a televised committee hearing turned the American public against him.

5. B

When it was clear that the "new look" military was not a "one size fits all" strategy, Kennedy sought to strengthen the American response to world crises by reinstituting conventional tactics, along with building the U.S. nuclear arsenal.

CHAPTER 27: A SPLIT AMERICA, 1950–1959

Exec Order 9981

THE EARLY CIVIL RIGHTS MOVEMENT

Segregation and discrimination against African Americans was nothing new in American society, and neither was the voice of protest. The social climate was changing, however. President Truman desegregated the armed forces in 1948. Before that, in 1947, Kennesaw Mountain Landis had encouraged the Brooklyn Dodgers to break the color line in professional baseball by drafting Negro American League champion Jackie Robinson. As African Americans moved into Northern cities during the migrations of the World Wars, they began to exercise the rights granted them by the Fourteenth and Fifteenth Amendments, with no barriers. There was an internal struggle within the American psyche—the country had just fought a war to liberate people to make their own decisions, but it could not offer that same freedom to some of its citizens. African Americans had experienced welcoming societies in Europe when they fought in two world wars and wanted that same treatment from their home country.

Brown v. Board of Education and the Little Rock Nine

The Civil Rights movement gained an indispensable ally when President Eisenhower appointed former California Governor Earl Warren as Chief Justice of the Supreme Court. Unbeknownst to Eisenhower, the **Warren Court** would be one of the most liberal in history. As early as the mid-1940s, the NAACP had begun to challenge segregation in Southern colleges, making modest gains in breaking down the wall of segregation. Not until the organization found a test case involving an elementary school student in Topeka, Kansas, did any real progress take place. Linda Brown, a first grader, had to leave her home an hour and a half early to travel across town to attend the all-black school, when there was a white neighborhood school less than a mile from her house. The NAACP encouraged the Brown family to file suit against the Topeka school board on the grounds that Linda's right to equal protection had been violated by the segregation policy. The case made it to the floor of the Supreme Court in 1954. NAACP lawyer (and later, the first African American to serve on the Supreme Court) Thurgood Marshall represented the Brown family. He argued that the Fourteenth Amendment guaranteed all citizens equal protection under

Early Civil Rights | Affluent Society | Conformity | Nonconformists | Revolutions the law, which translated into equal opportunity. The Warren Court agreed with Marshall, and in ***Brown v. Board of Education*** (1954) the ruling overturned the 1896 decision of *Plessy v. Ferguson*. The Court decision read that "separate facilities were inherently unequal" and had no place in public education. The Court soon ordered the desegregation of all public school facilities with "all deliberate speed."

ie – "Do it whenever the hell you please"

The decision was not well-received by Southerners. Many states claimed they would simply close the public schools if they had to integrate. White families refused to send their children to integrated schools, and some state legislatures even passed laws to resist the ruling. In 1957, the situation came to a head in Little Rock, Arkansas, as the governor of the state, Orval Faubus, ordered the National Guard to bar the entrance of nine black students into the all-white Central High School. The "**Little Rock Nine**" were allowed entrance to the campus by a Federal Court ruling, but violent protests immediately broke out in the city. President Eisenhower looked on with despair—he had no desire to get enmeshed in the civil rights fight. However when it looked like the situation was spiraling out of control, he was forced to intervene. The president ordered federal troops into the city to restore order and escort the students to their classes. Within a year of the forced integration, all Little Rock public schools had been shuttered; white families sent their children to segregated private schools or public schools outside of the city. It was not until another Warren Court ruling that the Little Rock School Board finally relented and integrated the public schools.

Rosa Parks → Montgomery Bus Boycott

ROSA PARKS AND A BUS BOYCOTT

A petite NAACP secretary would soon make headlines when she was arrested in Montgomery, Alabama, for refusing to give up her bus seat to a white patron. The Southern city prided itself as the most segregated in the nation. The black population of almost 65 percent drank from separate water fountains, rode at the back of buses, and ate in the back of restaurants. **Rosa Parks**, a recent volunteer for the local chapter of the NAACP, had seen many African American men and women arrested and mistreated for refusing to comply with the Jim Crow laws that ruled the bus system. Parks decided enough was enough when, on December 11, 1955, she refused to give up her seat to a white man on a city bus. Arrested and fined, Parks had started the ball rolling for the NAACP. A young minister from Georgia, **Dr. Martin Luther King, Jr.**, along with other black leaders, organized a bus boycott by the black community until the buses were desegregated. This would be an enormous blow to the city's revenues, as African Americans made up of about 95 percent of bus riders. The boycott lasted some 400 days, with the black community organizing car pools and walk buddies for the hundreds of people needing to get to school, work, and home. The Warren Court ruled that segregation on public buses was unconstitutional and soon the boycott was over. It was the negotiations by Dr. King with city managers and downtown business owners that truly desegregated the bus system in Montgomery.

Entire Civil Rights Movement

Early Civil Rights — Affluent Society — Conformity — Nonconformists — Revolutions

Dr. King and Protests Across the Country

Martin Luther King, Jr., and the Southern Christian Leadership Conference (SCLC) took the torch from the Montgomery boycott and began to challenge more Jim Crow laws in Alabama and other Southern cities. King believed in the teachings of Henry David Thoreau and Mahatmas Gandhi, following the tenets of civil disobedience and nonviolent resistance. He believed that engaging whites in violence would only feed the stereotype that African Americans were savages. Other boycotts emerged as followers across the country took King's message to heart. Greensboro, North Carolina, became the stage for a new kind of protest in 1960, when local college and high school students entered a local Woolworth's drug store and sat at the whites-only lunch counter, refusing to leave until they were served. Beginning with four students, the sit-ins grew to involve more than a thousand students, who rotated on and off lunch counter seats until the store owners gave in six months later. Several other sit-ins occurred across the nation in motel lobbies, beaches, public pools, and libraries. Students became the torchbearers for Dr. King, as the **Student Nonviolent Coordinating Committee** (SNCC or "Snick") was formed to keep the movement alive among the nation's young population. *MLK's link to black young*

President Eisenhower was a reluctant participant in the Civil Rights movement, preferring to maintain the support of Southerners and the status quo. He did sign two modest civil rights bills as president, however. The Civil Rights Bill of 1957 sought to ensure that African Americans would be able to vote by supporting new division within the federal Justice Department to monitor civil rights abuses. Furthermore, a joint report was to be written by representatives of both major political parties on the issue of race relations. By the time the bill was enacted as law, it had been watered down so as to not have much impact. The Civil Rights Act of 1960 was aimed at extending the life of the Civil Rights Commission and giving the U.S. Attorney General the authority to inspect local and state voting records for federal elections. After an intense fight in Congress, the final bill was just as weak as its predecessor in dealing with voting rights for African Americans.

Neither are of these facts did much for the cause.

THE "AFFLUENT SOCIETY"

As Eisenhower looked to balance the federal budget and maintain the prosperity that flourished in the 1950s, the gap between the rich and poor seemed to widen. The country as a whole experienced economic growth, with stable inflation and employment rates. The average American family saw its income more than triple during the decade and enjoyed the world's highest standard of living. Modern conveniences became cheaper for Americans to purchase. "Keeping up with the Joneses," or keeping pace with the prosperity of one's neighbors, became the American mantra. As a result, America experienced the second major consumer revolution as cars, televisions, and household appliances were snatched up from store shelves. The mass-consumption culture of the 1920s would be eclipsed by spending of the 1950s. Since consumer goods were in short supply during the war, Americans had savings burning holes in their pockets and were ready to spend.

Early Civil Rights | **Affluent Society** | Conformity | Nonconformists | Revolutions

[handwritten margin notes: Mass-produced houses's think Edward Saiserbands' "Suburbia"]

The National Highway Act and the GI Bill impacted the growth of the American suburb and construction business, as young families moved out of the city and into prefabricated starter homes. The American dream of two kids, a dog, and a manicured front lawn was now reality for an increasing number of Americans.

That American dream remained elusive for a large number of citizens, however. As "**white flight**" drained American cities of upper- and middle-class white families, poor and minority families and singles moved in to take their places. Once-booming downtown areas in cities such as Chicago and Detroit became rife with crime and poverty. Businesses often moved their headquarters out of the city and into the suburbs where workers lived, leaving empty buildings behind. African Americans in Northern cities were often unaffected by the gains made in the South through the work of Dr. King and others. Even though they were able to vote and lived with relatively less discrimination, they still were stuck in low-paying jobs and substandard housing due to "redlining" practices, which shut them out of better white housing areas.

CONFORMITY IN MIDDLE-CLASS SOCIETY

The stereotypical view of the 1950s usually consists of teenagers sipping ice cream malts and dancing at the sock hop and men in grey flannel suits coming home to a pipe, newspaper, and beautiful wife after work. Just as Americans looked to keep up with the mass consumption of goods that surrounded them, they also strove to blend in to the middle-class mold. Television was a major contributor to the American myth, as viewers often consumed as many as five hours a day of the "boob tube." Situation comedies such as *Father Knows Best* and *I Love Lucy*, along with advertisements for branded products, painted portraits of the "perfect" American family, wife, and household. Corporate America had an impact on society, as middle-class, white-collar workers donned the same suit, tie, and hat and left each day to make enough money to live the "American dream."

BEATNIKS AND NONCONFORMISTS

[handwritten margin note: Beat Generation]

Not all Americans bought into the middle-class, suburban myth. Many in the academic field called the conformity of the era into question through essays, books, and research papers. While most Hollywood films celebrated the "carefree" lifestyle of the 1950s, some filmmakers challenged the notion with films such as *The Man in the Grey Flannel Suit*. Artists such as Andy Warhol and Jackson Pollock shocked the world with paintings that did not follow form or function and initiated the beginning of the modernist movement. Novelists of the era often did not reflect the American dream, attempting to challenge readers to think for themselves. J. D. Salinger's *The Catcher in the Rye* shocked American parents as teens greedily read about the adventures of the troubled teen Holden Caulfield.

Another group of nonconformists rocked the Greenwich Village area of New York City with their poetry and wild culture. The "**beatniks**," led by people such as writer Jack Kerouac and poet Allen Ginsberg, spoke to an audience that encouraged individuality in an age of conformity.

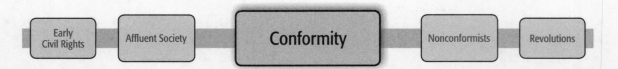

Early Civil Rights — Affluent Society — **Conformity** — Nonconformists — Revolutions

WOMEN AND THE CULT OF DOMESTICITY

Women of the 1950s were expected to take care of the "baby boom" generation as outlined by the baby care book by the nationally renowned Dr. Benjamin Spock. Homemaking was venerated as a noble "profession," and women working outside the home were looked down upon by their more traditional counterparts. The "cult of domesticity" was alive and well in the 1950s, but not all women were content with their situation. Alcoholism became a feminine problem, as bored housewives looked to liven up the hours they spent alone when their husbands and children were away for the day. Depression was also a burgeoning problem for American women, but it was often considered a "weakness" and left untreated.

Freely using mind-altering drugs and rebelling against the social standards of the day, beatniks studied art, poetry, and philosophy and publicly criticized the society in which they lived. Poetry readings often included "free verse," where participants were invited to the open microphone and encouraged to speak their minds. The terms *groovy* and *far out*, along with snapping instead of clapping, became synonymous with the beatnik movement. These young people would be the mold from which the "hippy" movement of the 1960s would emerge.

Women too joined the protest, as conformity to traditional roles created a climate that stifled free thought and individuality. In her book *The Feminine Mystique* (1963), author Betty Friedan encouraged women to leave the myth of homemaking behind and pursue fulfillment outside of the home. She called into question the notion that women were meant to remain at home to care for a husband and children and instead spoke of opportunities for women to become successful in the business world.

REVOLUTIONS IN SCIENCE, TECHNOLOGY, AND MEDICINE

The electronics industry experienced the most growth in the 1950s. As 95 percent of American homes were electric powered, the industry worked to keep up with the demand for new and innovative products. Record players, refrigerators, and the new "transistor radio," which was hand-held and ran on batteries, revolutionized the lives of Americans. Hand-held calculators and super computers opened up doors for engineers and designers in space, aeronautics, and automobiles. What once took weeks to calculate, the computer could churn out in the matter of hours. Air travel was no longer just for the ultra wealthy, as commercial airlines began to fly Americans across the nation and around the world.

Americans and people worldwide experienced an increase in their life expectancy as new discoveries and inventions emerged in the 1950s. Another discovery in 1940s improved the

chances of someone surviving infection by bacteria. Penicillin, an antibiotic, became widely available to doctors in the United States. It soon became very rare that an American would die from a simple bacterial infection.

DR. SALK AND THE POLIO VACCINE

Polio was a constant threat to people all over the world. The debilitating disease could cripple children and adults and confine them to a life of pain. In 1955, **Jonas Salk** discovered the serum that would immunize humans against polio. Using a live strain of the virus, Salk was successful in developing a vaccine that would almost eradicate the disease within the United States by the 1960s.

KEY TERMS	
Names	Dr. Martin Luther King, Jr.
	Rosa Parks
	Jonas Salk
Groups	Warren Court
	Little Rock Nine
	Student Nonviolent Coordinating Committee
Documents and Laws	*Brown v. Board of Education*
	The Feminine Mystique
Vocabulary	white flight
	beatniks

Affluent Society   Conformity   Nonconformists   Revolutions

Key Terms

REVIEW QUESTIONS

1. The ruling in *Brown v. Board of Education*

   (A) called for all public facilities to be desegregated.
   (B) protected the right of African Americans to vote.
   (C) overturned *Plessy v. Ferguson*.
   (D) ordered the Montgomery bus boycott unconstitutional.
   (E) demanded the immediate desegregation of all public schools.

2. Dr. Martin Luther King, Jr., advocated the tactic of

   (A) violence when necessary.
   (B) assimilation into white society.
   (C) economic compliance.
   (D) nonviolent resistance.
   (E) massive resistance.

3. Conformity was aided by all of the following EXCEPT

   (A) television.
   (B) advertisements.
   (C) corporate America.
   (D) growth of suburbs.
   (E) shared affluence of Americans.

   Not everyone was rich, dude.

4. The beatniks challenged the conformity of 1950s society by

   (A) protesting violently.
   (B) writing poetry and novels.
   (C) demanding integration in the South.
   (D) shunning alcohol and drugs.
   (E) widely publishing their tirades in national newspapers.

5. Corporate America altered the job market as

   (A) more white-collar jobs were created.
   (B) it hired women to serve as secretaries.
   (C) the number of factory workers outnumbered management.
   (D) union membership was banned.
   (E) it actively recruited minority employees.

ANSWERS AND EXPLANATIONS

1. C

The opinion of the Court deemed separate public schools to be inherently unequal and, thus, a violation of the Fourteenth Amendment. As a result, the precedent set in the *Plessy v. Ferguson* case was overturned.

2. D

Dr. King followed the teachings of Henry David Thoreau and Mahatma Gandhi in guiding his followers. Preaching "love one's enemies" and civil disobedience, King hoped to draw a distinct line between angry Southern whites and his protesters.

3. E

Unfortunately, not all Americans shared in the affluence of the 1950s. Middle-class whites could conform to the televised images they viewed, as their standard of living rose as never before. Poor and minority citizens were not able to live the "American dream," as they struggled to live from day to day.

4. B

In a small movement that was mostly contained in New York City, the beatniks wrote poetry and novels to express their disdain for the conformist society around them. Encouraging individuality and spontaneity, the beats freely used mind-altering drugs and wore unusual clothes so as to not blend into American society.

5. A

The American middle class grew, as big business created white-collar jobs and decreased the number of factory jobs. As America became franchised and mechanized, more and more people found themselves behind a desk rather than on the assembly line.

CHAPTER 28: TURBULENT TIMES, 1960–1969

KENNEDY TO JOHNSON—CHANGING IDEOLOGIES

Despite leaving the presidency more popular than ever, Eisenhower was unable to pass on that enthusiasm to Republican candidate **Richard M. Nixon** in the 1960 election. A former vice president, "Commie fighter," and foreign diplomat, Nixon believed his campaign would be an easy one, as the Democrats chose **John F. Kennedy** as their candidate, a young senator from Massachusetts. Kennedy's charisma and good looks carried him through the primaries to the Democratic convention, where he chose Texas Senator Lyndon Baines Johnson as his running mate. The campaign was an uphill battle for Kennedy—he was from a wealthy Bostonian family, was Roman Catholic, and would be the youngest elected president in history. The choice of Lyndon Johnson was a shrewd one because it secured the support of Southerners. And Kennedy's youth actually played in his favor, as Americans were drawn to his style and vitality. His religion would be the most difficult hurdle to jump. Many questioned whether or not a Catholic president could effectively rule a country without the influence of the Pope. Kennedy laid all fears to rest when he reassured an audience of Protestant ministers that he would in no way allow his religious beliefs to interfere with his role as executive.

"Ask not what your country can do for you; ask what you can do for your country." With these words from his inaugural address, John F. Kennedy began a shift in the White House that would deeply impact American society. His domestic policy was named the **"New Frontier,"** with promises of equality, employment, and aid to the poor. The young president would run into many roadblocks as he attempted to pass his plans through Congress. Republicans and conservative Democrats, a coalition that had earlier stalled the New Deal in 1938 and thwarted Truman's attempts to expand it in the late 1940s, repeatedly blocked the president's attempts to provide federal support to cure urban blight and reduce income taxes. Kennedy did have some success in increasing the minimum wage and battling the steel giants to keep prices regulated. Aside from these instances, the majority of Kennedy's domestic policies were not passed until after his assassination.

| Kennedy to Johnson | Civil Rights Expansion | Cold War Gets Hot | Counterculture & Antiwar | Key Terms |

NIXON AND KENNEDY DEBATE ON TV

For the first time in U.S. history, the four presidential debates were televised nationally. These debates sealed the election for JFK. Kennedy's poise and vitality proved effective weapons against the seemingly nervous Nixon. Americans who watched the debates believed that Kennedy had won, while those who listened on the radio gave their nod to Nixon. It was clear that Kennedy would benefit from press coverage, and he used it to his advantage as the election neared. In a narrowly contested race, Kennedy edged Nixon by the slimmest margin ever in an American presidential election. Despite cries of election fraud and ballot tampering from the Republicans, JFK was declared the next president.

KENNEDY'S ASSASSINATION

While on a trip to Texas to gain support for his domestic programs, John F. Kennedy was assassinated as his motorcade made its way through the streets of Dallas. On November 22, 1963, Lee Harvey Oswald shot the president from a book depository window across the street from the motorcade route. Americans sat riveted to their televisions as they waited for news of their beloved president. It was with great sadness that news anchors announced the president's passing and the swearing in of Lyndon Baines Johnson (LBJ) aboard Air Force One. As his first act as president, LBJ ordered the appointment of a special investigatory commission to study the assassination of JFK. The **Warren Commission**, headed by the Chief Justice, concluded that Oswald was the lone gunman who killed the president. Many conspiracy theories abounded after the commission delivered its final report, and to this day many question the conclusions of the Warren Commission.

LBJ AND THE GREAT SOCIETY

President Johnson had big shoes to fill once he took the oath of office. After winning the presidency in his own right in 1964, LBJ was determined to continue the liberal path of his predecessor and expand upon some of the New Frontier ideas he thought too modest. Johnson named his plan **The Great Society**, and was determined to expand civil rights, cut income taxes, and rid society of poverty. The president was heavily influenced by a controversial book by Michael Harrington titled *The Other America*. In it, Harrington asserted that 20 percent of Americans and more than 40 percent of all African Americans lived in poverty. The president created the **Office of Equal Opportunity** (OEO), which oversaw the creation of the Job Corp program that provided career training to inner-city and rural citizens. The OEO was also in charge of the Head Start program, which provided free or low-cost preschool to disadvantaged children to ready them for elementary school. In many ways, LBJ continued and strengthened the New Deal programs started by FDR. The Great Society saw the creation of Medicare and Medicaid, which provided low-cost medical care for the elderly and poor. **The Department of Housing and**

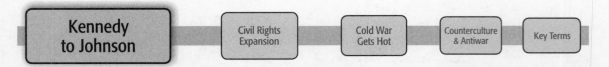

Kennedy to Johnson | Civil Rights Expansion | Cold War Gets Hot | Counterculture & Antiwar | Key Terms

Urban Development was founded in 1966 to provide low-cost housing and federal funding to rid cities of urban blight. **The Immigration Act of 1965** repealed the discriminatory practices of the Quota Acts of the 1920s by allowing first-come, first-serve entrance into the United States. This monumental law helped change the face of America by allowing millions of immigrants from Latin America and Asia to live in the United States over the course of the next four decades. President Johnson oversaw the creation of the National Endowment for the Humanities, which provided federal funding for artistic and cultural endeavors. The Johnson administration created the Department of Transportation, increased funding for universities and colleges, and enacted laws to protect consumers and the environment. Aside from FDR, no other president had overseen this amount of legislation and increase in the role of the federal government.

THE CIVIL RIGHTS MOVEMENT EXPANDS

In his early days as president, Kennedy was reluctant, as many before him, to take a stand with regard to African American civil rights. The Democrat desperately needed the support of Southern Democrats to get critical legislation passed and did not want to lose their support. As a result, JFK sat by for the first two years of his presidency while the civil rights movement continued to gain momentum. The president was pushed to act in 1961 when "**Freedom Summer**" was declared by the Congress of Racial Equality (CORE). They boarded integrated buses in the North bound for the Deep South to show their support for the desegregation of public transit and bus stations, as it had been ruled by the Supreme Court. As the buses reached Alabama, waiting mobs firebombed and severely beat the Freedom Riders as state troopers and local police stood by and watched. Attorney General Robert Kennedy at first asked the Freedom Riders to stop, but more and more boarded buses and traveled south. The attorney general then sent federal marshals to protect the bus riders, signaling a victory for CORE.

MARTIN LUTHER KING'S PEACEFUL PROTESTS

In 1962, JFK sent in federal marshals to protect University of Mississippi student James Meredith as he attended classes on the once all-white campus. All the while, Dr. Martin Luther King, Jr., began an all-out peaceful assault on the town of Birmingham, Alabama. The city had closed all public facilities to avoid integration. King and his followers staged a march on Good Friday 1963 and were arrested and jailed. While spending two weeks in his cell, Dr. King penned his "Letter from Birmingham Jail," which he wrote to explain to other black ministers why he and his followers could not "wait" for the whites to come around. Upon his release, Dr. King began using children in his protests and staging them where they would get the most media attention and most violent reaction from Birmingham whites. The nation and world watched in horror as Birmingham police commissioner Eugene "Bull" Connor used dogs, fire hoses, and cattle prods to disperse the nonviolent protesters, many of whom were children. Pressure was mounting on the president to take a more vigorous stand. Federal troops were once again summoned to the state of Alabama, as Governor George Wallace attempted to stop African American students

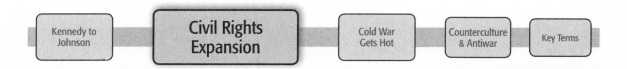

Kennedy to Johnson | **Civil Rights Expansion** | Cold War Gets Hot | Counterculture & Antiwar | Key Terms

from attending the University of Alabama in 1963. This was the last straw for JFK. After the Birmingham marches and the debacle with George Wallace, the president actively began to seek legislation to protect African American civil rights. On August 28, 1963, Dr. King organized the single most successful march in U.S. history to show support for the civil rights legislation on the Mall in Washington, D.C. His "I Have a Dream" speech touched audiences and lawmakers, and the civil rights bill made its way to passage just after JFK was assassinated.

THE CIVIL RIGHTS ACT AND THE VOTING RIGHTS ACT

Continuing and expanding the scope of civil rights was a major goal for Lyndon Johnson. LBJ saw the ratification of the Twenty-Fourth Amendment, which abolished another barrier to voting rights by outlawing the poll tax. Having years of congressional experience under his belt aided the president as he worked to get Kennedy's civil rights bill pushed through the Senate. The monumental **Civil Rights Act of 1964** outlawed segregation of public accommodations; established the Equal Employment Opportunity Commission to enforce the law; made the federal government responsible for finding instances of discrimination; and made illegal discrimination based on race, religion, ethnic origin, or gender. The greatest legislative success of the civil rights movement signaled the end of *de jure* (by law) segregation in all cities and towns across America. Unfortunately, the Civil Rights Act did not effectively address many problems associated with voting rights. To show lawmakers just how serious the problem was with voting, Dr. King organized a march from Selma to Montgomery, Alabama, in 1965. The march came to a violent end outside of Selma, as state police beat and taunted marchers. King tried again but was stopped just outside Selma. This time President Johnson sent an urgent message to King asking him to stop marching until he could finalize work on a voting rights bill. As promised, the **Voting Rights Act of 1965** was passed, making literacy tests illegal and more or less nationalizing the voter registration system in states where African Americans were denied voting rights.

MALCOLM X AND THE BLACK PANTHERS

Even though African Americans had won great battles from within the white political system, many within the black community were not convinced that integration and nonviolence were the way to success. Radical African American groups rose up, as many blacks grew tired of the "love thy enemy" rhetoric of Dr. King. **The Nation of Islam** (Black Muslims) followed the teachings of Elijah Muhammad as spoken by his disciple **Malcolm X**. Malcolm X openly criticized Dr. King and his followers as "Uncle Toms" who had sold themselves out to whites. While not advocating the use of violence, Malcolm X did encourage followers to respond to violence perpetrated against them with violence in self-defense. Malcolm X took his requisite Hajj (pilgrimage) to Mecca and returned a changed man in 1964. Preaching love and understanding, Malcolm X left the Nation of Islam and was assassinated by members of the Nation as he spoke to a congregation in February 1965. Meanwhile, the once nonviolent SNCC changed course under the leadership of **Stokely Carmichael** in 1966, when it rejected integration and began touting "Black Power." Carmichael left SNCC for the Oakland, California-based Black Panthers, who openly carried weapons and clashed with police on a regular basis. Despite their violent history, the Black Panthers were successful in organizing the community of Oakland to serve as a self-sufficient network for black citizens, providing free day care for working mothers and food for the poor. The Panthers finally succumbed to arrests and the deaths of major leaders by the 1970s.

MARTIN LUTHER KING IS ASSASSINATED

Evidence of the frustration of blacks in urban areas resulted in race riots that broke out during the "long hot summers" from 1964 to 1968 in cities such as Los Angeles, Chicago, and Atlanta. Instead of radical black groups inciting the violence, the Johnson-appointed **Kerner Commission** concluded in 1968 that frustration over extreme poverty and lack of opportunity had sparked the riots. The commission report stated that there were two Americas—one white and one black. Dr. Martin Luther King, Jr., was assassinated as he stood on a Memphis motel balcony in April 1968. Dr. King had lost some support when he publicly opposed increased American involvement in the war in Vietnam, but in reaction to his death, riots broke out across the country as African Americans expressed their frustration and anger with society.

THE COLD WAR GETS HOT

President Kennedy had taken on Eisenhower's belief that Asian countries would fall like dominos if left alone and unprotected from communism. Therefore, when it became clear that the French were pulling completely out of Vietnam, Kennedy increased financial and military assistance to the regimes in that country and surrounding regions.

THE GULF OF TONKIN RESOLUTION

The Ngo Dinh Diem regime, which Eisenhower had worked to prop up with SEATO, was becoming more and more of a liability. Buddhist monks in the South Vietnamese capital set themselves on fire in protest of Ngo's policies discriminating against fellow Buddhists and the poor, which made up more than 75 percent of the country's population. Just before JFK's death, a CIA-assisted assassination was carried out to remove Diem from power. Lyndon Johnson refused to become the president who allowed Vietnam and Southeast Asia to fall to communists. Yet the unstable country was falling apart just as he took the oath of office. Johnson's Secretary of Defense Robert McNamara urged the president to take more forceful action to prevent the fall of Vietnam. In August 1964, LBJ announced that a North Vietnamese gunboat had carried out an unprovoked attack on two U.S. destroyers in the Gulf of Tonkin off the coast of North Vietnam. The president immediately used the incident to ask Congress for an increase in his authority to wage war in Vietnam without an actual war declaration. The **Gulf of Tonkin Resolution** greatly increased the power of the executive branch to engage in war. It was later discovered that the U.S. destroyers were actually assisting the South Vietnamese in attacking their northern neighbor and,

Built upon terms of Formosa Reso [handwritten margin note]

| Kennedy to Johnson | Civil Rights Expansion | Cold War Gets Hot | Counterculture & Antiwar | Key Terms |

thus, the attacks were not "unprovoked." Johnson used the Gulf of Tonkin Resolution to widen the war further after he won re-election in 1964.

JOHNSON HEIGHTENS AMERICAN INVOLVEMENT

As Vietnam sank further and further into chaos, Johnson had no other choice but to escalate American involvement in the war. It was not a viable option to back out of Vietnam, as the country would have certainly fallen into communist hands. But then again, escalation meant diverting resources from his beloved Great Society programs—funding was needed to fuel the war machine. He hoped the war would be a quick one, as the first-strike Operation Rolling Thunder in 1965 called for bombing raids over North Vietnam. A quick victory was not in the cards, however, as **Ho Chi Minh's Vietcong** and Vietminh continued to bounce back with more supplies and more men in the face of the American assault.

The United States relied on air and ground forces to fight in the heavily forested jungle of Vietnam. U.S. tactics focused on destroying the "**Ho Chi Minh Trail**," which linked the South Vietnamese Vietcong fighters with the North Vietnamese supply lines. The United States dropped more artillery on North Vietnam than in all of World War II. The ground war would prove to be much more difficult and dangerous for Americans. The heavy rainforest canopy and moist tropical climate made fighting a conventional war impossible. General William Westmoreland developed a "search and destroy" method of rooting South Vietnamese Vietcong sympathizers out of villages by burning homes to the ground. Finding the enemy proved to be most difficult, as Vietcong soldiers dressed in the same peasant clothing as ordinary villagers. In an attempt to clear the countryside, the United States uprooted villagers and moved them to cities. Controversy at home escalated as the "hawks" (those who supported the war) and "doves" (those opposed to the war) battled it out in Congress and across America. As the election of 1968 loomed, events in Vietnam would change course.

THE WAR CHANGES COURSE

Vietnamese Lunar New Year, known as Tet, marked the beginning of a massive Vietcong offensive that moved the war from the rural areas to the streets of Saigon. In January 1968, Vietcong forces surprised American troops by attacking military bases and regional capitals. Just as General Westmoreland had said that the war's end was near, it was clear to those watching on television that the communists had no intention of surrendering. Losses for the Vietcong were large, but ultimate victory would be theirs. The psychological impact of the Tet Offensive would change the course of the war both in Vietnam and at home. American public opinion now opposed the war and increasingly demanded that the United States pull out of the war-torn country. In effect, Tet was the beginning of the end of U.S. military involvement in Vietnam. Having lost almost half of his support in presidential approval ratings, LBJ decided that he would not run for re-election in 1968.

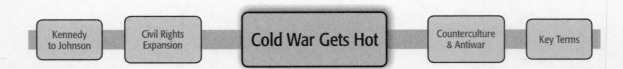

THE COUNTERCULTURE AND ANTI–VIETNAM WAR MOVEMENTS

As the 1950s became the 1960s, America's "baby boomers" were now teenagers hoping to break away from the conformity that their parents subscribed to. Many American teens grew their hair longer or wore clothing that their parents did not approve of. Only a small percentage of the teen and young adult population was truly involved in the counterculture and antiwar protests. Nonetheless, these students were outspoken and willing to protest publicly wrongs they saw in American social, economic, and political policy.

College students met in Port Huron, Michigan, in 1962 to form the Students for a Democratic Society (SDS), led by Tom Hayden. The meeting yielded the **Port Huron Statement**, in which the students demanded a greater voice in the course of their lives. This signaled the birth of the "New Left." Soon afterwards, the Free Speech Movement (FSM) would begin in 1964 on the campus of the University of California, Berkeley. Berkeley students staged sit-ins in administration buildings to protest university policies and teach-ins to hear speeches and lectures regarding issues from civil rights to the Vietnam War. Students across the nation took cues from SDS and the FSM to form protest movements of their own and demanded a greater role in determining their futures.

Nothing typified the youth movement like the 1969 counterculture festival on a farm in New York State called **Woodstock**. Hippies gathered at the concert for a three-day party that involved sex, drugs, and rock and roll. Artists such as Jimi Hendrix and Janis Joplin wowed the crowd that lived together in the dirt and mud of the farm. Young people found a connection with the work of folk singers such as Bob Dylan and Joan Baez, whose protest songs galvanized the counterculture. The flower children of Woodstock would soon change course to protest the Vietnam War with their shouts of "Make Love, Not War."

The counterculture led to a sexual revolution in which American's views regarding sexual relationships and gender roles softened. With the advent of the birth control pill and the beginnings of the feminist movement in the mid-1960s, many Americans believed that the old sexual mores of their parents were old-fashioned. Casual sex and multiple partners became more openly practiced. The feminist movement also gained momentum as a result of the liberal nature of the counterculture. After the founding of the **National Organization for Women** (NOW) in 1966 by Betty Friedan, women began to become more vocal with regard to their desire for a greater role in American society. With the Civil Rights Act of 1964 already making discrimination on the basis of gender illegal, women looked to strengthen their place by amending the Constitution. In 1972, Congress passed the **Equal Rights Amendment**, which would disallow states and the federal government to discriminate on the basis of sex. Unfortunately for the women's movement, the amendment fell short of the required number of ratifying states and died in the 1980s.

KEY TERMS

Names	Richard M. Nixon John F. Kennedy Malcolm X Stokely Carmichael Ho Chi Minh
Groups	Warren Commission Office of Equal Opportunity The Department of Housing and Urban Development The Nation of Islam Kerner Commission Vietcong National Organization of Women
Events	New Frontier Freedom Summer Woodstock Tet Offensive
Places	Ho Chi Minh Trail
Documents and Laws	The Great Society Immigration Act of 1965 Civil Rights Act of 1964 Voting Rights Act of 1965 Gulf of Tonkin Resolution Port Huron Statement Equal Rights Amendment

REVIEW QUESTIONS

1. With regard to domestic issues, Presidents Kennedy and Johnson can be characterized as

   (A) unwilling to challenge tradition.

   (B) open to possibilities, yet cautious.

   (C) reckless to the point of hurting the nation.

   (D) uninterested in expanding the role of the federal government.

   (E) able to secure support for a wide range of social programs.

2. The Civil Rights Movement gained its greatest success in the

   (A) founding of the Department of Housing and Development.

   (B) passage of the Twenty-Sixth Amendment.

   (C) enactment of the Civil Rights Act of 1964.

   (D) Kerner Commission report.

   (E) New Frontier.

3. The rise of radical African American groups and race riots can be attributed to

   (A) pent-up frustrations over discrimination and poverty.

   (B) the failure of the enforcement of the Civil Rights Act.

   (C) a return to the ideals of Booker T. Washington.

   (D) the jailing of Dr. Martin Luther King, Jr.

   (E) the end of the Civil Rights Movement.

4. The Gulf of Tonkin Resolution

   (A) ended U.S. involvement in South East Asia.

   (B) created the South East Asian Treaty Organization.

   (C) led to the assassination of Ngo Dinh Diem.

   (D) gave the executive broad powers to wage war.

   (E) was hotly contested in Congress.

5. The counterculture of the 1960s promoted all of the following EXCEPT

   (A) a deeper connection with the nuclear family.

   (B) loose attitudes in regards to sexual behavior.

   (C) the questioning of authority.

   (D) the quest for self-fulfillment.

   (E) broader rights for all Americans.

ANSWERS AND EXPLANATIONS

1. E

Kennedy and Johnson were both proponents of expanding the role of government to ensure the health of the nation. By expanding civil rights, cutting income taxes, and overseeing government agencies such as Medicare and Medicaid, these Democratic presidents continued New Deal government intervention but were not afraid to buck tradition along the way.

2. C

Finally able to achieve legislative success, the Civil Rights movement celebrated the enactment of the Civil Rights Act of 1964 and the Voting Rights Act of 1965. With the passage of these two bills, African Americans could finally realize the rights that had been granted to them 100 years before with the passage of the Fourteenth and Fifteenth Amendments.

3. A

The Kerner Commission reported in 1968 that the race riots and rise of radical African American groups could be attributed to urban dwellers releasing their frustrations over years of discrimination and a seemingly never-ending cycle of poverty.

4. D

President Johnson asked for an expansion of his ability to commit U.S. troops to Vietnam after the "unprovoked" skirmish in the Gulf of Tonkin. Congress basically handed the executive branch its power to declare war.

5. A

The counterculture is mostly known for a tolerance of loose sexual mores, drug use, self-realization, and resistance to authority. In many cases, these young people alienated their mothers and fathers, leading to a breakdown of the traditional nuclear family structure of the 1950s.

CHAPTER 29: THE THAWING OF THE COLD WAR, 1970–1990

THE ELECTION OF 1968

John F. Kennedy's younger brother Robert decided to continue the Kennedy legacy and entered the race for president in 1968. RFK had shown an uncanny ability to garner the votes of working-class and liberal Democrats. Therefore, it came as no surprise when he won the California Democratic primary in June 1968. The events after his victory speech were a surprise, however, when a young Palestinian nationalist by the name of **Sirhan Sirhan** shot and killed RFK as he left the podium at the Ambassador Hotel in Los Angeles. The Democrats eventually gave the ticket to Vice President Hubert Humphrey.

THE CONVENTION RIOT OF 1968

The Democratic National Convention was held in Chicago that year. Mayor Richard Daley made sure his city was prepared for possible trouble. Antiwar protesters had mobilized to the convention to express their distaste for a candidate (Humphrey) whom they believed would continue to support Johnson's war in Vietnam. A massive number of demonstrators lined the streets of downtown Chicago, with an equal number of police present to keep the peace. In an event that would be broadcast on national television, Chicago police harassed and beat protesters, resulting in a riot that caused the nation to question both Daley and Humphrey.

The Republicans decided to give Richard M. Nixon another try at the presidency, with vice presidential candidate and Southerner Spiro Agnew at his side. A third party rose to prominence; the **American Independent Party** chose Alabama Governor George Wallace as its candidate. Wallace, most known for his attempt to keep two black students from entering the campus of the University of Alabama in 1963, wished to tap into the base of Americans who supported the troops but did not agree with Democrats on domestic issues. Nixon won the election with a slim

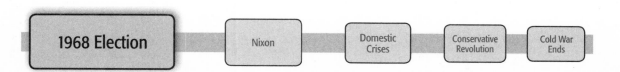

| 1968 Election | Nixon | Domestic Crises | Conservative Revolution | Cold War Ends |

margin over Humphrey, while Democrats maintained their majority in Congress. Without a clear mandate from American voters, Nixon would struggle at the start of his presidency to gain legitimacy.

NIXON FACES THE WORLD

Richard M. Nixon promised the United States change and a return of "law and order." First and foremost on the new president's agenda was the Vietnam War.

SLOWLY LEAVING VIETNAM   *Vietnamization*

Over 500,000 American men and women were serving overseas in a very unpopular war; Nixon wished to get out, but on his terms. He needed a way to pull back slowly but still end the conflict with an "honorable peace." Even as he promised during the 1968 presidential campaign that he had a "secret" plan to end the war, Nixon really had no idea how he was going to accomplish this task. Soon after his inauguration, Nixon announced a plan to turn the war over to those who should be fighting it—the Vietnamese. This process of Vietnamization involved the U.S. military instructing the South Vietnamese how to fight the war on their own. The number of U.S. troops in the country slowly decreased. Within the span of three years, the number of U.S. troops in Vietnam decreased from over 500,000 in 1969 to just under 30,000 in 1972.

PROTESTS, SECRETS, AND STAGGERING LOSSES

Nevertheless, many Americans were not pleased with the president's plans. He seemed to be talking out of both sides of his mouth—he wished to reduce the number of troops in Vietnam, but then he escalated the war by secretly bombing Cambodia in 1970 to shut down the Ho Chi Minh Trail, which facilitated the massive flow of men and goods from North Vietnam into the South. Protests across the nation broke out as news of the secret bombing missions reached the airwaves. The nation did not know that the bombings had already occurred. Four students at Kent State University in Ohio (who happened to be innocent passers-by during the protest) and two students at Jackson State in Mississippi were shot and killed by National Guard troops sent to keep the peace. The nation was shocked again when news of a 1968 massacre of Vietnamese women and children by U.S. troops in the village of My Lai was revealed in 1969. Eventually, the lieutenant in charge was court-martialed, convicted, and sentenced. However, his sentence was soon reduced from life in prison to 10 years. News of this aroused even more protesters, who now dubbed U.S. troops in Vietnam as "baby killers." To add insult to injury, secret documents regarding the Vietnam War under the Johnson administration were leaked to the *New York Times* by a former Defense Department analyst, Daniel Ellsberg. The documents showed that Congress had been lied to about the war in Vietnam during the presidency of LBJ, proved that the reason for the war was to avoid embarrassment, and revealed the truth behind the Gulf of Tonkin incident. All the while, Nixon had Secretary of State **Henry Kissinger** meet secretly with

[handwritten margin notes: My Lai Massacre (1968); Pentagon Papers]

the North Vietnamese to negotiate a settlement. It was clear to Nixon that the South Vietnamese would not be able to hold the communists off for very long on their own, and he wanted to get out quickly.

As the talks ground to a screeching halt, Nixon ordered some of the heaviest bombings yet to get North Vietnam to the negotiating table. In 1973, the sides returned to the table in Paris to hammer out an agreement. The North Vietnamese regained control of areas in the South, while the United States agreed to pull out troops in exchange for prisoners of war (POWs). March 29, 1973, saw the last of the U.S. troops pull out of Vietnam. The South Vietnamese capital of Saigon fell to the communist forces in April of 1975, with the United States evacuating the last of their troops and South Vietnamese sympathizers. In the end, the war caused the deaths of 58,000 Americans with 300,000 wounded and almost 2,600 missing in action. The Vietnamese lost over 2 million people, both military and civilian. The United States had spent a staggering $176 billion on the war through the Kennedy, Johnson, and Nixon administrations. After learning of the secret bombings of Cambodia, Congress decided in 1973 to repeal the Gulf of Tonkin Resolution by enacting the **War Powers Act**, which would severely limit the president's ability to wage war without the consent of the legislative branch.

DÉTENTE WITH CHINA AND RUSSIA

President Nixon and Secretary of State Kissinger did make headway in another part of Asia with results that would alter the very fabric of world affairs. Together they crafted **_détente_**, or the relaxing of tensions among the United States, the Soviet Union, and China. In February 1972, Nixon became the first U.S. president to visit communist China in an attempt to discuss policy with Mao Tse-Tung. Kissinger and Nixon had been mediating between the two communist superpowers behind the scenes, as the nations had split over differing opinions of how communism should work in practice. In a rare reversal, president Nixon agreed to support China's bid to be admitted to the United Nations and officially recognized the Chinese Revolution. Moscow watched this all with fascination and concern. Nixon visited Moscow in 1972 to encourage the USSR to sign a nuclear arms limitation treaty. In the **Strategic Arms Limitation Treaty** (SALT I), signed by the United States and the USSR in May 1972, each nation agreed to reduce the number of nuclear missiles in its arsenal in exchange for the United States supplying the Soviets with much-needed grain over the next three years. While not ending the arms race, détente did do much to relieve the world of the tension created by the struggle among the three world superpowers.

THE YOM KIPPUR WAR AND GAS SHORTAGES

In October 1973, war broke out on the Jewish holy day of Yom Kippur between Israel and the coalition of Syria and Egypt. President Nixon reacted by sending aid to Israel. The war was over quickly, as the aid from the United States greatly boosted Israeli forces. The war was far from over for the United States, however. The **Organization of Petroleum Exporting Countries**

1968 Election   Nixon   Domestic Crises   Conservative Revolution   Cold War Ends

6 Days War

OPEC Embargo

(OPEC) initiated an embargo of oil to the United States as punishment for its involvement in the **Yom Kippur War**. Immediately, the U.S. and world supply of gasoline and petroleum products plummeted. Americans waited in lines that stretched as much as a mile long at gas stations to purchase the coveted liquid. The impact of the gas shortage was most devastating to the economy—the nation fell into a deep recession as companies decreased investment, laid off workers, and reduced inventories. Inflation was growing at an alarming rate, and there was little the government could do.

DOMESTIC CRISES

Nixon's presidency is now known as an "imperial presidency," after the theory of historian Arthur Schlesinger. At various times, President Nixon abused his power as executive by claiming a right to protect documents from Congress and refusing to spend funds appropriated by Congress by "impounding" them. President Nixon also inherited economic problems that began when President Johnson refused to raise taxes while he escalated both the war effort and government domestic spending. The 1970s saw the emergence of a new economic phenomenon called "**stagflation**," in which high inflation was coupled with high unemployment.

The stagnant economy was difficult to repair, and Nixon first attempted to curb inflation by cutting government spending. He did not know this would prove to be disastrous—there was nothing the government could do to rid the country of this new form of economic crisis. Fortunately, the president enacted monetary policy near the end of 1971, taking the country once again off the gold standard to bring its value down relative to foreign currencies. This stimulated foreign investment and spending in the United States and helped in the economic recovery.

NIXON AND WATERGATE

Nixon struggled to gain legitimacy after his slim victory in the 1968 election. To garner more support from conservatives across the nation, he appealed to the so-called "silent majority"—conservative Democrats who were likely Southern, working-class, or elderly citizens who had become disenchanted by the liberalism of their party. He appealed to these voters by attempting to block a proposal to initiate forced busing of students to integrate public schools and becoming more vocal in his disdain for antiwar protesters.

The Nixon presidency would be damaged beyond repair, however, after the election of 1972. A break-in of the Democratic Party National Headquarters at the Watergate Hotel in Washington, D.C., in June 1972 seemed at the outset to be innocent of political intent. Through the investigations of *Washington Post* journalists Bob Woodward and Carl Bernstein, it was discovered that the burglars were connected to the **Committee to Reelect the President** (CREEP) and were attempting to bug the headquarters. The Nixon White House had hoped to stop "leaks" (so as to avoid another fiasco like the *Pentagon Papers*) by hiring a team of "plumbers," who used wiretaps, coercion, and threats to keep people quiet. Eventually the duo of Woodward and Bernstein

| 1968 Election | Nixon | **Domestic Crises** | Conservative Revolution | Cold War Ends |

uncovered evidence that the Watergate break-in was just the tip of an iceberg of illegal activities linked all the way to the Oval Office. As the chips began to fall, the president insulated himself with an ever-shrinking circle of supporters. A voice-activated tape system was discovered in the Oval Office and led to Congress's insistence that the tapes be released for investigation. President Nixon refused by claiming he was protected by *executive privilege* and fought with Congress for over a year. Just as things could not get worse, Vice President Spiro Agnew was convicted of tax evasion during his tenure as governor of Maryland and was forced to resign. The newly ratified Twenty-Fifth Amendment kicked in, as Nixon had to name a new vice president. He chose Representative Gerald R. Ford.

Facing certain impeachment and conviction by Congress on the charges of obstruction of justice, abuse of power, and contempt, President Nixon resigned the office on August 9, 1974. The Oval Office tapes, finally released due to a Supreme Court ruling in *Nixon v. United States* in July 1974, contained the "smoking gun" that directly linked the president to the Watergate scandal. Vice President Gerald R. Ford took the oath of office and became the only president in history who was not elected.

President Ford did not make friends in his first days in office when he pardoned former president Nixon of all charges (even though he had not been charged with a crime). Ford's next task was to try to repair the economy by asking for tax cuts and the reduction of government spending. Nothing he did touched inflation for very long. President Ford witnessed the failure of U.S. foreign policy in Asia, as Saigon and Cambodia both fell to the communists in 1975.

HIGHS AND LOWS OF CARTER'S PRESIDENCY

The Democrats seized on Ford's liabilities by choosing a "Washington outsider" to run for the office of president in 1976. Former Georgia governor and peanut farmer Jimmy Carter was a conservative Democrat from the South who appealed to Americans still reeling from the lies of the previous administrations. Carter squeaked out a narrow victory by garnering 51 percent of the popular vote, managing to take 97 percent of African American ballots. The Democrats also were able to secure majorities in both houses of Congress. Carter would be one of the most intelligent presidents ever to serve but was plagued from the start by his genial style and his inability to play politics. His dedication to human rights issues made him successful in the realm of foreign policy but also served as a liability when it came to domestic crises.

Carter's greatest success occurred when he crafted a peace agreement between Egypt and Israel in 1978. The president invited Egyptian President **Anwar Sadat** and Israeli Prime Minister **Menachem Begin** to meet at the presidential retreat at Camp David in the state of Maryland. Sadat and Begin discussed peace options while Carter acted as mediator. A peace agreement was signed in September 1978. The **Camp David Accords** served as the first step toward peace in the Middle East since the founding of the state of Israel in 1948.

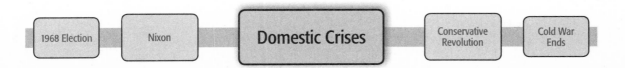

1968 Election — Nixon — **Domestic Crises** — Conservative Revolution — Cold War Ends

[handwritten margin notes: Iranian Hostage Crisis]

Unfortunately, another peace would soon be shattered as Islamic fundamentalists overthrew the Shah and seated the **Ayatollah Khomeini** as ruler in 1979. The United States now had no ally in the oil-rich region, and the Ayatollah suddenly cut off the flow of petroleum to OPEC, causing yet another gas shortage. As if this was not enough, later that year, Iranian college and high school students, angry over U.S. protection of the shah, seized the American embassy in the capital of Tehran and took hostages, many of whom were women. After a few days, the women and African Americans were released, but 52 white men were held captive for 444 days. President Carter froze Iranian assets in the United States and ordered a rescue mission that became an embarrassing failure.

[handwritten margin notes: SALT I: 1971 SALT II: 1979]

Carter also had to deal with increasing tensions between his country and the Soviet Union. SALT I was set to expire in 1977, so Carter and the Soviets were set to sign a renewal treaty. **SALT II** was negotiated and sat ready for ratification when another world crisis got in the way. The USSR invaded the nation of Afghanistan in December 1979 in a move to play a greater role in the Middle East. Americans were now certain that the Soviets intended to take control of the precious oil transportation region of the Persian Gulf. The United States immediately ceased supplying the USSR with grain shipments and withdrew SALT II from the table.

In protest, President Carter also boycotted the 1980 Olympic Games, which were held in Moscow. President Carter would be plagued by this decision and the Iran hostage crisis, which cost him the election in 1980. Domestically, Carter had difficulties eclipsing the troubles he was facing in foreign policy. He did uphold his promise to grant amnesty to the 10,000 young men who had fled the country during the Vietnam War draft. He created the Department of Education to address the problems of the nation's public schools and the Department of Energy to try to deal with the nation's energy crisis. The nation's energy woes were coupled with staggering inflation and high unemployment (*stagflation*), but even with the most conservative monetary policy, the nation did not emerge from the depths of the economic crisis until the mid-1980s.

CONSERVATIVE REVOLUTION

President Carter faced stiff competition from the right when Republicans chose former California Governor Ronald Reagan as their candidate for the election of 1980. The Democrats were reeling from the notion that Carter was ineffectual both domestically and abroad amidst a severe economic downturn. Conservatism was gaining popularity across the nation. as taxpayers sought to control where their money was spent. Christian fundamentalists became more influential, and Americans looked to "traditional family values" for strength. Americans cast their ballots for the former movie star and elected Ronald Reagan as their 40th (and oldest) president.

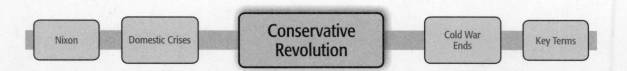

Nixon · Domestic Crises · **Conservative Revolution** · Cold War Ends · Key Terms

[handwritten margin notes: "Antithesis to New Deal's and New Frontier's and Great Society's liberalism"]

REAGAN BRINGS NEW POLICIES

The "**Reagan Revolution**" ended the old New Deal guard and ushered in a new era of conservative policy making in Washington. Reagan promised lower taxes, smaller government, and a stronger military. Helped by the sudden release of the Iranian hostages on the day of his inauguration, Reagan set forth to build trust and support by following through with his promises.

First the new president looked to repair the broken economy by rejecting Keynesian demand-side theory and adopting the classical supply-side model. Much like Andrew Carnegie of the 1920s, Reagan believed in the trickle-down concept of offering tax cuts and encouraging investment from the wealthy, thereby increasing the demand for new workers, who would then spend money for consumer goods. Congress agreed and passed a federal bill in 1981 that would cut taxes by 25 percent over a three-year period. As a result, many federally funded social programs were either cut or killed altogether, while defense spending increased.

During his first term, President Reagan enacted deregulation of telephone services and the truck transport industry. Other government regulations were lifted to help struggling industries, such as clean air standards for automobiles and large factories. Due to the release of government regulations on the savings and loan business, many in the 1980s began making risky investments to increase profits. By the mid-1980s, many of these institutions were in danger of collapsing, taking Americans' dollars with them. Not until 1989 would taxpayers have to foot the bill for the failure of the government to regulate the savings and loans. A potentially dangerous strike for the American economy and safety loomed over the president in August 1981 as the nation's air traffic controllers decided to walk off the job illegally. In a tough stand, Reagan fired every one of the controllers and replaced them with military personnel until civilians could be trained to take their place permanently. As a result, the air traffic controller's union was destroyed.

It had been a goal of Reagan to reconfigure the Supreme Court to carry on a more conservative legacy, and he more than fulfilled his promise. Reagan successfully seated the first woman on the Court, Sandra Day O'Connor, and placed conservatives Antonin Scalia and Anthony Kennedy on the bench as well. The new court pleased the conservative establishment by pulling back on laws protecting legal abortions, women, and African Americans.

REAGAN'S SECOND TERM

Against the first woman vice presidential candidate on the Democratic ticket, Reagan and Vice President George H. W. Bush successfully won re-election in 1984. Reagan's second term would be marked by continued conservative policy, as Congress worked to lower taxes even further and to limit illegal immigration. But the **Iran-Contra Scandal** left a mark on Reagan's presidency. It was discovered that money had been secretly diverted to the sale of American weapons to the Nicaraguan "Contras" to whom Congress had specifically forbidden aid. It was soon discovered that the United States had also secretly sold military equipment to Iran in exchange for the release

Nixon | Domestic Crises | **Conservative Revolution** | Cold War Ends | Key Terms

THE CHALLENGE DISASTER

Reagan had to soothe Americans when on February 1986, the NASA space shuttle **Challenger** exploded upon takeoff, killing all seven astronauts aboard, including the first teacher in space, Christa McAuliffe.

of the American hostages. This money was illegally diverted to pay for the weapons and aid to the Contras. The president denied any knowledge of the scandal.

Reagan also witnessed the largest drop of the stock market since the Great Depression on Black Monday, October 19, 1987. Congress reduced taxes further, fearing a return of recession.

THE COLD WAR ENDS

After the invasion of Afghanistan and the boycott of the 1980 Olympic Games, it was clear that détente was a thing of the past. President Reagan promised Americans a stronger military and had some tough words for what he called the "evil empire" of the Soviet Union. The president delivered on his promise of increased defense spending by pushing for funding of the Strategic Defense System (SDI), more popularly known as "Star Wars." The system was designed to station battle "ships" in orbit that could defend the United States against nuclear attack with lasers. While critics and many in the scientific community spoke of the impossibility of SDI, Reagan used the idea of the system as a scare tactic against the Soviets. The United States shifted its focus to taking the upper hand in nuclear endeavors rather than simply keeping pace with the other world powers. This intense buildup of both military and nuclear capacity put intense pressure on the Soviet economy, as it struggled to keep up.

GORBACHEV'S GLASNOST AND PERESTROIKA

In 1985, a new face came to power in the USSR who intended to change his country. Mikhail Gorbachev introduced two new ideas into the world vocabulary—*glasnost* and *perestroika*. The first reform, *glasnost*, or "openness," was designed to rid the country of the old Stalin totalitarianist state by easing laws designed to limit the freedoms of Russians. Secondly, *perestroika*, or "restructuring," was aimed at opening up the once-closed Soviet economy to free-market interactions to repair the sluggish economy. Gorbachev made the difficult decision to cease the arms buildup in his country to ease the shift toward his new vision. In December 1987, President Reagan and Premier Gorbachev signed an agreement to rid the world of intermediate-range missiles. From this point on, the two superpower leaders worked side-by-side to ease tensions not only between themselves but among many other nations around the world.

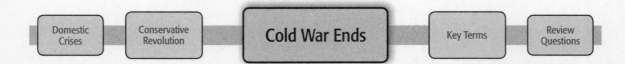

Domestic Crises | Conservative Revolution | **Cold War Ends** | Key Terms | Review Questions

GEORGE H. W. BUSH, THE BERLIN WALL, AND COLLAPSE OF THE SOVIET UNION

The United States was in a very interesting position on the cusp of the election of 1988. With the Cold War now almost at an end, what would happen to the hyper-military society Ronald Reagan had set up? The Republicans ran Vice President **George H. W. Bush** as their candidate against the Democrat Michael Dukakis. Bush was able to take the presidency easily, with his promise to be tough on crime and his statement of "Read my lips, no new taxes." However, the Republicans were not successful in uniting government, as the House and Senate went to the Democrats.

Communism was under fire from the moment George Bush took the oath of office. In the spring of 1989, China experienced a student uprising that demanded democracy. Beijing crushed this notion with a fierce fury. Hundreds were killed and many more imprisoned for their role in the protests. On the other side of the globe, the Eastern Bloc countries were experiencing troubles and challenges of their own. Needing to cut back on military spending, Gorbachev warned communist governments in countries such as Poland, Hungary, and Czechoslovakia that the Soviet Union would no longer be providing them assistance. With the "**Solidarity**" movement, the rise of Lech Walesa in Poland, and the collapse of the Romanian government in 1989, the "iron curtain" was coming down in Europe. President Reagan's famous words, "Mr. Gorbachev, tear down this wall," became a reality, as the **Berlin Wall** was torn down by protesters in October 1989. Despite his attempts, Gorbachev watched as his own country collapsed under the weight of protest. The Soviet republics of Estonia, Latvia, and Lithuania declared their independence in the spring of 1990. Gorbachev was forced from power, as the Soviet Union collapsed on Christmas Day, 1991. Boris Yeltsin became president of Russia, which joined with the 14 other former Soviet republics to create the temporary **Commonwealth of Independent States**. Presidents Bush and Yeltsin immediately began to dismantle the nuclear war machine that had been built up over the past four decades. They signed **START I** in 1991, which drastically reduced the number of nuclear warheads in both countries. **START II** was signed by both men in 1993 to reduce further the number of warheads, with an added promise of U.S. aid to the Russian economy. More importantly, however, both Bush and Yeltsin stood by as former Soviet republics fell into rebellion or economic collapse.

KEY TERMS

Names	Sirhan Sirhan Henry Kissinger Anwar Sadat Menachem Begin Ayatollah Khomeini George H. W. Bush
Groups	American Independent Party Organization of Petroleum Exporting Countries Committee to Re-elect the President Commonwealth of Independent States
Events	Yom Kippur War Reagan Revolution Iran-Contra Scandal Solidarity movement
Documents and Laws	War Powers Act Strategic Arms Limitation Treaty (SALT I) Camp David Accords SALT II START I
Places	Berlin Wall
Vocabulary	Vietnamization détente stagflation *Challenger* Star Wars *glasnost* *perestroika* executive privilege

REVIEW QUESTIONS

1. The violence at the 1968 Democratic National Convention

   (A) was viewed by most Americans with anger towards the establishment.

   (B) signaled the apex of the Civil Rights Movement.

   (C) occurred because of provocation of local law enforcement.

   (D) caused President Johnson to refuse the party's nomination.

   (E) drove the party to abandon antiwar rhetoric.

2. Détente was Nixon's attempt at

   (A) softening the relationship among the United States, USSR, and China.

   (B) opening China to the possibility of capitalist trade.

   (C) mediating between feuding racial groups.

   (D) responding to the South's disgust with forced integration.

   (E) insulating himself from a Senate investigation.

3. The events surrounding the Watergate scandal signaled

   (A) a stronger executive branch.

   (B) that the nation stood behind its president.

   (C) the end of talks to limit armaments.

   (D) that the executive branch was not above the law.

   (E) weakness in the legislative and judicial branches in dealing with the crisis.

4. President Reagan gained quick and lasting popularity through his

   (A) ability to reduce government spending in all sectors.

   (B) increase of governmental agencies to care for the poor.

   (C) soft approach to the Soviet Union and Cuba.

   (D) belief in traditional family values and Christian morals.

   (E) enactment of legislation to protect working-class citizens.

5. President George H. W. Bush struggled with all of the following issues EXCEPT

   (A) an economy in recession.

   (B) democratic revolutions in Eastern Europe.

   (C) dismantling of the military economy built by Reagan.

   (D) growing tensions in the Middle East.

   (E) the invasion of Grenada.

ANSWERS AND EXPLANATIONS

1. A

Mayor Richard Daley and the Chicago police reacted violently to provocations by the antiwar protesters that arrived at the Democratic National Convention in 1968. As a result, the nation watched in horror as protesters were beaten and abused by law enforcement on national television.

2. A

President Nixon sought to use his relationship with China to influence the USSR and cool the tension among all powers involved. While détente was short-lived, it did much to calm world pressure for at least a few years. Détente resulted in the USSR and China putting pressure on North Vietnam to negotiate an end to the Vietnam War.

3. D

The legislative and judicial branches made it perfectly clear that the president of the United States was not above the law during the investigation into the Watergate break-in and scandal. Through impeachment hearings and the Supreme Court's ruling in *Nixon v. United States*, it was clear that executive privilege had limits.

4. D

President Reagan was the prime spokesperson for the resurgence of conservatism in the United States in the 1980s. Through his keen wit and handsome charm, Reagan spoke of the importance of family, tradition, and faith, thus gaining support across the nation. The media dubbed him the "Great Communicator."

5. E

It was Bush's predecessor, Ronald Reagan, who ordered the U.S. Marines to invade the tiny island of Grenada in 1983 to prevent a communist take-over there.

CHAPTER 30: CHANGES IN POST–COLD WAR AMERICA

DEMOGRAPHIC SHIFTS

Many domestic and foreign changes altered the demographic makeup of the United States after 1965. First and foremost, the Johnson-era passage of the **Immigration Act of 1965** opened the doors to foreigners seeking a new life or an escape from oppression. Cubans fleeing the oppressive dictatorship of Fidel Castro, Vietnamese fleeing communist rule, Filipinos seeking economic opportunity, and Mexicans looking for a better life all came ashore between 1965 and 2000. While these were the largest groups seeking asylum, many others joined their ranks from countries such as India, Pakistan, Korea, China, and the Dominican Republic. States with coastlines such as Texas, California, Arizona, and Florida experienced massive growth. As immigration continued to flow uninterrupted, local and state governments struggled to keep pace with the influx of needy citizens taxing the already struggling welfare system. To provide education, medical care, and housing to documented residents as well as undocumented aliens, states and municipalities required funding well beyond what the federal government was providing. Aiming to put a damper on illegal immigration, Congress passed the **Immigration and Control Act** in 1986, which occurred mainly at the country's southern border with Mexico. Even with this restriction, illegal immigration into the United States continued, allowing some 12 million undocumented aliens into the country by 1990.

Americans were also on the move during this period, as they picked up from the former "steel belt" states and moved to the *Sunbelt*. Steel-producing states, such as Michigan, Pennsylvania, and Ohio, became known as the *Rustbelt*, as large steel mills closed due to decreasing domestic demand and increasing competition in the global market. Americans flocked to California, Texas, Arizona, Florida, and New Mexico to take advantage of the newly invented air-conditioning, as well as aerospace jobs that lured the nation's best and brightest. Americans were on the move, due to the the Interstate Highway Act, which provided easy-to-navigate freeways that connected every point across the United States from Newport, Rhode Island, to Newport Beach, California.

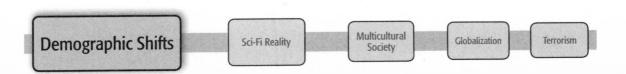

Demographic Shifts | Sci-Fi Reality | Multicultural Society | Globalization | Terrorism

PRESENT-DAY GRAYING OF AMERICA

The United States is today experiencing a unique phenomenon, as the "baby boomers" of the post–World War II era begin to reach the later stages of life. The "graying" of America began in the mid-1990s and will continue through the 2050s. Taxing the Social Security system set forth by FDR during the New Deal and the nation's health care system, the number of Americans over 65 will skyrocket as the baby boomers age and health care improves the average life span. By the year 2030, about 25 percent of all Americans will be over 85 years old. The effects of such a demographic shift are still being debated among sociologists and historians, but certainly the nation will experience struggles with regards to care giving, familial relationships, and economics.

SCI-FI BECOMES REALITY

What was once the stuff of science fiction movies became reality through the years 1965 to 2000. Advances in biotechnology, mass communications, and computers have made the world a much smaller place, bringing excitement and danger along with progress.

ADVANCES IN HEALTH

The average life span of an American well exceeds the life expectancy of just 50 years ago. Through advances in medicine, such as organ transplant, artificial life support, and advanced drug therapy, human life can be extended and even saved through the miracles of modern science. Previously deadly cases of bacteria can now be treated with a single regimen of antibiotics. Polio, which once ravaged the American psyche, has been all but eradicated from the North American continent. Other diseases have taken its place, though, with much deadlier force and with no cure in sight. In an effort to find cures for diseases such as AIDS, cancer, and diabetes, researchers in the United States successfully completed mapping the entire human genome in 2003. The medical research community has been experimenting with human stem cells in an effort to regenerate damaged cells to cure a variety of illnesses. Stem cell research has proven to be highly controversial in the United States.

THE AIDS CRISIS

The outbreak of Acquired Immune Deficiency Syndrome, or **AIDS**, in the 1980s descended upon urban areas and soon spread worldwide. By 2006, the known cases of AIDS in the United States was predicted to reach 1 million, with the number doubling throughout the world.

Demographic Shifts — Sci-Fi Reality — Multicultural Society — Globalization — Terrorism

ADVANCES IN COMMUNICATION

The idea of portable communication in the 1960s usually appeared in spy stories such as those featuring James Bond or Maxwell Smart, who used tiny telephones that could be hidden in a watch or shoe. The first consumer portable telephones were introduced in the 1980s at prices that only the very wealthy could afford. The phones looked more like two-way radios and needed the frequent charging of a huge battery pack. Currently, "cellular phones" seem to be everywhere. These telephones are small, lightweight, and virtually disposable. The advent of pay television revolutionized the airwaves in the late 1970s and early 1980s as consumers scrambled to get cable television. Not held to the decency standards of broadcast television, cable networks pushed the boundaries with more explicit programming. Cable news stations soon eclipsed the standard network stations, changing the face of television news coverage. Satellite communications opened up the world to television audiences, as news from around the globe could be transmitted in seconds to the television set in the living room.

No technological revolution has impacted society more than the information boom caused by the Internet. Although the **World Wide Web** gained prominence when it moved from the academic world into the public arena, the system (ARPANET) had been in place since the mid-1960s. Used mostly by universities and government officials, the small network of computers that were linked together to communicate would be the foundation for what is now a global system. A young computer science student named Bill Gates, who dropped out of Harvard University, revolutionized the computer industry by inventing an operating system that was independent of a mainframe computer. Mainframes, long the industry standard, could take up entire floors of office buildings and ran several computers hooked to them. Gates's MS-DOS software made it possible to operate a computer independently of a mainframe as a stand-alone machine. IBM soon adopted MS-DOS for its personal computer line in 1980 and began the personal computing revolution. More companies entered the business, producing their own operating systems and advancing the speed of computers through microprocessors. By the mid-1990s, personal laptop computers had the ability to outperform their mainframe predecessors by a hundred-fold. In 1990, the once-cumbersome network of computers opened up as sites were given domain names and hypertext links that made navigation quick and easy. By the late 1990s, nearly every American had used the Internet at some point. With the ease of **Internet** use came many challenges as well. There was no "policing" of the content or use of the Internet, making it difficult to manage misinformation, information theft, and other criminal activities. Users were left to control their own computer environment and protect themselves from dangers that lurked online.

LIVING IN A MULTICULTURAL SOCIETY

As the world got smaller through mass communication and the Internet, America became more diverse, as immigrants and birth rates increased from 1965 to 2000. For example, in the city of Los Angeles in 1990, a full third of residents were foreign born. California boasted residents from all over the world, with a majority from Southeast Asia and Mexico. Californians reacted to

the surge of immigrants by enacting laws restricting access to welfare, medical care, and public education for illegal aliens. There was even a push to make English the state's official language, which would limit the use of other languages on government forms, such as driver's license applications and business tax forms.

RIOTS ON THE STREETS OF LOS ANGELES

The city of Los Angeles exploded in riots in 1992 after the announcement that a jury had acquitted white policemen of beating an African American man named Rodney King. The nation had witnessed the brutality—the videotape of the arrest of Mr. King had been broadcast nightly since the start of the trial. Television viewers again stood watch as the city's minority communities erupted in violence. Three days of looting, arson, and murder caused over $500 million in damage and cost 40 lives. While some believed that the rioting resembled that of the Watts Riots in 1965, others saw different underlying tensions that were highlighted by those the rioters targeted.

AFFIRMATIVE ACTION DEBATES

California and Texas continued to be in the forefront of multicultural clashes, as laws were passed to overturn the progress made during Johnson's Great Society. Affirmative action had already taken a blow when the Supreme Court ruled in *Bakke v. UC Board of Regents* that the program resulted in "reverse discrimination," where qualified white applicants were being denied admission in favor of less-qualified minority applicants. Later, in an effort supported by an African American member of the University of California Board of Regents, Ward Connerly, **Proposition 209** sought to end affirmative action laws in the state of California for good. After the passage of the proposition, government contracts and college admissions boards could no longer use gender or race as a factor in awarding jobs or acceptance. As a result, minority enrollment in the UC system plummeted, with classrooms not reflecting the ethnic diversity of the state as a whole. Several other states followed suit, enacting laws abolishing affirmative action. The cycle of poverty continues to plague the nation's ethnic minority and immigrant population. While unemployment and the standard of living remains relatively high for white Americans, blacks are twice as likely to be unemployed, and almost 20 percent live below the poverty line.

CLINTON'S INTERNAL STRUGGLES

Winning the election for president in 1992, **President William (Bill) Clinton** worked to reform health care and the welfare system amid remaining vestiges of Reagan conservatism on Capitol Hill. Clinton faced the challenge of not having a united government—Congress sat in the hands of Republicans under the leadership of House Speaker Newt Gingrich. The president and speaker were headed for a showdown, as Clinton threatened to veto the Republican budget and force the closure of all government offices until a new budget could be drawn up. Twice the federal government closed. The Republican stand-off proved to be ineffective—they ultimately were forced to back down, opening the doors for Clinton to compromise and pass a federal budget.

Demographic Shifts | Sci-Fi Reality | **Multicultural Society** | Globalization | Terrorism

GLOBALIZATION IN THE UNITED STATES

As in no time before, the United States in the 21st century is linked to a broader global economy. Economic crises in distant lands can impact the stock market in the United States before most Americans have had their morning coffee. The late 1990s brought financial terror to many who invested in stocks and futures overseas, as Asian financial markets plunged into the depths of recession. Japan, the Philippines, and Korea experienced economic slides caused by the overvaluing of real estate transactions and risky investments. Thailand soon followed by closing banks across the nation, causing a ripple effect of bank patrons rushing to withdraw their deposits across Asia. Within minutes, once-vast fortunes became worthless as currency and stock values crashed in many countries. Countries that relied on Asian consumption soon suffered as supply of goods rose and prices fell. Oil-producing nations soon found themselves strapped with large amounts of crude and no buyers. The Russian and Venezuelan economies took a hard hit, with organized crime rings taking full advantage of the crisis. The **International Monetary Fund** (IMF) supplied billions to faltering nations. Some rebounded quickly, but there was concern over the possibility of the fund collapsing under the weight of a future global economic crisis.

President Clinton worked in his first term to deal with globalization as it pertained to protecting American jobs and welfare. His **North American Free Trade Agreement** (NAFTA) would open free trade with Canada and Mexico, allowing the flow of more goods, services, and jobs across the international borders. NAFTA was hotly contested by organized labor and conservative groups, who saw the agreement as selling American jobs to cheap labor across the border while compromising America's sovereignty to international arbitration boards. NAFTA was signed in 1993, reducing restrictions and tariffs on goods and services transported among the United States, Canada, and Mexico.

THE FEAR OF TERRORISM

Throughout the 20th century, Americans had watched from afar as other nations dealt with terrorism. Occasionally, American lives were lost at the hands of a hijacker or suicide bomber, but for the most part, the mainland United States would remain isolated from terrorists. That all changed in 1995, when the Murrow Federal Building in Oklahoma City, Oklahoma, was attacked by a large bomb that killed 168 people. Immediate reports pointed to Islamic fundamentalists, but soon it was discovered that the terror in Oklahoma was homegrown. Right-wing extremist **Timothy McVeigh** and a set of accomplices had driven a U-Haul truck loaded with explosives near the building and set the charge by remote. Americans were stunned by the nature of the attack and grieved over the loss of so many innocent lives.

In the meantime, fundamentalist Islamist coalition groups opposed to the American protection of Israel were forming in countries such as Saudi Arabia, Iran, Syria, and Afghanistan. While some were established solely for protest purposes, others took the next step in creating a paramilitary network of fighters across the world to fight the American "infidels." One such group had

Sci-Fi Reality | Multicultural Society | Globalization | **Terrorism** | Environmental Issues

already attacked Americans both on and off U.S. soil. **Al-Qaeda**, led by **Osama Bin Laden**, a Saudi national, had formed a military training camp in Afghanistan to prepare warriors to attack Western targets. Using American funding and training from the 1980s, Bin Laden had successfully trained a multinational force of fighters and terrorists by the early 1990s. Al-Qaeda began by attacking the World Trade Center in New York in 1993, killing six people but inflicting minimal damage. From that point on, Americans grew increasingly concerned as more and more attacks were carried out against them around the world. Soon, al-Qaeda and Bin Laden would become household words for every American.

SEPTEMBER 11 AND A NEW AMERICA

September 11, 2001, began as a normal workday in New York City, as employees of the businesses in the World Trade Center rushed off the subways and streets into their offices. At 8:46 A.M. Eastern Time, American Airlines Flight 11 crashed into the north tower of the World Trade Center. The flight had originated in Boston's Logan Airport and was supposed to be en route to Los Angeles with a belly full of fuel, 81 passengers, and a full flight crew. Many thought this was a freak accident, until approximately 15 minutes later, when United Flight 175 crashed into the south tower of the World Trade Center. It was clear that the United States was under attack. Two planes remained unaccounted for until American flight 77 crashed into the Pentagon and United flight 93 crashed into a wooded area of Pennsylvania. All flights were immediately grounded and the airspace over the entire country closed to any traffic. Pledging immediate action, **President George W. Bush** promised that the perpetrators would be caught and justice would be served. The towers soon collapsed, killing occupants and rescue workers who had rushed in to save anyone they could. In the end, some 3,000 lives were lost in the **9/11** attacks, and the city of New York faced over $80 billion in damages. The impact on American business was staggering—commercial airlines begged for assistance to avoid bankruptcy, and travel destinations around the country remained empty. Lost too was the innocence of the American public, who had previously considered themselves safer here than anywhere else in the world.

The immediate concern for the Bush administration was fighting terrorism and protecting Americans. The Bush administration enacted the **PATRIOT Act**, which broadly expanded the government's ability to monitor the activities of Americans and conduct investigations of people suspected of terrorism. Americans would face another scare when a white powdery substance containing anthrax was discovered in letters sent to members of Congress and national news organizations. Hundreds of illegal and legal immigrants soon found themselves under arrest or under suspicion of terrorist activities in post-9/11 America. Congress was quick to send troops to Afghanistan, the home of Osama Bin Laden and al-Qaeda, immediately after the attacks. Under the banner of the "**War on Terror**," American troops invaded the Muslim country in October 2001 to find Bin Laden. The ruling party of Afghanistan, the Taliban, was sympathetic to al-Qaeda and had provided safe haven for its activities. The U.S. military was successful in

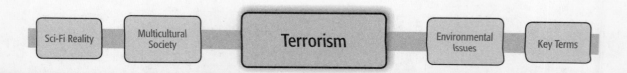
Sci-Fi Reality | Multicultural Society | Terrorism | Environmental Issues | Key Terms

removing the Taliban from power and assisted in the establishment of a coalition government in its place. Bin Laden remained elusive, however, escaping many times.

WAR ON IRAQ

President Bush insisted on invading another Arab country in March 2003 in an effort to remove a potentially threatening dictator and his cache of "**weapons of mass destruction**." Iraq had been a thorn in the side of the Bush family since his father's attempt to liberate Kuwait back in 1991. With **Saddam Hussein** still in power and refusing to cooperate fully with United Nations weapons inspections, Bush, along with Prime Minister Tony Blair, convinced Congress and most of the United States that Iraq posed a serious threat to the United States and the world if left in power. The official invasion of Iraq was not sanctioned by the United Nations and was condemned by many of U.S. allies around the world.

ENVIRONMENTAL ISSUES

The worldwide community continues to grow at an alarming rate. It is a mystery whether or not the planet will be able to sustain the sheer number of human beings that are currently living or will live on earth. Issues such as biodiversity, genetically engineered foods, overpopulation, global warming, natural conservation, and natural disasters will continue to plague human beings for hundreds of years to come.

Domestically, the United States has experienced its fair share of environmental problems since 1965. President Carter was one of the first presidents to address the issues surrounding the natural environment and energy sources when he created the Department of Energy and superfund sites. The superfund sites were former chemical waste dump sites that the federal government would acquire and then clean for future use. Carter encouraged the use of solar power in place of nonrenewable energy sources and started the **Drive 55** plan to reduce the amount of gasoline expended by the average American.

Nuclear power seemed to be another alternative until 1979, when the nuclear plant at **Three Mile Island** in Pennsylvania sent a cloud of radioactive gas into the air. It was soon discovered that in a rush to get the plant online, many shortcuts had been taken that ultimately threatened the safety of the plant. Nuclear power was no longer a viable option for most Americans.

Many of the strides made to help the environment would be reversed by Presidents Reagan and George H. W. Bush in an effort to stimulate the nation's business climate by lifting restrictions on waste dumping and pollution emissions. Now, many Americans live in cities that have air that is not completely safe 90 percent of the year. Ironically, Los Angeles and Sacramento, California, have the nation's dirtiest air and some of the strictest emission standards for gasoline and automobiles. The nation has had to come to grips with dirty oceans, lakes, and rivers; deteriorating national parks; and declining natural resources. The strain on natural resources

does not stop at the nation's borders, however. India and China now have the bulk of the world's population and are the largest users of nonrenewable fuel sources and clean water. These nations do not have the same environmental restrictions on business and consumers as Western countries and will, thus, continue to negatively impact the world's environment.

KEY TERMS	
Names	William (Bill) Clinton
	Timothy McVeigh
	Osama Bin Laden
	George W. Bush
	Saddam Hussein
	Hillary Clinton
	Barack Obama
	John McCain
	Sarah Palin
Groups	Al-Qaeda
	Taliban
Events	"War on Terror"
	9/11
	Watts Riots
	Hurricane Katrina
	2008 financial crisis
Documents and Laws	Immigration Act of 1965
	Immigration and Control Act of 1986
	Proposition 209
	International Money Fund (IMF)
	North American Free Trade Agreement (NAFTA)
	PATRIOT Act
	Drive 55
Places	Three Mile Island
Vocabulary	AIDS
	weapons of mass destruction
	World Wide Web
	Internet
	reverse discrimination

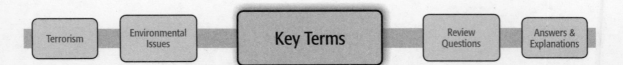

REVIEW QUESTIONS

1. Demographic shifts in the United States impacted all of the following EXCEPT

   (A) welfare systems.

   (B) housing projects.

   (C) public education.

   (D) race relations.

   (E) Social Security.

2. The Supreme Court ruling in *Bakke v. UC Regents* limited

   (A) racial discrimination in admissions.

   (B) affirmative action.

   (C) corporate emission standards.

   (D) high tariffs on Mexican goods.

   (E) tax-supported welfare programs.

3. The predecessor to the Internet was

   (A) the World Wide Web.

   (B) MS-DOS.

   (C) ARPANET.

   (D) the information superhighway.

   (E) mainframes.

4. Sunbelt states will be impacted by all of the following EXCEPT

   (A) minority majorities.

   (B) population growth.

   (C) declining school enrollment.

   (D) health care shortages.

   (E) racial tensions.

5. The North American Free Trade Agreement (NAFTA) was supported by

   (A) organized labor.

   (B) conservative Republicans.

   (C) liberal Democrats.

   (D) large business owners.

   (E) Southerners.

Environmental Issues | Key Terms | **Review Questions** | Answers & Explanations | Essays

ANSWERS AND EXPLANATIONS

1. E

The age of "baby boomers" will impact Social Security more than immigration and other demographic shifts.

2. B

In its 1978 ruling, the Court curbed the use of quotas in the admission of students to the state's university system. Claiming "reverse discrimination," Bakke had been refused admission to the university in favor of a less qualified minority student.

3. C

ARPANET was developed by academians to link together research computers all over the world in the mid-1960s. Through the development of HyperText Markup Language (HTML), computer code could be translated and viewed by computers around the world through phone modems. MS-DOS was the brainchild of Bill Gates, who was able to separate the desktop computer from mainframes, which sometimes filled entire floors of large office buildings. The World Wide Web and "information superhighway" are names for the millions and millions of individual pages of code that are seen when the Internet is used.

4. C

States such as California, Arizona, Texas, and New Mexico will all be impacted by an increase in population. Many of the people moving into these states are immigrants from foreign countries fleeing poverty, oppression, and overcrowding. With the increase in the number of citizens who are likely to live at or below the poverty line, Sunbelt states will face troubles with health care, schooling, and racial tensions.

5. D

NAFTA was difficult for President Clinton to pass due to the large numbers of groups opposed to its provisions. Conservatives feared a loss of jobs and a weakening of the border, while liberals worried about globalization issues that would cripple the development of Latin American nations. Organized labor lamented the loss of factory jobs to cheap labor in Mexico, while Southerners worried about border problems.

UNIT V SAMPLE ESSAYS

The following are sample free-response questions that you might see on the AP U.S. History exam. Listed under each question are important terms that would greatly add to your answer. AP Readers will look for you to mention at least several of the listed people, places, and things.

1. What impact did the Persian Gulf War have on U.S. foreign policy in the Middle East?

    Study List
    Camp David Accords
    President Jimmy Carter
    Iran/Iraq War
    U.S. policy towards Israel
    Saddam Hussein
    Kuwait
    oil production in the Middle East
    UN Resolution 678
    Operation Desert Storm
    global terrorism
    UN weapons inspections
    weapons of mass destruction
    economic sanctions against Syria
    U.S. relationship with Saudi Arabia and Jordan

2. What significant social, political and economic challenges will the United States face through the next half century?

    Study List
    the graying of America
    Social Security
    health care
    welfare
    immigration
    minority-majority
    equal pay for equal work
    gay rights
    religious rights
    global terrorism
    homeland security
    nuclear threats from rogue nations
    global debt
    environmental protection
    depletion of fossil fuels

Environmental Issues | Key Terms | Review Questions | Answers & Explanation | **Essays**

SAMPLE FRQ RESPONSES

What impact did the Persian Gulf War have on U.S. foreign policy in the Middle East?

The United States's foreign policy in the Middle East has changed greatly since the Persian Gulf War. The United States was initially involved financially and politically in Middle Eastern conflicts but not overtly involved militarily. The Persian War marked the beginning of military conflict between the United States and Iraq that continues today, and it initiated the downswing of relations between the United States and the entire Middle East. With that erosion of relations has come a much more hostile and adversarial brand of foreign policy.

The United States was involved in Middle Eastern foreign policy long before the Persian Gulf War. In 1978, then-president Jimmy Carter hosted the Camp David Accords, which led to a peace treaty in 1979 between Egypt and Israel. The United States was involved heavily with the formation of Israel and continued to be a close political ally, causing tension between the United States and the Middle East to some degree. But for the most part, the U.S. remained on good terms with the Middle East politically and economically, thus ensuring access to Middle Eastern oil.

The Iran-Iraq War, also known as the First Persian Gulf War, marked a change in the United States's previously more hands-off foreign policy. The war began in September 1980 and lasted until August 1988. After a long history of border disputes between the two countries, the war started when Iraq, led by Saddam Hussein, invaded Iran. The war was mostly a stalemate from 1982 until 1988. Having long distrusted Iran after the 1979–81 Iranian hostage crises, the United States began backing Iraq in 1982, possibly even supplying it with weapons. Both the United States and Iraq attacked oil tankers in the region, and under international law, the U.S. could view an attack on its ships as permission to engage in the war. The U.S. provided military protection for its ships going into Iraq, thus protecting the valuable Iraqi oil industry's ports. However, the U.S. was simultaneously involved in the Iran-Contra Affair, where the Reagan Administration secretly sold arms to Iran. In effect, the U.S. government had a vested interest in befriending whoever might win the Iran-Iraq War, since both controlled key oilfields. Up until 1990, U.S. companies profited from selling Iraq weapons technology.

The U.S. friendship with Israel, its financial agenda, and its previous backing of Iraq was put to the test when, in August 1990, Iraq invaded Kuwait and the Persian Gulf War began. After the invasion, King Fahd of Kuwait met with Richard Cheney to ask for U.S. help, and Israel discussed with the U.S. government their fear that they would be Iraq's next target. In November, UN Resolution 678 was passed, authorizing the use of any means necessary to get Iraq out of Kuwait. In January of 1991, Congress authorized the use of force by the U.S. military, and the Allies, made up of 38 nations, began their attack, often known

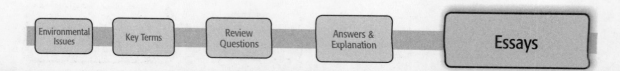

as Operation Desert Storm. In the battles that followed, U.S. and European technology previously sold to Iraq was used against them. But by July of 1991, the Allied forces had won the war. However, they had not disposed of Saddam Hussein.

On September 11, 2001, terrorists took over four American commercial airplanes and crashed them in Pennsylvania, Washington, D.C., and New York City, killing thousands. This prompted a war with Afghanistan and also led to fear of Iraq's involvement with terrorists. In 2002, Saddam Hussein agreed to a UN resolution allowing them to do weapon inspections of Iraq, looking for "weapons of mass destruction." The resolution also proposed the possibility of lifting a 12-year sanction stating that Iraq could not sell its oil on the international market and could only import food and medicine. While the UN failed to find evidence of weapons of mass destruction and asked that they be permitted to conduct another inspection, the United States refused and declared war on Iraq in 2003.

The war in Iraq has not yet been resolved. In May of 2004, the United States imposed economic sanctions against Syria, accusing it of having weapons of mass destruction and occupying Lebanon. Upon discovery that the majority of 9/11 terrorists were Saudi Arabian nationals, the traditionally strong relationship between the United States and Saudi Arabia has been strained. Relations with Jordan are complicated by the U.S. continued relationship with Israel. Even though Israel and Jordan signed a peace accord in 1994, they are still home to many Palestinian refugees who had to leave under Israeli occupation of the West Bank, which was previously Jordan's as well, and tension still exists.

The Persian Gulf War marked a turning point in U.S. foreign policy toward the Middle East. Before the war, the United States favored the brokering of peace, as in the 1978 Camp David Accord, and political machinations in order to retain economic advantages, as seen in the Iran-Iraq War. However, because of the U.S.'s historical backing of Israel and need for a stable Middle Eastern oil supply, Iraq's invasion of Kuwait led America to become involved in actual military conflict in the Middle East and to a more defensive and adversarial foreign policy that continues today.

What significant social, political, and economic challenges will the United States face through the next half century?

The most important political, social, and economical challenges that the United States will face in the coming half century will all stem from one key issue—oil. As the population of the world swells, global demand for oil will grow as well. If global production cannot keep up with global demand, then the entire world will be faced with massive shortages, price increases, and the possibility of another world war. The United States, the largest consumer of oil in the world, will be hardest hit by any fluctuations in the supply of oil.

Current global production of refined oil is not meeting demand. Americans see proof of this at gas stations across the country. The rise in cost is not due to a dwindling oil supply.

Instead it is caused in part by the emerging need for refined oil in China, which is stressing global refining capacity. High prices now show what happens when the global market cannot keep up with global demand. Though oil industry experts cannot agree on when the world's oil reserves will be exhausted, they all agree on one thing—that it will happen. As the oil supply dwindles, it will no longer be enough for the huge U.S. economy. At first prices will rise, like what is happening now. But prices will not level off after a temporary adjustment period, as they are predicted to after the current price increase. They will keep rising, first handicapping the mass population, then small businesses, and finally large businesses. Our economy, which has come to rely on cheap and abundant fuel, will suddenly have neither. This is what happened during the gas crisis of 1973, only world oil production was intentionally cut by OPEC. The result of the gas crisis was a year-long recession for the United States and the rest of the world. If a relative hiccup in oil production did that much damage to the U.S. economy back then, what will happen to the future economy when production can no longer support the demand?

The lack of oil will change the political sphere of the United States as well. Because oil is of paramount importance to the economy, it has the potential to become a significant issue in political campaigns. As the supply decreases, differing opinions will emerge on what to do about the coming crisis. Politicians will align themselves with philosophies that range from extreme conservation to threatening war on other oil-rich countries. Already, U.S. foreign policy is geared toward placating powerful oil-producing countries and subjugating less powerful ones. Just look at U.S. relations with Saudi Arabia, a country with a dubious, but conveniently overlooked, human rights record, and Iraq, a country that has been literally recreated by a U.S. occupation following a preemptive war with an equally dubious justification.

Oil will also affect American society. Oil is used for a lot more things than gasoline. Oil is a key ingredient in such widely used materials as plastics, pesticides, fertilizers, lubricants, and many other chemicals. If the supply of oil were to evaporate, not only would the American consumer not be able to fill up the gas tank of his car, he would have a car with a significantly smaller amount of plastic (a larger component of a modern car than is obvious to the naked eye), and his car would need to run on synthetic lubricant. Alternatives to petroleum products already exist, but the demand for such products will increase exponentially once oil becomes a rarity. Americans will have to rethink their daily lives. They will need to use more public transportation in a country that has been developed around the family car since the era of Henry Ford. People who live in colder areas will need to find a way to heat their homes without oil or gas. And because there doesn't seem to be a quick and easy replacement for oil in a world that depends on it, the cost of available energy from other sources will be far beyond the average consumer's reach, creating a whole new societal class, the nonmobile, educated workforce.

Though the loss of oil is only one challenge that the United States will face in the coming 50 years, it is the linchpin of our society, and its absence will have devastating effects on our way of life politically, culturally, and especially economically.

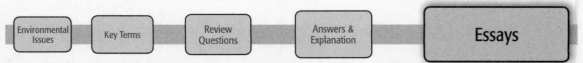

Environmental Issues | Key Terms | Review Questions | Answers & Explanation | **Essays**

Part Four

PRACTICE TESTS

HOW TO TAKE THE PRACTICE TESTS

The next section of this book consists of two full-length practice tests. Taking a practice AP exam gives you an idea of what it's like to answer these test questions for a longer period of time, one that approximates the real test. You'll find out which areas you're strong in and where additional review may be required. Any mistakes you make now are ones you won't make on the actual exam, as long as you take the time to learn where you went wrong.

The two full-length practice tests in this book each include 80 multiple-choice questions, one Document-Based question, and your choice of two (out of four) Free-Response questions. You will have 55 minutes for the multiple-choice questions, a 15-minute reading period, and then 115 minutes to answer the three essay questions. Before taking a practice test, find a quiet place where you can work uninterrupted. Time yourself according to the time limit at the beginning of each section. It's okay to take a short break between sections, but for the most accurate results, you should approximate real test conditions as much as possible. Use the 15-minute reading period to plan your answers for the essay questions, but don't begin writing your responses until the 15 minutes are up.

As you take the practice tests, remember to pace yourself. Train yourself to be aware of the time you are spending on each problem. Try to be aware of the general types of questions you encounter, as well as being alert to certain strategies or approaches that help you to handle the various question types more effectively.

After taking a practice exam, be sure to read the detailed answer explanations that follow. These will help you identify areas that could use additional review. Even when you answered a question correctly, you can learn additional information by looking at the answer explanation.

Finally, it's important to approach the test with the right attitude. You're going to get a great score because you've reviewed the material and learned the strategies in this book.

Good luck!

HOW TO COMPUTE YOUR SCORE

SCORING THE MULTIPLE-CHOICE QUESTIONS

To compute your score on the multiple-choice portion of the two sample tests, calculate the number of questions you got wrong on each test, then deduct $\frac{1}{4}$ of that number from the number of correct answers you got on each test. For example, if you got 6 multiple-choice questions wrong, you would deduct 1.5 ($6 \times \frac{1}{4}$) from 74 (the number of questions correct). Your score would then be a 73 (72.5 rounded up) for the multiple-choice portion of the exam. The multiple-choice section accounts for approximately one-half of your test score.

SCORING THE FREE-RESPONSE QUESTIONS

This section accounts for the other half of your test score. Of course, it will be difficult for you to score your own essays accurately. Review the key points listed for each essay and the sample essays offered. Refer to the scoring chart in chapter 2 to assign yourself a grade of 0 to 9 for how well you think you did.

CALCULATING YOUR COMPOSITE SCORE

(4.5 × _____) + (2.75 × _____) + (2.75 × _____) = _____

    DBQ points   First essay score   Second essay score   Free-Response Raw Score

      (0–9)   (0–9)   (0–9)

COMPOSITE SCORE

Multiple-Choice Raw Score + Free-Response Raw Score = Composite Score

CONVERSION CHART (APPROXIMATE)

Composite Score Range	AP Grade
117–170	5
96–116	4
79–95	3
51–78	2
0–50	1

Practice Test 1 Answer Grid

1. Ⓐ Ⓑ Ⓒ Ⓓ Ⓔ
2. Ⓐ Ⓑ Ⓒ Ⓓ Ⓔ
3. Ⓐ Ⓑ Ⓒ Ⓓ Ⓔ
4. Ⓐ Ⓑ Ⓒ Ⓓ Ⓔ
5. Ⓐ Ⓑ Ⓒ Ⓓ Ⓔ
6. Ⓐ Ⓑ Ⓒ Ⓓ Ⓔ
7. Ⓐ Ⓑ Ⓒ Ⓓ Ⓔ
8. Ⓐ Ⓑ Ⓒ Ⓓ Ⓔ
9. Ⓐ Ⓑ Ⓒ Ⓓ Ⓔ
10. Ⓐ Ⓑ Ⓒ Ⓓ Ⓔ
11. Ⓐ Ⓑ Ⓒ Ⓓ Ⓔ
12. Ⓐ Ⓑ Ⓒ Ⓓ Ⓔ
13. Ⓐ Ⓑ Ⓒ Ⓓ Ⓔ
14. Ⓐ Ⓑ Ⓒ Ⓓ Ⓔ
15. Ⓐ Ⓑ Ⓒ Ⓓ Ⓔ
16. Ⓐ Ⓑ Ⓒ Ⓓ Ⓔ
17. Ⓐ Ⓑ Ⓒ Ⓓ Ⓔ
18. Ⓐ Ⓑ Ⓒ Ⓓ Ⓔ
19. Ⓐ Ⓑ Ⓒ Ⓓ Ⓔ
20. Ⓐ Ⓑ Ⓒ Ⓓ Ⓔ

21. Ⓐ Ⓑ Ⓒ Ⓓ Ⓔ
22. Ⓐ Ⓑ Ⓒ Ⓓ Ⓔ
23. Ⓐ Ⓑ Ⓒ Ⓓ Ⓔ
24. Ⓐ Ⓑ Ⓒ Ⓓ Ⓔ
25. Ⓐ Ⓑ Ⓒ Ⓓ Ⓔ
26. Ⓐ Ⓑ Ⓒ Ⓓ Ⓔ
27. Ⓐ Ⓑ Ⓒ Ⓓ Ⓔ
28. Ⓐ Ⓑ Ⓒ Ⓓ Ⓔ
29. Ⓐ Ⓑ Ⓒ Ⓓ Ⓔ
30. Ⓐ Ⓑ Ⓒ Ⓓ Ⓔ
31. Ⓐ Ⓑ Ⓒ Ⓓ Ⓔ
32. Ⓐ Ⓑ Ⓒ Ⓓ Ⓔ
33. Ⓐ Ⓑ Ⓒ Ⓓ Ⓔ
34. Ⓐ Ⓑ Ⓒ Ⓓ Ⓔ
35. Ⓐ Ⓑ Ⓒ Ⓓ Ⓔ
36. Ⓐ Ⓑ Ⓒ Ⓓ Ⓔ
37. Ⓐ Ⓑ Ⓒ Ⓓ Ⓔ
38. Ⓐ Ⓑ Ⓒ Ⓓ Ⓔ
39. Ⓐ Ⓑ Ⓒ Ⓓ Ⓔ
40. Ⓐ Ⓑ Ⓒ Ⓓ Ⓔ

41. Ⓐ Ⓑ Ⓒ Ⓓ Ⓔ
42. Ⓐ Ⓑ Ⓒ Ⓓ Ⓔ
43. Ⓐ Ⓑ Ⓒ Ⓓ Ⓔ
44. Ⓐ Ⓑ Ⓒ Ⓓ Ⓔ
45. Ⓐ Ⓑ Ⓒ Ⓓ Ⓔ
46. Ⓐ Ⓑ Ⓒ Ⓓ Ⓔ
47. Ⓐ Ⓑ Ⓒ Ⓓ Ⓔ
48. Ⓐ Ⓑ Ⓒ Ⓓ Ⓔ
49. Ⓐ Ⓑ Ⓒ Ⓓ Ⓔ
50. Ⓐ Ⓑ Ⓒ Ⓓ Ⓔ
51. Ⓐ Ⓑ Ⓒ Ⓓ Ⓔ
52. Ⓐ Ⓑ Ⓒ Ⓓ Ⓔ
53. Ⓐ Ⓑ Ⓒ Ⓓ Ⓔ
54. Ⓐ Ⓑ Ⓒ Ⓓ Ⓔ
55. Ⓐ Ⓑ Ⓒ Ⓓ Ⓔ
56. Ⓐ Ⓑ Ⓒ Ⓓ Ⓔ
57. Ⓐ Ⓑ Ⓒ Ⓓ Ⓔ
58. Ⓐ Ⓑ Ⓒ Ⓓ Ⓔ
59. Ⓐ Ⓑ Ⓒ Ⓓ Ⓔ
60. Ⓐ Ⓑ Ⓒ Ⓓ Ⓔ

61. Ⓐ Ⓑ Ⓒ Ⓓ Ⓔ
62. Ⓐ Ⓑ Ⓒ Ⓓ Ⓔ
63. Ⓐ Ⓑ Ⓒ Ⓓ Ⓔ
64. Ⓐ Ⓑ Ⓒ Ⓓ Ⓔ
65. Ⓐ Ⓑ Ⓒ Ⓓ Ⓔ
66. Ⓐ Ⓑ Ⓒ Ⓓ Ⓔ
67. Ⓐ Ⓑ Ⓒ Ⓓ Ⓔ
68. Ⓐ Ⓑ Ⓒ Ⓓ Ⓔ
69. Ⓐ Ⓑ Ⓒ Ⓓ Ⓔ
70. Ⓐ Ⓑ Ⓒ Ⓓ Ⓔ
71. Ⓐ Ⓑ Ⓒ Ⓓ Ⓔ
72. Ⓐ Ⓑ Ⓒ Ⓓ Ⓔ
73. Ⓐ Ⓑ Ⓒ Ⓓ Ⓔ
74. Ⓐ Ⓑ Ⓒ Ⓓ Ⓔ
75. Ⓐ Ⓑ Ⓒ Ⓓ Ⓔ
76. Ⓐ Ⓑ Ⓒ Ⓓ Ⓔ
77. Ⓐ Ⓑ Ⓒ Ⓓ Ⓔ
78. Ⓐ Ⓑ Ⓒ Ⓓ Ⓔ
79. Ⓐ Ⓑ Ⓒ Ⓓ Ⓔ
80. Ⓐ Ⓑ Ⓒ Ⓓ Ⓔ

PRACTICE TEST 1

Section I: Multiple-Choice Questions

Time: 55 Minutes
80 Questions

Directions: Choose the best answer choice for the questions below.

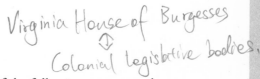

Virginia House of Burgesses
↕
Colonial Legislative bodies.

1. Four people were killed and 11 wounded at Kent State University in Ohio when

(A) protests grew violent, leading to clashes with federal troops.

(B) Nixon ordered all local police departments to crush student antiwar protests.

(C) male students fought with campus feminists.

(D) National Guard troops fired into a crowd of students at an antiwar protest.

(E) students protested the admittance of a black student into the university.

2. The wealthiest colonists on the eve of the American Revolution were

(A) doctors and lawyers.

(B) merchants.

(C) farmers.

(D) clergymen.

(E) skilled artisans.

3. Which of the following statements best describes the importance of the Virginia House of Burgesses?

(A) It failed miserably in establishing colonial rule.

(B) It was abolished immediately by King James I.

(C) It set the standard for more colonial legislative bodies that would follow.

(D) It established Puritanism as the official religion.

(E) It controlled the economy of all English colonies.

4. The population of the Southern United States increased dramatically between 1810 and 1860 due to

Slaves

(A) the Louisiana Purchase.

(B) the natural birth rate of African slaves.

(C) an increase in the number of imported slaves.

(D) Indian removal policies.

(E) the advent of the Lowell system.

GO ON TO THE NEXT PAGE ⟶

5. Advocates for peace such as Jane Addams won a temporary victory with the

(A) American entrance into the League of Nations.

(B) ratification of the Treaty of Versailles by the United States.

(C) annexation of Hawaii.

(D) Destroyers-for-Bases deal.

(E) signing of the Kellogg-Briand Pact.

1928 illegal of offensive warfare.

6. The best example of rising sectional tensions caused by westward expansion in antebellum America can be seen in

(A) the Treaty of Guadalupe-Hildago.

(B) the Bear Flag revolt.

(C) the Clayton-Bulwer Treaty.

(D) the Wilmot Proviso. — *Slavery should be banned*

(E) the failure to annex Texas.

ended Mexican war

admitted Main

7. The Compromise of 1820 (Missouri Compromise) provided for

(A) the end of slavery in the District of Columbia.

(B) admission of Maine as a free state and Missouri as a slave state.

(C) gradual emancipation of slaves south of the 36°30' line.

(D) slavery to be decided by popular sovereignty.

(E) the balance of power in the Senate to favor the South.

8. War Hawks in 1810 usually hailed from

(A) the South and West.

(B) New England.

(C) elite Federalist families.

(D) Middle states.

(E) the Deep South.

9. In the presidential election of 1984, Ronald Reagan

(A) barely escaped losing to Walter Mondale.

(B) won the election in a landslide.

(C) lost votes from women and youth.

(D) struggled to maintain his hold after the Iran-Contra scandal.

(E) gained a large following of African American voters.

10. President Lyndon Johnson struggled to keep his Great Society program afloat due to

(A) his desire to reduce voting rights for African Americans.

(B) congressional opposition to a withdrawal from Vietnam.

(C) government spending to keep missiles out of Cuba.

(D) increased protections of the environment.

(E) his failure to increase taxes to offset the cost of war and his programs.

11. The North American Free Trade Agreement (NAFTA)

(A) stipulated that Mexico and Canada agree to buy goods exclusively from the United States.

(B) set "most-favored-nation status" with China.

(C) began the development of a unified economic community like the European Union.

(D) attempted to lift most tariffs on goods sold across the international borders of the United States, Mexico, and Canada.

(E) was highly praised by organized labor in the United States

GO ON TO THE NEXT PAGE

12. The debate between the Federalists and the Anti-Federalists concerning the ratification of the Constitution mainly concerned

(A) allegiance to European allies.

(B) power of the states over power of a central government.

(C) slavery in the new nation.

(D) judicial review.

(E) a Bank of the United States.

13. U.S. involvement in the Vietnam War was

(A) approved by the UN Security Council.

(B) designed to root out Soviets in Asia.

(C) based on decisions by Republican presidents.

(D) born from a sense of responsibility stemming from the Truman Doctrine.

(E) officially declared a war by the Gulf of Tonkin resolution.

14. In the 1950s, the recording industry experienced massive growth because of

(A) crooners such as Frank Sinatra and Bing Crosby.

(B) Hollywood musicals.

(C) the advent of FM radio.

(D) transistor radios.

(E) rock and roll.

15. Hamilton's financial plan was designed primarily to

(A) prepare the new nation for a possible war with Britain.

(B) help protect the wealthy.

(C) improve the nation's credit standing and financial stability.

(D) find ways to export more products from the South.

(E) increase the country's industrial capacity.

16. By the end of the 17th century, the rise in the African slave trade could be attributed to

(A) the number of indentured servants who had served their contracted time and were now free.

(B) the low cost of African slaves as compared to white servants.

(C) revolts in Haiti and the Dominican Republic.

(D) the decline in the plantation economy.

(E) the rise of cotton as a cash crop.

17. Large numbers of Mexican immigrants were forced to return home during the

(A) 1860s.

(B) 1880s.

(C) 1910s.

(D) 1930s.

(E) 1960s.

GO ON TO THE NEXT PAGE

18. The Great Awakening had all of the following effects on American colonial society EXCEPT

(A) increased respect for traditional ministers.

(B) construction of universities to train clergy.

(C) establishment of new Protestant sects.

(D) greater emotion in church services.

(E) common religious experiences in various colonies.

19. The Puritans believed that their purpose in the colonies was to

(A) become an example of faith for the world to see.

(B) create a democracy that would model that of ancient Greece.

(C) abide by the rules of the Church of England.

(D) earn riches to send back to the mother country.

(E) forge an alliance with natives in order to gain power for England.

20. In response to the Great Depression, Franklin D. Roosevelt's initial policy for the agricultural sector aimed to

(A) keep agricultural goods priced low to encourage consumer purchase.

(B) stimulate farm production by paying for new equipment.

(C) encourage farmers to destroy their crops in order to increase prices.

(D) artificially stabilize prices with price ceilings and floors.

(E) cut federal aid to farmers in the Dust Bowl.

21. U.S. foreign policy in the years following World War II sought to

(A) cool down tensions between the United States and the Soviet Union.

(B) contain communism where it currently existed.

(C) appease Stalin by giving into small demands.

(D) provoke the Soviets into limited war situations.

(E) negotiate for the eventual Soviet takeover of Eastern Europe.

22. "I have the honor to state that I have carefully considered, in communication with my colleagues, the proposal . . . that a declaration should be made by foreign powers claiming "spheres of interest" in China as to their intentions in regard to the treatment of foreign trade and interest therein."

—British Foreign Minister, 1899

The statement above was prompted by the

(A) issuance of the Open Door Policy.

(B) annexation of the Philippines by the United States.

(C) U.S. involvement in the Boxer Rebellion.

(D) restatement of the Monroe Doctrine.

(E) signing of the Ostend Manifesto.

23. The approval by California voters in 1994 of Proposition 187 signaled

(A) public outrage over high property taxes.

(B) a desire to provide medical care for the poor.

(C) underlying tensions between whites and immigrants in the state.

(D) a desire to provide all immigrants with state services.

(E) the necessity of reforming urban ghettos to calm racial tensions.

GO ON TO THE NEXT PAGE

24. As a result of heavy debts left from the French and Indian War, the British Parliament decided to

(A) remove all British military posts in the colonies.

(B) hand Canada and Louisiana to the French.

(C) shift their attention to a war with the Netherlands.

(D) force the colonists to pay for the protection they had been provided.

(E) remove heavy tariffs on imported goods to stimulate the economy.

25. Which of the following statements best describes the reaction of the Kennedy administration to the Freedom Rides?

(A) It tried to remain noncommittal as the vote on the Civil Rights Act was approaching.

(B) Kennedy risked his political career by authorizing the use of force against violators of the Fifteenth Amendment.

(C) At the urging of his brother Robert, President Kennedy finally sent federal troops to end the violence.

(D) It denounced the freedom rides as a publicity stunt and asked for them to stop.

(E) Kennedy personally greeted the riders as they completed their last stop.

26. The fight for "bread-and-butter" economic issues was organized by

(A) the Populists.

(B) the Republican Party.

(C) the Knights of Labor.

(D) the American Federation of Labor.

(E) the Women's Christian Temperance Union.

27. Laissez faire economic policies of the late 19th and early 20th centuries encouraged

(A) high tariffs.

(B) powerful labor unions.

(C) tighter monetary policy.

(D) horizontal and vertical integration.

(E) fair trade and labor practices.

28. The Carter administration faced its greatest policy challenges in the realm of

(A) energy conservation.

(B) social programs.

(C) economic issues.

(D) Latin American affairs.

(E) relations between Egypt and Israel.

29. Which conflict is generally considered to be the end of Indian Wars?

(A) Battle of Little Bighorn

(B) Battle of Tippecanoe

(C) Battle of Fallen Timbers

(D) Battle of Wounded Knee

(E) Second Seminole War

assimilation of natives.

30. The Dawes Severalty Act of 1887 was designed to

(A) place tribes back on federally granted reservations.

(B) protect the culture and traditions of Native Americans.

(C) force the assimilation of Native Americans into "American" society.

(D) end the protective relationship between the federal government and the tribes.

(E) sever the ties between warring tribes to promote peace.

GO ON TO THE NEXT PAGE

31. All of the following were proponents of "manifest destiny" EXCEPT

    (A) voters for James K. Polk.
    (B) Whig Party members during the Mexican War.
    (C) Southern slave owners.
    (D) Northern Democrats.
    (E) supporters of the Treaty of Paris (1898), which ended the Spanish-American War.

32. Which of the following statements BEST reflects President Eisenhower's stance on civil rights in the 1950s?

    (A) He invited Martin Luther King, Jr., to the White House to strengthen the connection between government and civil rights leaders.
    (B) He publicly stated that he thought segregation should be protected.
    (C) He made it a point to place civil rights issues high on his presidential agenda.
    (D) He reluctantly sent in federal troops to integrate a high school in Little Rock.
    (E) He asked the Supreme Court to take a more active role in deciding civil rights cases.

33. The Pentagon Papers were

    (A) a series of articles written by two young *Washington Post* reporters regarding the Watergate break-in.
    (B) the blueprints for the design of the Pentagon building.
    (C) classified Vietnam War-related documents leaked by Daniel Ellsberg to the *New York Times*.
    (D) transcripts linking the CIA to the coup overthrowing Ngo Dinh Diem.
    (E) plans for the invasion of Cuba.

34. John Foster Dulles is most closely associated with which of the following?

    (A) MAD (mutually assured destruction)
    (B) Massive retaliation
    (C) The Bay of Pigs Invasion
    (D) Containment
    (E) Détente

35. Throughout the 1970s, the gross domestic product (GDP) in the United States

    (A) grew dramatically.
    (B) stagnated.
    (C) declined rapidly.
    (D) diversified with new innovations.
    (E) outpaced that of Japan and Germany.

36. Americans who were most likely to approve of the Articles of Confederation were

    (A) wary of a central government wielding too much power.
    (B) against strong states' rights.
    (C) New England merchants.
    (D) enlightened members of the Northern elite.
    (E) antislavery Quakers.

37. The Employment Act of 1946 was significant in that it

    (A) protected the rights of union members to bargain collectively.
    (B) outlawed child labor.
    (C) prevented discriminatory hiring practices based on race.
    (D) established the federal goal of full employment.
    (E) formed the Job Corps.

GO ON TO THE NEXT PAGE

38. All of the following statements correctly characterize the United States in the 1920s EXCEPT

(A) There was a rebirth of African American literature, art, and culture.

(B) The Volstead Act was followed by all Americans.

(C) The average American saw an increase in standard of living.

(D) American farmers fared worse than before World War I.

(E) Mass consumption of consumer goods by the middle class increased dramatically.

39. The settlement of the Jamestown Colony in Virginia survived as a result of

(A) adherence to a strict Puritan work ethic.

(B) the planting of tobacco as a cash crop.

(C) the ability of the settlers to avoid confrontation with Native Americans.

(D) the leadership of Jonathan Edwards.

(E) financial assistance from England.

40. The Roosevelt Corollary to the Monroe Doctrine sought to

(A) maintain U.S. influence over the affairs of Latin American countries.

(B) keep China open to foreign trade markets.

(C) force the Spanish to leave the Philippines.

(D) end the Russo-Japanese War.

(E) establish a U.S. presence in the building of the Panama Canal.

41. The main purpose of Black Codes was to

(A) ensure justice for freemen.

(B) guarantee emancipation for slaves.

(C) provide free public education to freedmen.

(D) grant land and mules to ex-slaves.

(E) limit the ability of ex-slaves to integrate into Southern society.

42. The World Wide Web

(A) had been in use by governments all over the world since the 1960s.

(B) was the brainchild of Bill Gates.

(C) was invented by Al Gore when he served in Congress.

(D) originated in 1989 as a method to connect the computers of physics researchers.

(E) was the predecessor of the Internet.

43. Writings that encouraged individualism and a connection to nature were most evident in the works of

(A) George Whitefield.

(B) Elizabeth Cady Stanton.

(C) Washington Irving.

(D) Henry David Thoreau.

(E) Booker T. Washington.

GO ON TO THE NEXT PAGE

44. The Triangular Trade network of the 18th century sought to

   (A) cut out the middleman in trade transactions.

   (B) increase the reliance of the French on American goods.

   (C) circumvent the Navigation Acts by engaging in illegal trade.

   (D) provide protection for Spanish gold runners in the Caribbean.

   (E) halt the importation of African slaves.

45. The Great Compromise (Connecticut Compromise) provided for

   (A) a balance of power between the states and the federal government.

   (B) checks and balances among the three branches of government.

   (C) complete abandonment of the Articles of Confederation.

   (D) a plan for apportionment of congressional representatives.

   (E) the levying of income taxes.

46. The period of high inflation and high unemployment in the 1970s was commonly referred to as

   (A) depression.

   (B) recession.

   (C) a trough.

   (D) supply-side economics.

   (E) stagflation.

47. European contact with Native Americans between 1500 and 1700 did all of the following EXCEPT

   (A) encourage the use of European farming techniques.

   (B) lead to the formation of new tribes.

   (C) force once large native settlements to disband.

   (D) prove lethal as new diseases were introduced into the population.

   (E) lead to the extensive enslavement of natives for work on plantations.

48. The 1954 Supreme Court decision in *Brown v. Board of Education* overturned

   (A) *Plessy v. Ferguson.*

   (B) *Marbury v. Madison.*

   (C) *Dred Scott v. Sandford.*

   (D) *Worcester v. Georgia.*

   (E) *Sweatt v. Painter.*

49. As a result of advancements in transportation in the 1820s,

   (A) agriculture overtook industry in the North.

   (B) once viable cities along the Erie Canal became ghost towns.

   (C) regional specialization developed in the United States.

   (D) the federal government became more involved in funding internal improvements.

   (E) transport of cotton to New England became more viable on canals.

GO ON TO THE NEXT PAGE

CITY AND RURAL DWELLERS 1860–1920

Year	City	Rural
1860	6,216,518	25,226,803
1870	9,902,361	28,656,010
1880	14,129,735	36,059,474
1890	22,106,265	40,873,501
1900	30,214,832	45,997,336
1910	42,064,001	50,164,495
1920	54,253,282	51,768,255

50. Which of the following statements is supported by the information provided in the chart above?

(A) The Civil War had a major impact on population growth.

(B) Immigration quotas helped to stem the growth of urban areas.

(C) Western states did not experience as much growth as the North.

(D) The rise of industry did much to fuel the move from the farm to the city.

(E) City growth significantly slowed after World War I.

51. "You cannot possibly have a broader basis for government than that which includes all the people, with all their rights in their hands, and with an equal power to maintain their rights."

—William Lloyd Garrison

These words would most likely have come from

(A) the Free-Soil Party platform.

(B) sermons of the Second Great Awakening.

(C) the abolitionist paper *The Liberator*.

(D) the book *Cannibals All*.

(E) Reconstruction congressional records.

52. Operation Desert Storm in 1991 began after

(A) Libyan militants attacked a discotheque in Lebanon, killing 283 U.S. Marines.

(B) the United Nations Security Council authorized the use of force against the Iraqi invasion of Kuwait.

(C) American hostages were taken by Iranian revolutionaries at the U.S. Embassy.

(D) Congress declared war against Iraq and Saddam Hussein.

(E) terrorists bombed the USS *Cole* in Yemen.

GO ON TO THE NEXT PAGE

53. The clearest reason why the United States entered World War I was

(A) the failure of European colonies.

(B) the Central Powers capture of Poland.

(C) to ensure adherence to the Monroe Doctrine.

(D) to protect Britain so she could pay her war debts.

(E) continued violations of U.S. neutrality by German U-Boats.

54. Shays' Rebellion worked to convince many Americans that

(A) excise taxes should be lowered.

(B) the United States needed to have a stronger relationship with France.

(C) frontier settlers should arm themselves against British troops in the west.

(D) the central government of the United States should be stronger.

(E) Native American tribes could not be trusted.

55. An important factor contributing to the Great Depression in the United States in the 1930s was the

(A) large military expenditure in the 1920s.

(B) decline in farm prosperity during the 1920s.

(C) redistribution of wealth due to stock market successes.

(D) increased importation of foreign goods.

(E) increase in population due to immigration.

56. All of the following occurred during the Second World War EXCEPT

(A) a dramatic increase of married women entering the paid workforce.

(B) the forced relocation of Japanese-Americans from the West Coast to camps in the interior.

(C) the prohibition of interstate travel without government permission.

(D) the federal rationing of gasoline and sugar.

(E) an increase in African American immigration to urban areas.

57. All of the following were provisions of Henry Clay's American System EXCEPT

(A) high protective tariffs.

(B) the building of a national road.

(C) federal subsidies to Southern farmers.

(D) the recharter of the Bank of the United States.

(E) federally financed internal improvements.

58. All of the following were factors in the failure of the United States to join the League of Nations after the First World War EXCEPT

(A) fear of further involvement in foreign wars.

(B) personal and political rivalries between President Woodrow Wilson and Senator Henry Cabot Lodge.

(C) President Wilson's illness.

(D) a group of U.S. senators who opposed American participation on any terms.

(E) the influence of the Soviet Union within the League.

GO ON TO THE NEXT PAGE ⇨

59. Cherokee Indians who had been told to move from their homelands found significant support from

(A) settlers of the Great Plains.

(B) abolitionists such as Garrison.

(C) the Supreme Court.

(D) the executive branch.

(E) the legislative branch.

60. The Salem Witch Trials in 1692 were

(A) a product of poisoning of the colonists by native tribes.

(B) indicative of social and economic tensions among colonists.

(C) a phenomenon isolated to Salem.

(D) attacks by elite women on poorer citizens.

(E) isolated to the hunting of female victims.

61. The "Revolution of 1800" was significant because

(A) power was peacefully passed from the Federalists to the Democratic Republicans.

(B) the United States finally ended the threat of Native Americans in the west.

(C) Jefferson was elected by popular vote.

(D) American foreign policy strengthened towards Britain.

(E) Southerners successfully defended their right to hold slaves.

62. Which of the following led to the Soviet cancellation of peace talks with President Eisenhower in 1960?

(A) The Kitchen Debate

(B) The U-2 incident

(C) The launch of Sputnik

(D) The creation of NASA

(E) The end of détente

63. The Equal Rights Amendment (ERA)

(A) was a new amendment proposed in 1970 by Betty Friedan and NOW.

(B) was pocket-vetoed by President Eisenhower.

(C) split the feminist movement, with moderates and radicals disagreeing over the scope of the provisions.

(D) was passed and ratified in 1986.

(E) was passed in 1972 but failed to get the necessary number of state ratifications to become an Amendment.

64. All of the following correctly describe the Lend-Lease program of the early 1940s EXCEPT

(A) It was welcomed and accepted by all Americans.

(B) It was a public agreement rather than a secretive prewar deal.

(C) It was intended to send a strong message to the Axis powers.

(D) It signaled the end of American neutrality.

(E) It started the real mobilization effort in American industry.

GO ON TO THE NEXT PAGE

65. The stock market crash of 1929 was precipitated by

(A) a rapid rise in unemployment.

(B) plunging farm prices.

(C) a decrease in buying on credit.

(D) a drop in the standard of living.

(E) decreased supplies of large consumer goods.

66. The treatment of native populations by Spanish explorers in current-day Mexico and the American Southwest is best described as

(A) congenial and helpful.

(B) purely driven by Christian motives.

(C) harsh and unprincipled.

(D) open to the possibility of cohabitation.

(E) curious and analytical.

67. Originally, the convention that led to the drafting of the Constitution was called to

(A) scrap the Articles and begin anew.

(B) establish more stringent foreign policy.

(C) create a system to handle disputes with Native Americans.

(D) finalize the independence of the nation from Britain.

(E) revise the Articles of Confederation.

68. President's Reagan's use of supply-side economics presupposed that

(A) wealth needed to be redistributed to close the poverty gap.

(B) the first priority should be to balance the federal budget.

(C) increased government spending was needed to stimulate the economy.

(D) tax cuts to middle- and high-income Americans would stimulate investment.

(E) the government needed to lower interest rates.

69. The tariff controversy that began in 1828 rekindled the

(A) discussion of a federal income tax.

(B) fight over the reelection of Martin Van Buren.

(C) spirit of open trade between the United States and Britain.

(D) argument over federal involvement into internal improvements.

(E) controversy over the doctrine of nullification.

70. The Emancipation Proclamation had the immediate impact of

(A) weakening the morale of troops in the Confederacy.

(B) shifting the purpose of the war to a moral fight.

(C) turning more would-be Democrats into Republicans in the Border States.

(D) reducing Union troop desertions.

(E) abolitionists celebrating the success of immediate emancipation.

GO ON TO THE NEXT PAGE

71. Despite a surge in popularity due to the success of Operation Desert Storm, President George Bush's political momentum suffered from

    (A) a lack of attention to domestic issues.
    (B) a resurgence of communist aggression.
    (C) failure to sign SALT II.
    (D) embarrassment over the failure of an invasion of Panama.
    (E) the hostage crisis in Iran.

72. After the Civil War, the railroad industry boomed because of

    (A) mass immigration of Chinese to the west.
    (B) vertical integration.
    (C) the rise in the cost of capital goods.
    (D) the success of the Interstate Commerce Commission.
    (E) massive government land grants.

73. Tension and fighting between Britain and France spilled over to North America during the

    (A) War of Polish Succession.
    (B) Metacom's War.
    (C) Seven Years' War.
    (D) Anglo-Franco War.
    (E) French Wars of Religion.

74. President Truman furthered the cause of civil rights by

    (A) authorizing Jackie Robinson to play baseball in the Major Leagues.
    (B) integrating public schools.
    (C) desegregating the armed forces.
    (D) ordering the desegregation of all public facilities.
    (E) demanding the resignation of Huey P. Long.

75. Native American tribes experienced a cultural shift before Columbus landed in the New World when

    (A) domesticated horses were introduced.
    (B) intricate irrigation systems were created.
    (C) outbreaks of smallpox ravaged the continent.
    (D) contact with Asians brought firearms to the continent.
    (E) knowledge of the growing of corn moved up from Mesoamerica.

76. In the late 19th century, various groups of Americans responded to the influx of large numbers of "new immigrants" by

    (A) opening better processing centers at ports of entry.
    (B) offering opportunities to immigrants who were seeking jobs.
    (C) establishing strict "quota" laws that limited immigration.
    (D) allowing for a speedy gain of U.S. citizenship.
    (E) welcoming Jews and Catholics more than in previous times.

GO ON TO THE NEXT PAGE

77. Nativists were primarily interested in

   (A) decreasing taxes and tariffs.

   (B) protecting the rights of organized labor.

   (C) lifting immigration restrictions on Asians.

   (D) rights for former slaves.

   (E) restricting privileges for immigrants.

78. In the Supreme Court decision in *Roe v. Wade*, it was ruled that

   (A) there are no protections of a woman's right to abortion in the Constitution.

   (B) states have the right to ban all methods of abortion.

   (C) the Constitution protects a woman's right to privacy in the matter of abortion.

   (D) states cannot regulate the distribution of contraceptives by doctors and clinics.

   (E) states have no right to set laws prohibiting the sale of pornographic material.

79. The cartoon shown above was drawn by Benjamin Franklin in 1756 to gain support for

   (A) the Declaration of Independence.

   (B) the Albany Plan of Union.

   (C) the Hartford Convention.

   (D) the Stamp Act Congress.

   (E) the Revolutionary War.

80. The Mayflower Compact is best described as

   (A) an intricate framework of central government.

   (B) a royal charter.

   (C) a declaration of freedom from the bonds of England.

   (D) a foundation for self-government.

   (E) an allegiance to the Church of England.

STOP

Section II: Free-Response Questions

Time—130 minutes

This section contains five free-response questions. Answer the Document-Based question in Part A, one of the essay questions in Part B, and one of the essay questions in Part C. The first 15 minutes of the 130 minutes allocated for Section 2 is a reading period. During this period, you should read the Document-Based question and plan what you will write, including taking many notes. However, you cannot begin to write your essay until the 15-minute reading period has ended.

PART A: DOCUMENT-BASED QUESTION

Suggested writing time: 45 minutes

The following question requires you to write a coherent essay incorporating your interpretation of the documents and your knowledge of the period specified in the question. To earn a high score, you are required to cite key pieces of evidence from the documents and draw on your knowledge of the period.

1. Using your knowledge of the periods 1830–1850 and 1880–1900 and Documents A–I, construct a coherent thesis that compares and contrasts antebellum and Progressive reform movements. Be sure to address the social, political, and economic impact of each movement in your answer.

DOCUMENT A

Extracted from the dying Declaration of Nicholas Fernandez, who, with nine others, was executed in front of Cadiz Harbor in December 1829 for piracy and murder:

"Parents into whose hands this my dying declaration may fall will perceive that I date the commencement of my departure from the paths of rectitude and virtue, from the moment when I become addicted to the habitual use of ardent spirits—and it is my sincere prayer that if they value the happiness of their children—if they desire their welfare here, and their eternal well being hereafter, that they early teach them the fatal consequences of Intemperance!"

DOCUMENT B

William Lloyd Garrison, 1830

"Even the 'glorious gospel of the blessed God,' which brings life and immortality to perishing man, is as a sealed book to his understanding. Nor has his wretched condition been imposed upon him for any criminal offence. He has not been tried by the laws of his country. No one has stepped forth to vindicate his rights. He is made an abject slave, simply because God has given him a skin not colored like his master's; and Death, the great Liberator, alone can break his fetters!"

DOCUMENT C

Angelina Emily Grimke, Letter XII (October 2, 1837), *Letters to Catherine E. Beecher* (Boston: I. Knapp, 1838)

"The regulation of duty by the mere circumstance of sex, rather than by the fundamental principle of moral being, has led to all that multifarious train of evils flowing out of the anti-Christian doctrine of masculine and feminine virtues. By this doctrine, man has been converted into the warrior, and clothed with sternness . . . whilst woman has been taught to . . . sit as a dollar arrayed in "gold, and pearls, and costly array," to be admired for her personal charms, and caressed and humored like a spoiled child, or converted into a mere drudge to suit the convenience of her lord and master . . . ."

DOCUMENT D

Brigham Young, 1854 letter to Thomas Kane

"In our Mountain home we feel not the withering sources of influence of political or even fashionable despotism. We breathe free air, drink from the cool mountain stream, and feel strong in the free exercise of outdoor life. I have traveled on several hundred miles this season among the native tribes, to conciliate their hostile feelings, and cause them to become friends. I have found the satisfaction of having been eminently successful, and peace again smiles upon all our settlements, and that too without a resort to arms."

DOCUMENT E

Eyewitness Account of the Triangle Shirtwaist Factory Fire, 1911

"I was upstairs in our work-room," said he, "when one of the employees who happened to be looking out of the window cried that there was a fire around the corner. I rushed downstairs, and when I reached the sidewalk the girls were already jumping from the windows. None of them moved after they struck the sidewalk. Several men ran up with a net which they got somewhere, and I seized one side of it to help them hold it.

"It was about ten feet square and we managed to catch about fifteen girls. I don't believe we saved over one or two however. The fall was so great that they bounced to the sidewalk after striking the net. Bodies were falling all around us, and two or three of the men with me were knocked down. The girls just leaped wildly out of the windows and turned over and over before reaching the sidewalk.

"I only saw one man jump. All the rest were girls. They stood on the windowsills tearing their hair out in the handfuls and then they jumped . . . ."

DOCUMENT F

Jane Addams, 1885

"Teaching in a Settlement requires distinct methods, for it is true of people who have been allowed to remain undeveloped and whose facilities are inert and sterile, that they cannot take their learning heavily. It has to be diffused in a social atmosphere, information must be held in solution, in a medium of fellowship and good will. . . . It is needless to say that a Settlement is a protest against a restricted view of education."

DOCUMENT G

The Volstead Act, 1919

"The term 'War Prohibition Act' used in this Act shall mean the provisions of any Act or Acts prohibiting the sale and manufacture of intoxicating liquors until the conclusion of the present war and thereafter until the termination of demobilization, the date of which shall be determined and proclaimed by the President of the United States. The words 'beer, wine, or other intoxicating malt or vinous liquors' in the War Prohibition Act shall be hereafter construed to mean any such beverages which contain one-half of 1 per centum or more of alcohol by volume."

DOCUMENT H

The Moral Thermometer,
Benjamin Rush, 1790

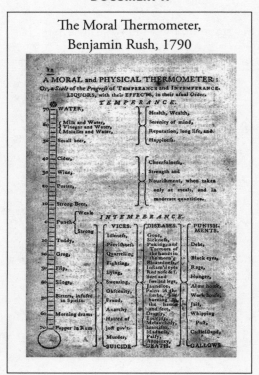

DOCUMENT I

Temperence Poster, 1874

PART B

Suggested time: 35 minutes

Directions: Choose ONE question from this part. You are advised to spend 5 minutes planning and 30 minutes writing your answer.

2. Assess the impact of TWO of the following with regard to the formation of American foreign policy.

   George Washington

   Thomas Jefferson

   James Monroe

3. British colonies had distinct views with regard to gender and social status. Compare and contrast the views of the New England colonies to those of the Middle Colonies in terms of women, the poor, and slaves.

PART C

Suggested time: 35 minutes

Directions: Choose ONE question from this part. You are advised to spend 5 minutes planning and 30 minutes writing your answer.

4. Popular sovereignty seemed to be the perfect solution to the problem of slavery in new territories. Analyze the problems with popular sovereignty and explain why it was not successful.

5. The Monroe Doctrine became the basis of American foreign policy in the late 19th century. Evaluate the validity of this statement, giving specific examples to support your thesis.

STOP

PRACTICE TEST 1 ANSWER KEY

1.	D	21.	B	41.	E	61.	A
2.	B	22.	A	42.	D	62.	B
3.	C	23.	C	43.	D	63.	E
4.	B	24.	D	44.	C	64.	A
5.	E	25.	C	45.	D	65.	B
6.	D	26.	D	46.	E	66.	C
7.	B	27.	D	47.	E	67.	E
8.	A	28.	C	48.	A	68.	D
9.	B	29.	E	49.	C	69.	E
10.	E	30.	C	50.	D	70.	B
11.	D	31.	B	51.	C	71.	A
12.	B	32.	D	52.	B	72.	E
13.	D	33.	C	53.	E	73.	C
14.	E	34.	B	54.	D	74.	C
15.	C	35.	B	55.	B	75.	E
16.	A	36.	A	56.	C	76.	C
17.	D	37.	D	57.	C	77.	E
18.	A	38.	B	58.	E	78.	C
19.	A	39.	B	59.	C	79.	B
20.	C	40.	A	60.	B	80.	D

ANSWERS AND EXPLANATIONS

MULTIPLE CHOICE

1. D

An otherwise peaceful rally became bloody when National Guards troops fired upon student protesters and passers-by at Kent State University in 1970. As students marched to protest the newly discovered secret bombings of Cambodia, nervous National Guards stood watch, and someone fired a shot. It is still not clear who fired. In the end, four young college students died.

2. B

Men who dealt in the buying and selling of manufactured goods were by far the most revered and moneyed in the colonies by 1775. Doctors and lawyers had little to no schooling, and many considered them to be crooks and liars. Even though 90 percent of all colonists were involved in agriculture, very few were making any sizable amount of money from it. Skilled artisans, such as carpenters and cobblers, relied on merchants to get their goods to market, often losing profits along the way.

3. C

Following the lead of the House of Burgesses, many more small legislative bodies formed to establish some form of "self-rule." While not fully in control of their own destiny, the House of Burgesses did allow for colonials to establish some law and order that resembled that of a sovereign nation.

4. B

The African slave population in the United States more than tripled between 1810 and 1860 due to natural birth rates. The Louisiana Purchase did not add many new citizens but rather land and the Native Americans living on that land. Slave importation actually dropped in the time period mentioned. The Lowell System was in New England and concerned the textile industry.

5. E

The Kellogg-Briand Pact of 1928 was an agreement of 62 participating nations to make illegal the use of offensive warfare. Unfortunately, the pact did not have any provisions for enforcement or punishment for offenders. The United States never entered the League of Nations, nor did it ever ratify the Treaty of Versailles. The annexation of Hawaii in 1896 and the Destroyers-for-Bases deal in 1940 would not have pleased Addams or other peace advocates.

6. D

As the United States spread westward, adding new territories, tension rose over the balance between free and slave states in Congress. The Wilmot Proviso dramatically contributed to those rising tensions when it proposed that slavery should be banned from all of the territories gained from the Mexican Cession. Although the Wilmot Proviso did not pass the Senate—as the Southern states successfully engineered its defeat—it nonetheless stood as a dangerous symbol in the eyes of Southerners that Northerners sought to tip the sectional balance in favor of the free states. The Treaty of Guadalupe-Hildago ended the Mexican War but did not stipulate any language regarding slavery. The Bear Flag revolt was a small coup staged by American settlers in California in 1846, where they drove the Mexican governor from the region. The Clayton-Bulwer Treaty was the first attempt by the United States to secure the building of a canal through the Isthmus of Panama. Texas was annexed by the United States in 1845.

7. B

When Missouri petitioned for admission as a slave state in 1819, tensions ran high, as the delicate balance of power between North and South was about to tip in the South's favor. Congressman James Tallmadge crafted a two-part compromise that would allow for the admission of two states (one free and one slave) to maintain the balance, as well as the prohibition of slavery north of the 36°30' line. Slavery was ended in the District of Columbia as a result of the Civil War. The slave trade in the nation's capital and popular sovereignty in the Mexican Cession were instituted by the Compromise of 1850.

8. A

Those who wished to defend American rights, gain more territory, and rid the nation of the Native American threat mostly lived in the West and South. War Hawks demanded a response to the continued violations of U.S. neutrality and arming of natives on the frontier by the British. New Englanders and Federalists were among the most ardent opponents to war, as they stood to lose valuable trade relationships with Britain if war occurred. The Middle and Deep South states were divided in their opinions over a possible war.

9. B

President Reagan's popularity was riding high by the time the election of 1984 rolled around. He handily defeated former Vice President Mondale by maintaining his hold on votes from conservatives, women, and the young. News of the Iran-Contra Affair did not break until 1986. African American voters were largely not fond of President Reagan.

10. E

President Lyndon Johnson struggled with his passion for improving American society and his refusal to let Vietnam fall to the communists. Upon taking office after the assassination of John Kennedy, Johnson passed a massive income tax cut that would severely limit the government's ability to fund both a war on poverty at home and a war on ideology overseas. He decided to focus on the war in Vietnam by escalating U.S. involvement, which eventually led to inflation and a premature end to many of Johnson's Great Society dreams.

11. D

President Clinton had a tough time selling NAFTA to conservative Republicans, moderate Democrats, and organized labor during the 1990s. The agreement, finally ratified in 1994, sought to create a tariff-free zone on the North American continent.

It was not an attempt at an EU-type system, in that the three participating countries still had autonomy over their own currencies and economic systems. "Most-favored-nation" status or "normal trade relations" has been granted to China under a special presidential waiver since 1980.

12. B

Federalists, led by men such as George Washington and James Madison, were quick to point out the necessity of a strong central government. The Anti-Federalists, led by George Mason and Patrick Henry, were fearful that a strong central power would diminish the rights of men that Americans had won in the American Revolution. Problems with European allies became an issue very soon for the new nation. The slavery debate had been temporarily settled in the drafting of the original Constitution with the Three-fifths Compromise and the agreement to abolish the slave trade in 1808. Judicial review and the development of the Bank of the United States were issues dealt with after the ratification of the Constitution in 1789.

13. D

It was the Truman Doctrine that set Cold War foreign policy with regard to communism. By pledging to intervene on behalf of any country under threat of communist takeover, the United States became the world's policeman for democracy. The aim in Vietnam was not to remove Soviets but to prevent the regime of Ho Chi Minh from influencing South Vietnam. The blame for the war can be placed on both Republicans (Eisenhower and Nixon) as well as Democrats (Truman, Kennedy, and Johnson). The Vietnam War was never declared an official war by Congress.

14. E

A form of music that came from African American jazz and blues, with some country style mixed in for good measure, rock and roll created a sound that made parents across the nation shake their heads in distaste. The baby boomers were becoming teenagers during the 1950s and flooded to local record shops to pick up the latest singles from Elvis Presley and Buddy Holly. FM and transistor radios did not gain popular use until the 1960s and 1970s.

15. C

While Alexander Hamilton was a friend of industry and the wealthy, his main goal was to get the new nation on its feet financially. He believed that no nation could be successful if it did not have a sound economy.

16. A

Wealthy landowners had to find new sources of labor when white indentured servants ended their time of service and became free. While African slaves were not cheap, they were easier to manage than white servants, who felt superior simply due to the color of their skin. As the plantation economy grew, so did the need for more and more labor.

17. D

Mexican immigrants had flooded California's San Joaquin Valley in order to help pick the bumper crops of the 1920s. As the number of white migrants, or "Okies," increased during the Dust Bowl years of the 1930s, many Mexicans were forcibly removed from the American West and Southwest to make room.

18. A

The Great Awakening served to deteriorate the respect of traditional ministers, also known as "Old Lights." "New Lights," such as Jonathan Edwards and George Whitefield, preached a different religious view that encouraged the expression of emotion and united colonists in common religious experience. Universities such as Harvard and Yale were established to train the large number of new clergy demanded.

19. A

John Winthrop's desire for the Puritans to build a "City on a Hill" (outlined in his *Model of Christian Charity*) best described the goals of the Puritans as they set sail for the Massachusetts Bay Colony. To be a beacon of hope, faith, and Godliness was the number one goal for the Puritans.

20. C

The Agricultural Adjustment Act (1933) worked to encourage farmers to plow under surplus crops to cause a supply dip, which would increase the price of goods. Farmers were paid subsidies to supplement the difference between the loss of crops and market prices.

21. B

Soviet expert and advisor to President Truman, George Kennan, insisted on a policy that would keep communism contained within its existing areas of Europe. His hope was that eventually the communists would have to back away from their aggressive goal of world domination and that democracy would prevail.

22. A

Secretary of State John Hay issued the Open Door Policy to protect regions of China falling victim to European and Japanese colonization. He was also concerned in the protection of American trade with China. Technically, the United States never annexed the Philippines but ruled it instead as a protectorate. The United States was involved in the rescue effort during the Boxer Rebellion, which occurred in 1900. The Monroe Doctrine was not applicable to Asia. The Ostend Manifesto (1854) dealt with U.S. insistence that Cuba was better off in U.S. hands rather than left on its own.

23. C

Proposition 187 was passed in 1994 to keep illegal immigrants from using state public services, such as public schools, medical care, and welfare. The law served to highlight the fears of whites and conservatives in California of becoming a minority in their state. The law was challenged in court immediately and was eventually repealed by Governor Gray Davis.

24. D

To shoulder the war debts left from the Seven Years' and French and Indian Wars, Britain needed the colonists to pay a share of the burden. The French surrendered all territorial claims in North America in the peace settlement that ended the war. The Netherlands was not a concern of the British in the 1750s. Tariffs would actually be increased to bleed revenue further from the colonies.

25. C
Much like his Democratic predecessors, Kennedy needed the Southern vote to secure many of his proposals for social and political reform. Therefore, he was reluctant at first to become involved in the civil rights debate. After violence that left many injured, some critically, Robert Kennedy urged his brother to act. It was at that point that the Kennedy White House was no longer noncommittal with regard to civil rights.

26. D
Samuel Gompers, founder and leader of the American Federation of Labor, prided himself on the union's goal of fighting for shorter working hours, better pay, and safer workplaces, or what he called "bread-and-butter" issues. The Knights of Labor had become a bit more radical in their bid for recognition by asking for change that sounded more socialist than most Americans were comfortable with. The Republican Party was not a friend of organized labor; rather it traditionally protected big business. The Populists were involved in agricultural issues, while the WCTU focused on alcohol prohibition and women's rights.

27. D
Integration of American businesses led to the huge trusts and monopolies of the 1880s and 1900s. The hands-off policy of the federal government enabled men such as Carnegie and Rockefeller to grow their fortunes unfettered.

28. C
The Carter administration never got itself out from under the horrible economic recession that had begun during the Nixon/Ford years. Some of President Carter's lasting contributions were the Department of Energy, Social Security reforms, and the Camp David Accords, which calmed relations between Egypt and Israel.

29. D
The Battle of Wounded Knee, 1890, is generally considered to be the end of Indian Wars in the United States. All the other Native American battles happened earlier: Battle of Little Bighorn,

1876; Battle of Tippecanoe, 1811; Battle of Fallen Timbers, 1794; Second Seminole War happened in the late 1830s.

30. C
The main goal of the Dawes Act was to assimilate Native Americans forcibly into white society by removing them from their reservations and opening up schools to teach them typical American etiquette. As a result, many native cultures and traditions were destroyed. By this time, there were few tribes left to be at "war."

31. B
Whigs, who largely opposed manifest destiny, claimed that the Mexican War was being waged purely to protect the interests of slave expansionists. Those who voted for Polk in 1844 wanted a president who would expand the borders of the country. Southern slave owners and Northern Democrats both believed that expansion would be good for the economy. The Treaty of Paris, which ended the Spanish-American War, extended manifest destiny overseas with many island acquisitions.

32. D
Integrating Central High School was the first nationally recognized test of the Supreme Court ruling in *Brown v. Board* (1954). When it looked as if violence would erupt in the face of integration, President Eisenhower reluctantly ordered federal troops to protect and personally escort the nine African American students to their classes. In all other cases, Eisenhower avoided the civil rights issue and even remarked that his appointment of Earl Warren to the Supreme Court had been "the biggest damn fool mistake I ever made."

33. C
Former Department of Defense employee Daniel Ellsberg leaked the Pentagon Papers to the *New York Times* in 1971. President Nixon sought to prevent them from being published but was overruled by the Supreme Court. The release of the papers increased the credibility gap in the eyes of the American public, as it was discovered that the Johnson

administration in the 1960s had lied with regard to American intentions in Vietnam.

34. B

Brinksmanship, the "New Look" military, and massive retaliation were all hallmarks of Dulles's foreign policy during the Eisenhower administration and were designed to deal directly with the communist threat. MAD was largely formulated during the 1960s by Secretary of Defense Robert McNamara. The Bay of Pigs invasion is most commonly attributed to President Kennedy. Containment lies with Truman and détente with Nixon.

35. B

The 1970s would be known for "stagflation," a period of high unemployment and high inflation that the government was virtually powerless to control.

36. A

Southern representatives to the Second Continental Congress held fast to the notion of preserving strong states' rights and a weak central government. New Englanders were not sure that a weak central government would be most effective but opted to compromise to start the nation off on the right foot. Slavery was very much a states' rights issue, one that Quakers would be against.

37. D

By firmly establishing the goal of federal government fiscal policy as maintaining full employment, the Employment Act of 1946 more or less "depression proofed" the American economy. Child labor was banned in 1938 by the Fair Labor Standards Act. Discriminatory hiring practices were not addressed until the Civil Rights Act of 1965. Collective bargaining was protected with the Wagner Act of 1935, and the Job Corps was part of Johnson's Great Society program.

38. B

The Volstead Act was the legislation passed to enforce the Eighteenth Amendment, or Prohibition. Most Americans simply ignored Prohibition and

drank alcohol they made themselves or bought from "bootleggers." The Harlem Renaissance was the scene of a dramatic increase in African American culture in the 1920s. The average American family did see a rise in its standard of living and, as a consequence, was able to purchase consumer goods at a rate not seen before. Unfortunately for America's farmers, these financial rewards would not come their way. They suffered under the weight of a depressed worldwide market and massive debt.

39. B

Through the leadership of Captain John Smith and the planting of tobacco as a viable cash crop, the Jamestown colony was able to escape the fate of the earlier Roanoke colony, which disappeared.

40. A

Many Latin American countries were deep in debt to European nations at the beginning of the 20th century. As nations such as Great Britain began sending military force to collect these debts, President Theodore Roosevelt intervened on behalf of Latin American countries, declaring that European force to collect debts was a violation of the Monroe Doctrine. Thus, the United States would occupy these Latin American countries until the debts were paid. The other issues all involved Theodore Roosevelt but were not connected to the Roosevelt Corollary.

41. E

Black Codes, passed during Reconstruction, were enacted by Southern legislatures to inhibit the ability of former slaves to gain socioeconomically in the South. The Black Codes were designed to keep a low-cost, stable workforce to care for cash crops. The other answer choices were goals of the Freedmen's Bureau.

42. D

Invented by Timothy Berners-Lee to aid in the connection of computers for a physics research team, the World Wide Web rapidly became the industry standard and was in use by 1991. The precursor to the Internet and World Wide Web was ARPANET, which was designed for academic and government use in 1969. Bill Gates revolutionized the computer world with his MS-DOS operating system, which separated individual computers from a mainframe. In the early '90s, Al Gore started a fervor when he said that he was instrumental in the development of the Internet, which some took to mean he was claiming to have invented the technology.

43. D

Henry David Thoreau and his contemporaries, such as Ralph Waldo Emerson, were known as Transcendentalists who believed in the power of the individual human spirit and the undeniable connection between man and nature. Whitefield was a minister of the First Great Awakening. Stanton was a women's rights activist of the antebellum era. Irving was a member of the Knickerbockers of New York, who began writing truly American literature. Washington would have written about individualism as an abolitionist but not of nature.

44. C

After the British Parliament began to enforce the old Navigation Acts in an attempt to regain control over their colonies, colonial merchants began devising ways to get around the laws. By trading rum and sugar for slaves, the trade network that formed a triangle from the American South to the Caribbean to the west coast of Africa successfully operated under the nose of the British government.

45. D

A great discussion ensued between large and small states over representation to the two houses of the legislative branch. It was finally decided to accept the compromise drafted by Roger Sherman of Connecticut to have equal representation in the upper house (the Senate) and proportional representation in the lower chamber (the House of Representatives). Checks and balances within the government and between states had been remedied in the drafting of the Constitution. The Articles had already been abandoned wholly with the drafting of the Constitution. Income taxes did not become an official fixture in the United States until the ratification of the Sixteenth Amendment in 1913.

46. E

In the 1970s, high prices and high unemployment coupled to bring America its first bout with stagflation. The usual tools government employed to combat inflation, cut taxes, and increase government spending did nothing to offset the massive rise in prices for energy and consumer goods.

47. E

Europeans brought silent killers among their ranks as they arrived in the New World. Diseases such as small pox decimated native tribes, as they did not have any immunity against the viruses. The Spanish attempted to enslave natives but soon found that they were not hardy enough to work under these conditions.

48. A

The 1896 Supreme Court decision of *Plessy v. Ferguson* set the precedent of allowing separate public facilities for whites and blacks. This case was overturned by the 1954 *Brown* decision, which determined that separate schools were inherently unequal. *Marbury v. Madison* was decided in 1803 and set the precedent of judicial review. The *Dred Scott* case, heard by the Court in 1856, determined that slaves were not citizens. *Worcester v. Georgia,* decided in 1832, determined that the Cherokee Nation was exempt from the laws of the state of Georgia. Finally, *Sweatt v. Painter* in 1950 allowed the admission of a black student to the all-white University of Texas.

49. C

The country began to experience separation, as canals and railroads divided the regions geographically. Northern states were known for manufacturing and the South for agriculture, while the west was a mixed bag. Agriculture always remained second to industry in the North, and canals worked to make cities along the Erie much more viable. The federal government did not become involved in internal improvements until well after the Civil War.

50. D

Because of the rise of plentiful factory jobs available in big cities, many Americans fled their farms, and immigrants flocked to American shores in search of better opportunity. The Civil War, which ended in 1865, did little to impact population growth. Some immigration restrictions were put in place as early as 1880, but most did not take effect until 1920 and beyond. Western states did experience growth due to the influx of Asian immigrants looking for a "mountain of gold." City growth increased rapidly after World War I, as veterans and blacks moved to cities for more opportunity.

51. C

William Lloyd Garrison published his abolitionist paper *The Liberator* from 1831 to 1865, before Reconstruction, to demand the immediate emancipation of slaves on the basis of the Constitution. Free-Soilers were interested in preventing the extension of slavery into the west. While abolitionism was prompted by the Second Great Awakening, sermons given during this time would not be concerned with African American rights. *Cannibals All* was written by slave apologist George Fitzhugh, who justified slavery as a necessary evil.

52. B

In November 1990, the UN Security Council voted to authorize the use of military force against Iraq for its unauthorized invasion of the tiny, oil-rich country of Kuwait. Operation Desert Storm, later called the Persian Gulf War, was launched on January 16, 1991, as U.S. warplanes attacked Baghdad and other targets around the Persian Gulf. The disco attack, carried out by Libyan extremists, occurred in Berlin in 1986, killing two American servicemen. The hostage crisis in Iran occurred in 1979. Congress never declared war against Iraq or Saddam Hussein. The *USS Cole* was attacked in 2000 by Al Qaeda operatives.

53. E

German U-boats had sunk a number of American merchant and passenger liners between 1914 and 1917. Germany's policy of unrestricted submarine warfare and the subsequent sinking of U.S. ships in early 1917 prompted Wilson to ask for a declaration of war. Wilson had attempted to negotiate with the Germans to stop the carnage, but after the interception of the Zimmerman note, all negotiations were dead.

54. D

Daniel Shays and his band of followers stormed the Springfield arsenal in 1787 to protest what they believed to be excessive taxes and the imprisonment of debtors. While the insurrection lasted only a few days, it did much to frighten local elites of the possibility of a popular uprising if a stronger central government was not put in place to regulate such a large nation. France had all but been removed as a threat in North America due to the Treaty of Paris that ended the French and Indian War, and British troops in the qest did not attack American settlers (although they did help to arm native tribes, some of whom attacked white frontier settlements).

55. B

The signs of economic collapse were all evident before the Great Depression hit in the 1930s. Farmers struggled throughout the interwar years due to worldwide depression and the inability to pay for goods on credit. Military expenditures actually fell during the 1920s. Wealth was not significantly redistributed, as the gap between rich and poor widened. Import of foreign goods and immigration both slowed during the 1920s.

56. C

Married women entered the workforce in response to the massive "Rosie the Riveter" campaign, which encouraged women to do their part to support the war effort. Women also had to endure rationing of staple goods such as butter and sugar, as well as gasoline and silk (used for stockings). People of Japanese ancestry were forcibly relocated to internment camps by Executive Order 9066. Finally, African Americans moved in great numbers to urban centers in the North and the west to find factory jobs vacated by men leaving to serve overseas.

57.   C

Henry Clay hoped to improve the economy just as Hamilton did before him by protecting infant American industry with high tariffs and by improving the country's infrastructure with a national road and other federally funded projects. Like many Federalists of an earlier era, Clay did not see the need to provide assistance to agriculture, which his plan ignored.

58.   E

Russia (the Soviet Union) was conspicuously absent from the meetings at Versailles to discuss post–World War I Europe. The country had backed out of the war earlier due to domestic issues. Americans feared becoming too connected to European affairs and the consequence of being pulled into another world crisis. Wilson and Senator Lodge never saw eye to eye on the issue of the League. Wilson's seven-month absence due to his stroke had a negative impact on those who supported his position, as they lacked leadership. The "Irreconcilables" refused to accept the treaty with the provision for the League of Nations.

59.   C

The Supreme Court actually ruled on the side of the Cherokee tribe in their bid to maintain jurisdiction over their homeland. In *Worcester v. Georgia* (1832), John Marshall and the Court ruled that the laws of the state did not apply within the Cherokee territory, as it was an independent nation. This prompted President Andrew Jackson to have allegedly said "John Marshall has made his decision. Now let him enforce it." Abolitionists were just gaining ground at this time and did not get involved in Native American affairs. The legislative branch was basically at the will of President Jackson and did not intervene. In fact, Congress had passed the Indian Removal Act in 1930.

60.   B

Accusers were usually young women living in Salem's inner "town," while the accused were typically older widowers living in Salem's outer "countryside." It was clear from the start that there were social and economic tensions that brought on the accusations and wild behaviors of the witch trials.

61.   A

The election of 1800 is known as a "Revolution" simply because it was now clear that power could be passed from one faction to another without violence. Thomas Jefferson was chosen by the House of Representatives as president after he tied with his running mate, Aaron Burr. The Native American threat did not end until well into the late 1800s. Southerners would continue to fight for their right to continue to hold slaves until the Civil War. American relations with Britain did not improve until after the War of 1812.

62.   B

U-2 spy planes had been flying routine missions over the Soviet Union since 1955 but at an altitude that was undetectable to Soviet radar until May 1960. Then an American U-2 spy plane flown by Francis Gary Powers was shot down flying over Soviet airspace. Powers was captured, and Moscow was angry at this "war effort." Khrushchev immediately called off peace talks amid Eisenhower's insistence that he had no knowledge of such spy missions. The so-called Kitchen Debate occurred between Vice President Nixon and Khrushchev at the World's Fair in 1959. Sputnik was launched in 1957 and impacted American policy. NASA was created in 1958 in response to the launch of Sputnik. Détente ended with the Soviet invasion of Afghanistan in 1979.

63.   E

In a defeat for the feminist movement, ERA was passed by Congress but failed to garner the necessary three-fourths of state ratifications to finally become an Amendment to the Constitution. It died in 1982 when the requisite number of states failed to ratify the Amendment.

64.   A

Isolationists, such as Charles Lindbergh, were not pleased with the Lend-Lease program, because it signaled the end of neutrality and the beginning of mobilization for war. Enacted as a measure to warn the Axis powers of U.S. intentions, lend-lease helped Britain get back on her feet after the Battle of Britain. The United States remained politically neutral as a nonbelligerent, but Lend-Lease was tantamount to an economic declaration of war against the Axis powers.

65. B
Signs of economic trouble were evident in the years prior to the Crash of 1929. The American farmer was struggling under the weight of falling agricultural prices and rising debts. Employment did not take a significant dip until the early 1930s. Other reasons for the economic collapse that would soon follow the Crash were massive increases in business inventories for large consumer goods, an increase in the amount Americans were purchasing on credit, and a relative increase in the standard of living over the past decade.

66. C
Spanish conquistadores were known for their brutal and exploitative treatment of native populations, driving many to extinction. On their quest for "God, gold, and glory," European explorers exploited "uncivilized" natives for riches and power.

67. E
The Founding Fathers met at the Philadelphia convention to discuss revisions of the existing Articles of Confederation. Due to lateness on the part of many delegates, however, Virginians and other dignitaries were able to draft a new document prior to the arrival of the rest of the attendees. This new document would become the new Constitution. American, foreign, and Native American policies developed throughout the post-Revolutionary period through various political dealings with France, Britain, and Native American tribes. Independence from Britain had been declared and finalized in 1776.

68. D
Supply-side or, as Reagan called it, "trickle-down" economics, provided deep tax cuts for the middle and upper classes to stimulate investment that would "trickle down" to the poor. Economists today disagree on whether Reagan's tax cuts actually helped improve the economy or if the real cause was the massive increase of government spending in the defense industry. Shrinking the poverty gap and balancing the federal budget were not priorities of the Reagan administration. Increasing government spending is connected more with demand-side, or Keynesian, economics. The government cannot influence interest rates; only the Federal Reserve can manipulate monetary policies.

69. E
John C. Calhoun secretly penned the document that led his home state of South Carolina to protest against the "tariff of abominations," otherwise known as the Tariff of 1828. By nullifying federal law, the state of South Carolina refused to comply, driving President Jackson to threaten the use of military force to enact the law.

70. B
The Emancipation Proclamation had the immediate effect of turning the war into a moral fight rather than purely an offensive war to save the Union. The Proclamation actually strengthened the resolve of Confederate troops, as they fought to preserve their way of life. Democrats in the Border States were angered by the Proclamation, as it endangered their ability to keep slaves. The Union Army actually experienced more desertions after the issuance of the Proclamation, because many soldiers who had been willing to fight for preserving the Union were now unwilling to give their lives for the abolitionist cause. Meanwhile, many abolitionists complained that the president had not gone far enough when he issued the Proclamation.

71. A
President George H. W. Bush was haunted by a campaign promise he made in the 1988 election—"Read my lips. No new taxes." Faced with a government bailout of failed savings and loan institutions and an increase in the national debt, President Bush accepted a congressional tax hike, thus alienating many Republican voters. This, coupled with an impending recession and questions

surrounding the nomination of Clarence Thomas as a Supreme Court justice. further damaged Bush's chances at re-election in 1992. The third-party campaign of billionaire Ross Perot split the Republican vote, enabling Bill Clinton to win the presidency with only 43 percent of the popular vote.

72. E

Due to massive land grants by the federal government, the railroad industry exploded after the Civil War. Chinese immigration had been steadily on the rise since the discovery of gold in California in 1849 but did little to fuel the growth of the railroad industry. Andrew Carnegie is best known for his use of vertical integration in amassing a significant market share in his industry. Capital goods actually dropped in price, as inventions such as the Bessemer process made the manufacture of steel cheap and fast. The Interstate Commerce Act sought to end unfair pricing practices by the railroads but lacked enforcement mechanisms to be effective. The Interstate Commerce Commission was not successful in curbing monopolies until the early 20th century.

73. C

The Seven Years' War was known as the French and Indian War in North America, as colonists allied with British militia. The War of Polish Succession was a Continental European fight that lasted between 1733 and 1738. Metacom's War (also known as King Philip's War) was a Native American insurrection that occurred 1675–1676. The French Wars of Religion were fought in that country in the late 16th century. There were a series of Anglo-French Wars; the Seven Years' War was the last and the only one fought in North America.

74. C

By executive order 9981 in 1947, President Truman desegregated the armed forces and added a spark to the fledgling civil rights movement. Jackie Robinson did not need presidential approval to play for the Brooklyn Dodgers in 1947, breaking the color line in professional sports. It was not until the 1954 ruling in *Brown v. Board* that public schools were integrated. Public facilities would not be integrated until 1965. The Civil Rights Act of 1964 ended

segregation in public facilities. Huey P. Long was assassinated in 1935.

75. E

The nutrition of Native American tribes vastly improved with the spread of information regarding the cultivation of corn as a staple crop. Mesoamericans in current-day Central America had long depended on the versatile crop, and they shared that knowledge with their neighbors to the north through trade networks along the Mississippi River.

76. C

Unfortunately, many of the so-called "new immigrants" coming to the United States after 1880 were not greeted by a welcome mat as they disembarked from their arduous journeys. Americans restricted immigration from southern and eastern European countries by establishing "quotas" and rigorous entry requirements for all immigrants. This new wave of people seeking refuge were mostly eastern European Jews fleeing persecution or southern European Catholics seeking a better life. Citizenship was not something readily handed out by the U.S. government.

77. E

Nativism began in the late 1840s with the American or Know-Nothing Party, which resented the increase in immigrants from Germany and Ireland. These feelings resurfaced at the turn of the 20th century and into the 1920s, as Americans turned against the large number of "new" immigrants from southern and eastern Europe entering the country before and after the First World War. The other answer choices have nothing to do with nativism.

78. C

The Court ruled that a woman's decision to have an abortion was protected by the Constitution up to the last three months of pregnancy. Neither the federal government nor states can outlaw all methods of abortion. The Court decided in 1965 that states did not have the authority to prohibit the sale or use of contraceptives. The Court has left the issue of decency up to states to regulate.

79. B

As the editor of the *Pennsylvania Gazette* and the sponsor of a plan to unite the colonies in a common defense during the French and Indian War, Franklin used the muscle of the press to try to persuade colonists to agree to the Albany Plan of Union. The Declaration of Independence, Stamp Act Congress, and Revolutionary War all occurred in the years after the French and Indian War; the Hartford Convention did not occur until the War of 1812.

80. D

The Mayflower Compact, penned by separatist Pilgrims and non-Pilgrims as they landed at Plymouth Bay, held the cornerstone of colonial self-rule. Far from being a constitution or a declaration of independence, the Compact bound the citizens of Plymouth Colony together under rule of law.

DBQ Analyses

Document A:

Inferences: These criminals acted due to their addiction to "ardent spirits," or alcohol. Mr. Fernandez is imploring those watching the execution to teach children to remain temperate and not consume alcohol. This document was widely used by the early temperance movement as evidence of the evils of drinking alcohol.

Document B:

Inferences: This excerpt was taken from Garrison's *The Liberator* in one of its earliest printings. It is clear that the author is a religious man and likens the liberation of slavery to a Christian moral duty. One may see the connection between this document and the Second Great Awakening.

Document C:

Inferences: Impacted by the Second Great Awakening and the abolitionist movement, the Grimke sisters soon took up the charge of women's rights. Angelina Grimke is writing this letter to fellow abolitionist and feminist Catherine Beecher bemoaning the state of the pampered woman. It is clear from this document that Grimke feels the new stature of women is far from "Christian."

Document D:

Inferences: One would have to know that Brigham Young was the second major leader of the Mormons and moved his people across the country to "Deseret," or Utah, to find their sacred homeland. Colonel Thomas Kane was a lifelong friend of the Mormons, fighting for political protections and even physical war for them. Late in his life, he converted to Mormonism. The Mormon movement can be viewed as an example of people searching for a utopia to practice their faith and life style in peace, much like Oneida and Brook Farm.

Document E:

Inferences: One of the most deadly industrial fires in U.S. history occurred at the Triangle Shirtwaist Factory in 1911. Young girls and women were locked inside the factory behind locked windows and fire escapes. Girls as young as 15 jumped from the high-rise windows to escape the fire and ultimately met their fate on the sidewalk below. The 148 girls and women who perished in the fire sparked a wave of reform aimed at better working conditions and laws to limit the work hours of women.

Document F:

Inferences: Jane Addams was a new breed of Progressive in that she was one of a new stock of college-educated women. Taking her knowledge of life and society to Chicago, Addams opened Hull House as a way to provide a clean respite to the destitute of the city. She also offered courses in manners, decorum, and reading at the house to teach indigents how to succeed in society.

Document G:

Inferences: This document can be used with Document A to explain that the temperance movement had not disappeared by 1919. The Volstead Act was the legal arm of the Eighteenth Amendment, thus enforcing Prohibition. It was widely thought that alcohol was the root of all evil and to ban it would solve the country's problems with crime and poverty.

Document H:

Inferences: Benjamin Rush was a member of the Sons of Liberty, signed the Declaration of Independence, and attended the Constitutional

Convention. Later in his life, he became a professor of medical theory and published one of the first textbooks dedicated to the study of mental illness. Rush was one of the first to recognize the dangers of addiction, especially alcoholism. This document shows how "spirituous liquor" affects a person's ability to cope with life and eventually leads to death. Students may link this to documents A, F, and I.

DOCUMENT I:

Inferences: Francis Willard and the Women's Christian Temperance Movement took up the reins of the old temperance movement and gave it new life in the post-Reconstruction era. Beginning in 1874, the WCTU worked to eradicate the evils of alcohol in American society through educational campaigns such as the one illustrated on this poster. Students may be able to see that this poster is designed to address American children and speak to their patriotic spirit. The movement has changed to make alcohol "un-American". This may be linked to documents A, F, and H.

DBQ INFORMATION AND STUDY LIST

As you approach this prompt, you should begin by "dissecting" the question. Underline directions and other words that give you clues as to the intent of the prompt. This prompt clearly asks the writer to consider two periods of reform and their social, political, and economic impact on the United States. It is important to note that the directions specify that you compare and contrast the time periods; use the documents and address the categories of PERSIA discussed in chapter 2.

Now, before looking at the documents, formulate a thesis based solely on your own background knowledge. If this step gives you trouble, then you know you will not have much outside information to draw upon. Remember, outside information is *required* on the DBQ.

Next, do a quick brainstorm of the social, political, and economic factors you remember from the time periods mentioned. You may wish to create lists of terms and people under each heading to aid you in writing your body paragraphs. Your list may include some of the following: abolitionists, William Lloyd Garrison and *The Liberator,* the Grimke sisters, Women's Christian Temperance Movement, utopian societies, Mormons, Andrew Jackson, Second Great Awakening, Market Revolution, rise of industry, child labor laws, white lung, Prohibition, settlement house movement.

You now need to move to the documents. Quickly use the SCIT method from chapter 2: *S* equals scan, *C* equals catalog, *I* equals infer, and *T* equals tie it together. By the time you take the AP exam, you should be able to complete SCIT for all of the documents in 10 minutes or less.

Finally, it is time to write your thesis. A possible answer may postulate that the antebellum and Progressive reform movements were very much alike in that they both involved middle-class whites trying to better society through influencing the government. You may also choose to say that the movements were very different in that the antebellum movements were more driven by religious beliefs and a need for perfectibility, while the Progressives were simply trying to protect themselves from massive social and economic change. Either way, you would need to make sure that you provide enough information from the documents and your own list to support your thesis.

SAMPLE DBQ RESPONSE

Both the antebellum (1830–1950) and Progressive (1880–1990) reform movements worked hard for their campaigns in order to create a better society for people to live in. The two movements are similar in goals, objectives, and impacts but differ in the methods they use in order to achieve their goals as well as a broader pattern of organization pertaining to their goals. Antebellum and Progressive movements were created to combat the vices existent in American life, but in order to fight this evil, the antebellum reform movements attempted to persuade people's minds by appealing to their conscience and emotions, where Progressive reformers went straight to the government to achieve their goals. Progressives also used muckraking to get the attention of the people and government in order to meet their goals. In terms of overall patterns, the antebellum reform movements had sprung from the Great Awakening and had more to do with changing the United States into a Christian ideal. Conversely, the Progressive reforms were centered around the idea of creating a fair and perfect society for every American. Because of this, the antebellum reformers had a greater social impact on society, whereas the Progressive reformers had more of a political and economic influence. But in spite of all of this, the two reform movements had much in common, as many of the original antebellum campaigns repeated themselves in the Progressive era.

The antebellum and Progressive reforms had much in common in the area of goals, objectives, and overall impacts. Both movements aimed to remedy society's ills, and they both achieved part of their goal in some way, by making the United States a better place to live in at least for a while. The two movements had similar campaigns, such as temperance and women's rights. Also, both the antebellum movement and Progressive movement were created as a backlash to the rise of cities and industry. In the cities were vice, in industry there was immoral practices, and corruption existed in American society, government, and economic system. Both reform movements had campaigns that existed solely to combat these evils in American society. Another similarity between the two movements is that both antebellum reformers and Progressives were from the middle class. The antebellum middle class wanted to save both the lower and upper classes from sin and vice, whereas the Progressive middle class acted out because they were hurting from the big trusts existing above them as well as the hordes of immigrants from below who worked for cheap prices, and so were a job threat. Just the fact that both were reform movements shows the similarity between the two in trying to remedy the bad side of American society and life. Overall, the movements were most similar to each other in terms of the goals and objectives they shared, as well as the fact that both made impacts on important aspects in the lives of American citizens.

The differences in methods of campaigning clearly separate the antebellum reformers from the Progressive reformers because the former used more social means to achieve their goals; hence, they had a greater social impact in the United States, whereas the latter used aggressive political, economic, and muckraking techniques, so their major influences lie mostly in the political and economic area (though it is true that the antebellum movement of temperance had political and economic impacts and the Progressive muckraking had social impacts). The Antebellum reform movements were created as a result of the Second Great Awakening, the second Christian revival to hit the United States. The middle class saw the corruption in the cities and vowed to spread Christian morals throughout society. As a result, feelings of tolerance, equality, and compassion created the Abolitionist Movement, who fought against Garrison's description of an African American's life in Document B. Alcohol addiction, which caused the "departure from the paths of rectitude and virtue" (Document A), was another vice that Christians felt it was their duty to warn society about. The early temperance movement began even before the Second Great Awakening with advocates such as physician Benjamin Rush who warned of dangers of alcoholism with leaflets designed to frighten potential drinkers. (Document H) The utopian movements where people set up communes in places where the evils of society could not touch them (Document D) were also started by groups who were looking to preserve certain moral and/or Christian values. The reform movement concerned with education was partially caused by the Christian goal to reduce violence in society; in this case, the means of which was education at a young age in order to steer the youth away from lives of crime. Dorothea Dix's work for better mental health treatment was motivated by the Christian teachings of love and compassion for other human beings, no matter how different they are. Even the women's rights movement of the antebellum era was working toward making the modern woman into a better Christian, rather than " 'a spoiled child'" who is made " 'to suit the convenience of her lord and master . . .'" (Document C). From these examples it is obvious to see that most of the antebellum reforms were created as a response to the Second Great Awakening and the new sense of Christianity it brought to middle-class citizens.

Conversely, most of the Progressive movements were caused by a want to improve society for everyone. It was more concerned with human welfare than creating a Christian society. A similarity between the reform movements was in the crusade against alcohol which continued until the passage of the Eighteenth Amendment. Frances Willard of settlement house fame also fought against the consumption and sale of "spirited beverages" with posters aimed at the young. (Document I) Many called the 18th Amendment a success of the Progressive movement; however, the noble experiment of prohibition failed and the amendment was finally repealed in 1933. The labor movements fought against the exploitation of men, women, and children workers through unfair wages, hours, and working conditions, and they fought for this in order to create a workplace for Americans. Jane Addams' work in offering people shelter from the vices of the city helped people out by giving them a place to go to where they could escape the harshness of city life (Document G). The muckraking about the meat industry helped all American people by warning them about what "food" they were putting into their bodies; and the environmental muckraking assisted the public by making them aware of how their world was being violated and showing them what they could do to stop it. The women's rights movement was a reform designed to help American women by giving them more control over their lives and the lives of their loved ones. The battles fought against trusts kept the consumers and producers from getting trampled on by big businesses. Though both these Progressive reform movements and antebellum reform movements helped create a better, cleaner United States, there is a fine line of difference between them. The antebellum reform movements were motivated by a public want to spread Christianity, while the Progressive reform movements were driven by the desire of the people not to be taken advantage of, exploited, or made inferior.

Another contrast between the two reform movements is their plans of action. The antebellum reformers relied on the conscience and heart of the public to get their changes made. They appealed to society to change their ways by using religious, moral, logical, and emotional arguments. For instance, a typical argument used against alcohol would be that it causes people to act violently and irresponsibly, which could result in harm to both the alcoholic and his loved ones. This technique would emotionally guilt-trip people into not drinking, because they did not want to be the reason for their family's demise. Because of their tactics, the antebellum reformers had a great social impact on the people, because they worked hard to change the point of view of American society as a whole. They used their Christian arguments to appeal to people's hearts, which is something the Progressives could not do, because most of their reforms were not based around Christianity. The antebellum reformers had to be very persuasive, and use society as their method to get their goals accomplished, and in some cases it worked.

Contrastingly, the Progressive reformers used the government and economy to accomplish their goals. Instead of appealing to the emotions and minds of society, the Progressives went straight to the government to get what they wanted. For example, after the Triangle Shirtwaist Factory Fire in 1911 (Document F), the Progressives were able to make political headway that included laws protecting both women and children laborers (Document E). Overall, the government actions the Progressives wrangled had more meaning and weight than the social support gained by the antebellum reformers. As shown in the discrepancies between the two temperance movements, the antebellum reformers were only able to achieve a no-alcohol, or dry policy, in several states; whereas the more politically aggressive progressives achieved a nationwide Prohibition law (Document H). Though neither the state nor the nation prohibition laws lasted, the groundwork made by the Progressives was clearly much more far-reaching than the work of the antebellum reformers. The Progressives' political successes (initiative, referendum, and recall) gave the American people a chance to play a larger role in the government, and their economic successes (through labor movement successes and Roosevelt's Progressive-inspired trust-busting) enabled people to have more economic opportunity and helped them not to be exploited by powerful businesses. Because of the difference between the plan of action of antebellum reforms and Progressive reforms, the two groups also differed in their effectiveness. The antebellum movements were less aggressive, and appealed to the people, and consequently they had a big social impact on American society. However, the more aggressive political strategy of the Progressives earned political and economic successes which last longer and were more solid in the lives of the American people.

The antebellum reform movement and Progressive reform movement took place only 30 years apart from each other, and consequently they shared the same goals of important matters of the centuries, but differed in strategies because those corresponded to the particular decade. The government response achieved in the Progressive era would probably not have been possible 30 years earlier, and similarly, the change in the minds of the public would have been harder to achieve in the time of the Progressives. Both movements acted in accordance to the United States they lived in, and though the reforms were backed by a different reasoning, they both attempted to better the lives of American citizens. The people who participated in both movements were from the same class, but their motivations differed, as well as the effectiveness of their campaigns. Overall, there are many similarities and differences between the antebellum movement and Progressive movement that paradoxically both link and separate the two reforms at the same time.

FRQs

2.

Study List:

Washington
Neutrality Declaration 1789
Farewell Address

Jefferson
Louisiana Purchase
remained neutral during Napoleonic Wars
Tripolitan War

Monroe
Spanish Florida
proposition from Great Britain
Monroe Doctrine

SAMPLE ESSAY

As a developing country, the United States had to approach foreign affairs with caution. It did not have the military power or stability needed to go to war; the avoidance of war would keep the United States safe from destruction. This situation led to the birth of isolationism, which George Washington set rolling when he was president and James Monroe maintained when he became president later on. Both men had a significant impact on foreign policy; they set the precedent for generations after them.

As the first president of the United States, George Washington wielded a lot of power in many areas of American government. He would be the prototype, the example which presidents after him would follow. When Washington accepted presidency, there were already growing feelings of isolationism, and Washington supported and approved this policy. Still fresh from their own revolution, the French Revolution had quite an impact on Americans. Some brought up the Franco-American alliance, and called for Americans to help France fight. Washington, however, saw this as dangerous for a country still wobbling on its new-born legs. He saw that the United States could not handle a war with Britain and issued his Neutrality Declaration which proclaimed the American government's official neutrality. With this declaration also came a warning to the American people to remain impartial towards both. By choosing to stay out of European affairs, Washington backed the idea of isolationism that would serve as the cornerstone to American foreign policy. He emphasizes this once again in his farewell address when he warns the American people against "permanent alliances," insisting that "temporary alliances" in "extraordinary emergencies" were best for the country. By staying out of European affairs, the United States was allowed to thrive in trade and continue to grow without hindrance. This idea of isolationism that Washington supported proved to benefit the country.

James Monroe followed the example set by Washington and also took it further. When Monroe sent Andrew Jackson into American Florida to act as a police force, Jackson proceeded to go into Spanish Florida and seized two important Spanish ports. When Monroe heard this he was alarmed; he had not wished to get involved with Spain at all. As a result of Jackson's actions, Spain ceded Florida to the United States on the agreement that Americans would stay out of Texas. This was not an idea of Monroe's. Government officials had to convince him not to punish Jackson, which demonstrates that he still supported isolationism and had not wanted to get involved with Spain. Also, many European countries were banding together to take back the Latin American countries that had rebelled against their European colonizers. Britain saw this as a threat to the trade that it and the United States had with these Latin American countries and attempted to strike a deal. It proposed that the United States create a joint declaration with Britain that renounced any interest in acquiring Latin America and that warned the other European powers to keep their hands off of the United States. This goes against American isolationism and the advice of Washington, so in response to this proposition, Monroe, with the aide of John Quincy Adams, issued the Monroe Doctrine. The Monroe Doctrine was a message to Europe that stressed noncolonization and nonintervention. The European countries could keep their existing colonies but could no longer acquire land in the Western hemisphere. If isolationism was not obvious in American foreign policy before, no one could ignore it now. This would keep European Powers from encroaching on land that Americans believed destined for them. Monroe had hammered the final nail into the American foreign policy of remaining free from entanglement in affairs of the "Old World."

Both of these presidents were faced with difficult decisions to make when it came to interaction with the European countries. Because of the decisions they were faced with, they were able to define American foreign policy. Washington laid the foundation of isolationism with his adamancy in remaining neutral when it came to wars and alliances in Europe. Monroe had taken it a step further by essentially banning European Powers from having any influence in the Western hemisphere. Isolationism and the Monroe Doctrine would stay alive in American foreign policy for many years to come, and these men are the reason. Their importance in the formation of American foreign policy is immeasurable.

3. **Study List**

	Women	Poor	Slaves
New England	Women had very specific roles that were defined by the Bible and customary practices. Women were not allowed to hold property unless widowed or unmarried. Wives had few rights in regards to property, child rearing, or household decisions.	Wealth was a sign that an individual was of the "elect." Therefore, the poor were not respected within the community. No special arrangements were made for care of the poor. Many found themselves in debtors' prisons.	Puritans justified slavery through the Bible and economics. However, in New England there was very little need for many slaves, and few families owned any. Many, such as Jonathan Winthrop, were outspoken critics of slavery.
Middle Colonies	In Quaker society, women were held in equal standing to men. Women were allowed to speak in church services and serve as ministers.	Quakers believed it was their spiritual duty to care for the poor. They established "almshouses" where the poor could live until they were ready to move on.	Quakers were the first group to demand for the abolition of slavery. Their doctrine determined that slavery was unjust and needed to be abolished. Being radical Christians, they believed that all were equal in the eyes of God.

4.

Study List:

Compromise of 1850

Kansas-Nebraska Act

Bleeding Kansas

Lecompton Constitution

Stephen A. Douglas

Manifest Destiny

expansionism

"Beecher's Bibles"

border ruffians

Lawrence, Kansas

John Brown's Raid

Sample Essay

As western expansion became highly popular in the 1840s and 1850s, the question of slavery came into question continuously. Though many excused this migration as a result of Manifest Destiny, it mainly was a race between the North and the South to acquire states to provide their wants and needs in regards to slavery. One major conflict between the North and the South came up over the issue of popular sovereignty, which was the ability of a new territory to decide if it was to become a free or slave state. The passage of both the Compromise of 1850 and the Kansas-Nebraska Act of 1854 created many problems, such as conflict, between the North and the South because both contained the component of popular sovereignty. Eventually, popular sovereignty was declared unconstitutional. It was this trial (i.e., Dred Scott Trial) that explained why popular sovereignty turned out to be unsuccessful.

Problems resulting from popular sovereignty were mostly centered around tensions between the North and the South. The Compromise of 1850 and the Kansas-Nebraska Act provided some territories, such as Utah, New Mexico, and Kansas, with popular sovereignty to decide whether the territory would become a slave or free state. This meant that all of those territories were open to either of the two options. This created high sectional interests for the North and the South. In specific, the Kansas-Nebraska Act provided that Nebraska would most probably become anti-slavery because it was a territory above the 36°30′ line that the previous Missouri Compromise had provided. Since this would shift the balance of pro- and anti-slavery officials in Congress in favor of the North, Kansas became a battleground for Northern and Southern interests. People from both of these regions rushed into Kansas to shift the local elections in their favor.

Eventually, violence followed, and this territory was dubbed the name Bleeding Kansas. In general, popular sovereignty was such a big problem mainly because of the conflict it created between the North and the South, and it partially was this serious tension that would lead to its failure.

Though serious conflicts between the North and the South, such as what happened in Bleeding Kansas, made popular sovereignty unsuccessful, it was mainly the Dred Scott Trial that led to its downfall. In reaction to the violence that happened at Bleeding Kansas, President Buchanan was looking for a court ruling in regards to slavery's expansion. He found the Dred Scott Trial, delivered by Justice Roger B. Taney, to provide the resolution. Dred Scott was a slave taken to free territory by his master, but was kept a slave. Taney said that slaves were merely property, even if they lived in a free territory. This led to Taney's ruling that Congress couldn't ban slavery in U.S. territory because it would violate the Fifth Amendment by taking away property (in this case, slaves) without due process. Taney also said that popular sovereignty, which allowed territory's governments to ban slavery, thus violated this Amendment. Thus, the Compromise of 1850 and the Kansas-Nebraska Act were declared unconstitutional. With this declaration came the downfall of popular sovereignty.

In conclusion, popular sovereignty seemed like an excellent solution to the problem of slavery in new territories. However, its introduction caused a tension-filled and violent confrontation between the anti-slavery North and the pro-slavery South. Because of this tension and conflict, along with the ruling in the Dred Scott Case, popular sovereignty resulted in failure and downfall.

5.

Study List:

Dollar Diplomacy

Open Door Policy

Roosevelt Corollary

jingoism

Alfred Maher

aggressive foreign policy

coaling stations

Spanish-American War

Panama Canal

SAMPLE ESSAY

At the close of the 19th century, many Americans were eager to begin expansion and keep up with the imperialistic ways of Japan and other countries. Colonization of the western hemisphere awakened the Monroe Doctrine, which was the basis of American foreign policy. However, the United States also twisted the Monroe Doctrine into other forms, such as the Roosevelt Corollary, in order to justify interference where it was unwanted.

The Monroe Doctrine warned European Powers to keep their hands away from land in the Western hemisphere; European colonization and intervention in the Western hemisphere was over. But as the nineteenth century was coming to a close, other world powers began to colonize again. There was no way the United States would be left behind. Alfred Mahan came up with a response; he helped create and develop the expansionist movement and wanted to expand the U.S. Navy and establish colonies to protect U.S. political and economic interests. This plan would give the Monroe Doctrine muscle and attempt to keep the other countries at bay. This aggressive expansionism lead to the Spanish-American War, when the United States succeeded in getting Spain out of the Western hemisphere and gaining Cuba, Puerto Rico, Guam, and the Philippines. This was an offensive move by the United States and was justified by expansion of overseas markets, a want for a stronger navy, and "civilizing" those of "uncivilized" areas. The Monroe Doctrine was used to serve the purpose of the United States, allowing it to get involved where it had banned the other Powers.

When Roosevelt became president, he created his own corollary to the Monroe Doctrine which he used to justify interference in Latin American countries when it wasn't wanted and wasn't needed. This Roosevelt Corollary said that the United States would interfere on Latin American affairs on behalf of other countries. How thoughtful of Roosevelt to make it easy on European countries to follow the Monroe Doctrine. This perversion of the Monroe Doctrine justified the building of the Panama Canal. When Colombia shot down the Hay-Herrán agreement, Roosevelt enlisted the help of Frenchman Phillipe Bunau-Varilla to organize a revolution. The revolution was successful and the Panama Canal began construction. What had started as a means to protect the United States from encroaching European countries had morphed into a means for the United States to use the Latin American countries to its advantage.

The United States wanted full control of its own colonies in order to give it the advantage and benefit U.S. interest. But when China was threatened with carving up, the U.S. insisted on the Open Door Policy which requested the countries with a stake on China keep fair competition open to all countries. This prevented the carving up of China, but displayed the hypocrisy of the U.S. and the mutation of the Monroe Doctrine. The United States had holds on Latin American countries, which of course were not completely open to fair trade, but the U.S. requested that China be left for all to benefit from. The United States had become very skilled in protecting its interests, and using the Monroe Doctrine as a basis for foreign policy and then manipulating it to serve expansionism desires allowed for justification.

Practice Test 2 Answer Grid

1. Ⓐ Ⓑ Ⓒ Ⓓ Ⓔ	21. Ⓐ Ⓑ Ⓒ Ⓓ Ⓔ	41. Ⓐ Ⓑ Ⓒ Ⓓ Ⓔ	61. Ⓐ Ⓑ Ⓒ Ⓓ Ⓔ
2. Ⓐ Ⓑ Ⓒ Ⓓ Ⓔ	22. Ⓐ Ⓑ Ⓒ Ⓓ Ⓔ	42. Ⓐ Ⓑ Ⓒ Ⓓ Ⓔ	62. Ⓐ Ⓑ Ⓒ Ⓓ Ⓔ
3. Ⓐ Ⓑ Ⓒ Ⓓ Ⓔ	23. Ⓐ Ⓑ Ⓒ Ⓓ Ⓔ	43. Ⓐ Ⓑ Ⓒ Ⓓ Ⓔ	63. Ⓐ Ⓑ Ⓒ Ⓓ Ⓔ
4. Ⓐ Ⓑ Ⓒ Ⓓ Ⓔ	24. Ⓐ Ⓑ Ⓒ Ⓓ Ⓔ	44. Ⓐ Ⓑ Ⓒ Ⓓ Ⓔ	64. Ⓐ Ⓑ Ⓒ Ⓓ Ⓔ
5. Ⓐ Ⓑ Ⓒ Ⓓ Ⓔ	25. Ⓐ Ⓑ Ⓒ Ⓓ Ⓔ	45. Ⓐ Ⓑ Ⓒ Ⓓ Ⓔ	65. Ⓐ Ⓑ Ⓒ Ⓓ Ⓔ
6. Ⓐ Ⓑ Ⓒ Ⓓ Ⓔ	26. Ⓐ Ⓑ Ⓒ Ⓓ Ⓔ	46. Ⓐ Ⓑ Ⓒ Ⓓ Ⓔ	66. Ⓐ Ⓑ Ⓒ Ⓓ Ⓔ
7. Ⓐ Ⓑ Ⓒ Ⓓ Ⓔ	27. Ⓐ Ⓑ Ⓒ Ⓓ Ⓔ	47. Ⓐ Ⓑ Ⓒ Ⓓ Ⓔ	67. Ⓐ Ⓑ Ⓒ Ⓓ Ⓔ
8. Ⓐ Ⓑ Ⓒ Ⓓ Ⓔ	28. Ⓐ Ⓑ Ⓒ Ⓓ Ⓔ	48. Ⓐ Ⓑ Ⓒ Ⓓ Ⓔ	68. Ⓐ Ⓑ Ⓒ Ⓓ Ⓔ
9. Ⓐ Ⓑ Ⓒ Ⓓ Ⓔ	29. Ⓐ Ⓑ Ⓒ Ⓓ Ⓔ	49. Ⓐ Ⓑ Ⓒ Ⓓ Ⓔ	69. Ⓐ Ⓑ Ⓒ Ⓓ Ⓔ
10. Ⓐ Ⓑ Ⓒ Ⓓ Ⓔ	30. Ⓐ Ⓑ Ⓒ Ⓓ Ⓔ	50. Ⓐ Ⓑ Ⓒ Ⓓ Ⓔ	70. Ⓐ Ⓑ Ⓒ Ⓓ Ⓔ
11. Ⓐ Ⓑ Ⓒ Ⓓ Ⓔ	31. Ⓐ Ⓑ Ⓒ Ⓓ Ⓔ	51. Ⓐ Ⓑ Ⓒ Ⓓ Ⓔ	71. Ⓐ Ⓑ Ⓒ Ⓓ Ⓔ
12. Ⓐ Ⓑ Ⓒ Ⓓ Ⓔ	32. Ⓐ Ⓑ Ⓒ Ⓓ Ⓔ	52. Ⓐ Ⓑ Ⓒ Ⓓ Ⓔ	72. Ⓐ Ⓑ Ⓒ Ⓓ Ⓔ
13. Ⓐ Ⓑ Ⓒ Ⓓ Ⓔ	33. Ⓐ Ⓑ Ⓒ Ⓓ Ⓔ	53. Ⓐ Ⓑ Ⓒ Ⓓ Ⓔ	73. Ⓐ Ⓑ Ⓒ Ⓓ Ⓔ
14. Ⓐ Ⓑ Ⓒ Ⓓ Ⓔ	34. Ⓐ Ⓑ Ⓒ Ⓓ Ⓔ	54. Ⓐ Ⓑ Ⓒ Ⓓ Ⓔ	74. Ⓐ Ⓑ Ⓒ Ⓓ Ⓔ
15. Ⓐ Ⓑ Ⓒ Ⓓ Ⓔ	35. Ⓐ Ⓑ Ⓒ Ⓓ Ⓔ	55. Ⓐ Ⓑ Ⓒ Ⓓ Ⓔ	75. Ⓐ Ⓑ Ⓒ Ⓓ Ⓔ
16. Ⓐ Ⓑ Ⓒ Ⓓ Ⓔ	36. Ⓐ Ⓑ Ⓒ Ⓓ Ⓔ	56. Ⓐ Ⓑ Ⓒ Ⓓ Ⓔ	76. Ⓐ Ⓑ Ⓒ Ⓓ Ⓔ
17. Ⓐ Ⓑ Ⓒ Ⓓ Ⓔ	37. Ⓐ Ⓑ Ⓒ Ⓓ Ⓔ	57. Ⓐ Ⓑ Ⓒ Ⓓ Ⓔ	77. Ⓐ Ⓑ Ⓒ Ⓓ Ⓔ
18. Ⓐ Ⓑ Ⓒ Ⓓ Ⓔ	38. Ⓐ Ⓑ Ⓒ Ⓓ Ⓔ	58. Ⓐ Ⓑ Ⓒ Ⓓ Ⓔ	78. Ⓐ Ⓑ Ⓒ Ⓓ Ⓔ
19. Ⓐ Ⓑ Ⓒ Ⓓ Ⓔ	39. Ⓐ Ⓑ Ⓒ Ⓓ Ⓔ	59. Ⓐ Ⓑ Ⓒ Ⓓ Ⓔ	79. Ⓐ Ⓑ Ⓒ Ⓓ Ⓔ
20. Ⓐ Ⓑ Ⓒ Ⓓ Ⓔ	40. Ⓐ Ⓑ Ⓒ Ⓓ Ⓔ	60. Ⓐ Ⓑ Ⓒ Ⓓ Ⓔ	80. Ⓐ Ⓑ Ⓒ Ⓓ Ⓔ

PRACTICE TEST 2

Section I: Multiple-Choice Questions

Time: 55 Minutes
80 Questions

Directions: Choose the best answer choice for the questions below.

1. The Ku Klux Klan of the 1920s differed from the KKK of the 1860s in that it

(A) included members of law enforcement among its ranks.

(B) remained solely in the South.

(C) restricted group activities to only legal ones.

(D) shunned the Bible as a source of inspiration.

(E) added Jews, immigrants, and communists to hate list.

2. President Ford justified his pardoning of Richard Nixon by

(A) stating that a trial of Nixon would be too painful for the American public.

(B) explaining how mentally and physically fragile Nixon was.

(C) claiming to be interested in protecting national security secrets that might have leaked during trial.

(D) arguing that the former president had suffered punishment enough by resigning as president.

(E) vowing to clean up Washington and the Republican Party.

3. The main purpose of the Wagner Labor Relations Act of 1935 was to

(A) end the sit-down strike in Flint, Michigan.

(B) settle the struggle between the AFL and the CIO.

(C) ensure workers' right to organize and bargain collectively.

(D) guarantee workers a minimum wage.

(E) exempt organized labor from the Sherman Antitrust Act.

4. Sharecropping in the South after the Civil War led to

(A) a never-ending cycle of poverty and debt for tenant farmers.

(B) better use of the soil on former cotton plantations.

(C) the beginning of integration of former slaves into white society.

(D) higher crop yields, which translated into greater wealth.

(E) more families living beyond the subsistence level.

GO ON TO THE NEXT PAGE

5. President Carter successfully ended a long feud when he

   (A) negotiated a treaty providing for the eventual turnover of control of the Panama Canal to Panama.

   (B) formally recognized Cuba as a sovereign nation.

   (C) supported the regime of Manuel Noriega.

   (D) agreed to send aid to rebels fighting communist takeover.

   (E) boycotted the 1980 Olympic Games.

6. New England's tightly knit colonial societies in the 17th century began to experience trouble when

   (A) indentured servants ended their contracts and demanded work.

   (B) many began to question the strict adherence to Calvinist doctrine.

   (C) Puritans intermarried with natives.

   (D) the birth rate among Puritan families began to drop.

   (E) Parliament revoked the Royal Charter in 1658.

7. President George H. W. Bush was hurt politically when he

   (A) continued the policies of his predecessor.

   (B) reneged on his promise by enacting the largest tax increase in history.

   (C) cut back social programs in order to balance the budget.

   (D) dramatically cut defense spending.

   (E) refused to negotiate with Saddam Hussein.

8. Many critics of the Warren Court argued that

   (A) the Court ignored the Constitution in favor of its own social agenda.

   (B) the justices were pawns for a liberal Congress.

   (C) decisions handed down by the Court were too conservative.

   (D) civil rights abuses were being ignored.

   (E) it had succumbed to the influence of big business.

9. President Abraham Lincoln's primary motive for entering the Civil War was

   (A) to emancipate the slaves.

   (B) to preserve the Union.

   (C) to punish the South for secession.

   (D) to enforce the Fugitive Slave Law.

   (E) to mend the rift in the Democratic Party.

10. President Kennedy's policy toward South Vietnam involved

   (A) rapidly escalating the number of American troops in the region.

   (B) planning the eventual withdrawal of American troops by Vietnamization.

   (C) avoiding any involvement in the affairs of the Vietnamese.

   (D) supporting Ngo Dinh Diem's regime with funding while seeking immediate withdrawal.

   (E) sending in advisors to assist in the winning of the "hearts and minds" of the Vietnamese population.

GO ON TO THE NEXT PAGE

11. During the midterm elections of 1994, the Republican "Contract with America" included

    (A) provisions for increased deficit spending.

    (B) a balanced-budget amendment.

    (C) health care reform.

    (D) decreased defense spending.

    (E) plans to decrease the size and scope of the federal government.

12. Radical Reconstruction ended in 1877 with the

    (A) successful integration of freed slaves into Southern society.

    (B) compromise agreement that removed federal troops from the South.

    (C) Treaty of Guadalupe Hildago.

    (D) slave revolt in Santo Domingo.

    (E) immigration of freedmen to Northern cities.

13. Disagreements over Hamilton's financial plan resulted in

    (A) the wholesale rejection of the plan by states.

    (B) passage of the Bill of Rights.

    (C) the immediate abolishment of excise taxes.

    (D) the failure of the National Bank.

    (E) the development of political parties.

14. The case of John Peter Zenger is significant in that it

    (A) found a member of the press guilty of slander.

    (B) upheld the rights of Englishmen.

    (C) outlawed any public discourse against government officials.

    (D) banned the printing of political cartoons critical of the Crown.

    (E) set the standard for future free speech and press rights.

15. As a "strict constructionist," President Jefferson had the most difficulty justifying his

    (A) ownership of African slaves.

    (B) sending the U.S. Navy to the Barbary Coast.

    (C) attempt to impeach Justice Samuel Chase.

    (D) relationship with Aaron Burr.

    (E) purchase of the Louisiana Territory from Napoleon.

16. During the confirmation hearings for Supreme Court nominee Clarence Thomas,

    (A) he admitted to involvement in the Iran-Contra Affair.

    (B) he was accused of supporting affirmative action laws.

    (C) more attention was given to the problem of sexual harassment.

    (D) Anita Hill was charged with obstruction of justice.

    (E) the nominee removed his name for consideration.

GO ON TO THE NEXT PAGE

17. The New Right gained its greatest number of new members in the late 1980s and 1990s from

    (A) conservative Catholics.
    (B) immigrant Muslims.
    (C) Orthodox Jews.
    (D) Southern Blacks.
    (E) western women.

18. "... whether they will or no, ... must now begin to look outward. The growing production of the country demands it. An increasing volume of public sentiment demands it."

    —Alfred Thayer Mahan in "The Influence of Sea Power Upon History" (1890)

    The statement above had the greatest impact on

    (A) increased demands for isolationism.
    (B) public sentiment supporting overseas imperialism.
    (C) the connection between the United States and its European allies.
    (D) a decrease in military spending.
    (E) America's entrance into World War II.

19. Progressive reformers supported all of the following causes EXCEPT

    (A) direct democracy.
    (B) free silver.
    (C) government regulation of big business.
    (D) child labor reform.
    (E) prohibition.

20. The Maryland Act of Toleration (1639) was passed to

    (A) encourage diversity in the colony.
    (B) maintain a safe haven for Catholics in the colonies.
    (C) expand the religious freedom of non-Christians.
    (D) protect the right of free speech in the colony.
    (E) dissuade racism between whites and slaves.

21. The Voting Rights Act of 1965

    (A) authorized literacy tests for all applicants.
    (B) had no "teeth" for enforcement.
    (C) allowed for millions of black voters to vote for the first time.
    (D) kept "grandfather clauses" in effect.
    (E) was overturned by the Supreme Court as unconstitutional.

22. The United States showed its willingness to sign unenforceable "paper agreements" without obligating itself to military enforcement in the

    (A) Lend-Lease Program.
    (B) Sherman Silver Purchase Act.
    (C) Open Door Policy.
    (D) Washington Naval Conference.
    (E) Roosevelt Corollary.

GO ON TO THE NEXT PAGE

23. *Glasnost* and *perestroika* were viewed by Americans as

    (A) potentially threatening to Soviet-U.S. relations.

    (B) a sign that the Cold War was nearing an end.

    (C) a sign that China and the USSR were rekindling their relationship.

    (D) the beginning of World War III.

    (E) a renewal of Stalinesque policies that would cause tension with the United States.

24. J. D. Salinger's *The Catcher in the Rye* addressed which of the following issues of the 1940s and 1950s?

    (A) Employment discrimination against women

    (B) Growing unemployment caused by increased imports from an economically recovering Europe

    (C) Alienated youth in a conformist world

    (D) Environmental problems brought about by postwar industrialization

    (E) African Americans' limited access to the middle class

25. "The duty of holding a neutral conduct may be inferred, without anything more, from the obligation which justice and humanity impose on every nation, in cases in which it is free to act, to maintain inviolate the relations of peace and amity towards other nations."

    —George Washington, 1796

    The quote above illustrates President Washington's concern over

    (A) the development of political parties.

    (B) the nation's preparation for warfare.

    (C) the power of the Bank of the United States.

    (D) the signing of the Jay Treaty.

    (E) U.S. neutrality and avoidance of alliances.

26. The Monroe Doctrine

    (A) was intended to limit European intervention in the Western hemisphere.

    (B) received great praise from world leaders upon its issuance.

    (C) was strongly enforced by the United States prior to the Civil War.

    (D) signaled a dramatic shift in U.S. foreign policy.

    (E) committed the United States as the "world's policeman."

GO ON TO THE NEXT PAGE

27. Despite public concern and mounting causalities, President Johnson

 (A) announced to the American public that he would personally take responsibility for the war.

 (B) refused to be the president that saw Vietnam go the way of China.

 (C) immediately arranged for peace negotiations with Ho Chi Minh.

 (D) considered immediate withdrawal of U.S. forces from Vietnam.

 (E) publicly agreed the United States was losing.

28. In 1963, a book by Betty Friedan

 (A) patronized women working outside the home.

 (B) exposed the boredom and myth of the American housewife.

 (C) explained the impact of pesticides on humans.

 (D) informed women how to care for babies and toddlers.

 (E) celebrated the civil rights movement.

29. Colonial New England women were able to

 (A) skip attending church if domestic matters dictated.

 (B) enjoy control over matters of the household, such as finances and purchases.

 (C) own property and enter legal contracts only as a widower or spinster.

 (D) divorce a husband due to infidelity.

 (E) control the religious education of their children.

30. "Among the numerous advantages promised by a well constructed Union, none deserves to be more accurately developed than its tendency to break and control the violence of faction."

—James Madison, *Federalist 10*, 1787

In the quote above, James Madison is warning against the danger of

 (A) states losing power to the federal government.

 (B) a "mobocracy."

 (C) political parties.

 (D) an overpowering executive branch.

 (E) voting rights for the uneducated.

31. The 1963 March on Washington

 (A) encouraged Congress to approve the civil rights bill swiftly.

 (B) failed due to low turnout and little enthusiasm.

 (C) ended in tragedy, as King was assassinated as he delivered his speech.

 (D) became a historic event as the speeches focused on the ideals of democracy.

 (E) was secretly planned by the Kennedy administration.

32. The focus of the Democrats in the 1992 presidential election was

 (A) civil rights.

 (B) cuts in defense spending.

 (C) health care reform.

 (D) welfare reform.

 (E) the economy.

GO ON TO THE NEXT PAGE ⇨

33. "There is nothing in our book, the Koran, that teaches us to suffer peacefully. Our religion teaches us to be intelligent. Be peaceful, be courteous, obey the law, respect everyone; but if someone puts his hand on you, send him to the cemetery. That's a good religion." (1963)

    The quote above was most likely spoken by which of the following?

    (A) James Farmer
    (B) Malcolm X
    (C) Martin Luther King, Jr.
    (D) H. Rap Brown
    (E) Roy Wilkins

34. "The wrath of God burns against them, their damnation does not slumber; the pit is prepared, the fire is made ready, the furnace is now hot, ready to receive them; the flames do now rage and glow. The glittering sword is whet, and held over them, and the pit hath opened its mouth under them."

    —Jonathan Edwards, 1741

    The quote above embodies the spirit of the Great Awakening in that

    (A) the sermon attempts to emote feelings of angst among listeners.
    (B) traditional Calvinist teachings are being shared.
    (C) only the elite would hear such speeches.
    (D) predestination is valued above faith.
    (E) it shows that emotion has no place in worship.

35. American attitudes regarding the Holocaust are best illustrated by

    (A) Congress's unwillingness to lift immigration restrictions on Jews fleeing to the United States.
    (B) the large amounts of funds sent for assistance of European Jews.
    (C) the speeches of Charles Lindbergh.
    (D) the greeting of the *St. Louis*.
    (E) widespread acceptance of Jews across the nation.

36. The Embargo Act of 1807 was enacted to

    (A) incite a war with Britain.
    (B) protest British and French violation of U.S. neutrality.
    (C) punish the South for trading with the French.
    (D) protect New England manufacturers from cheap British goods.
    (E) open shipping trade to non-American ships.

37. When the Soviet Union invaded Afghanistan in 1979, President Carter

    (A) derided the Soviet action but did little to protest publicly.
    (B) continued his efforts to make inroads with Chinese leaders.
    (C) curtailed grain sales to the Soviet Union and imposed a boycott of the 1980 Olympics in Moscow.
    (D) sent U.S. troops to Pakistan to launch an offensive.
    (E) implored NATO to step in to intervene in the crisis.

GO ON TO THE NEXT PAGE

38. Eli Whitney's invention of the cotton gin was significant in that it

    (A) increased the number of slaves in the South.

    (B) decreased the need for slave labor.

    (C) fueled the new reliance on steam power.

    (D) led to the development of the first textile mill.

    (E) was important in the progress of the turbine engine.

39. The Marshall court strengthened the power of the judicial branch by

    (A) declaring U.S. neutrality before the War of 1812.

    (B) acquitting Aaron Burr for the killing of Alexander Hamilton.

    (C) overturning convictions under the Alien and Sedition Acts.

    (D) urging a tariff on imported British and French goods.

    (E) establishing the precedent of judicial review by overturning the Judiciary Act of 1789.

40. At the time of the first wave of European settlers to North America, most Native American populations

    (A) could be found concentrated along the eastern seaboard.

    (B) had large, citylike societal structures.

    (C) were widely spread across the continent.

    (D) enjoyed the protection of confederations.

    (E) had similar languages and customs that unified them.

41. The Hartford Convention led to

    (A) a return to U.S. neutrality.

    (B) the death of the Federalist Party.

    (C) the election of James Madison.

    (D) a shift in demographic support for the War of 1812.

    (E) the dissolution of the Bank of the United States.

42. The national debt tripled during the 1980s due to

    (A) the expansion of the federal government.

    (B) increased federal income taxes.

    (C) protective tariffs.

    (D) the lowered value of the dollar in the world market.

    (E) loss of federal revenue and increased foreign borrowing.

43. President Andrew Jackson demonstrated the increasing power of the presidency through all of the following EXCEPT

    (A) deterring the rise of national third-party campaigns.

    (B) vetoing the building of the Maysville Road in Kentucky.

    (C) ignoring the Supreme Court ruling in *Worcester v. Georgia*.

    (D) standing up to South Carolina during the nullification crisis.

    (E) killing the Second Bank of the United States.

GO ON TO THE NEXT PAGE

44. In the interwar period (1919–1939), there was a strong push for an amendment to the Constitution to

(A) limit the president to two terms.

(B) disallow a declaration of war without a public referendum.

(C) change the date of inauguration to January 20.

(D) prohibit the sale of alcoholic beverages.

(E) give women the right to vote.

45. The pamphlet *Common Sense* by Thomas Paine aided the cause of American revolutionaries because it

(A) encouraged France to join in the war on the side of the Americans.

(B) led to the ultimate repeal of the Stamp Act.

(C) forced the king to consider the Olive Branch petition.

(D) created the government that would take hold after the revolution ended.

(E) pushed undecided Americans to join the fight for independence.

46. Passed in 1972, Title IX did which of the following?

(A) Barred discrimination in employment.

(B) Provided for equal pay for equal work.

(C) Protected people of color from discrimination.

(D) Required equal funding of public school activities for boys and girls.

(E) Ended the mandatory draft.

47. All of the following are true about the *Dred Scott* ruling EXCEPT

(A) it negated the Missouri Compromise.

(B) African Americans were not considered citizens.

(C) it upheld the doctrine of popular sovereignty.

(D) it influenced the nomination of Abraham Lincoln.

(E) it determined that Congress never had the right to ban slavery.

48. Congress refused to ratify the Treaty of Versailles on the grounds that

(A) it did not assign enough war blame to Germany.

(B) membership in the League of Nations could interfere with U.S. sovereignty.

(C) Italy and France were given territories in South America.

(D) self-determination was not enforceable.

(E) Germany needed military protection to rebuild after the war.

49. During the Cuban missile crisis,

(A) President Kennedy relied only on his diplomatic tools to solve the problem.

(B) President Johnson panicked and ordered immediate retaliation.

(C) Soviet submarines had already attacked the island of Grenada.

(D) the two nations stood at the brink of nuclear disaster.

(E) Premier Khrushchev ordered a naval blockade of all ships leaving the United States.

GO ON TO THE NEXT PAGE

50. The daily life of a U.S. soldier in Vietnam involved

(A) facing highly trained, uniformed Vietcong troops in the cities.

(B) constant barrages of shells and small arms fire.

(C) shorts bursts of action with long periods of boredom.

(D) easily rooting out the enemy from among civilians.

(E) slowly gaining territory from the North Vietnamese.

51. The concept of popular sovereignty held that

(A) Congress had the sole right to determine where slavery would exist.

(B) citizens living within the new territory would decide for themselves on the existence of slavery.

(C) individual property holders would decide whether or not to hold slaves.

(D) a national referendum vote would decide the slavery issue for new states.

(E) state courts had the right to overturn citizens' decisions regarding slavery.

52. The Proclamation of 1763 was designed to

(A) punish the colonists.

(B) cause a rift between the Native Americans and the colonists.

(C) protect the colonists from Native Americans in the west.

(D) draw more taxes from the South.

(E) open up western lands to more British settlement.

53. The main goal of the Granger movement was to

(A) extend civil rights protections for African Americans.

(B) aid farmers in the fight against unfair storage and shipping practices.

(C) take the United States off the silver standard.

(D) protect the laissez-faire policies of the Republicans.

(E) give land grants to displaced Native Americans.

54. President Eisenhower's policy toward South Vietnam can be characterized as

(A) giving it little attention after Ngo Dinh Diem took power, which allowed the French to stage a comeback.

(B) viewing it as vital to American security, as he feared the "domino effect."

(C) proactive, as he established more military outposts in the Pacific.

(D) aggressive, with his increased involvement of the U.S. military in South Vietnamese affairs.

(E) ignorant, as he continued to allow the French to call the shots in regards to policy.

55. By the mid-1960s, Northern support for the civil rights movement was

(A) improving after the 1963 March on Washington.

(B) fading in the face of forced school busing for integration.

(C) declining, as race riots and militancy frightened whites.

(D) supplanted by concerns over Watergate.

(E) unchanged from its 1955 level.

GO ON TO THE NEXT PAGE ⟩

56. Television in the United States in the late 1940s and the 1950s

(A) had no government regulations.

(B) had few advertisements for goods and services.

(C) broke down the American identity.

(D) furthered the mass-consumption culture of post-WWII Americans.

(E) was mostly filled with high quality cultural programs.

57. The environmental movement experienced new life after the release of

(A) the Pentagon Papers.

(B) Jacob Riis's *How the Other Half Lives*.

(C) information regarding the disaster at Three Mile Island.

(D) water test results from Love Canal, New York.

(E) Rachel Carson's *Silent Spring*.

58. The Strategic Defense Initiative (SDI)

(A) was proposed by the Reagan administration as a system of space satellites to intercept incoming missiles.

(B) would have violated the provisions of SALT I.

(C) called for the erection of large intercontinental missile bases in Alaska and Antarctica.

(D) involved building a large magnetic web that would shield the United States.

(E) was a portion of Kennedy's military strategy of flexible response.

59. Public education was MOST encouraged by which of the following colonies?

(A) Massachusetts

(B) Virginia

(C) Georgia

(D) New York

(E) Maryland

60. Forced busing of public school children

(A) helped stem the number of white families leaving urban areas for the suburbs.

(B) was met with acceptance by most Americans.

(C) eventually declined when the courts stopped enforcing the law..

(D) was a provision of *Brown v. Board of Education*.

(E) was more successful in the North than the South.

61. During World War II, the United States decided to lend and lease munitions to the Allies after

(A) Hitler invaded Poland.

(B) the Atlantic Charter.

(C) Germany invaded the Soviet Union.

(D) the Battle of Britain.

(E) Stalin entered the secret nonaggression pact.

62. By the Civil War, the South differed from the North in that the South

(A) had a more developed transportation system.

(B) boasted a more educated white citizenry.

(C) contained more cities than the North.

(D) attracted fewer European immigrants.

(E) allowed women to vote in local elections.

GO ON TO THE NEXT PAGE

63. The compromise made in the Kansas-Nebraska Act (1854) served to irritate sectional tensions further by

    (A) deeming the Missouri Compromise null and void.

    (B) throwing out the Fugitive Slave Law.

    (C) admitting Maine as a free state and Kansas and Nebraska as slave.

    (D) making popular sovereignty unconstitutional.

    (E) ending the old Republican Party.

64. In his pamphlet *Common Sense,* Thomas Paine argued that

    (A) government should derive its authority from the consent of those governed.

    (B) divine right is tantamount to natural rights.

    (C) the colonists had no right to declare independence from Britain.

    (D) government was inherently corrupt.

    (E) humans are naturally corrupt, necessitating a strong absolute ruler.

65. The principal reason for the economic boom in the United States after the Second World War was

    (A) full employment, because the United States kept 10 million men in the armed services as a precautionary measure.

    (B) the continual production of war materials on a round-the-clock basis.

    (C) the continuance of the federal government's operation of some basic industries, such as railroads.

    (D) a shortage of consumer goods during the war, combined with a reserve of purchasing power in the form of accumulated savings.

    (E) strong action by the federal government on behalf of organized labor.

66. Bacon's Rebellion led to

    (A) a reduction in slave trafficking.

    (B) a decrease in reliance on indentured servants for labor.

    (C) stricter laws adhering to church doctrine.

    (D) deportation of religious heretics.

    (E) improvement of relations between natives and colonists.

67. The largest group of immigrants outside of England in colonial America by 1775 were

    (A) Irish.

    (B) German.

    (C) African.

    (D) Scots-Irish.

    (E) French.

68. One possible early advantage for the Confederacy during the Civil War was

    (A) potential British and French intervention in favor of the South.

    (B) greater ability to fight an offensive war.

    (C) advanced industry.

    (D) better river and land transportation.

    (E) successful naval blockade.

69. The U.S. economy during the Carter presidency

    (A) was improving after the Nixon recession.

    (B) showed signs of failing though consumer confidence soared.

    (C) had lower rates of inflation than in the previous administration.

    (D) was boosted by the lifting of the oil embargo.

    (E) had high inflation and high unemployment.

GO ON TO THE NEXT PAGE

70. President Nixon's vice president, Spiro Agnew, was forced to resign from office because he

(A) lied about his involvement in the Watergate scandal.

(B) was indicted for tax evasion and bribery that occurred while he served as governor of Maryland.

(C) covered up his direct orders to the "plumbers" to break into Daniel Ellsberg's doctor's office to steal records.

(D) was believed to be a liability to the Republican Party.

(E) attempted to bribe members of the House during investigations into his alleged obstruction of justice.

71. The Free Speech Movement

(A) ended sit-in protests in the South.

(B) was concerned about the censorship of television and radio.

(C) was a group organized by Timothy Leary.

(D) was formed due to activities at the University of California.

(E) was the group responsible for the violence at the 1968 Democratic Convention.

72. The headright system

(A) established the right to import African slaves into the Chesapeake.

(B) provided for the seizure of any ship carrying indentured servants to the colonies.

(C) gave women legal the right to claim their husbands' property upon his death.

(D) granted acreage to any person who paid the passage of servants to the colonies.

(E) gave land to struggling debtors to cultivate cash crops.

73. The 1992 Los Angeles riots

(A) cost the city almost $1 billion in damages and more than 50 lives.

(B) were sparked by a jury's refusal to convict O. J. Simpson of murder.

(C) resulted in the destruction of affluent white neighborhoods.

(D) led to the investigation by the Kerner Commission.

(E) were not as violent as the earlier Watts riots in 1965.

74. President Reagan's most lasting legacy was his

(A) continuance of New Deal social programs.

(B) ability to limit defense spending.

(C) management of the national debt.

(D) conservative appointments to the judicial branch.

(E) protection of women's rights.

75. A major difference between Congressional and Presidential Reconstruction was

(A) the congressional plan was much tougher on Southerners than the presidential plans.

(B) the presidential plans did not seek to restore statehood to Southern states quickly.

(C) the congressional plan provided for Black Codes to be instituted in the South.

(D) the presidential plans placed the South under military occupation.

(E) the congressional plan allowed for individual "pardons" for former Confederates.

GO ON TO THE NEXT PAGE

76. In the decision of the Supreme Court in the case *Marbury v. Madison* (1803), Chief Justice John Marshall argued that

(A) the Court could rule acts of Congress unconstitutional, thereby establishing the principle of judicial review.

(B) the judicial branch could remove federal government appointees if found to be incompetent.

(C) cases involving states suing other states were protected under the Constitution.

(D) the executive branch had the authority to purchase land without congressional consent.

(E) the Court could override presidential vetoes.

77. President Nixon's strategy to end the Vietnam War was to

(A) keep the war going until he won re-election in 1972.

(B) reduce American troop involvement and teach the Vietnamese how to fight the war on their own.

(C) work with the nations of Laos and Cambodia to place diplomatic pressure on Ho Chi Minh to back down.

(D) use détente to pressure China into backing the United States.

(E) intensify the war so that South Vietnam would feel forced to negotiate a settlement.

78. The Civil Rights Act of 1964

(A) authorized the use of federal agents to enforce voting rights in the South.

(B) outlawed discrimination in employment on the basis of race, religion, national origin, or sex.

(C) banned the use of literacy tests and poll taxes.

(D) ordered the immediate integration of all public schools.

(E) did not end Jim Crow laws.

79. The War Powers Act (1973)

(A) ended the extended powers granted by the Gulf of Tonkin Resolution.

(B) was enacted to stop a possible "domino effect."

(C) was passed in response to the Tet Offensive.

(D) became null and void when overturned by the Supreme Court in 1975.

(E) immediately brought U.S. troops home from Vietnam.

80. The Pure Food and Drug Act of 1906 was the result of public pressure inspired by

(A) the Sherman Antitrust Act.

(B) the Wagner Act.

(C) *How the Other Half Lives.*

(D) food poisoning of American soldiers in Cuba.

(E) *The Jungle.*

STOP

Section II: Free-Response Questions

Time—130 minutes

This section contains five free-response questions. Answer the Document-Based question in Part A, one of the essay questions in Part B, and one of the essay questions in Part C. The first 15 minutes of the 130 minutes allocated for Section 2 is a reading period. During this period, you should read the Document-Based question and plan what you will write, including taking many notes. However, you cannot begin to write your essay until the 15-minute reading period has ended.

PART A: DOCUMENT-BASED QUESTION

Suggested writing time: 45 minutes

The following question requires you to write a coherent essay incorporating your interpretation of the documents and your knowledge of the period specified in the question. To earn a high score, you are required to cite key pieces of evidence from the documents and draw on your knowledge of the period.

1. To what extent did the African American Civil Rights Movement achieve its goals? Using the documents A through G and your knowledge of the period 1950–1978, construct a coherent essay that analyzes the outcomes of the Civil Rights Movement.

DOCUMENT A

A Drinking Fountain, 1943

GO ON TO THE NEXT PAGE

DOCUMENT B

Brown v. Board of Education, Topeka, 1954

"Whatever may have been the extent of psychological knowledge at the time of *Plessy v. Ferguson*, this finding is amply supported by modern authority. Any language in *Plessy v. Ferguson* contrary to this finding is rejected. We conclude that, in the field of public education, the doctrine of "separate but equal" has no place. Separate educational facilities are inherently unequal. Therefore, we hold that the plaintiffs and others similarly situated for whom the actions have been brought are, by reason of the segregation complained of, deprived of the equal protection of the laws guaranteed by the Fourteenth Amendment. This disposition makes unnecessary any discussion whether such segregation also violates the Due Process Clause of the Fourteenth Amendment."

DOCUMENT C

Martin Luther King, Jr., *Letter from Birmingham Jail*, 1963

"You may well ask: 'Why direct action? Why sit-ins, marches and so forth? Isn't negotiation a better path?' You are quite right in calling for negotiation. Indeed, this is the very purpose of direct action. Nonviolent direct action seeks to create such a crisis and foster such a tension that a community which has constantly refused to negotiate is forced to confront the issue. It seeks so to dramatize the issue that it can no longer be ignored. My citing the creation of tension as part of the work of the nonviolent-resister may sound rather shocking. But I must confess that I am not afraid of the word "tension." I have earnestly opposed violent tension, but there is a type of constructive, nonviolent tension which is necessary for growth. Just as Socrates felt that it was necessary to create a tension in the mind so that individuals could rise from the bondage of myths and half-truths to the unfettered realm of creative analysis and objective appraisal, we must we see the need for nonviolent gadflies to create the kind of tension in society that will help men rise from the dark depths of prejudice and racism to the majestic heights of understanding and brotherhood."

GO ON TO THE NEXT PAGE

DOCUMENT D

Voting Rights Act, 1965

"SEC. 2. No voting qualification or prerequisite to voting, or standard, practice, or procedure shall be imposed or applied by any State or political subdivision to deny or abridge the right of any citizen of the United States to vote on account of race or color."

DOCUMENT E

The Kerner Commission Report on Civil Disorders, 1968

"The typical rioter was a teenager or young adult, a life long resident of the city in which he rioted, a high school dropout; he was, nevertheless, somewhat better educated than his nonrioting Negro neighbor, and was usually underemployed or employed in a menial job. He was proud of his race, extremely hostile to both whites and middle-class Negroes, and although informed about politics, highly distrustful of the political system."

DOCUMENT F

Bobby Seale, 1975

"The first point was we wanted power to determine our own destiny in our own black community. And what we had done is, we wanted to write a program that was straightforward to the people. We didn't want to give a long dissertation."

DOCUMENT G

Excerpt from the majority opinion in *Bakke v. UC Regents*, 1978

"This case presents a challenge to the special admissions program of the petitioner, the Medical School of the University of California at Davis, which is designed to assure the admission of a specified number of students from certain minority groups . . . . For the reasons stated in the following opinion, I believe that so much of the judgment of the California court as holds petitioner's special admissions program unlawful and directs that respondent be admitted to the Medical School must be affirmed. For the reasons expressed in a separate opinion, my Brothers THE CHIEF JUSTICE, MR. JUSTICE STEWART, MR. JUSTICE REHNQUIST, and MR. JUSTICE STEVENS concur in this judgment."

GO ON TO THE NEXT PAGE

PART B

Suggested time: 35 minutes

Directions: Choose ONE question from this part. You are advised to spend 5 minutes planning and 30 minutes writing your answer.

2. Identify and analyze the development of industry between 1790 and 1850 with regard to technological advances, government involvement, and improvement of infrastructure.

3. Historians have labeled successful men of the Gilded Age as both "Robber Barons" and "Captains of Industry." To what extent do TWO of the following fit the names given them by historians?

   James Blaine

   John D. Rockefeller

   Andrew Carnegie

PART C

Suggested time: 35 minutes

Directions: Choose ONE question from this part. You are advised to spend 5 minutes planning and 30 minutes writing your answer.

4. Compare the impact of the railroad to the impact of the automobile on America with regard to the social, economic, and political in the 1870s and the 1920s.

5. Assess the degree to which American foreign policy shifted in the post–World War II era. Consider reactions to European, Asian, and Latin American nations in your response.

STOP

PRACTICE TEST 2 ANSWER KEY

1. E	21. C	41. B	61. D
2. A	22. D	42. E	62. D
3. C	23. B	43. A	63. A
4. A	24. C	44. B	64. A
5. A	25. E	45. E	65. D
6. B	26. A	46. D	66. B
7. B	27. B	47. C	67. C
8. A	28. B	48. B	68. A
9. B	29. C	49. D	69. E
10. E	30. C	50. C	70. B
11. B	31. D	51. B	71. D
12. B	32. E	52. C	72. D
13. E	33. B	53. B	73. A
14. E	34. A	54. B	74. D
15. E	35. A	55. C	75. A
16. C	36. B	56. D	76. A
17. A	37. C	57. E	77. B
18. B	38. A	58. A	78. B
19. B	39. E	59. A	79. A
20. B	40. C	60. C	80. E

ANSWERS AND EXPLANATIONS

MULTIPLE CHOICE

1. E

The KKK of the Reconstruction era stayed in the South, boasted police and local government officials among its ranks, used the Bible for inspiration, and committed many illegal acts against African Americans. As the 1920s dawned, the new KKK carried on these "traditions" but added other groups to its hate list. The KKK also did not remain restricted to the South—it had huge followings in Indiana, Ohio, and Illinois and even as far west as Oregon. It became a truly national movement.

2. A

On September 8, 1974, President Gerald Ford hoped to "end an American tragedy" by unconditionally pardoning Richard Nixon of all wrongdoing. Ford claimed that to see Nixon face a trial would be more painful than simply to put the episode in the past. The reaction was mixed, as many Americans felt betrayed by Nixon and wished to see him pay for his alleged crimes.

3. C

Having already made gains with the National Industrial Recovery Act (which was deemed unconstitutional in 1935), organized labor finally won its biggest legislative victory with the passage of the Wagner Act later that year. The sit-down strike at the GM plant in Flint occurred as result of the passage of the act. The AFL and CIO split over differences in ideology in 1936. The minimum wage was guaranteed in 1940 by the Fair Labor Standards Act. It was the Clayton Antitrust Act (1914), not the Sherman Antitrust Act, that exempted organized labor from trust regulations.

4. A

Unfortunately for former slaves and poor whites, sharecropping, or the crop-lien system, continued the cycle of poverty well into the 20th century. By owing the landowner rent, crops, and loans for supplies, the sharecropper was in constant debt due to low crop yields and an ever-changing market for agricultural goods. Most tenant farmers could barely live beyond subsistence and were more or less bound to the land.

5. A

Due to a provision that had the United States holding the Panama Canal indefinitely, the Caribbean nation long held that it should have eventual control over the canal. In 1977, President Carter successfully negotiated a treaty that would return control of the canal to the Panamanians in 1999. The United States formally recognized Cuba in 1898. Manuel Noriega was not a Panamanian concern until 1983, when he rose to power. Carter boycotted the 1980 Games in protest of the Soviet invasion of Afghanistan in 1979.

6. B

Puritan leaders grew increasingly concerned as younger generations of followers began to question the strict doctrine that ruled the lives of colonists. As a result, Puritan elders were forced to come up with ways to lure citizens back into the arms of the church.

7. B

In the 1988 presidential campaign, Bush had repeatedly stated, "Read my lips, no new taxes." This campaign phrase would haunt Bush throughout his presidency but most of all after he agreed to enact the largest tax increase in American history, coupled with massive spending cuts. It was Bush's continuation of Reagan's policies, such as military spending, that drove the national debt even higher and had Americans looking for relief. Most Americans were happy with the way Bush was cutting excess spending by eliminating programs and were pleased with his tough dealings with Iraq's Saddam Hussein.

8.   A

One of the most liberal Chief Justices ever to serve on the Supreme Court, Earl Warren made many enemies during his tenure. The Court handed down decisions upholding the civil rights of African Americans, the rights of the accused, and privacy protection. Many conservative critics charged that the Court was ignoring the Constitution in favor of advancing its own social agenda.

9.   B

To maintain the support of the border states, Abraham Lincoln declared that he sought to preserve the Union with or without slavery. He appealed for the exercise of restraint after the first states seceded from the Union, not wanting to provoke the South into a civil war. Anger over the enforcement of the Fugitive Slave Law and the passage of the Kansas-Nebraska Act soon led to the formation of a new political party, the Republicans, of which Lincoln was a member. Split North and South during their presidential nominating convention for the election of 1860, the Democrats sent forward two presidential candidates, driving a further rift within the party.

10.   E

Ever the optimist, Kennedy sought to remain in an advisory role in Vietnam and eventually leave the country to its own devices. He was killed before his true intentions regarding Vietnam could be articulated. Rapid escalation was the work of his successor, Lyndon Johnson, while Nixon championed the theory of Vietnamization.

11.   B

The "Contract with America" was designed to balance the federal budget, set term limits for members of Congress, offer large tax cuts, and reduce the overall size and scope of the federal government. Republicans intended to continue investing in building up the American military.

12.   B

Reconstruction effectively ended with the compromise agreement between Republicans and Democrats that settled the election of 1876. The election results were being contested between Democrat Samuel Tilden, who led in popular and electoral votes, and Republican Rutherford B. Hayes, who held that election fraud had occurred in several states. The compromise granted the presidency to Hayes, removed federal troops from the South, provided for the appointment of Democrats to Hayes's cabinet, and allocated funding for internal improvements.

13.   E

It was no secret that Alexander Hamilton and Thomas Jefferson did not see eye to eye with regard to the role of the federal government. Jefferson believed that small government was best, while Hamilton, a Federalist, believed in the importance of a strong central power. Political followers fell into two camps and eventually established the first two permanent political parties. Despite their disagreements, Jefferson did allow for most of Hamilton's ideas to remain throughout his presidency. The Bill of Rights was added to the Constitution to placate Anti-Federalists, who feared an overpowering central government.

14.   E

Despite handpicking the jurors who would hear the case, New York governor William Crosby was not pleased when all 12 delivered the verdict of "not guilty" for newspaper publisher John Peter Zenger. On trial for seditious libel, Zenger had overseen the printing of articles directly critical of Crosby. The Rights of Englishmen did not protect the press or speech. From this point on, many colonials felt it was well within their rights to protest against government.

15.   E

President Jefferson struggled with his decision to buy the Louisiana Territory, as no provisions explicitly existed in the Constitution authorizing a president to spend money not appropriated by Congress. Nonetheless, he followed through with the purchase in the best interest of the country. Each of the other answers gave Jefferson trouble either politically or personally, but none had as much to do with his interpretation of the Constitution as the Louisiana Purchase.

16. C
Anita Hill, a University of Oklahoma professor and former EEOC employee under Clarence Thomas, came forward with accusations of sexual harassment by the Supreme Court nominee as the final nomination went to the floor of the Senate. The event became a media spectacle as the "he said-she said" fight ensued. In the end, Thomas was confirmed and currently sits on the bench as one of the most steadfastly conservative justices, routinely voting against affirmative action and abortion rights.

17. A
Concerned over issues of abortion, homosexuality, and moral degradation, conservative American Catholics have been joining fundamentalist Christians in the New Right. This resurgence of conservatism began with the election of Ronald Reagan in 1980 and continued through the 2000s with the election of Republican George W. Bush.

18. B
Mahan's theory worked to shape public sentiment to agree that if America kept naval forces and acquired overseas posts for trade and docking purposes, the United States would emerge a world power.

19. B
While the Populists, who were mostly farmers had worked for "free silver," the Progressives were more interested in other reforms. They urged the direct election of U.S. Senators, governmental restrictions on big business, prohibition, and new laws that protected children in the workplace.

20. B
In an effort to encourage settlement, the Maryland Act of Toleration was passed to maintain a safe haven for persecuted Catholics. The act was quite punitive to other religions, suggesting arrest, expulsion, and even death for those who did not adhere to the divinity of Christ (e.g. Jews and atheists).

21. C
Thousands of first-time voters registered throughout the South after the passage of the Voting Rights Act of 1965. Literacy tests, grandfather clauses (a Reconstruction holdover), and poll taxes were now a thing of the past, opening the doors to all African Americans who wished to exercise their right to vote. The act revolutionized the American electorate.

22. D
President Harding was advised to host a conference designed to reduce the rapidly growing naval arms race after World War I. The conference ended with an agreement that limited the number of battleships each participating nation could have. The idea was that these kinds of self-regulations would keep the world free from conflict and the United States could remain relatively isolated. The Sherman Silver Purchase Act was in 1890, the Open Door Policy in 1899, the Roosevelt Corollary in 1904, and Lend-Lease in 1941.

23. B
Soviet Premier Gorbachev's policies of *glasnost* and *perestroika* were designed to give Russians more freedoms and reform the existing government. Americans saw this as a sign that the end of communism and the Cold War were a possibility.

24. C
Holden Caulfield, the main character in Salinger's novel, chose to rebel against the strong forces demanding conformity around him. *The Catcher in the Rye* was one of the most popular novels for American youth in the 1950s and 1960s.

25. E
In Washington's Farewell Address, the president made it clear that he recommended neutrality and avoidance of alliances with foreign powers. His concern was American self-interest and her ability to keep from getting caught between France and Britain. An ardent Federalist, Washington was in favor of the Bank of the United Sates. Though it was very unpopular, President Washington pressed for the ratification of the Jay Treaty to avoid a possible war with Britain.

26. A

Secretary of State John Quincy Adams, who served under President Monroe, was growing increasingly concerned over the possibility that new Latin American nations might not be able to survive if European powers intervened in their affairs. Adams was equally alarmed at the Russian insistence on its rights to occupy Alaska. Therefore, he drafted a message to Congress to be delivered by Monroe on December 2, 1823, to warn European nations that any incursion into the Western hemisphere would be seen as a threat and acted upon with force. This was not a well-received policy by the world, nor could it be effectively enforced by the United States at that time. Nor was it a particularly great departure from previous U.S. foreign policy.

27. B

President Johnson refused to watch Vietnam fall to the communists. He therefore escalated U.S. involvement in the conflict throughout his presidency. Johnson never took responsibility for the war, nor did he arrange for peace talks or withdrawal.

28. B

The Feminine Mystique by Friedan decried the lives of middle-class American housewives in the 1950s. This first step in the development of the modern women's movement would serve as the battle call for women all over the United States. In it, Friedan celebrated the need for women to have an identity outside the home and even a job. Pesticides were exposed in *Silent Spring* by Rachel Carson in 1962.

29. C

Puritan law dictated that a married woman obey her husband until she died or passed on. Therefore, these women had very little control of their own lives once they were married. Once widowed or if never married, women could own property and have some say in legal matters.

30. C

One of Madison's great fears was the development of "factions," or political parties, which he believed could destroy democracy. In *Federalist 10*, Madison warned against factions but also warned that to forbid the development of parties would be the end of true democracy. Throughout the *Federalist Papers*, the hallmarks of federalism, or the sharing of power between the federal government and states, was touted. While many feared a "mobocracy," or rule by the uneducated, the Founding Fathers of the Constitution protected the government by creating a representative system rather than a popular democracy.

31. D

Martin Luther King's "I Have a Dream Speech" riveted the 250,000-plus participants, making it the largest and most successful rally in American history up to that time. While it was planned in support of Kennedy's Civil Rights Bill, the administration had no hand in planning the event, nor did it do much to encourage the quick passage of the bill, which was promptly filibustered by Southern Democrats. King was not assassinated until 1968.

32. E

The Clinton camp knew that the way to win the election of 1992 was to focus on the recession and point their fingers at President George H. W. Bush as the culprit. Clinton had a strong following of African American voters and was able to reform health care and welfare during his time in office.

33. B

In 1963, the Nation of Islam (Black Muslims) followed the sermons of Malcolm X, who opposed the passive resistance tactics of men such as James Farmer of CORE, Martin Luther King, Jr., of the SCLC, and Roy Wilkins of the NAACP. H. Rap Brown was one of the leaders of another militant civil rights group that emerged in the late 1960s—the Black Panthers.

34. A

As one of the "New Lights" of the Great Awakening, Jonathan Edwards was known for delivering emotional sermons warning parishioners rich and poor of the eternal "fire and brimstone" of Hell that awaited sinners. Far from the traditional Calvinist "Old Lights," who emphasized predestination,

Edwards and others valued faith, good works, and prayer as the true path to Heaven.

35. A

Anti-Semitism ran high in the United States in the 1940s, as Jews were not accepted and were often discriminated against across the nation. Little funding went to the relief effort for European Jews from the United States. Speeches by men such as Lindbergh further fueled the fire, as Jews were blamed for the war. The story of the *St. Louis* is a tragic reminder of the scope of anti-Semitism; neither Cuba nor the United States would take the ship full of Jews fleeing assured death.

36. B

During the Napoleonic Wars, British and French naval ships continually violated U.S. neutrality by seizing cargo and impressing sailors into military service. In an attempt to avoid war and flex sovereignty, Jefferson rushed the Embargo Act through Congress; it prohibited all exports. Unfortunately, the embargo hurt New England merchants more than it hurt the British.

37. C

In a bold move to send a message to the world, President Carter boycotted the Olympic Games and ended sales of much needed grain stores to the USSR to protest the invasion of Afghanistan. The president was very public and vocal about his distaste for the move, which ended détente and the athletic careers of many American Olympic hopefuls. NATO had no jurisdiction to intervene, and no official dispatch of U.S. troops was ever made.

38. A

The cotton gin made cotton "King" in the South, thus increasing the reliance on slave labor to pick the crop.

39. E

Supreme Court Chief Justice John Marshall successfully increased the power of the judiciary branch in the decision handed down in *Marbury v. Madison* (1803). By overturning an act of Congress passed in 1789, Marshall established the doctrine of judicial review, giving the Court the power to decide the constitutionality of an act of Congress or action by the president. The Marshall court did not have a role in declaring neutrality, establishing tariffs, or overturning convictions under the Alien and Sedition Acts. John Marshall did preside over the trial of Aaron Burr, not for the killing of Alexander Hamilton but rather for Burr's treasonous role in a plot to have western territories secede from the Union and join with territory to be conquered in Spanish Mexico and Florida.

40. C

Archeologists estimate that the North American Native American population went from just under 1 million to a high of 10 million. These people were spread unevenly across the continent. Very few tribes lived in complex, citylike societies, and they varied greatly in both language and culture. Confederations of tribes did not develop until the massive increase of Europeans at the end of the 17th century. Native Americans had difficulty amassing a defense against European settlers because of their dispersion across a vast continent and their inability to communicate.

41. B

Members of the New England Federalists met at Hartford to suggest possible amendments to the U.S. Constitution in protest of the War of 1812. Some radical attendees even suggested that New England secede from the Union. Once the meeting was discovered and its resolutions made public, many Americans saw the attendees as unpatriotic traitors. The United States returned to a neutral position after the War of 1812, but this had nothing to do with the Hartford Convention. James Madison was a Jeffersonian Democrat and was already president at the time of the convention. The Bank of the United States did not "die" until around 1832.

42. E

President Reagan exempted Social Security, Medicare, and the military from the massive program cuts he made during his time in office. With the massive tax cuts, increased military spending, and massive borrowing to pay bills, the national debt eventually impacted the value of the dollar overseas due to high interest rates domestically.

43. A

As president, Andrew Jackson did more to strengthen the power of the office than any chief executive before him. However, he could not deter the growth of third parties in the United States to secure his position, as was evident in the third-party presidential run by the Anti-Masonic party in 1832. He vetoed more congressional bills than all presidents before him combined. Jackson dared the Chief Justice of the Supreme Court to enforce his decision regarding states' rights and Indian removal after the ruling in *Worcester v. Georgia*. By standing up to the "nullies," Jackson successfully avoided a potential secession of South Carolina from the Union. Finally, being an ardent Jeffersonian, Jackson believed that the Bank of the United States was a monopolistic money monster and worked tirelessly to kill it once and for all.

44. B

Many Americans were worn down by the impact of World War I and wished to limit the power of the government to declare war. In the wave of Progressive reforms that were passed prior to the outbreak of World War I, Americans were empowered with greater influence at the ballot box. They wished to extend this power by amending the Constitution to add a public voice to the declaration of war. The government stopped short of this request by issuing Neutrality Acts in the face of World War II. The amendment to limit the president to two terms did not emerge until after Franklin D. Roosevelt won his third term. During FDR's first term, the inauguration date was changed to January 20. Prohibition was enacted in 1920 and repealed in 1935. Women were given the right to vote in 1919.

45. E

In very plain terms, Paine appealed to Americans' "common sense" in his pamphlet, saying that rule by a single tyrant thousands of miles away was illogical. There was little discussion of what government would be like after the war in Paine's work. The Olive Branch Petition was sent to England on July 8, 1775, well before the July 1776 publication of Paine's pamphlet. The Stamp Act had been repealed 10 years before *Common Sense*.

46. D

Title IX required that public schools provide adequate funding to run sports programs for both boys and girls during the same season. Equal pay for equal work has not yet been achieved. Legal discrimination on the basis of color ended with the passage of the Civil Rights Act of 1964. A draft is still possible, as a "stand-by" list has been kept since 1980.

47. C

One of the most influential cases in U.S. history is *Dred Scott v. Sanford*, which was decided by the Taney Court in 1857. A slave who had been moved with his wife from free to slave territory by a series of masters, Scott finally sought freedom when he was transferred to a new owner in 1843. Winding its way through the Missouri court system to the federal courts, the case finally landed at the Supreme Court. The ruling determined that Scott, as a black man, had no right to sue in federal court due to the fact that he was not a citizen. Furthermore, the Court determined that the Compromise of 1820 was unconstitutional in that Congress never had the authority to regulate slavery in the territories. The decision so outraged Northerners that they called for the nomination of Abraham Lincoln as the Republican presidential candidate.

48. B

Unfortunately for President Woodrow Wilson, iArticle X of the League of Nations that kept the U.S. Congress from ratifying the Treaty of Versailles. Each member nation had to agree to become a part of a covenant in which all member nations would come to the aid of any other in times of peril. Senators such as Henry Cabot Lodge and his followers refused to sign the treaty without the addition of "reservations," whereas the "Irreconcilables," such as Hiram Johnson and William Borah, refused to sign the treaty regardless of additions or deletions.

49. D

It was clear to Kennedy that diplomacy alone would not stop the Soviets from placing nuclear missiles less than 90 miles off the coast of the United States. He therefore ordered a naval blockade of all Soviet ships on their way to Cuba in the hopes of intercepting the missiles before they arrived. His plan worked, and Khrushchev finally backed down and removed the missiles from Cuba. Kennedy had to pledge that the United States would never again attempt to invade Cuba and that American missiles in Turkey would be dismantled within six months. Khrushchev, in fact, may have gotten the better deal, although publicly, Kennedy seemed to have come out ahead.

50. C

Many U.S. soldiers complained of nothing more than the pure boredom they endured as they served their time in Vietnam. Until the Tet Offensive, the fighting remained largely in the countryside rather than in cities. Vietcong were disorganized and wore regular peasant clothing, making it very difficult for Americans to tell who was enemy and who was civilian. The Americans never really gained any sort of footing in Vietnam.

51. B

The decision-making process regarding slavery would be left to the citizens of a new territory under popular sovereignty. Congress wished to avoid involvement in the decision altogether, as slavery was seen as a states' rights issue.

52. C

In a show of support of colonists and friendship to the Native Americans, the British crafted the Proclamation Line of 1763 to protect the colonists from attack and extend a hand of peace to the native tribes. Some colonists, particularly veterans who had fought in the French and Indian War, were angry at this seemingly blatant attack on their freedom to live where they wished and simply ignored the line.

53. B

First founded as a social group for farmers, the Grangers soon evolved into a political organization that would work to protect farmers from price gouging and other ruthless business tactics of middlemen and railroad tycoons. The Grangers were more interested in protecting farmers economically than in taking on the social ills of the day. Later, the Populists would take over for the defunct Granger movement by asking for the free coinage of silver and removal of the gold standard.

54. B

President Eisenhower deeply feared what he called the "domino effect," where one Southeast Asian nation would fall to communism leading to the fall of the others. Therefore, he committed millions of dollars and "military advisors" to South Vietnam to keep North Vietnamese communists, led by Ho Chi Minh, from making headway in the South. By the time Eisenhower became deeply involved, the French had been defeated, and a puppet government in the South, led by Ngo Dinh Diem, sat in their place. Eisenhower was not terribly aggressive but allowed the puppet government to maintain control during his presidency.

55. C

By late 1965, the race riots of the Long Hot Summers and increased militancy sent shock waves throughout otherwise supportive white groups in the North. Support did rise slightly after the March on Washington but not significantly. Forced busing and Watergate did not occur until the 1970s.

56. D

The "boob tube," or "idiot box" as it was called by critics, became the new American pastime. Television was filled with ads for consumer goods furthering the mass consumption that fueled the postwar economy. Television was actually federally funded and heavily regulated. TV helped to create a national "persona" through shows and ads aimed at young families.

57. E

Writer Rachel Carson mobilized a new generation of environmentalists with her book *Silent Spring* (1962), which chronicled the dangers of the pesticide DDT. Carson was inspired to write the book when a friend from Massachusetts wrote her a letter describing the damage DDT sprayings were having on large bird species in the area. The Pentagon Papers were documents leaked to the *New York Times* by Daniel Ellsberg in 1971 regarding the Vietnam War. *How the Other Half Lives* was a piece of muckraking journalism written by Jacob Riis during the Progressive Era. Three Mile Island and Love Canal both occurred in the 1970s after the release of *Silent Spring*.

58. A
The Strategic Defense Initiative (SDI), or "Star Wars," was a plan that would build a space defense system of satellites and lasers that would detect and intercept Soviet missiles aimed at the United States. Kennedy's flexible response was a step away from Eisenhower's "New Look" military, because it included budgeting for conventional troops as well as nuclear capacity.

59. A
Puritans held nothing higher than the word of God and believed that one could not be truly "chosen" unless he or she could read the Bible. Therefore, once 50 families had established homes in an area of Massachusetts, it was mandated that the community provide a teacher to instruct students in reading.

60. C
State and federal judges began to step away from the forced integration of schools in the early 1970s, as violence and protests broke out in all parts of the nation over the issue. *Brown v. Board* only insisted on the desegregation of public schools with "all deliberate speed," but it did not specify how this was to happen. "White flight" occurred regardless of busing or other provisions to integrate schools and communities.

61. D
Distraught after the almost year-long shelling of London by the German *blitzkrieg* called the Battle of Britain, British Prime Minister Winston Churchill asked President Roosevelt for war assistance in 1941. Congress passed the Lend-Lease Act in April of 1941 to aid our friend overseas. Hitler did invade

Poland, Stalin did enter a secret nonaggression pact, and the Atlantic Charter involved both Britain and the United States, but none of these had an impact on Lend-Lease.

62. D
European immigrants flocked to Northern cities, where jobs could be found in the textile mills of New England and the Middle States. The South struggled with a primitive transportation system, a poorly educated white population, and few urban centers. Women were not allowed to vote in local elections in the South until 1920.

63. A
The Kansas-Nebraska Act killed the Missouri Compromise by instead instituting the doctrine of popular sovereignty in the newly organized territories of Kansas and Nebraska. This fueled sectional tension, as anti-slaveryites and slave proponents fought and sometimes killed each other over the elections to decide the slave issue in Kansas. Maine was admitted as a free state under the Missouri Compromise. The Republican Party was actually born from the crisis that stemmed from the Kansas-Nebraska Act.

64. A
Thomas Paine's pamphlet *Common Sense* echoed the teachings of Enlightenment thinker John Locke. The pamphlet argued that government, while supreme, must still derive its strength from the consent of those governed. Locke also argued that citizens had a obligation to rebel against a government that was failing to protect their natural rights, a sentiment echoed by Thomas Paine. The philosophy of divine right and absolute rule could be seen in the reigns of Queen Elizabeth I of England and Louis XIV of France.

65. D
Americans who stayed home during World War II had few consumer goods to buy and, therefore, stocked their earnings away. Once the war was over and goods were plentiful, Americans spent with reckless abandon.

66. B

Backwoods farmers who had previously been indentured servants had grown increasingly angry over repeated attacks by natives with no protection from the local government. In 1676, Nathaniel Bacon and his band of followers rose up in protest against the elite establishment, scaring it into finding more suitable (and docile) laborers.

67. C

Despite the fact that they were brought to the colonies against their will, the largest immigrant group by 1775 were African slaves. Making up nearly 80 percent of the population in the South, Africans clearly outnumbered whites in the region.

68. A

It was rumored that either the British or the French or both would recognize the legitimacy of the Confederacy and provide much-needed aid to the South. Unfortunately for the Rebels, this support never materialized. The South was in no position to wage an offensive war (although Antietam and Gettysburg were notable exceptions) and had much less in the way of industry and transportation. The Union established a successful naval blockade of the South.

69. E

Stagflation is an economic condition that government cannot repair and one that the Carter administration suffered under the entire term. There were no signs of improvement during the Carter years—inflation was as high as it had ever been. Another energy crisis caused by problems in the Middle East further strapped worldwide oil production.

70. B

Vice President Spiro Agnew was forced to resign in 1973 under charges that he had accepted bribes while serving as the governor of Maryland. Agnew had no real role in Watergate, but he had contended that Nixon released the information regarding his wrongdoings to divert attention away from Watergate.

71. D

September 14, 1964, signaled the beginning of the Free Speech Movement, when Dean Towle announced that political activities would be restricted on a section of the University of California–Berkeley campus normally reserved for such activities. The FSM actually used some of the tactics of the Civil Rights Movement with sit-ins, sleep-ins, and teach-ins. Timothy Leary was a Harvard professor who gained attention with his use and approval of LSD. The 1968 Democratic Convention was interrupted by antiwar protesters, not the FSM.

72. D

The headright system granted 50 acres of land to the sponsor for every indentured servant whose passage was paid to the colonies. The system made for some very wealthy landowners in the Southern colonies, and created a large underclass of whites, who would serve contracts between 7 and 10 years before they were free.

73. A

Sparked because of a white jury's failure to convict Los Angeles police officers of the beating of African American suspect Rodney King, the LA riots, which lasted three days, cost the city in lives and property. The city was ravaged by looters and vandals, but most of this remained well within the poor sections of Los Angeles. The Watts Riots of 1965 cost 34 lives and $100 million in damages. The Kerner Commission was appointed by Lyndon Johnson to investigate the causes of the race riots of the Long Hot Summers of 1965 and 1966.

74. D

Having appointed more judges to the federal bench than any other U.S. president, Ronald Reagan certainly made his mark on the judicial branch. His legacy is lasting due to the fact that all of his appointments had lifetime jobs. Reagan sought to dismantle some New Deal programs and had little interest in furthering women's issues. During his time in office, military spending was higher than at any other time in history, which increased the national debt.

75. A

The Presidential Reconstruction plans of Lincoln and Johnson sought to readmit the Southern states quickly back into the Union and offered pardons to many ex-Confederate military and political leaders (many of whom were wealthy plantation owners). Congressional Reconstruction, on the other hand, was a reaction to the leniency of Presidential Reconstruction and enforced much stricter laws in an attempt to punish ex-Confederates. Congress placed the South under military rule in 1867 through the Military Reconstruction Act.

76. A

Chief Justice John Marshall strengthened the power of the judicial branch during his 30 years on the Court. By declaring the Judiciary Act of 1801 to be unconstitutional, Marshall set the precedent of judicial review in which the Court could declare an act of Congress to be unconstitutional. The Court does not have jurisdiction over the removal of federal appointees and cannot override presidential vetoes. There are no provisions in the Constitution regarding the purchase of land, and it forbids state versus state cases.

77. B

The process Nixon called "Vietnamization" involved slowly decreasing the number of U.S. troops in the region and turning over the war effort to the South Vietnamese. Nixon promised an end to U.S. involvement even before his re-election. There were never any negotiations with Laos or Cambodia regarding their ability to place diplomatic pressure on Ho Chi Minh. It was the North Vietnamese that the United States needed to negotiate with, not the South.

78. B

The largest of the legislative victories of the Civil Rights movement, the Civil Rights Act, served to end discrimination across the nation. Jim Crow died with this act. The banning of literacy tests and poll taxes and the authorization of federal agents to enforce voting rights were instituted in the Voting Rights Act of 1965.

79. A

In response to information about secret bombing missions over Cambodia and other executive abuses of power, Congress passed the War Powers Act to curb the ability of a president to engage U.S. troops for long periods of time without congressional approval. The Tet Offensive occurred in 1968. U.S. troops were not brought home by the War Powers Act.

80. E

Upton Sinclair's muckraking exposé of the meatpacking industry sent Americans reeling and demanding government intervention to protect their health. President Roosevelt worked with lawmakers and the meatpacking industry to craft the Pure Food and Drug Act of 1906. Soldiers were struck with food poisoning while fighting the Spanish-American War in Cuba, but it did not lead to any legislation. The Sherman Antitrust Act was designed to end the stranglehold of monopolies on the American economy. The Wagner Act, not passed until the New Deal administration of Franklin D. Roosevelt, dealt with organized labor. *How the Other Half Lives* was a piece of muckraking by Danish immigrant and photojournalist Jacob Riis that dealt with poverty and immigration.

DBQ Analyses

Document A:

Inferences: Immediately your eye should be drawn to the signs and water fountain. This photo clearly shows the impact of Jim Crow laws in the South that segregated all aspects of life. The date is also of import, as it is before the *Brown* decision and the Montgomery Bus Boycotts.

Document B:

Inferences: This case ended segregation in public schools by overturning *Plessy*. This case is the starting point for the modern Civil Rights Movement. Here you may infer that the goal of the movement was to end racial segregation.

Document C:

Inferences: By this time in the movement, Dr. King has moved from the quiet of Montgomery to the most segregated city in the country to launch protest. It is important to know that King had begun to use children in his marches by this time to increase the impact of the protests on television and newspapers. He had been asked by fellow Southern pastors why he could not wait for the white man to make change. This letter is his response to them.

Document D:

Inferences: Having won a legislative victory the previous year with the passage of the Civil Rights Act, the movement experienced another win with the Voting Rights Act. Here, protections were guaranteed for voters regardless of race.

Document E:

Inferences: This report was written after the outbreak of racial violence during the Long Hot Summers of 1965–1966. You may infer that not all of the problems plaguing African Americans had been addressed by the Civil Rights Movement, as the riots clearly proved.

Document F:

Inferences: Bobby Seale was a leader of the Black Panthers, a militant group based in Oakland, California. This quote was written 10 years after the formation of the Panthers and shows a sense of determination of African Americans to have control over their own destinies and communities. Again, you may use this to show possible problems still in existence after the end of the Civil Rights Movement.

Document G:

Inferences: You would have to know that this case involved a white student suing the University of California because he was denied admission to the school based on race. This "reverse discrimination" case was aimed directly at the racial quotas some universities used to diversify their campuses. The court ruled in Bakke's favor by stating that race could not be used as a sole determination in the admission of a student to a publicly funded school.

Review the plan of action for DBQ #1 and the information regarding writing DBQs in chapter 2.

This prompt is asking you to evaluate the extent to which the African American Civil Rights Movement achieved its goals by 1978. You may choose to write a thesis that says that the movement was very successful in meeting its goals, or you may choose to say that the movement was not wholly successful by 1978. In either case, you must use information from the documents and your knowledge of the time period to support your assertion.

SAMPLE DBQ RESPONSE

The era of the mid- to late 1900s was a time when America was grasping its foothold in the world of society, politics, and economics. Socially, America was enduring a time of civil conflict among the races of the blacks and the whites. Civil Rights activists were starting their campaigns, and many succeeded by getting the nation to stop and acknowledge all the racial tensions of the time. By 1978, the African American Civil Rights Movement had achieved its goals, but not all of them to a full extent. There were still minute turmoils and anti civil rights movements taking place that kept a negative image. The year 1978 and the years to follow had a far better condition for the average African American, but there were still some issues that even today appear in society and deal with racial prejudices.

The extent to which the African American Civil Rights Movement achieved its goals by 1978 was a tremendous accomplishment. Around the 1880s the Jim Crow Laws were established in the South, legalizing segregation between the blacks and the whites. This resulted in legal suits, mass sit-ins, and boycotts to get rid of segregation. Southern whites responded by violent attacks, and in some cases federal troops were needed to keep order. The Civil Rights Act, Voting Rights Act, and Fair Housing Act ended the legal sanction of the Jim Crow Laws around the 1960s (Document A), which was a huge step forward from previous conditions. The Voting Rights Act of 1965 was an excellent contribution to the civil rights of African Americans. This win entitled a guaranteed vote to all citizens regardless of their race. The court case *Brown v. Board of Education in Topeka, Kansas* during 1954 had a massive impact on African American society and racial segregation as well. The result of this court case lead to desegregation of public schools when Chief Justice Earl Warren broke long tradition and overruled the "separate but equal" doctrine of the *Plessy v. Ferguson* case. For the first time he acknowledged that public schools violated the principle of equal protection under the law of the Fourteenth Amendment of the Constitution. This decision gave great facilitation to the civil rights movement and brought integration in public facilities and accommodations (Document B). Martin Luther King is one of the most influential and renowned African American activists during the civil rights movement, and his nonviolent approach to protesting brought a great deal of support. By the time he had moved from his quiet home in Montgomery to a segregated city, he had a dream to see equality among all colors. He used clever strategies such as involving the youth and children in protests that aired on the television and were printed in the newspaper. This led to a more highly interested public in the current issues of racial prejudices at the time. King was questioned by Southern pastors how or why "he could not wait for the white man to make change," and his responses always conveyed the same messages of non-violence, peace, and equality. He was imprisoned many times for his protests and beliefs and over time has grown to be a constant reminder of courage against racial prejudices (Document C). These factors all brought many wins to the battle of Civil Rights up to 1978.

Many benefits were received through the countless efforts of activists towards the Civil Rights Movement; however, some principles and ideas didn't give way and unfortunately hold true to some people even today. Like in any other category, there is always a case of bad apples. In the Civil Rights Movement, as in other movements, there were those blacks who opposed asking for equality and help from the opposite race and saw it as a means of demeaning oneself. These teenagers or young adults were mostly high school dropouts that were proud of their race and extremely hostile to both whites and middle-class Negroes (Document F). Not all problems that pestered African Americans were addressed by the Civil Rights movement, such as the rise of the Black Panther party in 1966, which lost its influence in the late 1970s. The Panthers were a militant group based in Oakland, California, who saw violent revolution as the only means of achieving black liberation. They armed themselves for the liberation and brought violence, showing that again, problems still existed after the end of the civil rights movement (Document G).

The Civil Rights Movement was a time of peaceful picketing, violent rioting, and life-changing political court cases. The time shaped a new era of opportunity for people of color. However, some racial prejudices still hold true today. There are many organizations that work against the racial discrimination of colored men, women, and children, such as the National Association for the Advancement of Colored People (NAACP). This organization is a current day group of American blacks, and whites, whose goal is to end racial discrimination and segregation among blacks. Founded in 1908, it still has its foothold in society and strives to achieve those same goals of the Civil Rights Movement. With strong mindset goals such as those of King and the NAACP of today, the racism in society will soon diminish and century-long goals of equality among all colors will be fulfilled.

FRQs

2.

Study List:

Technological Advances
steamboats
clipper ships
Conestoga wagons
trains
Lowell system

Government Involvement

Indian removal

tariffs

Clay's American System

Bank of the United States

Infrastructure Improvements

canals

railroads

turnpikes

national roads

SAMPLE ESSAY

Shortly after the American Revolution of 1776, the United States had a boom in its development of industry. Before the U.S. gained its independence, its industry, for the most part, relied on imports and exports from across the Atlantic. Throughout the colonial period, the colonies were relied on for their raw materials, such as cotton, tobacco, rice, and indigo. Because colonies such as the Carolinas and Virginia were rich in goods, they were all often seen as markets for British and West Indian goods. It was never thought of that the colonies would ever have their own independent industry. Yet, as the American Revolution was coming to a conclusion, an American industry was starting to form. Essentially, there are three categories that contributed to the development of industry during 1790 and 1850: technological advances, government involvement, and improvement of infrastructure. Through these three categories, the first independent American industry was formed and took the United Stated to the level of eventually being one of the biggest economic powers in the world.

To maintain a powerful industry, it is important to have generic technological advances. Indeed, the United States had many inventions that catalyzed the development of industry. Examples of these inventions include the steamboat and the clipper ship. Invented by Robert Fulton, the steamboat helped to accelerate trade throughout America. This invention allowed merchants to travel against river currents and send their products from the South to the North. This helped the Southern economy, because they were able to have a quick and reliable way to ship their goods. Next, clipper ships had the same sort of effect as steamboats, but in a bigger way. These ships, grand and large, had lateen sails and made the trip across the Atlantic Ocean easier for merchants. Technological advances not only took place on water, but also on land. Such inventions were trains and Conestoga wagons. Trains, arguably one of the biggest American technological advances, helped to develop an extremely fast way for goods and also people to travel across the United States. Conestoga wagons weren't exactly as easy as trains, but fit for the middle to lower classes. Overall, these advances helped escalate the development of industry and left the U.S. in a position where it held a legitimate amount of economic power.

Major development of industry can also be attributed to the involvement of government. Through many governmental acts, the United States was able to create a steady economy. Prior to the American Revolution, England placed many tariffs and duties on the United States that prevented the colonies from importing and exporting goods without the participation of England. Such acts were the Navigation Acts, Tea Act, Stamp Act, and the Declaratory Act. After the revolution, the U.S. was able to control the importation and exportation of goods that contributed to an independent economy. Government involvement in industry post-Revolution included the Removal Act of 1830, the Bank of US, and more. The Removal Act of 1830 (or Indian removal) was a demand by Andrew Jackson saying that Indians must surrender all their land to the government or die fighting for it. This was motivated by the fact that Jackson wanted to sell all land at a cheap price to white settlers, because he aspired to migrate west. In the end, he hoped to have a booming economy, in part because of westward expansion. Also, industry development may be attributed to the formation of a Bank of the US. The formation of this bank would help individualize the United States economy, while regulating and strengthening it. The government involvement in industry helped to develop a strong economy and also bring industry to the western United States.

Not highly publicized were the infrastructure improvements of the United States during 1790 and 1850. These infrastructure improvements include the formation of national roads, canals, turnpikes, and railroads. Most of these infrastructure improvements were put into action due to the inventions of trains, steamboats, etc. Although they may have not seemed important, they were the internal improvements that shaped our present-day United States. National roads were formed in response to wagons and later the invention of the automobile. Canals were formed for water transportation for steamboats. Canals were usually in coastal areas and fed into large ports. Turnpikes were much in response to the westward movement and also to improve transportation for large Conestoga wagons. Finally, the railroads were made for trains to travel. Later on, railroads became increasingly popular due to the formation of the Transcontinental Railroad. Overall, the infrastructure improvement of the United States helped form the industry and gave our American industry the ability to travel coast to coast.

3.

Study List:

Blaine

Implicated in the Credit Mobilier scandal, which involved the Union Pacific Railroad and bribery career in Congress
ran for president

Rockefeller

Standard Oil
trusts and monopolies
Ida Tarbell

Carnegie

US Steel
vertical integration
philanthropies
"Gospel of Wealth"

SAMPLE ESSAY

At a time when America was grasping its foothold in full-scale economics and when businesses were starting a new, trying to make it big in the market—two men by the names of Andrew Carnegie and James D. Rockefeller amassed great gains in their self-made industries. Their ambition and morals led them to rule some of the most profitable industries of their time. Rockefeller soon became the "robber baron" and "captain of industry" for Standard Oil, and Andrew Carnegie for steel. Both of these men used their tactics, power, and smarts to monopolize and gain control over their category of investment and push small businesses aside to reap full benefits and profit. They truly were, to the fullest extent, the captains of industry during their age.

By the early 1870s, John D. Rockefeller was know, to be an American capitalist well known for his success in the petroleum industry through the founding of the Standard Oil Company. With strong tactics in business, he came to guide Standard Oil towards its number one spot as the largest oil refinery business in the world. He even reached the title as the richest man in the United States. Being a great philanthropist, he gave a great amount of his wealth and earnings to private foundations of knowledge and research. By keeping his cost and wages at a minimum low, his business grew quickly. Because his business was most prominent and dominant over smaller businesses, he had a reputation of being a great holder of monopoly and trusts. During the anti-trust movement, the 1904 book The History of the Standard Oil Company by Ida Tarbell, whose father had been driven out of business by Rockefeller's business arrangements, was published. Great support of anti-trust laws was activated. Soon, Standard Oil gradually gained virtual control of oil production in America, leading Rockefeller to be greatly renowned for his success in his monopoly over oil production.

Andrew Carnegie established an industry dominant in the production of steel through vertical integration, meaning he owned all the industries that went through the process of building steel. Carnegie noticed the need of steel and steel production in America, so he geared towards founding and running the Carnegie Steel Company. He concentrated on production instead of the stock-market manipulations and expanded his plants.

By the 1990s his company was responsible for producing a 1/4th of U.S. steel. His vertical integration worked through his control over iron mines, coke ovens, ore ships, and railroads. His essay "The Gospel of Wealth" preached the idea that rich men are trustees of their wealth and should contribute for the good of the public. Thus, he was a well-known philanthropist who helped fund institutions of teaching as well as thousands of libraries. He, too, was a captain of industry and proved so by his bountiful success.

With such legends as Rockefeller and Carnegie as a part of our United States history, it is possible to see what hard work and determination can lead to. Both men were great captains of their industries, and in not such a good light of reputation, Robber Barons, as well. Their control over such a vast and important amount of industry led them to override smaller industries along the way and achieve maximum wealth. Their amazing capacity of wealth, production, and efficiency lead them to be well known and legendary even today.

4.

Study List:

	Social	Political	Economic
Railroad	Women could travel unaccompanied.	Sectional split between North and South.	Furthered the expansion of industry.
	People could travel great distances to see the nation.	Large land grants to build rail.	Aided in the rebuilding of the South.
	Class was clear in seating options on board.	Connection of the west with the rest of the nation.	Monopolies and problems with farmers.
	Rail towns grew along routes. Brought Irish and Chinese immigrants into the country.		
Automobile	Dating relations became more secretive.	Federal funding for the building of roads and road safety.	Henry Ford—price, assembly line
	Families could move away.	Shift in priority from from cities to suburbs.	Shipping of goods rail to auto.
	"White flight"	Protections of oil companies.	New industries—oil, rubber, tar, glass, chemical
	Cross-country travel linked Americans together.		

SAMPLE ESSAY

Every day, most Americans have some sort of daily routine. They wake up in the morning, take a shower, grab a cup of coffee, read the newspaper, and possibly do several other things. Yet there is one practice that finds its way into the daily routines of almost every person in the United States. This is that of walking out of the house and soon finding the way to a mode of transportation. Most commonly used in present times, the automobile is becoming so popular that it has its own industry. Whether it is a school bus, city bus, Toyota, or Ferrari, most Americans use an automobile sometime in their life to transport themselves. Yet, in the late nineteenth to early twentieth century, Americans most commonly used the railroads to get where they wanted to go. Both the railroad and automobile industries had tremendous impacts on the political, social, and economic aspects of life in the 1870s and 1920s, and it is the fact that their impacts were so influential among Americans that sets them apart from any other invention created in America. From catching the train to a weekend paradise in the year 1900, to cruising Pacific Coast Highway with the top down in 2005, both of these creations have had the same effect on our culture that precipitates into our world today.

Both the automobile and railroads, at the time of their creations, had everlasting effects on the social life of Americans, with an emphasis on the relationship between husband and wife, family to family, and also among all Americans. First off, the creation of the railroads came in a time of economic boom. This was the time of tycoons and birth of business and enterprise. The railroad only increased this boom by interconnecting much of the American culture. With railroads, Americans were able to travel great distances to see the nation. Along with that, rail towns were built along routes, which added to the expansion of the United States. Railroads didn't just affect Americans; they also affected cultures such as the Irish and Chinese. Railroads are a big contributor to the fact that many Chinese and Irish came into this country. About 50 years later came the birth of the automobile. The automobile had both positive and negative effects on the social aspect of America. One negative aspect is that dating relations became more secretive. Also, commonly known as one of the biggest environmental problems of the U.S. is the problem of smog emissions from vehicles. Aside from the negative aspects, automobiles have left Americans with a sense of unity due to the interstate highway systems, and also the fact that you can travel anywhere in the continental United States by traveling in an automobile (plus a lot of gas money!). Socially, both the trains and automobiles have benefited us Americans. Life is just a bit easier, and we are more productive human beings.

Politically, railroads and automobiles had modest effects, although there were some effects from these two modes of transportation. For example, the railroads added a sectional split between the Northern and Southern United States. Also, railroads were essentially the first easy connection between the west and the rest of the United States. This added to a sense of unity and also contributed to the population flow into the western region of America. In regards to automobiles, they had most of their effect on government spending. Automobiles demanded federal funding for the building of roads and road safety. Also, there was a shift in priority from rail to auto, which caused the government to place more emphasis on automobiles. Overall, the political comparisons run on the fact that they both didn't have a huge effect on the political side of the American spectrum.

Economically, automobiles and trains were a whole different brand on the market. They both formed booming new industries, in which a whole different kind of business would be pursued. Railroads furthered the expansion of industry after the era of industrialization and aided the rebuilding of the South. Because railroads were nationwide, people in the South were able to attain jobs closely after the war. But the railroads clashed with part of the Southern population, and some of the North, because farmers were very unhappy about the land that was being granted to the railroads. Therefore, there were many monopolies and problems with the farming population of the United States. The automobile industry hit the economy with much force. Henry Ford, one of the essential creators of the automobile, had a lot to do with this. He set the price for cars and also set the standard to which they were to be manufactured. He established the assembly line and elevated Ford Motors to the top of all automobiles. The car industry led to the creation of many new industries such as oil, rubber, tar, glass, chemical, etc. All of these goods are essential in running an automobile. Overall, railroads and automobiles had a positive economic effect, because they encouraged Americans to purchase durable goods.

Railroads and automobiles can be compared to many other famous American inventions, but truly not in the same way. The two contributed immensely to the formation of an American culture. In saying that, the social, political, and economic comparisons between railroads and automobiles are quite similar, because they are two of the most influential forms of transportation for Americans in the modern era.

5.

Study List:

General

massive retaliation
brinksmanship
"New Look"
MAD

Europe

Marshall Plan
NATO
"Iron Curtain"
Truman Doctrine
Berlin Blockade
NSC-68
U-2 incident
Berlin Wall

Asia

Korean War

fall of China

domino theory

Vietnam

SEATO

Latin America

Guatemala

Nicaragua

Cuba

Fidel Castro

Bay of Pigs

Cuban Missile Crisis

SAMPLE ESSAY

United States foreign policy changed a great deal after World War II. Prior to the Second World War, the United States had an isolationist foreign policy and only got involved with international affairs if they had a direct effect on the United States. The United States did not get involved with either of the first two world wars until direct harm came to American citizens. However, after World War II, the foreign policy of the United States changed to that of being very involved in international affairs, which can be seen through the relationship between the United States and Europe, Asia, and Latin America.

After World War II, Western Europe was left in shambles and badly in need of money to rebuild their devastated countries physically and economically. Since the United States entered the war late and had almost no fighting on home soil—unlike Western Europe—it suffered the least from the war. In 1945, Winston Churchill correctly assessed that the United States was the strongest economic and military power in the world (due to its monopoly on nuclear weapons). Consequently, through the Marshall Plan, the United States pumped money into Western Europe to get the countries economically stable again. This money also benefited the United States because Western Europe used it to buy products from the U.S. By 1953, 13 billion dollars had been sent into Europe—enough so that the countries there were back to being economically functional. On top of the Marshall Plan, the Truman Doctrine was created, which maintained that the United States would support "free peoples who are resisting attempted subjugation by armed minorities or by outside pressures," meaning that the United States would provide assistance to governments who are fighting communism, like the governments of Greece and Turkey. The Marshall Plan and the Truman Doctrine both firmly entangled the U.S. in the affairs of other countries, which was a huge shift in foreign policy compared to the traditional isolationism that the U.S. had always abided by. In addition, NATO (North

Atlantic Treaty Organization) was created as an alliance between the United States, European Countries, and Canada that provided for all members to respond if the Soviet Union or any of her allies attacked any member of NATO. The formation of NATO was a huge step for the United States in foreign policy, as it firmly aligned itself with Western Europe instead of staying traditionally isolationist. Because of NATO and the resulting link between the United States and Western Europe, a symbolic and physical boundary was set up known as the "Iron Curtain." To the east of it were the countries that were under the influence of the Soviet Union and communism, and to the west of the curtain were countries that had democratic governments (the United States and Western Europe). This curtain has since faded over time, but when it was first erected it served as a reminder that the United States had-created a bond with Western Europe, breaking its ties to isolationism forever.

The Berlin Blockade and resulting Airlift also show how far the United States transgressed from isolationism after World War II. Defeated Germany had been split into four occupational regions, and similarly, Berlin, the capital, had been split in two—the east side controlled by the Soviet Union and the west side controlled by Western Europe and the United States. The Berlin Wall had been erected to separate the eastern and western portions of the city from each other. During the Berlin Blockade, the Soviet Union blocked Western European and U.S. access to Western Berlin because of the three Western Germany zones' decision to end the use of occupational currency and instead use the deutsche mark—a decision which the Soviet Union was against. In response to this blockade, the Berlin Airlift took place, where Allied aircrafts landed in Berlin and delivered thousands of tons of supplies to the people there. The Soviet Union did not try to stop them, and the crisis ended there, but the important fact was that the United States went to such extreme means to establish its presence and keep the Soviet Union from getting in its way. This shows how far from isolationism the United States foreign policy came after World War II. The United States owning part of Germany and Berlin was extreme enough when compared to traditional foreign policy, but when coupled with the Berlin Airlift, it just illustrates even more how much U.S. foreign policy shifted in 1945.

U.S. foreign policy changed one more time in the post–World War II era, when the goal of containment of communism (the main reason behind the shift away from isolationism) changed from being defensive to offensive—meaning a huge military buildup during peacetime. This strategy was outlined in the NSC-68 report, which argued that the Soviet Union had a systematic plot to spread communism across the globe, and consequently, the United States must make their newly labeled goal of "containment" more aggressive than it was before. Truman did not sign the NSC-68 report until communist North Korea attacked South Korea in 1950, which made it seem as though the nation's worst fears about communism had been realized. In 1960 a United States U-2 aircraft was shot down over the Soviet Union. This plane was used by the U.S. to spy aerially on the Soviet Union, and because it was found out, relations between the United States and the Soviet Union became increasingly worse. By this time, United States foreign policy toward Europe had gone from isolationist, to internationalist, to aggressive containment—a huge shift from what it had been before World War II.

The U.S. vow to fight communism led it into the conflict of the Korean War. When communist North Korea invaded Western-supported South Korea, the United States saw the move as the Soviet Union using North Korea as a way to spread communism in Asia. The United States intervened on behalf of South Korea in order to protect its allies as well as contain its communist enemy. The United States becoming involved in this conflict was a big change from its normal foreign policies. Prior to World War II, the United States stayed out of foreign wars, unless they directly involved American citizens, in order to keep the United States safe from outside harm. After the Second World War, the United States still had self-preservation in mind, but its new enemy was communism, one it believed would have to be fought both domestically and abroad. Thus, isolationism was no longer a safe foreign policy for the United States. One of the new foreign policy beliefs was that of the "domino effect," which meant that if one country in a region falls to communism, then soon all of them will become communist as well. This is one of the reasons why the U.S. sprang into action so quickly in South Korea. When China fell to Communism, the United States was concerned about Taiwan falling as well, and so the U.S. also interfered and threatened China with nuclear weapons. This response was called massive retaliation, and it was used for a while so that the United States could get what it wanted—from other countries by threatening them with nuclear missiles. In the end, this policy didn't work very well, because it was reasoned that if used all the time, it would lose its threat, and it made the United States seem like a big bully. As it is, the tactic of massive retaliation shows how much force the United States was willing to use in order to contain communism. The "domino effect" theory was used in regard to the Vietnam War in order to explain that the U.S. got involved solely to prevent communism from spreading throughout Asia. But by this time, the American public was getting very fed up with containment. The fact that many Americans viewed it as an overzealous foreign policy that cost more than it was worth illustrates that by the time of the Vietnam War, the isolationist, detached foreign policy of several decades earlier was long gone, and the American citizens knew it. Furthermore, SEATO, the South East Asian Treaty Organization, was set up by the United States, Western European countries, and Asian countries in order to allow the United States to interfere in a way similar to that of the Truman Doctrine; and though in the end it was never functional, it is another instance of the United States acting in a very un-isolationist way after World War II. In Asia, the United States foreign policy shifted even more away from isolationism than the foreign policy toward Europe.

U.S. foreign policy also changed in regards to Latin America. The U.S. used the CIA to interfere in Guatemala in order to overthrow its democratic government with some help from the people. As a result, 100,000 Guatemalans were killed, and a long period of unrest was caused in the country. The United States foreign policy had never before included orchestrating internal sabotages of foreign governments, but after World War II, this happened at least twice. When Fidel Castro came to power in Cuba, the U.S. feared that communism would spread to a country close to home where missiles could be placed. Previously, U.S.-supported Fulgencio Batista ran Cuba, where many American investors owned property; but Castro redistributed this land when he came to power, showing that he was no ally of the U.S. The CIA then attempted the Bay of Pigs Invasion, using Cuban exiles and trained Guatemalans to try and overthrow Castro, but it didn't work and was criticized heavily. Later, during the Cuban Missile Crisis, the world was poised on the brink of Mutual Assured Destruction, or MAD. The crisis had started because the United States believed that Cuba had nuclear missiles. The U.S. knew these missiles pointed at the U.S. and Cuba, and the Soviet Union knew that the U.S. had missiles in Turkey pointed at the Soviet Union. If one country fired at the other, then the other country in retaliation would fire as well, which could have destroyed the entire world. This standoff lasted for 13 days until Khrushchev, the leader of the Soviet Union, backed off; ending the crisis. The world was saved from destruction, and afterward the Soviet Union took its missiles out of Cuba and the U.S. took its missiles out of Turkey and promised never to try and invade Cuba again. A direct phone line between Moscow and Washington, D.C., was also set up to head off any future crises. The Cuban Missile Crisis is an example of a time when the United States went as far as almost destroying the world in its foreign policy; once again showing how far the U.S. had came from traditional isolationism after WWII.

The United States also tried to use a mini-Marshall plan with Latin America to appease the countries it had angered by its attention to Europe, CIA interferences, and other events, but it was too little money and too late in time, and the Latin American countries were not satisfied. After WWII, the U.S. meddled a lot in Latin America. The United States used the CIA, money, and offensive techniques to achieve its goals of containment and appeasement, but it didn't always work out in the end. Just the fact that the U.S. used such means shows that the foreign policy after WWII shifted so much so that a country who never got involved in the affairs of other countries (save for fighting for democracy) now was seen as somewhat of a bully because of always becoming involved in other country's governments.

After World War II, the U.S. foreign policy shifted a great deal. The United States went from being isolationist to having a hand in most of the world's affairs. On one hand, the U.S. helped out other countries after World War II, because of its superior financial and military strength. On the other hand, the U.S. used its military and economic strength to take advantage of other weaker countries in order to contain communism and/or create better economic circumstances there for the United States. Either way, after World War II, the foreign policy of the United States shifted a great degree and has never been the same since.

GLOSSARY

abolitionist
one who favors the end of slavery

affirmative action
policies of the government aimed at increasing access to jobs, schooling, and opportunities to people previously discriminated against

agrarian
pertaining to farming or agriculture

anarchist
an individual who advocates the overthrow of all government

annexation
the act of taking a smaller territory to a larger one

antebellum
before the war; usually used with regard to the time before the Civil War

anti-Semitic
having or showing prejudiced against Jews

apologists
those in the South who justified slavery by claiming African Americans were better off under the current system than left on their own

appeasement
a policy of giving into modest demands of an enemy to hold off potential conflict

apportionment
The proportional distribution of the number of members of the U.S. House of Representatives on the basis of the population of each state

arbitration
the settlement of a dispute by a third, unbiased party

armistice
a suspension of fighting; a cease-fire

arsenal
a stockpile of weapons or a place for making and storing weapons

artisans
those considered skilled in certain industries such as metal work, carpentry, or printing

autocrat
a ruler having unlimited power; a despot

bandwagon
a political cause that draws increasing numbers of proponents due to its success

bicameral

composed of or based on two legislative chambers or branches

blasphemy

a contemptuous or profane act, utterance, or writing concerning God or a sacred entity

blitzkrieg

Hitler's tactic of "lighting war," which involved swift action against the enemy

bond

an interest-bearing note issued by the government that guarantees repayment at a set date

boycott

to refrain from engaging, purchasing, or trading with another in an expression of protest

bracero

a Mexican farm worker brought to the United States to work during World War II

buying on margin

the act of purchasing stock on credit

capitalism

an economic system in which the means of production and exchange are controlled by individuals

caravel

any of several types of small, light sailing ships, especially one with two or three masts and lateen sails used by the Spanish and Portuguese in the 15th and 16th centuries

carpetbagger

a Northern Republican who moved South for financial and political gain

ceded

given or surrendered to another, possibly by treaty

charter

a written grant from the sovereign power of a country conferring certain rights and privileges on a person, a corporation, or the people

closed shop

a workplace in which workers must join the labor union as a condition of employment

collective bargaining

the process by which employees and management negotiate wages, working conditions, and work hours

confederation

an alliance or body of states loosely united for common purposes

conscription

compulsory enrollment of men in the armed forces

constituents

the voters or citizens of a particular region who are represented by an elected official

conquistador

a Spanish conqueror of the Americas

conversion experience

a rite of passage for Calvinists who publicly confessed all sins to become one of the "elect"

corollary

an inference that follows proof from a previous instance

coup

the overthrow of a ruling party/person by a small group illegally and/or by force

de facto

"in fact"; usually with regard to segregation

de jure

"in law"; usually with regard to laws passed for segregation

demography

the study of the characteristics of human populations, such as size, growth, density, distribution, and vital statistics

depression

a prolonged period of declining economic activity characterized by rising unemployment and falling prices

détente

a period of relaxed tensions between countries

direct primary

an election in which registered members of the party elect who their party nominees for office will be

dissent

to object or disagree

domestic

of or relating to a country's internal affairs

duty

money collected by government from a tariff

foreclosure

the repossession of a property by a lender after a borrower fails to pay on the loan

egalitarian

upholding the equality of all people

elect

according to Calvinists, those who have been chosen by God for salvation

elite

a group or class of persons or a member of such a group or class enjoying superior intellectual, social, or economic status

emancipation

to free from slavery or bondage

embargo

a prohibition or ban; usually used with regard to trade or shipping

encomienda

the Spanish labor system whereby individuals were bound to unpaid labor but were not legally owned by a master

enfranchisement

giving the right to vote

entrepreneur

a person who engages in a risky business adventure

established church

a church that is officially recognized and protected by the government

excise tax

a fee collected on goods and services bought and sold within a country

executive privilege

the claim by a president that certain information should be kept from Congress

expatriates

individuals who have chosen to leave their native country in favor of living abroad

fascism

a dictatorial form of government that glorifies military service and nationalism

filibuster

the act of members of Congress of delaying a vote or action by refusing to release the floor during debate

Fire Eaters

term used by Northerners to name Southern slavery advocates

fugitive

an individual who flees danger or capture

fundamentalism

a religious movement or point of view characterized by a return to rigid adherence to fundamental principles

genocide

the systematic extermination of a race or ethnicity by another group

gentry

people of gentle birth, good breeding, or high social position; usually landowners

ghetto

an area where ethnic minorities are forced to live, either by law or discrimination

graft

the use of one's position to gain money or property illegally

greenback

paper currency in the United States that replaced specie before the founding of the Federal Reserve

Gross National Product (GNP)

the sum of all goods and services produced both within and abroad by citizens of a country in a given year

guerrilla warfare

irregular, paramilitary units operating in small bands in occupied territory using subversive tactics to surprise the enemy

hard money

limited currency with high value

headright system

a system of obtaining land in colonial times in which one received 50 acres of land for every emigrant to America one sponsored

heresy

an opinion or a doctrine at variance with established religious beliefs

hierarchy

a system that places things in graduated order, from lowest to highest

homestead

a single-family home or farm

horizontal integration

a single company controls one aspect of the manufacture of a product

ideology

the body of ideas and beliefs that characterize a culture or large group

impeach

to charge a government official with a criminal offense

imperialism

a policy of extending a country's authority over a foreign country by acquisition or colonization

impress

to force into military service

incumbent

an individual running for an office he or she currently holds

indentured servant

a person who is bonded or contracted to work for another for a specified time in exchange for learning a trade or for travel expenses

indigenous

native to a particular region

inflation

an increase in the volume of money, resulting in a decrease in the value of currency (i.e., rising prices)

infrastructure

the basic structure needed for the functions of a society; usually transportation, sanitation, and communication

initiative

process by which voters can propose legislation and place that law on a ballot in a popular election

insurrection

the act or an instance of open revolt against civil authority or a constituted government

isolationist

an individual who would rather remain uninvolved in world affairs

Jim Crow

the practice of legal racial segregation

jingoism

extreme nationalism coupled with an aggressive foreign policy stance

joint-stock company

a company that has some features of a corporation and some features of a partnership

laissez-faire

the belief that government should refrain from interfering in business and the economy

landslide

the winning of an election by a large margin

literacy test

an exam given to individuals to prove they were literate before they could register to vote

lynching

the illegal act of putting to death a person accused of committing a crime; usually conducted by mobs

mandate

a command or instruction given by the electorate to their representative

martial law

military occupation imposed upon an area when civilian resources have failed or collapsed

martyr

an individual who makes a great sacrifice to further a cause; one who chooses death rather than renounce beliefs

materialism

a belief that the accumulation of possessions is more important that spiritual pursuits

matrilineal

relating to, based on, or tracing ancestral descent through the maternal line

mercantilism

the belief that all economic activity should be for the good of the whole (country) rather than for the individual

mercenaries

foreign soldiers hired to serve in the military

mestizo

a person of mixed racial ancestry, especially of mixed European and Native American ancestry

mobilization

government organization of the nation for war

mudslinging

unsubstantiated accusations and attacks on a political opponent

mulatto

an individual of African and European ancestry

nation-state
a political society that combines a central government with cultural unification

nationalism
devotion to the interests or culture of one's nation

nativism
the policy of upholding the rights of native citizens over those of immigrants

naturalization
the process of immigrants gaining citizenship

nullify
to declare a law void

oligarchy
rule by a few

omnibus bill
a potential law that includes a variety of topics under one name

pacifist
an individual who is opposed to all war

pardon
the act of releasing an individual from responsibility for a crime

partisan
supporting a particular political party

patronage
the support of a cause through financial gifts

peculiar institution
a name given to slavery by Southern apologists

political machine
an organization controlled through spoils and patronage

poll tax
a tax levied on individuals before they can vote

pool
an alliance of competing companies to set prices and split profits by sharing customers

pork barrel
congressional appropriations for political gain in a particular constituency

precedent
a decision or action that establishes a standard for future instances

predestination
the doctrine that God has foreordained all things, especially that God has elected certain souls to eternal salvation

primogeniture
the right of the eldest child, especially the eldest son, to inherit the entire estate of one or both parents

proclamation
an official announcement

propaganda
information or materials provided by the proponents or opponents of an idea to influence public thought

proprietary colony
a settlement in a region granted by a king or queen to a legal owner

proviso
a clause within a document that stipulates an exception or restriction

pump priming
an increase in government spending to stimulate the economy

puppet government
a government that is controlled by outsiders

quota
a proportional share of something to a group or members of a group; an allotment

ratification

the act of approving and giving formal sanction of

recall

the act of removing a public official from office by a vote of a specified number of citizens

referendum

the submission of a law directly to the voters for approval or denial

reparations

money, goods, or services paid by a government for destruction and damage caused during a war

republic

a government whose power rests in a citizenry who is entitled to vote and is represented by those they vote for; usually has a president rather than a king as head

Rustbelt

states in the Northeast and Midwest that were once prosperous steel producers

scabs

replacement workers during a strike

scalawag

a white Southerner who supported Radical Reconstruction

secession

the withdrawal from an alliance or association

sect

a group of people forming a distinct unit within a larger group by virtue of certain refinements or distinctions of belief or practice

secular

of the world rather than the church or spirit

sedition

the act of incitement of rebellion against the government

segregation

the act of separating; usually regarding race and ethnicity

self-determination

the belief that people should have the opportunity to decide their own form of government

sharecropper

an individual who receives land on credit and pays back debt with a share of the crop yield

siege

the surrounding and blockading of a city, town, or fortress by an army attempting to capture it

socialist

an individual who believes that business and the economy should be controlled by the community, not individuals

soft money

plentiful currency with low value

sovereignty

power vested in an independent government

speakeasies

illegal bars and clubs where liquor was sold during Prohibition

specie

coined (gold, silver, or other metal) currency

speculation

risky business transactions on the bet of quick or considerable profit

sphere of influence

a region controlled by the influence of other powerful nations

spoils system

the practice of the winning political party rewarding supporters with jobs, regardless of qualifications

stagflation
a combination of high unemployment and high inflation

stalwart
an individual who has unwavering support for a party or cause

strike
an action by organized labor to stop work in order to force management to negotiate

subversion
a systematic attempt to overthrow or undermine a government or political system by persons working from within

suffrage
the right to vote

Sunbelt
states along the south and southwestern United States

tariffs
taxes placed on imported goods

temperance
the belief in moderation, particularly with regard to alcohol

tenant farmer
a person who leases land from a landowner

tenement
an urban multifamily housing unit

theocracy
a government by the church leaders

trust
an organization of corporations where stockholders have traded their stocks for trust certificates

tycoon
a wealthy and powerful businessperson

urbanization
the growth of cities

utopian
seeking perfection in society

vertical integration
control of all aspects of manufacturing by a single company

Vietnamization
President Nixon's policy of turning over the Vietnam War to the South Vietnamese

virtual representation
the political practice of a small group of people being elected to speak for a larger group

wildcat banks
uncontrolled and unregulated western banks of the 1800s whose speculation and unsafe practices helped spur the Panic of 1819

writ of habeas corpus
from the Latin "of the body," a formal order requiring the presentation of the accused before a judge to be charged with a crime or released from custody

yellow-dog contracts
agreements that forced employees to promise never to join a union in order to gain or maintain employment

yeomen
non-slave-owning farmers